Generic Innovation in Shakespeare and His Contemporaries

As ever, for Lisa and now for Sam too.

Generic Innovation in Shakespeare and His Contemporaries

Edward Gieskes

Edinburgh University Press is one of the leading university presses in the UK. We publish academic books and journals in our selected subject areas across the humanities and social sciences, combining cutting-edge scholarship with high editorial and production values to produce academic works of lasting importance. For more information visit our website: edinburghuniversitypress.com

© Edward Gieskes 2023

Edinburgh University Press Ltd
13 Infirmary Street, Edinburgh, EH1 1LT

Typeset in 11/13pt Sabon LT Pro
by Cheshire Typesetting Ltd, Cuddington, Cheshire

A CIP record for this book is available from the British Library

ISBN 978 1 4744 9673 5 (hardback)
ISBN 978 1 4744 9674 2 (paperback)
ISBN 978 1 4744 9675 9 (webready PDF)
ISBN 978 1 4744 9676 6 (epub)

The right of Edward Gieskes to be identified as the author of this work has been asserted in accordance with the Copyright, Designs and Patents Act 1988, and the Copyright and Related Rights Regulations 2003 (SI No. 2498).

Contents

List of Tables	vi
Acknowledgements	vii
Introduction	1
1. "Chaucer (of all admired) the story gives": Shakespeare, Medieval Romance, and Generic Innovation	37
2. "Mirrours more then one": Spenser, Shakespeare, and Generic Change	79
3. "King Cambyses' vein": Generic Change in the 1580s and 1590s	119
4. "Lies like truth": History, Fiction, Genre, Innovation	155
5. "What's aught but as 'tis valued": "History," Truth, and Fiction	197
6. "When the bad bleed": Tenants to Tragedy	239
Bibliography	282
Index	296

List of Tables

Table 1.1a:	Shakespeare's Plays, 1599–1602	54
Table 1.1b:	Chamberlain's Plays, 1599–1602	54
Table 1.2:	*DEEP* Records for Extant Professional Drama Printed, 1599–1602	55
Table 3.1:	Plays performed by Lord Strange's Men, February 1592–February 1593	147
Table 6.1:	Plays Which Include *Revenge* in the Title	244

Acknowledgements

This book is the end result of many years of work, and it is likely that I will miss some of the people to whom I owe thanks and recognition. The idea to write a book about genre and generic change emerged out of a graduate seminar I taught at the University of South Carolina organized around the putative break between the drama of the sixteenth century and that of the early seventeenth century.

Since then, I have benefited from the refinements to my thinking made possible by participating in a series of Folger Institute Seminars and Symposia led by Lynne Magnusson, Coppelia Kahn, Lorna Hutson, Christopher Brooks, and Kristen Poole. The Folger Shakespeare Library offers essential space and resources for long term scholarly projects, and I am always grateful to the Library and the librarians (all librarians!).

Elements of essentially every chapter were aired for the first time at meetings of the Shakespeare Association of America, and I am grateful to seminar leaders and fellow seminarians who provided encouragement and sage commentary on early arguments in the book.

Since joining the English Department at the University of South Carolina, I have had a supportive and intellectually exciting group of colleagues. I am grateful to all my colleagues but particularly to Holly Crocker, Mike Gavin, Brian Glavey, Anne Gulick, Scott Gwara, Cat Keyser, Nina Levine, David Miller, John Muckelbauer, Larry Rhu, Esther Richey, Bill Rivers, Andy Shifflett, Rebecca Stern, and Qiana Whitted.

Students in my graduate courses have helped refine arguments, clarify vaguenesses in my thinking and forced rethinking of positions. Jenna Adair, Barbara Bolt, Melissa Crofton, Rob Kilgore, Emily Murray, Emily Rendek, Jonathan Sircy, and Bhavin Tailor, among others, played an important role in this book. I have also been fortunate to have been able to teach many of the plays discussed in this book with many undergraduate students whose conversation has been important in my thinking as well.

The University of South Carolina has supported my work through Research and Productive Scholarship Grants, sabbatical leaves, and travel grants throughout the research and writing of this book. This support has been invaluable in providing time and space for this work.

In the broader world of early modern drama studies, I am grateful to Meghan Andrews, Rob Carson, Linda Charnes, Anneliese Connolly, Diana Henderson, Margo Hendricks, Adam Hooks, Lorna Hutson, Ros Knutson, András Kiséry, Naomi Liebler, Jim Marino, Lucy Munro, Cy Mulready, Tom Rutter, Lisa Starks, Holger Syme, Henry Turner, Andrew Tumminia, Brian Walsh, Chris Warley, Jessica Winston, and Linda Woodbridge. Like so many others, I owe thanks to the late Harry Berger and Arthur Kinney.

My longest debts in the profession are still owed to Jim Siemon, who introduced me to Bakhtin and Bourdieu in graduate seminars at Boston University; to Bill Carroll, who was and is an advocate for me and many others; and to Andrew Hartley, Sarah Lyons, and Kirk Melnikoff, all long-time interlocutors and friends.

The anonymous readers for Edinburgh University Press provided excellent and sympathetic feedback on the manuscript which is much the better for their commentary.

Introduction

I

Either for tragedy, comedy, history, pastoral, pastoral-comical, historical-pastoral, tragical-historical, tragical-comical-historical-pastoral, scene individable, or poem unlimited: Seneca cannot be too heavy, nor Plautus too light.

Shakespeare, Hamlet

Genre is both one of the oldest and the most slippery of literary historical concepts: the names of kinds are at once self-evident, even self-defining, at the same time that their specific content is always shifting as new works appear and as old works move from one category to another. Polonius' description of the players' repertory and qualifications trades on both of these characteristics in his invocation of historical genres and a series of increasingly large hybrids. Even his use of Seneca and Plautus points to a theory of genre as defined by major practitioners. In the contemporary book shop, library, or theatre, genre presents itself as given, a set of categories that have clear if, paradoxically, not always well-defined boundaries demarcating real, substantial distinctions between kinds of books.[1] It is a critical commonplace that early modern drama is free with generic mixing and innovation, while at the same time critics deploy traditional terms to mark kind off from kind. This book is concerned with developing an historical account of generic mixing and innovation

---

1. This paradox of boundaries that are blurry and clear at the same time lies at the very center of genre theory (and practice). The fact that books often appear in more than one section of a bookstore underscores the fictional quality of some of these distinctions.

that does not proceed from category to expression, but places what genres *do* before what they *are*.[2]

Noting that genre is one of the oldest fields of inquiry in literary studies is hardly an astonishing claim; indeed, it is almost obligatory in any work that deals with questions of genre. In fact, if there exists a genre of "genre criticism," such statements are a central marker of participation in it.[3] We can look to Aristotle's *Poetics* as one of the originary texts in a long series of arguments about form. Writers from Horace through the Renaissance and beyond have taken up the question of how to understand the "kinds" of literature from positions ranging from the rigidly prescriptive to the merely descriptive to the wholly dismissive.[4] It could be asked, given this long history, what the purpose of another investigation of generic change might be. The bulk of my answer to that question lies in the chapters that follow but this introduction offers some initial justifications for this project.

Genre theory, to quote Michael Prince,

> is not inherently about literary or rhetorical genres; it is about the decisions writers make to adopt some categories as opposed to others, the range of influences that help determine their choices, the steps writers take to defend or naturalize these categories, and the decisions historians and critics such as myself then make to study the past through one lens instead of another. (475–6)

In my argument, the choices Prince describes are both less deliberate and more focused on function than he suggests. Scholars

---

2. In his 1983 essay "Of Gentlemen and Shepherds: The Politics of Elizabethan Pastoral Form," Louis Montrose argues that the study of pastoral must not limit its inquiry "to what pastorals 'are' or what they 'mean;' it must also ask what they *do*" (419). My work extends this formulation by placing the question of what genres do before questions about substance.
3. David Duff's 2000 anthology of genre criticism might serve as an especially good example of this kind of statement, and not only as a function of being a collection of theoretical statements on genre theory.
4. One could include the varied programmatic poems found in the work of writers from Tibullus to Ovid to Propertius as examples of classical genre theory (see Farrell's discussion in his "Classical Genre Theory"). Benedetto Croce's is only the most well-known and discussed rejection of genre in interpretation. Derrida's often-cited (and almost as often misread) "Law of Genre" serves as another example of a questioning of the category. Adena Rosmarin's *The Power of Genre* (1985) argues that genre is the creation of the critic and more useful in producing new readings than new works. (While useful, I think that she minimizes the generative power of genre).

often describe early modern English drama in terms of innovation – the appearance of new forms, of new writers, of new audiences – and those innovations occurred in a complex series of contexts. Investigating genre means looking closely at the kinds of choices Prince writes of and attempting to situate them in the literary and social contexts of their origin.

This book comes out of a long-standing desire to locate innovations in both form and content in early modern English drama in the field of cultural production. Bourdieu describes this field as a system of relations between agents like playwrights and institutions like the theatre or the emergent publishing industry.[5] For Bourdieu, works of art emerge and find or fail to find audiences in this field which is defined by struggle: "the literary or artistic field is a *field of forces* but it is also a *field of struggles* tending to transform or conserve this field of forces" (*Field* 30, original emphasis). Narratives of rupture abound – we need only think about how the advent of Christopher Marlowe's "mighty line" has been understood in literary history – but these narratives misrepresent both the process and nature of changes in cultural production. Partly as an effect of the structure of anthologies and partly because of habits of thought deriving from influential works of criticism, scholars have often acted as though there were a meaningful distinction between the Elizabethan and Jacobean stage, a distinction that meant that there were clear differences of genre, of mood, and of structure.[6] Genres have histories and make histories, and this book considers the implications of this mutual and recursive shaping.

Bakhtin and Bourdieu, whose work on genre remains remarkably under-discussed, offer ways to account for innovation that avoid at least some of the problems in other approaches to the question of kind. Part of the danger, often recognized if not always

---

5. This term derives from the work of Pierre Bourdieu, whose sociology of culture is one of the theoretical underpinnings of this book. See, for example, *The Field of Cultural Production* (1993) and *The Rules of Art: Genesis and Structure of the Literary Field* (1996).
6. One example might be the break between Chambers's *Elizabethan Stage* (1923) and Bentley's *Jacobean and Caroline Stage* (1941–68), which both emplaces and implicitly endorses a distinction between epochs in the theatre based on who sits on the throne. English departments still structure courses based on this putative break, and books still point to Elizabethan or Jacobean as meaningful markers beyond a simple designation of time before or after 1603. Jeremy Lopez's recent work on the canon of early modern drama, discussed below, is a most welcome corrective to this.

avoided in genre criticism, lies in the way that genres imply a kind of transhistorical identity within one genre – as though "tragedy" or "comedy" remain the same in some fundamental way – which encourages anachronism. If genre is as unavoidable a category as its long history suggests, it behooves us to situate it as carefully as we can in literary history and not to grant more substance to generic categories than they can sustain. Taking the ferment and innovation of the period's drama not as a phenomenon to be described or labeled but on its own terms as a material practice embedded in the social field offers a better way to understand the dynamism of the ferment and to see relations between texts and institutions that can be obscured by approaches more focused on defining boundaries between kinds.

II

But besides these gross absurdities, how all their plays be neither right tragedies, nor right comedies, mingling kings and clowns, not because the matter so carrieth it, but thrust in the clown by head and shoulders to play a part in majestical matters with neither decency nor discretion, so as neither admiration or commiseration, nor the right sportfulness, is by their mongrel tragicomedy obtained [...]. So falleth it out that, having indeed no right comedy, in that comical part of our tragedy, we have nothing but scurrility, unworthy of any chaste ears, or some extreme show of doltishness, indeed fit to lift up a loud laughter, and nothing else: where the whole tract of a comedy should be full of delight, as the tragedy should be still maintained in a well-raised admiration.

Sir Philip Sidney, *A Defence of Poetry* (1579)

Gentlemen, so nice is the World, that for apparell there is no fashion, for Musique no Instrument, for Diet no Delicate, for Playes no Inuention but breedeth satietie before noone, and contempt before night. Come to the Taylor, hee is gone to the Painters, to learne how more cunning may lurke in the fashion, then can be expressed in the making. [...] Time hath confounded our mindes, our mindes the matter, but all commeth to this passe, that what heretofore hath beene serued in seuerall dishes for a Feast, is now minced in a Charger for a Gallimaufrey. If we present a mingle-mangle, our fault is to be excused, because the whole World is become an Hodge-podge. We are iealous of your iudgements, because you are wise; of our owne performance, because wee are vnperfect; of our Authors deuice, because he is idle. Onely this doth encourage vs, that presenting our studies before Gentlemen, though they receiue an inward mislike, wee shall not be hist with an open disgrace. *Stirps rudis vrtica est: stirps generosa, rosa.*[7]

John Lyly, *Midas* (1592)

WIFE: I have a plot in my head, son – i'faith, husband, to cross you.
SAM: Is it a tragedy plot or a comedy plot, good mother?
WIFE: 'Tis a plot that will vex him.

Thomas Middleton, *A Trick to Catch the Old One* (1605)

Scholars often ask Sam Lucre's question about his mother's plot of early modern plays, and critics have spent a great deal of intellectual energy in developing solutions to the problem of classification.[8] Her answer to this question is instructive, and her attention to effects will serve as a guiding principle of the discussion that follows. As far as Jenny Lucre is concerned, it does not matter whether the plot is comic or tragic, so long as it produces the desired effect of vexation on its intended audience.[9] Thus, her "plot" will be composed of whatever generic elements necessary to achieve her desired effect, and that effect is the plot's principle of structure rather than the other way around. Her use of *plot* to mean a plan of action leads her son to seek some qualification of the literary category. Her plot needs a genre, at least for her son to understand it. If the question of whether a play is comedy or tragedy (or tragicomedy or history or other variation) is a vexing one, it may be because it is not exactly the right question. We might more usefully begin, as Mistress Lucre does, with the effects of the plot and proceed to a discussion of how various generic elements contribute to those effects.

Sidney's complaint that the improper mingling of kings and clowns in the drama of the 1570s leads to neither right tragedy nor right comedy has less to do with a global condemnation of mixing genres than it does with the improper, indecorous, or gratuitous mixing of forms. The "mongrel tragicomedy" criticized by Sidney cannot achieve properly tragic "admiration or commiseration" or

---

7. "The base born is a nettle, the noble a rose." Lyly flatters the Paul's audience as being more gentle than the audiences of the amphitheaters.
8. City comedy alone has been the subject of many books since at least L. C. Knights's work on Jonson in *Drama and Society in the Age of Jonson* (1937). See also Jean Howard's *Theatre of a City: The Places of London Comedy, 1598–1642* (2007) and Nina Levine's *Practicing the City: Early Modern London on Stage* (2016).
9. That we never see what this plot is in the play adds a layer of irony here.

comic "sportfulness" because the hypothetical play is not judicious in its deployment of distinct generic types. His complaint is specifically that these mixtures, which are not dictated by the matter of the play, prevent the work from achieving the full effect of either tragedy or comedy. Indeed, it is the effects that define the genres – tragedy is to produce "right" admiration and comedy "sportfulness," not scurrility or doltishness – rather than some list of specific formal characteristics. This condemnation is sometimes taken to be absolute – particularly as it appears in the context of a broader critique of English drama's failure to observe the unities – but it is important to stress that Sidney's focus is on the effect such drama has on its audience and his criticism is not of mixing *per se*, but mixing with problematic results. Earlier in the *Defence*, he argues that mixing is not a problem if the parts "be good":

> Now in his parts, kinds, or species (as you list to term them), it is to be noted that some poesies have coupled together two or three kinds, as the tragical and the comical, whereupon is risen the tragicomical. Some, in the manner, have mingled prose and verse, as Sannazaro and Boethius. Some have mingled matters heroical and pastoral. But that cometh all to one in this question, for if severed they be good, the conjunction cannot be hurtful. (43)

The tragicomical is good because, unlike the works he criticizes later, it mingles good (or right) tragedy and comedy. It is only when the contrary is true that the hybridizing of genres is to be condemned.[10]

The prologue to John Lyly's play takes a somewhat different position with regard to the mixing of genres. Lyly admits that at one time the sundry dishes of comedy, tragedy, and pastoral were served as separate courses at the Ordinary of Literature but that now all of them are "minced" together "for a Gallimaufrey." Formerly firm distinctions between genres erode, and this erosion causes the players to present a "mingle-mangle" of forms: "If we present a mingle-mangle, our fault is to be excused, because the whole World is become an Hodge-podge." Where Sidney complains about the bad effects of careless mixing, Lyly shrugs and attributes it to the mingle-mangle condition of the world, requesting the audience pardon the play as being simply a reflection of the mixed nature of the whole world. *Midas*' gallimaufry refers at least in part to the blending of two dis-

---

10. Sidney's own practice is much less rigid than a narrow reading of the *Defence* suggests. To take one example, the *Arcadia* mixes all manner of forms in one longer work. In practice, mixing is both inevitable and productive.

tinct narratives about Midas – the tale of the golden touch and that of the ass's ears – linked not by plot but by a focus on Midas' flawed judgement in both stories. Lyly's mingle-mangle is a deliberate one, designed to appeal to and refine the tastes of his audience at Paul's. The Paul's prologue suggests that the generic mixing is part of what makes the play the *rosa* for the *stirps generosa* in the Paul's audience.

Middleton's 1605 comedy, *A Trick to Catch the Old One*, moves language from revenge tragedy into city comedy, transforming the content of revenge into business and at the same time calling expectations about generic conventions into question. In Act 2, Hoard sees an opportunity to take revenge by marrying Jane:

> Happy revenge, I hug thee! I have not only the means laid before me extremely to cross my adversary and confound the last hopes of his nephew, but thereby to enrich my state, augment my revenues, and build mine own fortunes greater (2.2.44–8).[11]

Revenge gets a hug here, and Hoard's satisfaction is not in, say, the death of his adversary but in angering him and in enriching himself. This revenge has a kind of social decorum – a usurer's revenge – if not a generic one and offers commentary on both social and generic expectations. The play's comedy depends on this playful disposition towards genre. Like Jenny Lucre, Middleton is interested more in the effect of the plot than its adherence to one or another set of conventions, which allows his play to comment on both social and generic structures.

While Sidney and Lyly posit the existence of more or less distinct genres that organize the production and reception of dramatic art, they both also allow that genres often mix and purity of kind is rarely seen. Middleton's play undercuts the class associations of genres that Sidney endorses in service of his comic plot.[12] As these examples demonstrate, generic categorization is a preoccupation of early modern authors. Anticipating Bakhtin, Lyly points out that generic mixing responds to the condition of the world and that the representation on stage mixes kinds in much same way that the times confound them under the pressure of a demand for the new. It is a critical commonplace that early modern English dramatists invented

---

11. I am quoting from Valerie Wayne's edition in *Thomas Middleton: The Collected Works* (2007).
12. See the discussion of Middleton's *Women Beware Women* in chapter six; the play places characters from city comedy into a tragedy, changing the parameters of tragedy.

genres, mixed existing ones, and generally treated more traditional notions of generic decorum with a certain amount of skepticism. Nevertheless, those received categories of classification and expression remained important for them and for later audiences, readers, and critics. The question is how they were important and what they did for writers and audiences.

III

Aristotle's *Poetics* exerts a powerful influence over genre theory and has often been taken as a prescription for the production of what Sidney might call "right tragedy." I do not propose to offer an extended reading of the *Poetics*, but I do wish to point to a few of the most salient features of that text as they structure much later thinking on genre. In particular, the definition of tragedy in chapter six has drawn a great deal of commentary. Aristotle writes:

> Tragedy, then, is a representation of an action that is worth serious attention, complete in itself, and of some amplitude; in language enriched by a variety of artistic devices appropriate to the several parts of the play; presented in the form of action, not narration, by means of pity and fear bringing about the purgation of such emotions. (38–9)

This passage combines a description of the form of tragedy – representation of a serious action of some significant size in appropriate language – with a definition of the effect this representation is meant to achieve. It is worth noting that the first part of Aristotle's description is vague enough to apply to any number of forms we would not call "tragic." Aristotle's central focus in on the effect tragedy ought to produce and in pointing out that successful tragedy is as much marked by these effects as by any particular element of structure it may possess.[13] Elsewhere in the *Poetics*, Aristotle discusses the history of the form, presenting a developmental narrative about tragedy. He does not, however, propose "to consider whether or not tragedy is now developed as far as it can be in its various forms, and to decide this absolutely and in relation to the stage" (36). Aristotle's reservation demonstrates that his approach to thinking about genre is historical: he does not suppose that trag-

---

13. For more developed commentary on the *Poetics*, see Gerard Else's work including *Aristotle's Poetics: The Argument* (1957).

edy (or, by extension, any particular genre) has or will reach some final form beyond which there is no further development. The only category of judgment that might remain fixed is the evaluation of what the effect of tragedy has: whether it produces and purges the emotions of pity and fear.

As Joseph Farrell has argued, ancient genre theory is, for the most part, far more rigid and prescriptive than the practice of the poets. It is also not as self-consistent or prescriptive as later theorists may have wanted it to be.[14] Farrell writes "classical genre theory, while always insisting on the essentializing nature of genre, was neither uniform nor wholly self-consistent in other respects; and this fact opened to door for poets to exploit the tendentiousness of such essentializing assumptions" (Farrell 383–4). One way that poets and other writers exploit this tendentiousness is their constant testing of the boundaries of genres even as they appear to accept them. Farrell points out that Roman poets were:

> demonstrably concerned, even obsessed with genre as a discursive device . . . But their interest in genre as a set of prescriptive rules – which is just about the only way in which they ever articulate their generic self-awareness – is powerfully undermined, even to the point of parody, by an attitude of practical inventiveness and what looks like nothing so much as an interest in the untenability of any position founded on the idea of generic essence. (396)

This obsession, balanced by the inventiveness of the poets, is, to my mind, an important if sometimes under-recognized element of the influence of classical Roman literature on early modern poets and playwrights. Ovid shared this disposition, and Marlowe's translation of the first elegy offers a good example:

> With Muse upreard I meant to sing of armes,
> Choosing a subject fit for feirse alarmes:
> Both verses were alike till Love (men say)
> Began to smile and tooke one foote away. (A2r)[15]

---

14. One example is the distance between Aristotle's descriptive account of tragedy and later prescriptive deployments of the *Poetics*, some of which depend on the assumption that Sophocles' work represents the fullest achievement of tragic form.
15. I have written on Marlowe, Jonson, and Shakespeare's adaptation of Ovid's work and disposition in "'materia conveniente modis': Early Modern Dramatic Adaptations of Ovid."

Ovid's desire to write epic is subverted by Love's removal of a foot from his verses, making it impossible to write epic, since epic is defined by its hexameters. This playful attitude to genres characterizes much of the practice of a writer like Sidney even as he offers what look like rigid prescriptions about what is or is not allowed of a poet.[16]

Interest in genre has waxed and waned throughout the twentieth century, as has critics' sense of its usefulness in approaching texts. Benedetto Croce (1909) dismissed the whole idea of genre as a kind of abuse of literature, preferring instead to talk only about books, not kinds. Croce's position, while undoubtedly influential and a useful corrective to overly prescriptive notions of genre, has correctly been set aside in favor of more nuanced versions of thinking about genre. Arguably the most well-known critic to offer a thoroughgoing account of genre is Northrop Frye, whose *Anatomy of Criticism* (1957), *A Natural Perspective* (1965), and *A Secular Scripture* (1976) continue to have considerable influence in thinking about the nature of genre.[17] Journals like *Genre* and *Narrative* place generic analysis in a central place in their publication programs, but substantial engagements with genre theory as such (rather than with particular genres) have been relatively rare.[18] As Ralph Cohen notes in his introductory essays to two special issues of *New Literary History* in 2003:

16. Sidney was always an ironist, and keeping that in view qualifies many of his more authoritarian sounding statements in the *Defence*. Rosalie Colie, in another important work of genre theory *The Resources of Kind* (1973), picks up this dynamic deployment of genre even as definitions and rules proliferate (see below).
17. I use the term "nature" advisedly since part of Frye's argument is that there are what amount to essences at the root of genres like tragedy or comedy. Frye's work influences any number of later critics' treatment of romance and comedy especially those interested in the "ritual" elements of plays that move towards social redemption by way of an interlude in a "green world" (a term still very much current in criticism). Frye's system naturalizes genres in terms of relations to seasons, and part of what I want to suggest, following Bourdieu, is that the "essences" of genres are *historical* universals, not the kind of abstract ones that Frye discusses.
18. Even such important books as Heather Dubrow's *Genre* (1982) in the Critical Idiom series work more as descriptions of genre theory rather than examples of it. John Frow's 2005 book on genre in the successor New Critical Idiom series is a better example of theorizing, but such books as Alistair Fowler's indispensable *Kinds of Literature* (1983) or Rosmarin's *Power of Genre* seem more the exception than the rule. Rosmarin's work argues that genre is more a product of criticism than a feature of texts, and, as this book as a whole will show, I respectfully disagree.

Many years have passed since Mikhail Bakhtin and later Tzvetan Todorov changed the direction of genre study from classification to its functions in human speech and behavior. And although much has been accomplished in the study of the novel and nonliterary writing, there have been few attempts to envision genre study as a theory of behavior or as one that can provide an insight into the arts and sciences. (v)

Genre study – especially of the kind imagined by Bakhtin – does provide insights into the structure of the field of cultural production, and in what follows I hope to make a contribution to the envisioning that Cohen calls for. As Cohen notes, the essays in these two special issues represent a kind of invitation to both a "generic reconstitution of literary studies" and a prompt to the need for a "reexamination of the nature, function, and significance of generic combinations" (xvi).[19] The persistence of received notions about the "history play" in early modern studies demonstrates that this reexamination has not happened (with the possible exception of recent work on the novel). This book takes up Cohen's invitation and reexamines some of the combinations he writes of and places them into the broader context of the cultural field of early modern England.

In her posthumously published collection of lectures, *The Resources of Kind* (1973), Rosalie Colie presents an extended consideration of the usefulness of genre to writers in the Renaissance and makes an argument for the similar usefulness of genre-theory for critics working in the period.[20] The title itself is a clear statement of that argument: for writers of the Renaissance, kind was a rich resource of forms that enabled rather than restricted expression. In contrast to what Barbara Lewalski in the introduction calls "the modern prejudice that genre is some kind of straightjacket" (vii),

19. Cohen's 1986 article "History and Genre," a kind of response to Derrida's "Law of Genre," also points in this direction and makes the vitally important point that "generic transformation can be a social act. Generic transformation reveals the social changes in audiences and the interpenetration of popular and elite literature. Within a common audience difference genres complement or contrast with one another" (216). It seems to me that this point is often lost. The fact that Cohen's introductions to special issues of the same journal published almost twenty years apart make very similar points shows that this is the case.
20. She uses Renaissance to designate a period that starts with Petrarch and ends with Swift. This deliberately broad designation of period encompasses multiple language traditions. Her contention is that any approach to questions about genre must be comparative.

Colie's book points out how essential genre is to communication, artistic or otherwise.[21] The prejudice Lewalski alludes to has faded somewhat since the publication of Colie's book, partly due to the strength of her argument, but it still exerts an effect in the way that genre criticism tends to be more descriptive and classificatory than analytical. Colie's book begins with a discussion of how rhetorical education encouraged Renaissance writers to think in terms not only of styles but of structures:

> Rhetorical education, always a model-following enterprise, increasingly stressed *structures* as well as styles to be imitated in the humane letters – epistles, orations, discourses, dialogues, histories, poems – always discoverable to the enthusiastic new man of letters by kind. (4)

This stress on structure, she argues, tended towards the development of treatises on poetry, which themselves became an important Renaissance genre. Colie's analysis of these texts along with the literature of her long Renaissance lead to a version of genre theory that serves as a means to account for "connections between topic and treatment within the literary system" as well as a way "to see the connection of the literary kinds with *kinds* of knowledge and experience" (Colie 29). She wishes to investigate, in her words, "what the *literary* gain may be, both in having genres and refusing to allow generic categories to dictate or predestine the size, scope, content and manner of any particular literary work" (103). This disposition – being aware of the usefulness of different genres for expression but skeptical about their determining power – allows for an approach to the question of genre that can account for both tradition and innovation. It is neither purely descriptive nor prescriptive, which makes it an important tool for thinking about the early modern theatre and the field of cultural production more generally because it mirrors the way genre seems actually to work.

Shortly after the publication of Colie's book, Fredric Jameson's essay "Magical Narratives: Romance as Genre" appeared in *New Literary History*. The essay complements Colie's approach by considering generic innovation as at least in part a response to historical change. In his account, romance emerges as an imaginative solution to historical contradictions. Jameson points out that:

21. In this, Colie's position is akin to Bakhtin's in the speech genres essay (see below), which holds that all expression depends on some notion of kind without which meaning would be difficult or impossible to produce (a commonplace of much genre theory).

> Traditional genre theory has been understood as performing the distinct but related functions of furnishing specifications for the production of this or that type of composition, and of providing a typology according to which the various existing compositions may be sorted out by genus and species. (136)[22]

This combination of functions is important to literary history, as Jameson concedes, but leads genre criticism to alternate between the functions of prescribing and sorting and eventuates in what he describes as an intractable division between a semantic and a syntactic approach to genre. Of the semantic approach, Jameson writes that "the object of inquiry is not the individual work but rather something like the comic vision, which may be seen as a more general or universal attitude towards life or form of being-in-the-world" ("Magical" 136). This kind of inquiry is interested in the meaning of a genre. The syntactic approach, in contrast, proceeds from:

> a view of comedy as a determinate laughter-producing mechanism with precise laws and requirements of its own, whose realization in the various media of theater or narrative, in film or in daily life, may be the object of analysis and synthetic reconstruction, resulting, not in the expression of a meaning, but rather the building of a model. ("Magical" 137)

Jameson's solution to the intractability of the distinction between these approaches is to attempt to turn the "dilemma into a solution" through an historical approach to genre. Jameson locates romance in the historical moment of its emergence and, in a passage worth quoting at length, describes it as an imaginative response to a specific historical contradiction:

> When, in the twelfth century, this kind of social isolation is overcome and the feudal nobility becomes aware of itself as a universal class, with a newly elaborated and codified ideology, there arises what can only be called a contradiction between the older positional notion of evil and this emergent class solidarity. Romance may then be understood as an imaginary "solution" to this contradiction, a symbolic answer to the question of how my enemy can be thought of as being evil, that is, as other than myself and marked by some absolute difference, when what is responsible for his being so characterized is simply the identity of his own conduct with mine, which – challenges, points of honor, tests of strength – he reflects as in a mirror image. ("Magical" 161)

22. The article becomes a chapter in Jameson's *The Political Unconscious* (1981).

We can see emergent genres as imaginative responses to historical developments, which makes an historical approach to genre essential. Early modern dramatic genres respond not only to developments within the theatre but also to external pressures and the work of thinkers like Jameson is profoundly important in understanding those responses.

Alistair Fowler's *Kinds of Literature: An Introduction to the Theory of Genres* (1982) is less explicitly political but is still deeply historical and offers an influential account of a range of genres, subgenres and modes.[23] Its argument has been so influential that it often seems that later writers forget the book's subtitle which describes the book as an introduction to genre theory, not a definitive statement. Fowler's position in general is that despite the complaints of those who regard genre as a limitation – an illegitimate restraint on the freedom of the author – genre serves as a primary aid to communication.[24] Fowler points to where he thinks genre theory has gone wrong:

> Genre criticism has tended to split into two quite distinct and almost unrelated activities. One is abstract speculation about permanent genres. It excited many during the Renaissance and for a century after, but is now regarded as unreal—unless of course, it is structuralist. The other activity is plodding chronicle history of individual genres that continually transform themselves without ever waiting long enough for generalization. (49)[25]

His position is that neither of these activities are adequate. The abstract speculation about "permanent" genres that characterized neoclassical thinking misrepresents the dynamism of literary change, as do the more doctrinaire and less flexible varieties of structuralism

---

23. This history is literary history, however. Fowler's book, though not hostile to the kind of historicizing that Jameson advocates, is not especially engaged in situating genre and generic change in extra-literary contexts. As he writes: "... we ought to be a little skeptical towards easy correlations of genres with immediate social contexts. The relation is almost certainly too complex to be explained by any simple model of 'superstructure'" (36).
24. See, for example, his second chapter. This position is, of course, close to that of Bakhtin and is, in many ways, entirely conventional, as Fowler himself acknowledges. Fowler's work keeps the roots of genre in communication in constant view, which helps prevent the genres he talks about from hardening into classifications with some kind of solidity or permanence.
25. It is hard not to see the reference to chronicle history as a kind of joke alluding to a "form" which has seen more than its share of chronicling.

of which he makes gentle fun. At the same time, "plodding chronicle history of individual genres" errs in its failure or refusal to generalize or compare.

When Fowler turns to the matter of generic transformation, he offers a schematic account that is worth noting for what it does not include. Discussing the mechanisms of change, Fowler argues that:

> Those that stand out may be identified as: topical invention, combination, aggregation, change of scale, change of function, counter-statement, inclusion, selection, and generic mixture. No doubt there are others; but these would be enough in themselves to cover the main changes known to literary history. (170)[26]

These mechanisms remain within the bounds of literary history and while Fowler would not argue that literary change happens in isolation from a broader history, he is less interested in the effects of changes in the whole field of cultural production – changes which, in a mediated way, do have a role in shaping mechanisms of innovation in particular moments. Significantly, *Kinds of Literature* closes with the hope that:

> Genre criticism may return us to problems shared by readers and critics—especially the problem of identifying literary works' total forms. For genre is an organizing principle of the redundancies by which it is possible to break the hermeneutic circle and to reconstruct old or difficult works. Above all, dealing in terms of changing genres offers frequent reminders that works of literature come to us from literary communities, with which we in our turn have to form a relation. (278)

This problem – of identifying the "total forms" of literary works – has always been a concern of genre criticism, and Fowler's book (as well as his later essay on generic formation in the Renaissance) contributes to this task of identification at the same time that his emphasis on communication offers important cautions against the danger of letting identifications become rigid and distorting classifications. Forming, or constructing, relations to literary (and other) communities helps enable the reconstruction of "old or difficult" works, and a relational approach reveals how changes internal to a literary field connect to external changes that, in however indirect and mediated a fashion, structure them.

26. "Change of function" is the only one of these with clear reference to use, to what a text might be for.

Another important strand of recent genre theory is represented by the work of Franco Moretti and other scholars like Wai-Chee Dimock which looks at developments in genre systems – mostly the novel – from a "distant" perspective that deploys tools from what has come to be called the digital humanities.[27] In Moretti's case, he seeks to develop very large scale descriptions of "world literature" that will "function as a thorn in the side, a permanent intellectual challenge to national literatures – especially the local literature" ("Conjectures" 68). By "local," Moretti appears to mean the work closest to the critic, and "world literature" functions as a challenge to the kind of critical chauvinism that privileges one's own preferred object as typical of literature as a whole. Moretti's project focuses so closely on the novel that other forms drop from consideration even as he argues for greater specificity about what "the" novel might be. In *Graphs, Maps, Trees* (2005), Moretti does address the question of generic change in the novel but, while pointing at the impact of extra-literary forces, seems peculiarly content to indicate a pattern of generational changes without going very far to characterize or account for them.[28]

This book intends not only to offer descriptions of generic change but also to speak to a wider range of genres, of the system of kinds that early modern writers found themselves engaged in. Distant descriptions of systems can only be a part of this project, and work like that inspired by Moretti's *Graphs, Maps, Trees* still explains literature in terms of literature. Moretti's book understands genre through what amounts to the "family resemblance" line of thinking deriving in however attenuated a way from Wittgenstein, though he does not use that precise language. Genre, he writes, ought to be thought of as "an abstract diversity spectrum," never fully represented by any one text (*Graphs* 76). Generic change, at least in the "Trees" chapter, is understood in immanent terms and through a cyclical movement of divergence leading to convergence and then to divergence among forms again:

> It is easy (in theory, at least) to envision how this cyclical matrix could be applied to the history of genres: convergence among separate lineages would be decisive in the genesis of genres of particu-

---

27. Dimock does differ from Moretti on the abandonment of close readings in favor of his "distant reading," but they do share an interest in broader systems that are made visible with digital tools.
28. The New Formalism, while interested in formalist readings, lacks, in my view, a more general theory about genre and generic change.

lar significance: then once a genre's form stabilizes, "interbreeding" would stop, and divergence would become the dominant force. (*Graphs* 80n13)

While this kind of model does have a certain amount of explanatory force, it grants genres a peculiar kind of agency by overplaying the biological metaphor. Genres, of course, do not interbreed by themselves; instead, writers acting at specific moments in history combine them under the pressures exerted by the shape of the literary field, which are themselves (in part) refractions of the forces structuring the broader field of power.

Given the range and richness of genre theory of the kind discussed above, this book turns to the work of the Bakhtin circle and the sociology of Pierre Bourdieu because of these thinkers' emphasis on the necessity of understanding literature in terms of social interaction, rather than understanding it in terms immanent to itself. Whether as what the Bakhtin circle thought of as "verbal interaction" or "ideological colloquy" or Bourdieu's argument about the cultural field as a site of position-takings and conflict linked to but also distinct from the general social field, they model the dynamic relationship between text and society. If genre criticism and theory is to account for change and innovation, approaches like those of Bakhtin and Bourdieu represent perhaps the best (if also most difficult) method of accomplishing that goal.

IV

> The novel as a whole is an utterance just as rejoinders in everyday dialogue or private letters are (they do have a common origin), but unlike these, the novel is a secondary (complex) utterance.
>
> The work, like the rejoinder in dialogue, is oriented towards the response of the other (others) [. . .] The work is a link in the chain of speech communion. Like the rejoinder in dialogue, it is related to other work-utterances: both those to which it responds and those that respond to it.
>
> M. M. Bakhtin, "The Problem of Speech Genres"

A concern with the social nature of discourse pervades all of the Bakhtin's circle's thought about language. Whether in Bakhtin's extended investigations of dialogic interactions in the book on Dostoevsky or in the essays collected in *The Dialogic Imagination* (1981) or in Voloshinov's work *Marxism and the Philosophy of*

Language (1986), their thought stresses the irremediably social nature of any kind of verbal communication. Voloshinov writes that:

> Utterance, as we know, is constructed between two socially organized persons, and in the absence of a real addressee, an addressee is presupposed in the person, so to speak, of a normal representative of the social group to which the speaker belongs. *The word is oriented toward an addressee.* (85, original emphasis)

All utterances presuppose the social existence of a real or notional audience. Voloshinov argues against an abstract notion of language, instead constructing an account that is profoundly historical and material. Utterance has to be understood historically – partly by understanding the social formations that give rise to it – and any account of change has to be situated in terms of these kinds of verbal interactions between "socially organized persons," actual or hypothetical. Voloshinov's argument points towards an idea of genre as practice, without meaning or existence outside of concrete utterance. He goes on to argue that the orientation of the word to the addressee has important consequences:

> Orientation of the word toward the addressee has an extremely high significance. In point of fact, *word is a two-sided act*. It is determined equally by *whose* word it is and *for whom* it is meant. As word, it is precisely *the product of the reciprocal relationship between speaker and listener, addresser and addressee* . . . a word is territory shared by both addresser and addressee, by the speaker and his interlocutor. (86, original emphasis)

Word, to adopt his phrasing, is not only socially organized, but is also the product and mechanism of a relation between addresser and addressee. This reciprocity means that the word is oriented not only towards the hearer, but to the hearer's potential response. It anticipates reactions from its hearers and that anticipation structures the utterance. I understand literary history as a part of the shared territory Voloshinov describes. In the same chapter of *Marxism and the Philosophy of Language*, Voloshinov explicitly includes books in the forms of verbal communication that share territory and inevitably have a kind of reciprocal relationship with potential responses:

> A book, i.e., a verbal performance in print, is also an element of verbal communication. It is something discussable in actual, real-life, dialogue, but aside from that, it is calculated for active perception. Involving attentive reading and inner responsiveness, and for organ-

ized *printed* reaction in the various forms devised by the particular sphere of verbal communication in question (book reviews, critical surveys, defining influence on subsequent works). Moreover, a verbal performance of this kind also inevitably orients itself with respect to previous performances in the same sphere, both those by the same author and by other authors. It inevitably takes its point of departure from some particular state of affairs involving a scientific problem or a literary style. Thus the printed verbal performance engages, as it were, in ideological colloquy of large scale: it responds to something, objects to something, anticipates responses and objections, seeks support, and so on. (95, original emphasis)

A book is something that can enter into communication as an object of discussion, as in the critical conversation about literature, and, equally as significant, it expects "active perception" by its immediate audience as well as the larger one of history. The book's material existence is part of this conversation: that it is a physical object, with its own set of involvements, whether physical or ideological, makes up part of this colloquy. When Voloshinov writes that a book (and I think it reasonable to extend this to include theatrical performance) "inevitably orients itself with respect to previous performances" and to succeeding ones, he is arguing that the work is taking part in a literary or scientific metadialogue (95). Works function as utterances in dialogue with their predecessors, contemporaries, and followers. This conception of literary works as part of an enormous dialogue of utterance and rejoinder suggests alternative ways to conceptualize relations between works and between writers.

Despite Bakhtin's alleged hostility to drama, his work offers productive ways to engage with the question of generic change in the dramatic field of the first decades of the seventeenth century.[29] This hostility has always been more putative than actual and does not apply to the plays of early modern playwrights. *The Dialogic Imagination*'s suggestion that drama is inherently monological seems to be referring specifically to plays of the nineteenth century. Shakespeare figures in Bakhtin as fundamentally dialogic and heteroglot. In "The Problem of Speech Genres," Bakhtin argues that while utterance remains the fundamental category of analysis in the study of language and that each utterance is irreducibly individual, language tends to develop "relatively stable types" of utterances: "these we may call *speech genres*" (60, original emphasis). As utterances,

---

29. For a more developed argument about Bakhtin and early modern drama, see James R. Siemon's *Word Against Word: Shakespearean Utterance* (2002).

literary works engage, like speech, in dialogue but with other works as interlocutors. In this conception, the work is necessarily oriented towards both its predecessors and its successors in the metadialogue of a literary history imagined as dialogue. Thus, individual plays can be usefully conceptualized as interventions in an ongoing debate or conversation about the nature, purpose, capacities and form of drama. In addition, the play-utterance is actively linked to both the play-utterances that come before and those that come after.[30]

Both genre and generic change, then, arise out of a literary metadialogue, wherein influence operates at the level of the word, at the level of structure, and between whole works. Bakhtin's conception of literary works as part of an enormous dialogue of utterance and rejoinder suggests alternative ways to conceptualize relations between works and between writers. Works orient themselves towards other works (not to mention audiences), and that orientation, like that of the rejoinder in spoken dialogue, comprehends in various ways the utterance to which it is responding. This idea is a consistent feature of the Bakhtin circle's theory from early texts like *Marxism and the Philosophy of Language* all the way to later works like the speech genres essay. As Bakhtin writes in that essay:

> Utterances are not indifferent to one another, and are not self-sufficient; they are aware of and mutually reflect one another. These mutual reflections determine their character. Each utterance is filled with echoes and reverberations of other utterances to which it is related by the communality of the sphere of speech communication. Every utterance must be regarded primarily as a *response* to preceding utterances of the given sphere . . . Each utterance refutes, affirms, supplements, and relies on the others, presupposes them to be known, and somehow takes them into account. After all, as regards a given question, in a given matter, and so forth, the utterance occupies a particular *definite* position in a given sphere of communication. It is impossible to determine its position without correlating it with other positions. Therefore, each utterance is filled with various kinds of responsive reactions to other utterances of the given sphere of speech communication. (91, original emphasis)

Utterances' mutual awareness and reflection of each other operates at both the level of the individual word and of the whole work. The refutations, affirmations, and supplements Bakhtin refers to

---

30. *Troilus and Cressida*'s armed prologue responds to the armed prologue of Jonson's *Poetaster*, among others.

comprise one of the primary engines of generic change, not least because they represent the taking of a position in a specific field of discourse.[31] "Refraction" better characterizes transformations of style or form across generic boundaries and stresses the ways that these responsive reactions are active rather than passive responses. This responsiveness operates across generic boundaries as much as within them. As an example, Jonson's *Poetaster* explicitly attempts to define the boundaries of good dramatic language by caricaturing and expelling bad dramatic verse while at the same time presenting a play that is a statement about dramatic form.[32] Verbal interaction, here at the level of the work, is thus oriented towards both past and future, and each intervention necessarily alters the genre in which it takes form.

Bakhtin argues that speech genres, and by extension all genres, develop over a long history and that literary genres represent an especially complicated example of this process:

> Historical changes in language styles are inseparably linked to changes in speech genres. Literary language is a complex, dynamic system of linguistic styles. The proportions and interrelations of these styles in the system of literary language are constantly changing. Literary language, which also includes nonliterary styles, is an even more complex system, and it is organized on different bases. In order to puzzle out the complex historical dynamics of these systems and move from a simple (and, in the majority of cases, superficial) description of styles, which are always in evidence and alternating with one another, to a historical explanation of these changes, one must develop a special history of speech genres (and not only secondary, but also primary ones) that reflects more directly, clearly, and flexibly all the changes taking place in social life. Utterances and their types, that is, speech genres, are the drive belts from the history of society to the history of language. ("Problem" 65)

These changes include educational developments, increasing (or alternative) access to literary traditions, developments in audiences and changes in sites of production among others.[33] Moving beyond

---

31. Bourdieu picks up on these insights and develops them further in *The Rules of Art*, and *The Field of Cultural Production* collects a number of essays on the cultural field. See discussion below.
32. See my *Representing the Professions* (2006) for an extended discussion of Jonson's play as this kind of position-taking.
33. See Bourdieu, *The Rules of Art* for an extensive account of the French literary field in the nineteenth century that operates along these lines.

"simple description" entails both that description and an extensive investigation into a far wider array of changes. Part of this effort must be to characterize the stylistic context and available resources at a given moment in the development of a specific variety of literary language as far as that is possible. Bakhtin's metaphor of a drivebelt can be more productively (and less reductively) replaced with the idea of refraction. Genre, in this account, is the primary link between language and society, and generic innovation occurs as a refraction of social change. If generic change at least partly results from social change, then generic innovation may serve as a marker of social change, but not in any direct or transparent way. Bakhtin also here identifies a central problem of genre theory – the way that discussion of genre has tended to function in a descriptive rather than an analytical or historical register – calling for a "special history of speech genres" that would move beyond what he criticizes as in the passage above as the "simple description of styles" (65).

V

> Few areas more clearly demonstrate the heuristic efficacy of *relational* thinking than that of art and literature. Constructing an object such as the literary field requires and enables us to make a radical break with the substantialist mode of thought (as Ernst Cassirer calls it) which tends to foreground the individual, or the visible interactions between individuals, at the expense of the structural relations—invisible, or visible only through their effects—between social positions that are both occupied and manipulated by social agents which may be isolated individuals, groups or institutions.
>
> Pierre Bourdieu, "The Field of Cultural Production,
or: The Economic World Reversed"

Bourdieu's most extended treatment of artistic production is found in *The Rules of Art*, a book that contributes to the development of a more clear and flexible history of genre. Bourdieu argues that upheavals within genres or in the hierarchy of disparate genres depend on the coincidence of historical developments with aesthetic innovations. In this view, generic change operates on a basis similar to other social changes, which depend on the coincidence of changes within a given field with external changes that open up room for innovations. Vacancies in a social system open up because of historical or economic shifts that new occupants struggle to occupy.[34] Writing of generic change in the *Rules of Art*, Bourdieu argues:

> Changes as decisive as an upheaval in the internal hierarchy of different genres, or a transformation within genres themselves, affecting the structure of the field as a whole, are made possible by the *correspondence between internal changes* (themselves directly determined by the transformation in the chances of access to the literary field) *and external changes* which offer to new categories of producers (successively, the Romantics, Naturalists, Symbolists, etc.) and to their products consumers who occupy positions in social space which are homologous to their own position in the field, and hence consumers endowed with dispositions and tastes in harmony with the products these producers offer them. (252, original emphasis)

Bourdieu's emphasis on this correspondence between such internal and external changes in this passage concerning generic upheaval bears a clear resemblance to Bakhtin's discussion of genre and, like Bakhtin's, offers a productive way to characterize generic change that moves beyond description or catalogue towards a more adequate historicization of generic change. This book takes up the question of internal transformation – such as the emergence of the so-called "tragedy of blood" with the broader category of tragedy – as well as changes that alter the shape of the literary field. For such transformations to occur, changes internal to the field like the advent of new playwrights with different dispositions and backgrounds must coincide with changes in audience that are dependent on external – social or historical – changes that alter tastes. Offering one example of such a change in both producers and consumers, Lynda Boose has discussed what she terms the "sexualization" of the Jacobean stage resulting from the 1599 ban on satire promulgated by the Archbishop of Canterbury and the Bishop of London. The ban legislatively closed the print market for verse satire which, Boose argues, led a group of writers including Middleton and Marston to turn to the stage. It is tempting to think that as authors turned to an alternative publication medium so too did their audience. What is striking, nevertheless, is the degree to which satirical railing of the kind that Middleton and Marston write before the Ban makes its way into the drama after 1600. Its presence sug-

---

34. Andrew Abbott's *The System of Professions: An Essay on the Division of Expert Labor* (1988) makes extensive use of this kind of model to describe how the titular system operates.

gests the existence of an audience well-suited to appreciate such productions.[35]

I have written on Bourdieu's social theory elsewhere, and here I want to contain my comments to his engagements with literature and the literary field.[36] *The Field of Cultural Production* and the *Rules of Art* contain the bulk of Bourdieu's work on literature – at least that which has been translated into English – and despite their relative neglect by English-speaking scholars, they represent a valuable resource for research into questions of generic change. In "Principles for a Sociology of Cultural Works," Bourdieu makes a concise statement of his approach to the study of literary works, and these principles structure my approach in what follows. The essay critiques what he characterizes as two of the primary approaches to literary study: the position exemplified by New Criticism which posits atemporal universals and a structuralist approach which, although more historical and "stronger" as a method, still refuses "external hermeneutics" (178). On the other hand, the classic version of an "external hermeneutic" – Marxist criticism – has historically made the links between outside and inside far too direct and simple. As he writes, Marxist analyses have attempted "to relate works to the world view or the social interests of a particular social class" (180).[37] This "short-circuit" ignores the mediation of institutions or other social structures. Internal approaches attempt to explain artistic change only (or mostly) in terms internal to art – refusing to consider effects from external forces – and thus cannot offer satisfactory accounts. Even structuralist approaches ignore forces outside "literature" when appealing to ideas like the "literary system" or "literary language" as though they are self-contained and self-referential systems. Instead of this variety of immanentist criticism, "one should study the genesis of systems of classification, names of periods, schools,

---

35. The success of stage satire has much to do with audiences from the Inns of Court, who were disposed both to appreciate and produce satirical works. See Jessica Winston's *Lawyers at Play: Literature, Law, and Politics at the Early Modern Inns of Court, 1558–1581* (2016). Adam Zucker's *Places of Wit in Early Modern English Comedy* (2011) locates the emergence of "town comedy" in a series of social, economic, and spatial changes that opened space for a new version of city comedy in the later sixteenth and seventeenth century.
36. See my *Representing the Professions*.
37. His examples include Lukács's work on the novel and others that depend on too easy a connection between base and superstructure. It is true that the essay does not attend to more subtle versions of Marxist criticism, but the central contention about an often too-direct link between specific classes (say) and specific forms seems not unfair.

genres and so forth that are actually the instruments and stakes of struggle" because without this work scholarship concludes where the research should start (180). The emergence of historicist criticism has at least partially addressed the problem Bourdieu is responding to in this essay, but his caution remains valuable, especially in the context of genre criticism which often proceeds as if genres precede their concrete instantiation.

Both the internal and external approaches Bourdieu criticizes ignore the mediating effects of what he calls the field of cultural production, which distorts their understanding of both individual works and their contexts of production. A *field*, a central category in Bourdieu's work, is a social space within which participants – like writers in the literary field – engage in a structured competition for position, a competition structured by the particular kinds of capital that field values.[38] The field of cultural production is the social space within which genre becomes meaningful, both as an expressive tool and as a stake in debates about the value of particular works. As he writes:

> A field may be defined as a network, or a configuration, of objective relations between positions. These positions are objectively defined, in their existence and in the determinations they impose on their occupants, agents or institutions, by their present and potential situation (*situs*) in the structure of the distribution of the species of power (or capital) whose possession commands access to the specific profits that are at stake in the field, as well as by their objective relation to other positions (domination, subordination, homology, etc.). (*Invitation* 97)

In the early modern context, the field of cultural production consists of (in part) the institutions through which cultural products like drama find audiences (acting companies, theatres, publishers) and the relations between writers working in those institutions. It is defined by the structure of relations between writers (and the institutions circulating their work) and the relative status of those writers based on the particular cultural capital they possess.[39]

---

38. Examples include the law, where lawyers find (or fail to find) positions of authority based not only on individual ability but on the capital conferred by what law school a particular lawyer attended, that lawyer's social background and so on. Each field has its own structure and stakes.
39. That status is internal to the field and not always directly analogous to other kinds of status. Bourdieu's example of the writer's writer who, while a "failure"

As the literary field becomes more autonomous, the criteria by which writers and their products are judged become increasingly "literary" and the right to define that category is the object of struggle. The value of works of art depends on this competition. As he writes of the field of cultural production:

> It is the field of production, understood as the system of objective relations between these agents or institutions and as the site of the struggles for the monopoly of the power to consecrate, in which the value of works of art and belief in that value are continuously generated. (*Field* 78)

The key aspect, one that is sometimes overlooked in the kinds of approaches Bourdieu criticizes, is that the value of works of art is a product of this structured struggle and that one important part of that struggle is in what he elsewhere calls the "production of belief" that works (and kinds of works) have value.[40]

Fields are dynamic because there is a constant struggle over the power to consecrate – the power to confer value on a particular work or author – and because new agents and institutions are constantly entering the field. The relative values of genres respond to these struggles. For example, the way that Jonson denigrates the long jars of Lancaster and York in *Every Man in His Humor* (1598) is an effort to assert the value his work in a new kind. In the induction to that play, Jonson denigrates poets made by "need," and states that he

> Hath not so loved the stage,
> As he dare serve the ill customs of the age:
> Or purchase your delight at such a rate,
> As for it, he himself must justly hate. (Ind. 3–6)[41]

Unlike others, Jonson will not debase himself because of need and will instead pursue a worthier project. Jonson is asserting that his work, while still commercial, aspires to distinguish itself from the "ill customs of the age" that he goes on to define by specific refer-

---

in terms of sales or general popularity, achieves fame and respect within the field points towards the specificity of these relations. See *Rules of Art*.

40. I have argued that the struggle Jonson, Dekker, and Marston engaged in around 1600 represents an example of such a struggle for the right to consecrate, to decide what counts as valuable or not, in the dramatic field. This struggle operates both explicitly in paratextual statements and implicitly in the way competing works are written. See *Representing the Professions*.
41. I am citing from *Ben Jonson: Five Plays* (1988).

ences to the historical drama of Shakespeare: the wars of York and Lancaster or the Chorus wafting audiences from London to France in *Henry V*. Rather than the squeaking thrones or squibs and rolled bullets of what he characterizes as crude spectacle, Jonson argues for the superior value of his mode of comedy, a mode he argues can "show an image of the times" (Ind. 23). Jonson's comedy strives to take up a place in a contention with other dramatic kinds and does so by downgrading and differentiating itself from an earlier and successful one. Francis Beaumont's *Knight of the Burning Pestle* (1607) and its representation of dramatic hierarchy offers another example, when the Prologue Boy asserts that Red Bull plays are lower in value than *The London Merchant*.[42] Any position in the field – like that occupied by Shakespeare – is defined only in relation to other positions in the field and those positions in turn are defined (and altered) by struggles to achieve "higher" positions in the field.[43] For example, commendatory poems like Jonson's poem in the First Folio (or Milton's in the Second) describe the field, staking a claim for their authors' positions at the same time. Constructing the field cannot be completed by either an immanent or an external approach on its own. Attending to works at the same time as the position of producers in a field is necessary because:

> the field exerts an effect of *refraction* (much like a prism) and it is only when one knows its specific laws of operation ... that one can understand what is happening in the struggles between poets. (Bourdieu, *Field* 182)[44]

Like struggles in other social spaces, struggles between poets (or other cultural producers) are structured by the positions they hold and those positions need to be attended to in order to understand

---

42. In many cases, the hierarchy is linked to social distinctions, though not always in straightforward ways.
43. "Higher" and "lower" have multiple definitions that depend on nature of the field. One of Bourdieu's examples is the avant-garde, where literary status stands in a more or less inverse relation to external markers of success like sales. In addition, not all of these struggles are conducted by their ostensible objects: Marlowe's position in the field after 1593 changes not because he is struggling for position, but because he becomes a reference point or species of capital.
44. It is worth noting that Bourdieu is far from hostile to Marxist or materialist approaches to literary study per se. His critique is focused on work that indulges in the short-circuit. Indeed, as a sociologist, his work is eminently materialist. To call him a post-Marxist is almost as inaccurate as calling him a post-structuralist.

and characterize changes in genres, the emergence of new works and new forms, and of new categories of producers:

> The impetus for change in cultural works—language, art, literature, science, etc.—resides in the struggles that take place in the corresponding fields of production. These struggles, whose goal is the preservation or transformation of the established power relationships in the field of production, obviously have as their effect the preservation or transformation of the structure of the field of works, which are the tools and stakes in the struggles. (Bourdieu, *Field* 183)

Finding the impetus for change in the field of production requires attending to as much of the structure of the field as possible, and while the kinds of reconstruction Bourdieu does for the nineteenth century French field of cultural production are far more difficult in early modern England because the cultural apparatus of reviews, newspapers and the like had not developed and because of the spottiness of the records that survive, this book will make an effort to characterize the field of production given the tools and resources available as a way of better understanding the nature and process of generic change and shifts in the hierarchy of dramatic genres.

VI

> What we need, in effect, is a form of structural history that is rarely practiced, which finds in each successive state of the structure under examination both the product of previous struggles to maintain or to transform this structure, and the principle, via the contradictions, the tensions, and the relations of force which constitute it, of subsequent transformations.
>
> Pierre Bourdieu, Invitation to Reflexive Sociology

Bourdieu argues for a historicism that attempts to locate elements of diachrony in the synchronic moment of study. Each successive state of a social structure thus must be thought of as containing both traces of the past and indications of possible future trajectories of change. This call for a "structural history" has special relevance to this book's examination of the changing generic system in the later sixteenth and early seventeenth centuries. Kyd, Marlowe, Shakespeare, Jonson, Middleton, and many others were writing plays that challenged and transformed more or less established boundaries of genre, literally confusing history, tragedy, and comedy. Any effort to investigate genre and generic change must also look to the materials this process of combination transforms. Thus, this effort at establishing a structural history of genre will necessarily be a kind of source study, but one that focuses on technique and narrative form in addition to specific textual or plot echoes.

Bakhtin argues that works interact in ways that go beyond more or less readily recognizable matters of verbal influence.[45] He writes:

> The work, like the rejoinder in dialogue, is oriented towards the response of the other (others), towards his active responsive understanding, which can assume various forms: educational influence on the readers, persuasion of them, critical responses, influences on followers and successors and so on. It can determine others' responsive positions under the complex conditions of speech communication in a particular cultural sphere. The work is a link in the chain of speech communion. Like the rejoinder in dialogue, it is related to other work-utterances: both those to which it responds and those that respond to it. At the same time, like the rejoinder in a dialogue, it is separated from them by the absolute boundaries created by a change of speaking subjects. ("Problem of Speech Genres" 76)

Works, in this account, engage in a conversation spanning histories of reception and production, and each work actively works to condition the kinds of responses it will receive as much as it influences the works to which it responds. Bakhtin imagines a dynamic and flexible version of literary history that attempts to account for the ways that work-utterances, to use his term, intervene prospectively and retrospectively in the "chain of speech communion" that is the literary field. The interventions, appropriations, and transformations under discussion in this book will necessarily be linked to changes both within and without the literary field. As Bakhtin reminds us, literary change necessarily relates to broader social changes and a fuller understanding (insofar as such things are possible) of generic changes and literary influence must include a consideration of historical developments that get refracted into literary work ("Problem of Speech Genres" 65).

Many early modern comic and tragic plays are set in distinct social and physical locations: comedy tends to either country or urban settings, while tragedy tends to be set at court. This pattern,

---

45. Even these matters end up being more complicated and difficult to identify than initially appears. Much of the literature on Shakespeare's Chaucer taken up in Chapter One points to this problem.

of course, has much to do with the social classes normally associated with the two genres.[46] Bakhtin uses the term chronotope in the essay "Forms of Time and the Chronotope in the Novel: Notes Towards a Historical Poetics" to describe the specific form that time and space take in particular works of literature. Chronotope describes the "intrinsic connectedness of temporal and spatial relationships that are artistically expressed in literature ("Chronotope" 84). There are, in this view, ways of representing space and time that are particular to particular forms. "Adventure time," for example, is a chronotope in which space and time function only as a background for the characters' adventures, exerting no particular influence over those adventures or the characters. Chronotopes necessarily stand in close relation to genres. If a speech genre (or literary genre) is the characteristic mode of speech of some specific sphere of communication, then chronotopes represent time and space characteristic of those spheres.[47] In much the same way that genres bring with them more or less stable expectations, so too do chronotopes.

Literary historians rarely discuss Bakhtin's essay "The Problem of Speech Genres," despite its English publication in 1986 (and its usefulness). Scholars of rhetoric, following the generic turn, have thoroughly examined it – albeit not in terms of literary history.[48] Likewise, Bourdieu's work on culture – particularly on the question of genre – has been relatively underdiscussed in both the subfield of genre studies and literary studies more generally.[49] There are a variety of reasons for this, the central one being the extraordinary difficulty of the project that both writers outline. In Bakhtin's case, building an account of how speech genres combine and recombine

---

46. Aristotle writes that comedy concerns people of the middling or lower sorts while tragedy concerns the better sort. Renaissance thinkers like Sidney pick up these social distinctions.
47. Bakhtin refers to spheres of communication in relation to speech genres in "The Problem of Speech Genres." I am using his language here as the most appropriate to this discussion.
48. See Amy Devitt, "Generalizing about Genre: New Conceptions of an Old Concept"; Helen Rothschild Ewald, "Waiting for Answerability: Bakhtin and Composition Studies"; or Kay Halasek, *A Pedagogy of Possibility: Bakhtinian Perspectives on Composition Studies* (1999).
49. John Speller's 2011 *Bourdieu and Literature* offers an introduction to Bourdieu's consideration of literature. A special issue of *Paragraph* on "Bourdieu and the Literary Field" was published in 2012, and there are scattered articles elsewhere. The *Paragraph* issue mentions genre only in passing in one article on form (Jeremy Lane's "Between Repression and Anamnesis: Pierre Bourdieu and the Vicissitudes of Literary Form").

into secondary genres through history demands a combination of philological, linguistic, and historiographic skills. To "give a full account" of the field requires a great deal of information but at the same time "it would quite unjust and futile to reject this demand for complete reconstitution on the ground (which is undeniable) that it is difficult to perform and in some cases impossible" (Bourdieu, *Field* 65). Complete reconstitution might well be impossible, given the nature of the records we have, but we can construct a reasonably complete picture.[50] Extending our attention to the broader field of print, as book history has been teaching us to do, is one way to build this more adequate picture. Following a Bourdieuvian approach akin to my own, Douglas Bruster's "The Representation Market of Early Modern England" concludes with the suggestion that "research could investigate the shapes of the representation market vis-à-vis specific months and years, writers and artists, purchasers of cultural goods, literary characters, works and genres" (23). Similarly, this book examines genres, years, and particular producers in an effort to understand the dynamics of innovation in the drama of early modern England. More generally, my intent is to contribute to the characterization of the field of cultural production. Moments of innovation in the generic system of early modern English "literature" offer a glimpse at that field and, at the same time, affords a space to consider genre theory more generally.[51]

VII

My method in the chapters that follow will be to attempt insofar as it is possible to reconstruct segments of the generic system in an effort to describe and account for innovation. My goal is to develop a sense of the shape of the field at given moments and for specific traditional genres like tragedy as well as for what have been seen as emergent forms like the history play or "romance." Bourdieu's sociology of

---

50. My own arguments about theatre professionals and Beaumont's *Knight of the Burning Pestle* represent an attempt to do this kind of work by locating the play in the context of theatrical crafts as well as more literary contexts. See *Representing the Professions*.
51. The matter of "literature" is the subject of a great deal of work, and scholars like Timothy Reiss, among others, have written on the emergence of literature as a category. See Timothy Reiss, *The Meaning of Literature* (1992). John Guillory's *Cultural Capital: The Problem of Literary Canon Formation* (1993) takes up the problem of the canon from a Bourdieuvian perspective.

art and the work of the Bakhtin circle subtends this work, but I will complement the more abstract work of characterizing a field with close readings of plays and poems. Each chapter takes up distinct kinds and approaches within the larger framework I am striving to develop, and I hope that the disparate nature of each chapter contributes to at least a sketch of a system of genres. I have deliberately chosen to examine a range of texts and kinds here rather than focus on one genre (however tempting that might be) in order to keep at least a portion of my attention on the system even in the midst of detailed discussions of literary and historical texts.

The chapters examine an array of putatively "new" forms and several moments typically recognized as especially innovative. Focusing on clusters of innovations rather than attempting to produce a chronology, I open with two chapters on Shakespeare's use of earlier narrative forms as resources for producing new modes of drama at the turn of the seventeenth century. In the traditional narrative, tragicomedy and "romance" emerge along with city comedy after 1600. My book examines the first two of these, leaving city comedy out since critics like Brian Gibbons, Theodore Leinwand, and Jean Howard among others have discussed it so well; city comedy is also a partially hybrid form by definition. In the third chapter, I examine the drama of the late 1580s and early 1590s, which, among other things, introduces blank verse to the public stage and represents another locus of innovation. I then turn to the history play, which in the standard narrative emerges in the 1580s and 1590s, flourishes briefly, and vanishes after about 1600. I discuss the tragedy of the seventeenth century sometimes called "the tragedy of blood," which is itself a hybrid form, willing to engage in self-parody. As evidenced by this brief description, my book cannot have a singular argument; rather, it offers a series of related ones. Each chapter shares a common interest in the shape and mechanisms of generic change, but the arguments differ in accord with the objects of study.

Chapter one, "'Chaucer (of all admired) the story gives': Shakespeare, Medieval Narrative, and Generic Innovation," examines Shakespeare's narrative debts to medieval poetry by reading *Troilus and Cressida* (1600–1) with Chaucer and Henryson and *Pericles* (1607–8) with Gower. I examine *Troilus and Cressida* as an instance of generic innovation at the turn of the century and argue that the play deliberately fails as a dramatizing of a medieval romance narrative as part of an intervention in contemporary struggles with dramatic form. *Pericles* was more popular than *Troilus and Cressida* despite sharing some of the same disjointed narrative structure and satirical content. The chapter accounts for the two plays' different receptions in terms of the dramatic field at the moment of production. As Bourdieu points out, generic transformations depend on innovative works finding receptive audiences, not on innovation itself. The narrative innovations of *Troilus and Cressida* and *Pericles* – ruptured narratives, inconclusive or "unsatisfying" endings – resonate with and respond to both their medieval sources and the contemporary dramatic field.

Chapter two, "'Mirrours more then one': Spenser, Shakespeare, and Generic Change," examines the influence of Edmund Spenser's *Faerie Queene* (1596) on Shakespeare's *Hamlet* (1600) and *Troilus and Cressida*. If Spenser's purpose in Book III of the *Faerie Queene* is to illuminate the virtue of chastity from multiple sides, shining light on it from various mirrors, reflecting it from those mirrors into a variety of more or less recognizable refractions, then Shakespeare's narrative intentions in such convoluted plays as *Hamlet* and *Troilus and Cressida* may be homologous: to reflect on a problem from multiple perspectives. Both *Hamlet* and *Troilus and Cressida* resist easy categorizing, and the chapter argues that that resistance is a product of developments like the emergence of dramatic satire and tragicomedy that blur distinctions between dramatic kinds. This blurring of generic boundaries marks changes in the structure of the field of cultural production attendant on the emergence of new forms, as does the different receptions of the two plays.

Chapter three, "'King Cambyses' vein': Generic Change in the 1580s and 1590s," takes up the question of generic change in the 1590s, situating that change within the traditions of public playing, civic and court drama, university neo-Latin drama, and the broader field of cultural production. The chapter addresses such examples as Gager's Latin play *Meleager* (1593), Preston's *Cambises* (1560/1?), Kyd's *Spanish Tragedy* (1590), and *Arden of Faversham* (c. 1592). Literary historians conventionally describe the 1580s as a moment of profound change in the drama, a moment that extends into the early years of the 1590s. One purpose of this chapter is to situate and evaluate those changes in a somewhat broader context, looking back into the 1570s and turning part of the critical gaze away from London and to the universities.

Chapter four, "'Lies like Truth': History, Fiction, Genre, Innovation," discusses the history play before roughly 1600. "The English History Play" is almost always discussed as a distinctively new and distinctively English dramatic genre. Through discussions of Marlowe's *Edward II* (1594) and Shakespeare's *2 Henry IV* (1600), this chapter looks at the form at its putative moment of origin. The history play is a notoriously hybrid form and this hybridity has, almost since the first attempts to label these plays, raised questions about what these plays "are" in terms of genre. The chapter argues that this effort, in many ways, obscures what is actually distinctive about this ad hoc grouping of plays. Through discussions of the intellectual context of an increased interest in history – Annabel Patterson's work on Holinshed is only one example of this – the chapter shows that the "genre" of the history is both less innovative than often argued and more durable and pervasive.

Chapter five, "'What's aught but as 'tis valued': 'History,' Truth, and Fiction," turns to historical drama of the seventeenth century. It opens by discussing Shakespeare's *Troilus and Cressida* as historical drama before turning to a series of "Tudor history plays," including *The True Chronicle History of the whole life and death of Thomas Lord Cromwell* (1600), Dekker and Webster's *Famous History of Sir Thomas Wyatt* (1602), Rowley's *When You See Me You Know Me* (1604), the two parts of Heywood's *If You Know Not Me, You Know Nobody* (1604, 1605), and Shakespeare and Fletcher's *All is True* (1613). The chapter concludes with Middleton's "late" historical drama *Hengist, King of Kent* (1621) and John Ford's *Perkin Warbeck* (printed 1634). The chapter argues that despite the commonplace narrative that the "history play" fades away after 1600, interest in plays on historical subjects remains high and that these later plays also engage in the project of historical representation despite being separated from the 1590s flourishing of the history play by almost three decades. Rather than proceeding from an assumption that these plays represent a genre because they share an interest in history, I ask why and how it made sense for working playwrights across the whole period to write plays drawing on the recalcitrant materials of history. In both of these chapters, I raise the problem of innovation and suggest that the story of the "history play" offers valuable ways to think about generic change more generally.

Chapter six, "'When the bad bleed': Tenants to Tragedy," turns to developments in early modern dramatic treatments of tragedy after the turn of the seventeenth century while also looking back to plays discussed in the first chapter. In Middleton's *Revenger's Tragedy*, Vindice calls vengeance a "tenant to tragedy," suggesting his awareness of revenge tragedy's status as a subgenre, or, perhaps, a sense that revenge is only one possible element of tragedy. This chapter examines Marston's *Antonio* plays (c. 1599, c. 1600), Chapman's *Bussy* plays (1603–4, 1610), Middleton's *Revenger's Tragedy* (1607) and *Women Beware Women* (Q 1657), before concluding with Shakespeare's *Timon of Athens* (1606–7). It discusses the various tenants to tragedy in these diverse plays – which include elements drawn from comic drama, history and satire – as another way to characterize both the dramatic field and generic change.

The book as a whole reflects on the work done by generic labels through time as well as looking at the varied effects produced by genre theory in literary history. Overtly prescriptive genre criticism that judges a work's value by how well it follows the "laws" set out by Aristotle's *Poetics* has gone by the wayside, but much genre criticism nevertheless proceeds from abstract ideas about what genres are, how they work, and how they interact. If genre is to be a useful category, it must not be assumed to have an existence outside of particular texts produced at particular moments in the history of the field of cultural production: there is no "tragedy," only tragedies. Genre and generic change instead come from the struggles and competitions that define the field of cultural production.

While Shakespeare's plays are important throughout my argument, it is my intention to locate Shakespeare among his contemporaries. Shakespeare's plays offer a way to characterize the complexity of the work of genre in the period, and at the same time I argue that his practice is typical of the period rather than being exceptional. Shakespeare's centrality to the field is at least partly an effect of our construction of his work as the defining work in English theatre of the period and to assume that the generic system revolves around Shakespeare is anachronistic and distorting. I proceed in this way because the category of "author" at least is under construction in the period: Ben Jonson appears to have come to think of himself as a "writer," but it's far from clear how many other playwrights did. Individual plays and playwrights do, of course, effect changes in the genre system in the period but only in relation to other plays and playwrights and the whole range of institutional and cultural contexts that define the field. This book's most general purpose is to consider in detail the background for the changes critics often talk about in the literary production of the period. Genre theory navigates between the Scylla of positivistic prescription and the Charybdis of impressionist description, both of which dangers tend to limit its use as explanation. By deploying the work of Mikhail Bakhtin and Pierre Bourdieu, I attempt to steer between these hazards and to locate generic change in the broad field of cultural production which itself is a part of the general social field.

Chapter 1

"Chaucer (of all admired) the story gives": Shakespeare, Medieval Romance and Generic Innovation

Edward Dowden, an Irish professor of English literature, is best known for having applied the term "romance" to four of Shakespeare's plays as part of two books of criticism published in 1872 and 1877 respectively, whose intent was to place the whole of Shakespeare's literary production into a developmental narrative tracing, to use Dowden's terms, the "growth of his intellect and character from youth to full maturity" (*A Critical Study* xiii). The two books, *Shakspere, A Critical Study of His Mind and Art* (1875) and *Shakspere* (1877), are the originary descriptions of four of Shakespeare's later plays as "romances" – a label that has since expanded to include other plays and the work of other playwrights. Dowden's work covers the whole Shakespearean corpus and divides the plays into a twelve part chronological sequence, from the "Pre-Shaksperian Group" (*Titus Andronicus* and *1 Henry VI*) to "Fragments" (*Two Noble Kinsmen* and *Henry VIII*).[1] The influence of the romance label far exceeds his other divisions because it introduces a term not found in the Folio that brings together plays which appear under the comedy and tragedy rubrics in the Catalogue in the First Folio in ways that recognizes their affinities in terms of content.[2] The other divisions add chronological labels to traditional genres (early, middle, late), and the plays of the Pre-Shaksperian Group and the Fragments have been more happily assimilated into the broader corpus of Shakespeare's plays than appears to have been the case in the later nineteenth century.

1. This last group is separate from the Romances because they are collaborations with Fletcher though they share the same "spirit." The groups overlap chronologically but not generically.
2. It speaks to the sense that something links these plays, something distinguishes them from others among Shakespeare's canon, and it offers a convenient and open label for them while not constraining the association with anything like specifics.

It is not news to argue that Shakespeare's contemporaries did not use the label "romance" for plays, despite it being an available and widely used term for long narratives in prose and verse dating back medieval literature. Nor should it be a shocking discovery that Dowden's description of romance does little to situate these plays in the dramatic context in which they were composed beyond considering Shakespeare's career and some cursory reference to some of the work of his contemporaries. Much of his lack of interest in plays other than Shakespeare is, of course, due to his time period and differences in the project of literary study in the nineteenth century. His biographical explanations of the shape of Shakespeare's career have not had much purchase, and most of the rest of both books have been forgotten. Nevertheless, Dowden's account of Shakespeare's romance remains important, if not always fully recognized, in discussions of these plays.[3] I want to discuss two passages, one from each of these books, in some detail here before proceeding to a broader consideration of the label *dramatic romance*, which has spread to encompass plays from several decades before the four identified by Dowden.

In *Shakspere, A Critical Study of His Mind and Art*, Dowden's discussion of romance is briefer and less specific than in the later book. He writes:

> The plays belonging to Shakespeare's final period of authorship, which I shall consider, are three: Cymbeline, The Winter's Tale, and The Tempest. The position in which they were placed in the first Folio (whether it was the result of design or accident) is remarkable. The volume opens with The Tempest; it closes with Cymbeline. The Winter's Tale is the last of the comedies, which all lie between this play and The Tempest. The circumstance may have been a piece of accident; but if so, it was a lucky accident, which suggests that our first and our last impression of Shakspere shall be that of Shakspere in his period of large, serene wisdom, and that in the light of his closing years all his writings shall be read. Characteristics of versification and style, and the enlarged place given to scenic spectacle,

---

3. Barbara Mowat's "'What's in a Name?': Tragicomedy, Romance, or Late Comedy" (2003) offers a very useful discussion of Dowden's influence and the deployment of other terms (like tragicomedy) to describe the plays of the period. Mowat points out that Dowden's inferences about Shakespeare's state of mind have not withstood criticism. Cyrus Mulready's *Romance on the Early Modern Stage* (2013) discusses Dowden's project and his impact in detail in his first chapter, "Romancing Shakespeare," and argues that romance has a much broader scope than Dowden's biographical project allows.

indicate that these plays were produced much about the same time. But the ties of deepest kinship between them are spiritual. There is a certain romantic element in each. They receive contributions from every portion of Shakspere's genius, but all are mellowed, refined, made exquisite; they avoid the extremes of broad humour and of tragic intensity; they were written with less of passionate concentration than the plays which immediately precede them, but with more of a spirit of deep or exquisite recreation. (402–3)[4]

The paragraph begins with a comment on the placement of the three plays he is interested in in the Folio, but he only alludes to the labels attached to the plays with his reference to *Winter's Tale* (1610–11) being the last of the comedies and does not note that *Cymbeline* is listed with the tragedies. He turns the order of the plays into a statement about how the Folio is meant to be read: "our first and our last impression of Shakspere shall be that of Shakspere in his period of large, serene wisdom, and that in the light of his closing years all his writings shall be read." The notion that the late Shakespeare was defined by "serene wisdom," of course, cannot be verified in any biographical way, but the idea that the *plays* display some kind of distinctive wisdom still has force in criticism.[5] More meaningful and more durable is the idea that these plays are linked by characteristics of versification and of "scenic spectacle." The "spiritual kinship" between the plays is, for Dowden, the most important and what makes them, to use his term, "romantic" rather than comic or tragic. Precisely what he means by romantic in this book is more difficult to say, but it has much to do with what Dowden sees as the "mellowed" and "refined" genius of the plays. Dowden is far more interested in the content and implication of the plays than any kind

---

4. In this work, Dowden does not italicize titles. In the same passage, Dowden justifies excluding *Pericles* out because it was not included in the first Folio: "The same remark applies to Shakspere's part of Pericles, which belongs to this period" (402–3). *Troilus and Cressida* figures as a comedy.
5. I do not mean to dismiss this position read in terms of the plays' engagement with philosophical questions, but to note that it has part of its roots in Dowden's criticism. Cloten's brutishness, the irrationality of Leontes' jealousy, and the submerged violence of Prospero's plan all agitate against straightforward serenity, of course, and the darker tone of these plays make such claims difficult to sustain. Stanley Cavell's work on *The Winter's Tale* represents a powerful example of reading the play through a philosophical lens. It is telling that, though Dowden does mention *Pericles* despite it not being in the Folio, he excludes *Two Noble Kinsmen*, a darker play but one as linked to "romance" as any of the plays he does link under that rubric.

of formal analysis or contextual interpretation of the plays' production or reception.

His 1877 work, more simply titled *Shakspere*, offers a more developed account of the plays, and there is where he explicitly applies the term *romance* to the four plays generally, though not exclusively, linked under that term.[6] After a discussion of what he terms "later tragedy," he turns to the romances.[7] He writes:

> **Romances.**—The transition from these to Shakespeare's last plays is remarkable. From the tragic passion which reached its climax in *Timon of Athens,* we suddenly pass to beauty and serenity; from the plays concerned with the violent breaking of human bonds, to a group of plays which are all concerned with the knitting together of human bonds, the reunion of departed kindred, the forgiveness of enemies, the atonement for wrong—not by death but by repentance—the reconciliation of husband with wife, of child with father, of friend with friend. *Pericles* is a sketch in which only a part of the subject of these last plays is clearly conceived; it is in some respects like a slighter and earlier *Tempest,* in which Lord Cerimon is the Prospero. It also contains hints later worked out in *The Winter's Tale*; the reunion of the Prince of Tyre and his lost Thaisa is a kind of anticipation of the re-discovery by Leontes of his wife who he had so long believed to be dead. Posthumus's jealousy, his perception of his error, his sorrow, and his pardon, may be contrasted with the similar series of incidents in *The Winter's Tale*, and the exquisitely impulsive and generous Imogen may be set over against the grave, statue-like Hermione, whose forgiveness follows long years of suffering, endured with noble fortitude. Prospero is also wronged; his enemies are in his power; but he has employed his ministers to bring them to penitence rather than to bring them to punishment. He has learned that the "rarer action is in virtue than vengeance." In these plays there are two sets of *dramatis personae*: the great sufferers, aged and experienced—Pericles, Prospero, Hermione, afterwards Queen Katherine; and the young and beautiful children in the brightness of the morning of life—Miranda, Perdita, Arviragus, and Guiderius; and Shakspere seems to render homage to both: to the great sufferers for their virtue, and patience, and sorrow; to the young men and maidens of for their beauty and their joy. There is a romantic element about these plays. In all there is the same romantic incident of lost children recovered by

---

6. It may also be worth noting that despite talking about romance, this book pays little attention to the narrative genre whose name Dowden gives to this group of plays.
7. For him, these are *Othello, King Lear, Macbeth, Antony and Cleopatra, Coriolanus*, and *Timon of Athens*.

those to whom they are dear—the daughters of Pericles and Leontes, the sons of Cymbeline and Alonso. In all there is a beautiful romantic background of sea or mountain. The dramas have a grave beauty, a sweet serenity, which seem to render the name "comedies" inappropriate; we may smile tenderly, but we never laugh loudly, as we read them. Let us, then, name this group, consisting of four plays, (xi.) Romances. (55–6)[8]

These plays strike Dowden as remarkably different from those that precede them – having nothing like the "tragic passion" of *Timon of Athens* or what he terms the later tragedy – since they are characterized by "beauty and serenity." They emphasize reconciliation, reunions of divided families, penitence rather than punishment, and what Dowden characterizes as a graver tone than the comedies which have similar themes. Dowden's rhetoric sets up contrasts between the thematics of the tragedies and his romances. The plays move from passion to serenity, from breaking bonds to making them, and from punishment to penitence. Dowden argues that the plays have two sets of characters – the "great sufferers" (which oddly includes Katherine of Aragon from *Henry VIII* which Dowden places with the "fragments") and the "young and beautiful children" – that both receive "homage" at the playwright's hands. The plays, in this view, value both the endurance of suffering and the brightness of youth. This interest in both suffering and youth, combined with the recovery of lost children, lends a "romantic element" to the plays, an element supported by the "beautiful romantic background" of sea and mountain. He does not quite invoke the sublime, but the way he presents nature is close to ideas about the sublimity of nature that run through Romanticism. This notion of the "romantic" has far more in common with Romanticism than with romance proper, and Dowden pays very little attention to the medieval material several of these plays draw on, nor is he much interested in their relations to other texts beyond fairly straightforward ideas about source material. "Romance" seems rather an idiosyncratic generic label that owes more to the immediate tradition of Romantic poetry and drama than to anything like more recent versions of literary history.

Perhaps encouraged by Prospero's lines quoted about virtue being the rarer action than revenge, critics still deploy the idea that these plays are interested in reconciliation. Allowing for differences in crit-

8. The *xi* refers to the group in which Dowden places the plays. The Romances are the eleventh of twelve.

ical vocabulary, it is difficult not to recognize more or less standard descriptions of the four plays in Dowden's account. Many more recent accounts of romance pick up on the moral and social rhetoric Dowden uses in discussing these plays and are typically more interested in offering readings of the plays than explanations of how they developed.[9] As one example, Christopher Cobb's *The Staging of Romance in Late Shakespeare* (2007) opens with a contention that derives from and exemplifies this tradition. He writes that his book "examines how ultimately beneficent human transformations can take place through performances of romance plays" (11).[10] These transformations are of the kind that Dowden and a line of critics have associated with these plays, and Cobb's intention is to examine how such changes take place through performance.

Barbara Mowat's essay in *A Companion to Shakespeare* (2003) states that these plays "belong together in a single genre is a given" (132). She goes on to note that there is no agreement about exactly what to call them, though romance continues to be the default term rather than something like "late Shakespearean comedy" despite that being a more accurate and less baggage-laden term (134).[11] Mowat's argument that the persistence of the label despite the difficulties inherent in it is a clue worth following leads her to an examination of other plays like *Clyomon and Clamydes* and the hugely popular *Mucedorus*, by way of Fowler's theory of family resemblances. These plays, and others carrying the label "heroical romance" in the Harbage *Annals*, clearly do shed light on these plays by Shakespeare and represent a dramatic tradition that was important to the field, though critics have considered it insufficiently.[12] At the same time, Mowat concedes that recognizing this oversight "does not answer the question underlying so much twentieth-century debate about the late plays: namely, what led Shakespeare to create these plays?" (143). Part of my goal in the following two chapters is to point at an answer

---

9. I do not mean to suggest that there is some direct line of inheritance but that the original characterization of these plays as "romance" brings certain concerns with it as an effect of the history of Shakespeare criticism.
10. The book's central focus is on *The Winter's Tale*.
11. Tragicomedy, as Mowat notes, is another term often used for these plays, and both labels, in her argument and the scholarship more generally, remain unsatisfactory.
12. The label *heroical romance*, like *romance*, seems not to have been used by writers, printers, or audiences in the sixteenth and seventeenth centuries. As with the plays we call romances in the Shakespeare canon, they were printed under quite different generic labels.

to that question that does not proceed from assumptions about the existence of "romance" as a genre with some kind of substantive existence outside of individual works. As I argue in the introduction, genres exist more as practices than as substances. The question is not so much what they *are*, but what they *do*.

Much thinking about romance comes out of works like Northrop Frye's *Anatomy of Criticism* and *A Secular Scripture*, which posit more or less transhistorical genres that structure literary expression. While this work is important and still provocative, it is not of much help in answering more specific questions about form, and, more pertinent to my interest in this book, it cannot speak to questions about why works in certain genres should or should not find audiences at specific moments in history. Why, for example, would Shakespeare have turned to medieval narrative poetry for material for his plays in the first years of the seventeenth century, and why would he have also, as I argue below, adopted certain narrative structures from that literature and its Renaissance successors in those plays? Why would a play like *Pericles* be a success, while a play like *Troilus and Cressida* was not?

Regardless of the utility of the label and of how it does seem to register something real about the later Shakespeare, it remains worth noting that no surviving printed play from the period uses "romance" on its title page. Stationers seem to have seen no value in attaching the description to plays (or to narrative romance for that matter), despite the popularity of the form and the availability of the term as a generic label.[13] The plays appear as comedies, histories, and the occasional tragedy, and the bulk of the printed prose and verse romances are called "histories" (with various adjectives attached).[14] Puttenham's *Art of English Poesy* (1589) uses *romance* to refer to "stories of old time, as *The Tale of Sir Topas*, reportes of *Beuis of Southampton, Guy of Warwicke, Adam Bell,* and *Clymme of the Clough* & such other old Romances or historicall rimes" (173). Puttenham uses the term to refer to old works, including Chaucer's parodic *Tale of Sir Thopas*, and suggests that the term is more or less

---

13. To my knowledge, the first play to use "romance" on the title page is Samuel Holland's *Don Zara del Fogo* (1656), and there it is a "mock-romance."
14. To take one example – one that Shakespeare was clearly aware of – Robert Greene's *Pandosto* (1588) is titled *The delightful history of Dorastus and Fawnia. Wherein is declared the cruelty of Pandosto to his fair Bellaria; and how the child Fawnia was put into a boat to be drown'd, but was taken up by the sea-side out of the boat, by a shepherd: and how he brought up the fair Fawnia to keep sheep; and how Dorastus fell in love with the fair Fawnia, &c.*

interchangeable with "historicall rimes." Romances do use the term inside the texts, but the term is strikingly absent from titles.

I

> Utterances are not indifferent to one another, and are not self-sufficient; they are aware of and mutually reflect one another . . . each utterance is filled with various kinds of responsive reactions to other utterances of the given sphere of speech communication.
> M. M. Bakhtin, "The Problem of Speech Genres"

Shakespeare's engagement with Chaucerian narrative responds to an idea of medieval narrative and, in re-interpreting or re-presenting that narrative, contributes to the production of generic innovations like the curiously anticlimactic *Troilus and Cressida,* the kaleidoscopic *Pericles,* and the collaborative *Two Noble Kinsmen.* These three plays had quite different early receptions and print histories that we can at least partially understand in the related contexts of the playhouse and printing house. Of the three, only *Pericles* was a clear theatrical and publishing success, eliciting Ben Jonson's scornful, if envious, "mouldy tale," in his 1629 "Ode: To Himself" and six quarto editions by 1635. *Troilus and Cressida* appeared in quarto and in the 1623 Folio, but its stage history is undocumented in the period and, as is well-known, one of the two states of the 1609 quarto claims the play was never performed, at least not for a general audience.[15] *Two Noble Kinsmen* does have a number of well-attested early performances and seems to have been in the repertory at least until 1625–6, but it was not printed until 1634 and, like *Pericles,* did not appear in any early collection of Shakespeare's plays. All three draw on medieval narratives but to different ends and to different receptions. A sense of the capaciousness of medieval narrative may be one of the forces producing such singularly unresolved plays as Shakespeare's *Troilus and Cressida* and such chaotically structured plays as *Pericles* as well as the more directly Chaucerian, if still unsettling, *Two Noble Kinsmen.*

Scholars have long discussed what Alice Miskimin's enormously useful book (1975) calls the "Renaissance Chaucer." Joseph Dane's

---

15. It is at least possible that the reference to never being "clapper-clawed by the palms of the vulgar" in the publisher's letter means that it was only performed for an elite audience such as at the Inns of Court.

Who Is Buried in Chaucer's Tomb? (1998) examines the history of Chaucer's books, including the early print history of the Chaucerian corpus, and suggests that both the history and the corpus itself are far from stable. More recently, Theresa Krier's 1998 edited collection, *Refiguring Chaucer in the Renaissance*, has engaged the question of the reception of Chaucer in the sixteenth and seventeenth centuries, focusing on the complex and conflicted relations of later writers to the figure of Chaucer. And in *The Chaucerian Apocrypha: A Counterfeit Canon* (2001), Kathleen Forni describes the ways that Chaucer's corpus was progressively purged of so-called spurious works. One of the implications of this body of work is simply that the "Chaucer" of *Two Noble Kinsmen*'s prologue is not the Chaucer of, for example, *The Riverside Chaucer*. Shakespeare's Chaucer is a composite – made up of an increasing number of poems of varying authorship – as well as a composite figure deriving not only from the various printed volumes of the poems but also from literary representations, such as Spenser's imagination of Chaucer and his language in *The Faerie Queene*.[16]

Early modern editions of Chaucer are curiously syncretic and expansive texts. The print history of Chaucer's work begins with Caxton in the late fifteenth century, and until Tyrwhitt's eighteenth-century editions that history is one of expansion and inclusion rather than what we might see as scrupulous editing. Such inclusions are less a mark of credulity among early modern printers and readers than of a different conception of what the "works" of an author should include. Various examples in early printings that clearly indicate that some of the included material is not Chaucer's belie the curious assumption on the part of some scholars that early modern readers must have believed the apocryphal material was his.[17]

Thomas Speght's 1598 black letter folio edition of the works includes materials from previous editions and appears under the title:

> The workes of our antient and lerned English poet, Geffrey Chavcer, newly printed. In this impression you shall find these additions: 1 His portraiture and progenie shewed. 2 His life collected. 3 Arguments to euery booke gathered. 4 Old and obscure words explaned. 5 Authors by him cited, declared. 6 Difficulties opened. 7 Two bookes of his neuer before printed.

---

16. Discussed in the following chapter.
17. E. Talbot Donaldson discusses this assumption in his *Swan at the Well*.

From Thynne's 1532 edition, Speght reprints the preface, genealogical materials, a glossary of obscure words, and a series of "arguments" to each individual poem collected in the volume. The edition also has a title page for the *Canterbury Tales* that surrounds the simply printed title with a rose briar representing a whole series of royal figures beginning with Henry IV and including an image of Elizabeth shaking hands with Henry VII. Richard II is conspicuously absent despite Chaucer's long association with the Plantagenet court. Clearly, the edition refigures Chaucer's connections to the monarchy so as to make him more aligned with the Tudor line than with Richard. The figure of Chaucer here is made to serve – or, better – fit into a particular historical narrative, and his "Englishness" becomes aligned with that of the current dynasty.

The author thus functions more as a token of cultural authority and less as a historical figure. Speght is apparently unworried about matters of historical accuracy and the presentation of the texts is likewise unconcerned with possible contradictions or problems of authorship. Speght's presentation of Chaucer's *Troilus and Criseyde* provides a good example of these attitudes. Speght's edition prints the five books of Chaucer's poem, and immediately following the end of book 5, the text tells us "thus endeth the fifth booke, and last of Troilus: and here foloweth the pitefull and dolorous Testament of faire Creseide" (fol. 164, Do ii recto). Henryson's *Testament of Creseide* (1593) follows without any attribution to Henryson, but the poem itself indicates that Chaucer did not write it. It opens with a discussion of how wintry weather suited itself to the composition of the tragic narrative of Creseide's fate and describes how the poet "toke a queare, and left all other sport / Written by worthy Chaucer glorious / Of faire Creseide, and lusty Troilus." Henryson raises the question of genre as he begins his work on the poem, invoking a kind of seasonal decorum that explains his turn to tragedy. Discussing the poem at hand, the author continues:

> Who wote if al that Chaucer wrate was trew
> Nor I wote nat if this narracion
> Be authorized, or forged of new
> Of some Poete by his invencion
> Made to report the lamentacion
> And woful end of this lusty Creseide
> And what distresse she was in or she deide. (fol. 164 v, Do ii v)

The poem goes on to report both – notoriously cursing Creseide with leprosy after her complaint to the gods about being abandoned by

Diomed and showing her receiving alms from a not-dead Troilus who fails to recognize her.[18] There are two crucial features of this introduction for my argument. First, the poet mentions taking down a "queare" of *Troilus and Criseyde*, making it very difficult to imagine a reader of the poem failing at least to question whether the *Testament* is Chaucer's work. Second, and more importantly, the poet expresses doubt about both what "Chaucer wrate" and whether the current poem "be authorized or forged of new." These uncertainties about the truth of Chaucer's account and the authority of the current one frame the whole of the *Testament* and, perhaps less than explicitly, leave the evaluation of the poem's judgment of Creseide to the reader.

Chaucer's own poem also expresses uncertainty about itself and how it might be taken (and even about potential sequels that Chaucer doesn't want to write).[19] He submits the "litel bok" to the judgment of poetry and worries about reception:

> Go, litel bok, go, litel myn tragedye
> Ther God thi makere yet, er that he dye,
> So sende myght to make in som comedye!
> But litel book, no making thow n'envie,
> But subgit be to alle poesye;
> And kis the steppes where as thow seest pace
> Virgile, Ovide, Omer, Lucan and Stace.
>
> And for ther is so gret diversite
> In Englissh and in writing of oure tonge,
> So prey I God that non miswryte the,
> Ne the mysmetre for defaute of tonge,
> And red wheresoo thow be, or elles songe,
> That thow be understonde, God I biseche! (5.1786–98)

The plea for understanding bespeaks an anxiety about ways the poem might be miswritten, mistaken, and "mysmetred" by later audiences. His expressed worry here suggests both an entirely rational anxiety

---

18. Chettle and Dekker's lost *Troilus and Cressida* (1599) appears to have drawn on Henryson's poem, especially this ending. See David Bevington's Arden edition for discussion of the play's sources, especially 393–4, and a valuable discussion on the *Troilus and Cressida* page on Lost Plays Database at the Folger Shakespeare Library. There are other possible references to Henryson's poem in *Twelfth Night* (Feste mentions that Cressida was a beggar in Act 3) and in *Histriomastix*.
19. At 5.1774–8, Chaucer asks that his female readers not be "wroth" with him but to read of Criseyde's guilt in other books. He says he'd much rather write about good women anyway. Quoted from *The Riverside Chaucer*.

about failed transmission – scribes unfamiliar with his "Englissh" might "miswryte" the poem – but also about appropriation and adaptation by later writers who might fail to "understonde" the poem. Nevertheless, the poem is subjected to "alle poesye" and sent off to be read and to be seen (bowing) in the presence of Virgil, Homer, Ovid, Lucan, and Statius. These lines, like the dedication to Gower and Strode that appears in the penultimate stanza of the poem, also situate the poem in the literary and cultural field in the moment of its production:

> O moral Gower, this book I directe
> To thee, and to the philosophical Strode,
> To vouchen sauf, ther nede is, to corecte,
> Of your benignistees and zeles gode. (5.1856–9)

Chaucer's submission of his book to Gower and Strode's editorial authority, following as it does a claim that it should be at least in the vicinity of those authoritative poets, links those writers to Chaucer's peers and helps create a picture of "alle poesye" that ranges from classical epic, to history, as well as contemporary poetry and philosophy. Chaucer's own "litel bok," his tragedy, takes its place among the work of these writers.

It is a relatively easy task to show that Chaucer's fears are an accurate prediction of the poem's reception by later readers (and Donaldson's *Swan at the Well* points to ways that many critics have mis-taken the poem), but I am more interested in the way that the poem explicitly defers judgment of its own value and the value of its characters to later readers. Henryson could be said to present a judgment, but even he frames the fate of Creseide with doubts about its veracity.[20] It is this doubt, this skepticism, that I am interested in as a legacy Shakespeare picked up along with the more explicit one of the story of Troilus and Cressida. That legacy is the subject of the following section.[21]

---

20. We can infer that Chettle and Dekker's play was less uncertain, and part of Shakespeare's intervention in his play is to foreground doubt and to satirize a familiar narrative.
21. The transmission of both poems is, of course, important to this argument. Indeed, the uncertainty that I argue has much to do with matters of transmission. Henryson's own question – "who knows if all Chaucer wrate was true?" – speaks to this.

II

> Take this for a warning, and, at the peril of your pleasure's loss, and judgment's, refuse not, nor like this the less for not being sullied with the smoky breath of the multitude; but thank fortune for the scape it hath made amongst you, since by the grand possessors' wills I believe you should have prayed for them rather than been prayed. And so I leave all such to be prayed for, for the states of their wits' healths, that will not praise it.
>
> Printer's preface, Shakespeare, Troilus and Cressida

The printer's preface in the second state of the 1609 quarto edition of *Troilus and Cressida*, while indicating nothing of the content of the play, calls attention to the play's distinction and states that the play will have a positive effect on the reader's wit and judgment. It argues for the play's stature as "passing full of the palm comical" and as more fitted for a discerning audience than the smoky breathed multitude – though it will have positive effects on that audience as well. The preface, of course, does little to prepare a reader for the play that follows, a play whose relentless questioning of received values has more recently become a primary interest of its critics. Donaldson's learned and witty review of the history of the critical discussion of the relations between Chaucer's and Shakespeare's versions of the Troilus and Cressida story stresses the ways that the play's critics have spent much of their energy on judging Cressida – most often focusing on her "false" nature (74–118). This obsession responds to the play's refusal to articulate unambiguous judgments of any character or action by offering an external evaluation. Here, I will focus on the problems of judgment raised in both narratives and the ways that those problems structure the narrative in Shakespeare. These aspects of the play derive not so much from the text of Chaucer's *Troilus and Criseyde* as from the judgment-deferring disposition of the text's conclusion. This disposition manifests in the play's structure: first in its refusal of any centered or authoritative source of evaluation and, second, in its striking refusal to represent (or even comment on) the fates of its titular characters. The play instead prefers to leave its audiences with Pandarus' legacy of diseases.

In the Trojan council scene, Shakespeare represents judgment as fundamentally unstable, if not impossible. When Troilus asks, "what's aught but as 'tis valued?" (2.2.52) in response to Hector's questioning the value of Helen in comparison to the Trojan blood spilled in keeping her, he treats judgment as both arbitrary and absolute at the same time.[22] Hector's response that "value dwells not in the particular will; / It holds his estimate and dignity / As well wherein 'tis precious of itself / As in the prizer" offers an essential notion of value (53–6), but Hector's own irrational reversal at the close of the scene subverts, as in other instances, this position. This oscillation characterizes the structure of the play as a whole and, as many critics note, tends to transform the iconic figures of the Trojan War into scurrilous, scheming, and unchivalric versions of themselves.[23] The multiple and contradictory characterizations of Ulysses, Achilles, Hector, Troilus, Cressida and others leave the audience to determine what, if any, value to attach to characters or the narrative.[24] The play, not unlike Chaucer's poem, even as it stages judgment, disavows or defers it by offering contradictory moments of evaluation.

One of the most striking of these moments is the play's ending, which is silent on the fate of both Cressida and Troilus. Where Chaucer's poem reveals that Troilus dies because of Achilles and finds his way to the eighth sphere where his spirit can look dispassionately down on the ensuing events (and on Criseyde) and Henryson's *Testament* gives a vivid picture of Creseide's post-Troilus trajectory, Shakespeare's play tells us nothing at all about what happens to either of the play's putative protagonists.[25] Indeed, the final act of the play refuses to settle on any one figure for long and represents the end of only one story – that of Hector (and, of course, it makes that end a problem in many ways by turning it into an unchivalrous ambush by Achilles' Myrmidons). By ending the play as he does, Shakespeare appears to be leaving everything about the play to the judgment or, perhaps, the literary memory of its audience. More radically than Chaucer's poem, *Troilus and Cressida* leaves its evaluation in the hands of an audience whose last encounter with the play is with Pandarus and his bequest of disease. That dis-ease, it seems to me, is not dissimilar to that left by Chaucer's poem, a lack of closure that prompts such works as Henryson's and may explain the inclusion of that explicitly non-Chaucerian poem in printed edi-

22. All quotations from this play are from the 3rd series Arden Shakespeare edition, edited by Bevington, and will be cited parenthetically in the body of the text.
23. See discussion in the next chapter.
24. See Linda Charnes's *Notorious Identity* (1995) for a discussion of the ways that characters are trapped by external and conflicting judgments of what their characters are or mean.
25. Chaucer's Troilus looks down and despises the "wrecched world" and "in himself he lough right at the wo / Of hem that wepten for his deth so faste" (5.1817, 1821–2).

tions of Chaucer's complete works throughout the sixteenth century. The doubting, questioning, and judgment-deferring dispositions of Chaucer's and Shakespeare's works seem akin, and I would argue that it is an important and overlooked way that Chaucer's influence appears in the later Shakespeare.[26]

Satire is undeniably a central feature of *Troilus and Cressida*, and Thersites' caustic commentary on both Greeks and Trojans shares a rhetoric with the Marston of the *Scourge of Villainy* (1598) and the later *Malcontent* (1604). Whether or not the play found an audience suited to appreciate its experimentation is a different question and one more difficult to answer. The paucity of evidence of actual performance and the epistle's claim that the play had never been "clapper-clawed with the palms of the vulgar" suggests one obvious answer. Moreover, Shakespeare does not produce another play quite like it until, perhaps, *Timon of Athens*, suggesting that the play may have been a less than fully successful experiment.[27]

As Bakhtin and Bourdieu's model suggests, the experiment represented by a play like *Troilus* may not have appeared at a felicitous moment (unlike, say, the historically-themed plays of the late 1580s and 1590s) and thus did not precipitate a transformation in the dramatic field. Comedy (broadly construed and including Latin Comedy, Satirical Comedy, and Romantic Comedy) held a consistent share of roughly 30 percent of the new plays produced between 1599 and 1602. History (again broadly understood and including plays labeled as Biblical History, Foreign History, Classical or English History, Foreign Pseudohistory, and Classical History) comprised 26 percent or the new plays, and tragedy (which includes *Troilus and Cressida*) comprised 13 percent of the new plays. The remaining 30 percent is a mixture of kinds from *Classical legend, Romance, Heroical Romance, Topical play* and others.[28] I have tabulated both Shakespeare's plays

26. Many of the *Canterbury Tales* close with either explicit or implicit invitations that the reader decide what the tale means. The *Franklin's Tale* and the *Wife of Bath's Tale* do make such invitations, and the occasion of the whole of the *Tales* is a competition to be judged.
27. Edward Dowden links *Troilus* to *Timon* in his *Shakspere*.
28. The generic labels in the *Annals* raise all manner of interesting questions and problems, not least because of how durable they have been despite the lack of period precedent. The specificity, while attractive and simplifying, produces various distortions of the field. Interestingly, "tragedy" gets significantly fewer modifiers than either history or comedy in the *Annals*. *Heroical Romance* is a good example: in the *Annals* it covers plays as diverse in form and content as Marlowe's *Tamburlaine* (1590) and the anonymous *Mucedorus* (1598). Wiggins and Richardson's *British Drama: 1533–1642, A Catalogue* simplifies them and

and the (surviving) plays produced by the Chamberlain's Men below using generic labels from the *Annals* for convenience and consistency as one way to characterize a part of the field of dramatic production between 1599–1602. This data cannot reflect the whole of the repertory, and it is not possible to be wholly confident about what plays were or were not being revived, but it is a glimpse at what new plays were appearing.[29] Roslyn Knutson argues that the "strategy of the Chamberlain's Men to distribute their offerings among new plays and old, select a mix of new and old story materials, and obtain plays in the most popular new dramatic formulas while keeping old favorites on the schedule" makes sense in the context of "a new playhouse, a burgeoning theatrical industry, and a consequent multiplication of play offerings in new and old dramatic forms" (*Repertory* 85). This context helps to account for Shakespeare's turn to old material (the Troilus story) but to house it in a new form, with a new, satirical disposition. Thersites' railing would not have been out of place in Marston's verse satires, and the skeptical treatment of the Troy story represents a more thorough critique of an originary myth than audiences were prepared to enjoy. While satire did move from print to stage after the Bishop's Ban, the Troy story appears to have been played fairly straight in Dekker and Chettle's play (and in Heywood's *1* and *2 Iron Age*), and the relentless undercutting of a famous story appears not to have resonated with audiences. That producing the play might have been a misjudgment in 1601 or 1602 is borne out by the play's alleged unpopularity on the stage and its relatively limited publication history.

Shakespeare contributed six plays over this four-year period to the Chamberlain's Men, as described below in Table 1.1b. Half were tragedies (counting *Troilus and Cressida*), two comedies, and *Henry V* his last play on English history until *Henry VIII*. These proportions are (with the exception of the number of tragedies) more or less in line with the field in general. The corpus of new plays added to the Chamberlain's repertory is also somewhat different in generic composition compared to the broader field with a higher proportion of tragedy and comedy, but it contains a similar proportion of history plays. The strategies of the acting companies in terms of the kinds

---

drops many, if not all, of the qualifying adjectives. I employ the *Annals* labels here as a shorthand.

29. See chapter three of Roslyn Knutson's *The Repertory of Shakespeare's Company, 1594–1613* for an extended discussion of the Chamberlain's repertory in 1599–1603.

of plays offered seem broadly consistent, and if the Chamberlain's Men offered more tragedies than the overall average that probably says more about having Shakespeare as a company playwright than anything else. In this context, *Troilus and Cressida* looks like an outlier in a number of ways. First, if these genre labels are a useful way to understand company and audience expectations, *Troilus* seems likely, if not calculated, to defy expectations for either of the kinds to which it has been assigned. It is a tragedy without the deaths of its protagonists, a comedy without a wedding, and, if we want to think of it as a kind of historical play, it defies expectations about the Troy story.

Out of these plays, *The Merry Devil of Edmonton,* a comedy about the magician Peter Fabell, was reprinted in quarto six times to 1655, one more quarto than *Hamlet. Troilus* was clearly less successful in the print market than *The Merry Devil, Hamlet, Every Man Out of His Humour,* and *Henry V.* Reprint rates are, as Alan B. Farmer and Zachary Lesser have argued in "The Popularity of Playbooks Revisited," one measure for print popularity, but popularity in print is a different matter than popularity on stage. Evaluating the "success" of the Folio-only plays is a complicated question as well.

Other examples of plays that initially failed in performance and later become successes include Beaumont's *Knight of the Burning Pestle.* As is well-known, its printer's preface asserted the play did not do well in early performances and blamed the audience's inability to see the "privy mark of irony" on it. The printer claimed that he saved it from oblivion so that readers might be able to have access to the play.[30] The shape of the justificatory arguments in Burre's letter resemble those found in the Troilus quarto since both make appeals to the better wit of the reading audience and position the publisher as saving the play from an undeserved oblivion. Like *Troilus and Cressida, Knight of the Burning Pestle* might signal a premature sign of a generic upheaval, in Bourdieu's terms, since it represents a new category of drama in search of an audience in print as much as on stage. This kind of archly metadramatic play becomes more common later in the century. Playwrights like Middleton, Massinger, Brome, and Jonson produce such plays, some of which found appreciative audiences, and some which did not. What is important here, and relevant to the situation of *Troilus and Cressida,* is the way in which the letter figures the Beaumont play's failure as a failure of the audience

---

30. See *Representing the Professions* for a discussion of the play. Lesser's "Walter Burre's *The Knight of the Burning Pestle*" discusses Burre's publishing strategy.

Table 1.1a Shakespeare's Plays, 1599–1602[a]

Title	Classified as	Editions
Hamlet	Tragedy	5 q, 2 f
Henry V	History	3 q, 2 f
Troilus and Cressida	Tragedy	1 q, 2 f
As You Like It	Comedy	2 f
Twelfth Night	Comedy	2 f
Julius Caesar	Tragedy	2 f
Total: 6 plays	3 tragedies (50%) 2 comedies (33%) 1 history (17%)	

[a] Drawn from Alfred Harbage, Samuel Schoenbaum, and Sylvia Stoler Wagonheim, editors. *Annals of English Drama, 975–1700*. 3rd ed., Routledge, 1989.

Table 1.1b Chamberlain's Plays, 1599–1602[a]

Title	Genre	Editions
Anon., *The Merry Devil of Edmonton*	Comedy	6 q
Shakespeare, *Hamlet*	Tragedy	5 q, 2 f
Jonson, *Every Man Out*	Comedy	3 q, 2 f
Shakespeare, *Henry V*	History	3 q, 2 f
Shakespeare, *Troilus and Cressida*	Tragedy	1 q, 2 f
W.S., *Thomas, Lord Cromwell*	History	2 q
Shakespeare, *As You Like It*	Comedy	2 f
Shakespeare, *Twelfth Night*	Comedy	2 f
Shakespeare, *Julius Caesar*	Tragedy	2 f
Anon., *A Warning for Fair Women*	Tragedy	1 q
Anon., *A Larum for London*	History	1 q
Dekker, *Satiromastix*	Comedy	1 q
Smith (William), *The Freeman's Honour*	Bourgeois Romance[b]	Lost
Anon., *Cloth Breeches and Velvet Hose*	Comedy	Lost
Wilson, 1 and 2 *Sir John Oldcastle*	History	Lost
Total: 16 plays	4 tragedies (25%) 7 comedies (43%) 5 histories (31%)	

[a] Drawn from Alfred Harbage, Samuel Schoenbaum, and Sylvia Stoler Wagonheim, editors. *Annals of English Drama, 975–1700*. 3rd ed., Routledge, 1989.
[b] For the purpose of my tally, I counted this play as a comedy.

Table 1.2 *DEEP* Records for Extant Professional Drama Printed, 1599–1602[a]

Genre	Number of plays	Percentage of total
Comedy	25	40%
History	22	35%
Tragedy	9	15%
Heroical Romance	2	3%
Pastoral	1	2%
Biblical Moral	1	2%
Tragicomedy	1	2%
Moral Interlude	1	2%
Total:	62	101%[b]

[a] Alan B. Farmer and Zachary Lesser, editors. *Database of Early English Playbooks*, created 2007, accessed 6 December 2022, http://deep.sas.upenn.edu.
[b] The total percentage is greater 100 because I rounded percentages to the nearest whole number.

and that failure is later rectified by print and also by well-received later performances.[31]

In the second state of the 1609 quarto, a letter addressed to a reading audience presumably equipped to cope with and appreciate the sophistication of the play prefaces *Troilus and Cressida*. Laden with anti-theatrical language, the preface suggests that the theatre is not the proper venue for such a play. It describes the play as new, "never staled with the stage, never clapper-clawed with the palms of the vulgar" (Pref. 1–2) and as full of wit as any of the playwright's other work. The "Never Writer" avers that:

> all such dull and heavy-witted worldlings as were never capable of the wit of a comedy, coming by report of them to his representations, have found that wit there that they never found in themselves and have departed better witted than they came, feeling an edge of wit upon them more than ever they dreamed they had brain to grind it on. (13–19)

Shakespeare's work, like a kind of intelligence-boosting supplement, makes even dull-witted auditors smarter. Indeed, the publisher continues, the play is the most witty of all Shakespeare's comedies: "amongst all there is none more witty than this." That the play

31. Jonson's complaints in his "Ode: To Himself" in 1631 voice a more obstreperous version of these sentiments.

has not been "sullied with the smoky breath of the multitude" or "clapper-clawed with the palms of the multitude" before publication is not a problem; instead, the letter writer instructs the readers to be grateful to have the play at all since the author's comedies are likely to become a scarce and enormously valuable commodity and the play's "grand possessors" would have held on to the play if they only could have (34).[32] The preface does not suggest that the play failed in production but rather that it was never produced at all. This distinction, articulated in one state of the quarto, explicitly targets the play towards a literate audience whose wit will benefit more from the play than the vulgar multitude, who profit all unwittingly from the author's gifts.

In the first state of the quarto, there is no such letter to introduce the play to its reading audience. Instead, the play is introduced only as "THE Historie of Troylus and Cresseida. *As it was acted by the Kings Maiesties servuants at the Globe.* Written by William Shakespeare." The authorial ascription is in the smallest type and, as is typical, follows the assertion that the play was acted and that this text faithfully reports that performance text. No other authorizing material appears and there is no indication at all of what kind of reception the play may have received.[33] This state of the quarto relies on the traditional authorizing practices of printed plays: the claim of performance, buttressed by the author's name. By itself, without the other state, this would be entirely unremarkable, a title page much like any other early Shakespeare quarto. However, in the presence of the other state, this title page takes on other potential resonances.

These two states and their attendant depictions of the audience for the play indicate the play's status as an intervention in the hierarchy of genres, in the struggle for legitimation that Bourdieu argues defines the structure and functioning of the literary field. The two states suggest that the play's publishers imagined the possibility or encountered the reality of a differentiated market for printed plays with tastes and desires formed by and responding to different models

32. By "grand possessors," the preface appears to mean the King's Men, though, like everything else about the play, this reference is open to question. That acting companies were reluctant to see plays published has come into question, and this exhortation may be only a marketing strategy. If the play really was a failure on stage, selling the script to a printer would at least have represented some kind of income.
33. Nor, of course, is there any outside evidence that the play appeared on stage. There is no data to confirm or deny the play's production.

of the theatre and, based on the distinct language of the paratexts, different generic preferences. Billing the play as a "tragical history" and leaving out the claim for its status as comedy locates the play in one theatrical mode, leaving the generic weirdness of the play to be discovered in the process of reading. Labelling the play a "famous history" (in the second state) and stressing its excellence as comedy points to the play's generic difficulties before the reading of the play properly begins and makes those difficulties, perhaps, part of the appeal. To be able to respond appreciatively to such a play elevates the reader above the clapper-clawing hands of the vulgar.

III

In the first decades of the seventeenth century, tragicomedy and what has come be called *romance* began finding audiences. At the same time, scholars have noted that the practices of printing and marketing printed plays were shifting, as the publisher's preface to *Troilus and Cressida* shows. Two of the pivotal historical events that have shaped our understanding of dramatic change are the publications of Jonson's *Workes* in 1616 and, perhaps more significantly, Shakespeare's 1623 Folio. These two volumes, embodying the best-known claims for the dignity of plays, intervene in and to some extent transform period conceptions of dramatic genre and literary hierarchy. Later readers have continued to categorize plays under the rubrics used by Shakespeare's Folio, and new designations (romance) owe much to the Folio's early formulation of generic categories. Romance, in particular, owes its origin to Dowden's construction of a narrative about Shakespeare's life and career. In this case at least, the genre label depends crucially on the making of "Shakespeare."

Critics have often discussed the difficulties of assigning an adequate generic label for *Troilus and Cressida*. It is usually anthologized with the comedies for lack of a better place to put it. The epistle attached to the second state of the 1609 Quarto states that the play is "passing full of the palme comicall," well suited to stand with work of Plautus, while the Folio labels it a tragedy – though not as part of the volume's catalogue. The play does lack the conventional markers of comic closure – no marriages occur in the play, no renewed social order rises at the play's close – and it leaves the audience with a bequest of diseases instead of laughter, but neither does *Troilus and Cressida* close with, say, the deaths of the protagonists (instead, only Hector dies). As I discussed above, Mowat argues that tragicomedy is an inadequate label for the play. She offers "late Shakespearean comedy" as a more accurate one. Even this label, however chronologically accurate, operates more as description than as a characterization of the play.

Howard Felperin's 1972 book, *Shakespearean Romance*, claims that an element of romance can be found throughout Shakespeare's plays. In his discussion of *Troilus and Cressida* as one of the "problem plays," Felperin argues that "in the problem plays generally, and *Troilus* in particular, the romantic imagination – be it Homer's, Chapman's, Troilus', or Shakespeare's own – is subjected on all sides to unprecedented stresses and strains" (76–7). Despite those stresses, Felperin goes on, "the play is ambivalent toward romance, not scornful of it." I am less convinced than Felperin of the play's ambivalent attitude towards romance, but his attention to the romance elements of the play point to its connections to later, perhaps less cynical, plays in the genre. As critics have often noted, *Troilus and Cressida* exposes chivalric ideals to corrosive criticism: it consistently and insistently punctures the pretensions of romantic love to purity and steadfastness, and it demystifies/desacralizes heroes on both sides of the Trojan War, while still operating within the confines of a narrative profoundly congenial to romance.

Troilus shares some of the characteristics of late sixteenth and early seventeenth century satirical comedy, plays that question values and forms while still working within them. John Marston's *The Malcontent* provides a useful analogue, one that Shakespeare must have been familiar with from its King's Men performances. Marston's play begins in the mode of revenge tragedy, with the banished Duke Altofront assuming the identity of the malcontented and satirical Malevole. Malevole lurks about the court, not unlike the lurking revenger Vindice in Middleton's *Revenger's Tragedy*, positioning himself to resume power by orchestrating the downfall of his rivals. However, despite the setup, none of the major players die at the end of the play, and the punishments meted out by the restored Altofront are hardly those characteristic of the retributive justice of tragedies like *Antonio and Mellida* or *Antonio's Revenge*. The play violates the formal expectations produced by its opening, and Marston's *Malcontent*, pervaded by satirical railing, develops a tragicomic mode which exposes and chastises corruption without that chastisement necessarily leading to death. Where tragedy seems inevitably to lead to death, these plays end with something else. Like Jonson's comical satires, which were successful at the same time, the play seems more interested in curing than destroying.[34]

Troilus, though seemingly uninterested in cures (Pandarus' bequest seems to imply the incurability, or at least the inescapability, of his diseases), is also invested in violating formal expectations. The play could be a love story, but the play consistently denies the audience any kind of romantic comedy satisfactions – even Troilus' anticipatory speech leading up to his assignation with Cressida is pervaded by strange allusions to death and meditations on his confusion. The play could be a heroic narrative, but the heroic characters are pompous, conniving, buffoonish, barbaric and otherwise unheroic. Achilles' killing of Hector by proxy is only the most notorious of examples. This list could continue, but what seems clear to me is that the elements of romance in this play are consistently qualified and exploded through the agency of a pervasively satiric or cynical mode of representation. In or around 1600, it appears as if Shakespeare was working with medieval materials but that the theatrical context – imbued with satire, seeing the early work of playwrights whose careers began in verse satire and the like – influenced him in such a way as to produce a play that experiments with form, that satirically questions the forms he had been working with, giving us a play that might be characterized as a failed comedy.

IV

> To sing a song that old was sung
> From ashes ancient Gower is come,
> Assuming man's infirmities
> To glad your ear and please your eyes.
> It hath been sung at festivals,
> On ember eves and holy ales,
> And lords and ladies in their lives
> Have read it for restoratives.
>
> Shakespeare, *Pericles*

Pericles explicitly looks back to medieval narrative for inspiration and, along with *Two Noble Kinsmen*, invokes the authors of those narratives to make appearances, whether as choric figures of absent yet anxiety-inducing Muses. Like a number of the later plays

---

34. I discuss Marston's play more fully in Chapter Six below.

(whether romances, problem plays, or even tragedies), *Pericles* shifts times, locations, and genres with at times confusing speed and decorum-violating abandon.[35] Unlike the later *Two Noble Kinsmen*'s Chaucer, who appears only as an absent author whose reaction the playwrights worry about, Gower is a resurrected and constant presence in the play, offering explanatory commentary and exposition (particularly at the end of the play where he reports Cleon's fate). *Pericles*' sources include Gower's *Confessio Amantis* (1532) as well as later versions of the story of Apollonius of Tyre, but that fact alone does not explain Gower's role as presenter. Many of Shakespeare's earlier plays have sources, but audiences do not get running commentary from their authors as part of the play. The closest analogue is the role of the Chorus in *Henry V*, but even there the Chorus is not an incarnate Holinshed filling in gaps in the narrative. Gower appears to authorize, guide, and structure a narrative whose shape is uncommonly loose and episodic – more like medieval narrative romance than the more tightly plotted plays that were also appearing in the first decade of the seventeenth century.[36]

To refer again to the capaciousness of Chaucer's book in the sixteenth and seventeenth centuries and its ever-expanding contents and to argue by analogy, it may be that the openness of many medieval narratives to asides, interruptions, and other diversions along with the openness of the books themselves to additional works contributed to the development of Shakespeare's play. Gower's presence in the play helps move the action along, clarifies events, and solves problems of representation in ways that make some aspects of the drama possible. The influence of medieval narrative thus operates at both the level of content and the more obscure one of form and structure. To demonstrate more fully how the figure of Gower introduces an *idea* of medieval narrative into the structure of *Pericles*, I will first sketch a description of the "Renaissance Gower" by examining the presentation of Gower as a character in Robert Greene's *Vision* and

35. Many of the later plays share this quality of geographic and temporal mobility. *The Winter's Tale* jumps over sixteen years and moves the action to the "coast of Bohemia," *Antony and Cleopatra* leaps back and forth between Egypt and Rome, and *Pericles* is something of a Mediterranean travelogue. *Hamlet* and *Troilus and Cressida* both offer shifting and multiple perspectives on a central narrative.
36. An obvious contrast would be Jonson's *Alchemist* (1612), in which the plot is so tightly constructed that the action is all but continuous. Jonson's complaints about audiences still wanting "mouldy tales" like *Pericles* may be a response to the older narrative style of the play delivered with his usual competitiveness.

the presentation of Gower's work in print. Greene's work reveals the considerable cultural capital associated with Gower, while printings of his work illuminate the fluid "meaning" of Gower in early modern England. Making use of this account of the meaning of Gower, I will then explore questions of narrative raised by *Pericles*' reliance on medieval romance and the authorizing figure of Gower.

Gower's cultural capital in early modern England emerges in the fact that Shakespeare was not the first early modern writer to resurrect Gower in a literary fiction. Robert Greene's *Vision*, one of the confessional publications that proliferated around the time of his death, features an argument between Gower and Chaucer over what kind of writing is best and most likely to secure one's permanent reputation. Occasioned by Greene's expressed doubts about his own production, the debate presented in *Greene's Vision* appears to set up a hierarchy of texts that privileges *sentence* over *solaas*. Although his hierarchy is itself set aside by the appearance of Solomon at the end of the pamphlet and his condemnation of every form of learning other than divinity, Greene clearly deploys the two medieval poets to represent two possible modes of poetic achievement.

In the *Vision*, Greene relates that, while thinking deeply about his repentance and how to maintain himself as a "reformed man from [his] former follies," he falls asleep and, in his dream, finds himself under an oak tree in a pleasant meadow being approached by two "ancient men" who bear on their chests cards with the names Chaucer and Gower (12:208).[37] Greene recognizes them only by their nametags, as he does not provide any description of their physical appearance until they join him in the shade under a tree. His need to identify their physical presence suggests the symbolic or representative nature of the figures: Greene is engaging in a kind of allegory rather than, say, literary history. Only Greene's ascriptions fix their identity, not some essential connection between their appearance and their names, and the necessity of the nametags marks this fluidity. After describing the two "ancient" men, Greene relates that Chaucer starts up and says, "Thy outward lookes bewrays thy thoughts, and thy outward lookes thy inward passions: for by thy face I see the figure of a discontented minde, and the very glaunce of thine eyes is a map of a disquieted conscience," inviting Greene to speak of his troubles (211). The conversation then turns to a debate over the value of different kinds of writing. Both of the ancient poets present tales on the same subject:

37. This and all subsequent quotations are from the 1964 compilation of Greene's work edited by A. B. Grosart.

the evils of jealousy. Both tales are intended as moral instruction – to delight and teach – but Greene finds Gower's more attractive and is inspired to emulate Gower rather than Chaucer in any future work.

Greene describes Chaucer first, dwelling extensively on his physical appearance and his clothing:

> *His stature was not very tall;*
> *Leane he was; his legs were small,*
> *Hos'd within a stock of red,*
> *A buttond bonnet was on his head,*
> *From under did hang, I weene,*
> *Silver haires both bright and sheene:*
> *His beard was white, trimmed round,*
> *His countenance blithe and merry found:*
> *A Sleeuelesse Iacket large and wide,*
> *With many pleights and skirts side,*
> *Of water Chamlet did he weare;*
> *A whittell by his belt he beare.*
> *His shooes were corned, broad before,*
> *His Inckhorne at his side he wore,*
> *And in his hand he bore a booke:*
> *Thus did this auntient Poet looke.* (12.209–10)

Chaucer is a short, thin, colorfully attired, and cheerful-looking person. He carries his inkhorn at his side, apparently ready to write at any moment, and holds a book in his hand. His readiness to write and his having to hand a book (not to mention being described as an "auncient Poet") associate him with "blithe and merry" writing – the witty literary production he champions in the conversation that follows.

Gower, on the other hand, appears as a stern and physically imposing figure, resembling the moralist Cato. The image likely derives from Chaucer's own addressing of *Troilus and Criseyde* to "moral Gower" as well as illuminations of Gower's manuscripts. His size, grave visage, and attire are the central features in Greene's description of him in the *Vision*:

> *Large he was, his height was long;*
> *Broad of brest, his lims were strong;*
> *But couller pale, and wan his looke,—*
> *Such have they that plyen theyr booke:*
> *His head was gray and quaintly shorne,*
> *Neately was his beard worne.*
> *His visage grave, sterne and grim,—*

> Cato *was most like to him.*
> *Thus* Iohn Gower *did appear,*
> *Quaint attired, as you heere.*
> *His Bonnet was a Hat of blew,*
> *His sleeves straight, of that same hew;*
> *A surcoate of a tawnie die,*
> *Hung in pleights over his thigh:*
> *A breech close unto his dock,*
> *Handsomd with a long stock;*
> *Pricked before were his shone,*
> *He wore such as others done;*
> *A bag of red by his side,*
> *And by that his napkin tide.*
> *Thus* John Gower *did appeare,*
> *Quaint attired, as you heere.* (210)

Gower thus appears as a daunting, scholarly figure in the *Vision*, and, as with the description of Chaucer, his appearance lines up with the poetic values he endorses. Unlike he does with Chaucer, however, Greene does not label him a poet here. Greene consistently calls them both poets throughout the text, but in the poem presenting Gower's physical appearance, Greene describes no implements associated with Gower's poetic vocation, specifically aligning him with stern moral figures like Cato.

Chaucer and Gower function iconically in the pamphlet – even their exemplary tales are meant to function more as representations of tales than as tales themselves – and signify what Greene posits as two distinct traditions. Gower consistently praises *sentence*, moral content, and *matere* in his oration and in his narrative about the evils of jealousy, while Chaucer praises quick invention, wit, and, essentially, *solaas* in his. In his pre-dream meditations, Greene has already suggested that matter is more important than what he terms "outward phrase": "so the outward phrase is not to be measured by pleasing the eare, but the inward matter by profiting the minde: the puffing glorie of the loftie stile shadowing wanton conceipts is like to the skin of a serpent that contrives impoysoned flesh" (202–3). His (stated) predisposition towards profitable matter helps explain the otherwise surprising preference for Gower he expresses at the end of the tale-telling and debate. In a passage worth quoting at some length, Greene addresses both poets, cap in hand:

> Learned & lawreat, whose censures are Authentical: I have noted your words with such attention, that my minde is cleared of that doubt, wherewith it hath beene long blemished: For now I perceive

> Father *Chawcer*, that I followed too long your pleasant vaine, in penning such Amourous workes, and that ye fame that I sought after by such travail was nothing but smoke.... Hence foorth Father *Gower*, farewell the insight I had into loves secrets: let *Venus* rest in her spheare, I wil be no Astronomer to her influence.... they which held *Greene* for a patron of love, and a second *Ovid*, shal now thinke him a *Timon* of such lineaments, and a *Diogines* that will barke at every amourous pen.... Thus father *Gower*, thy counsaile hath made me a convert & a penitent deeply sorrowfull for the follies of my pen, but promising heere that no idle fancies shall grow any more from my conceit. (272–4)

Greene then offers his hand to Gower, who takes it heartily. Greene appears to be won over by Gower's position since it resonates best with his own intentions to maintain his repentance, which is the issue the narrating Greene is pondering in the frame of the *Vision*. This endorsement of Gower's argument also points to the way that Greene is making use of an imagined medieval author to illustrate a broader point: it is less important how accurate a picture of Gower this is than how effective it is as an illustration. Greene clearly links Chaucer with a poetic pleasure that must be abandoned by those pursuing real fame, while Gower's work represents the achievement of that fame. As Jeremy Dimmick suggests in "Gower, Chaucer, and the Art of Repentance in Greene's *Vision*," Greene is doing something more complicated and interesting than simply endorsing a moralistic position (for one thing, he does make the claim that he has been known as a "second Ovid," which troubles any positioning as a "moral" poet) or even ironizing a hierarchy of value he inherits from the Horatian tradition. In addition to doing both of these things, he is, moreover, deploying and augmenting the specific cultural capital associated with the two writers to establish a position of his own. In 1592, Chaucer and Gower already stand for divergent kinds of poetry (whether or not their works easily map onto that distinction), and they appear in the text as synecdoches for those kinds. At the same time, Greene claims a position for himself in the poetic tradition by depicting himself as worthy of conversing with both "aunceint poets." Thus, we can see Chaucer and Gower as ironic celebrity endorsements for Greene, and the capital their names bring with them is a resource for Greene's own self-promotion. The poets and the works they are associated with authorize Greene and orient his readers towards the proper reading and understanding of his work.

Greene's Gower was likely a printed Gower, and several editions of the *Confessio Amantis* were available to early modern readers.[38] The three early printings are Caxton's in 1483 and Berthelette's editions of 1532 and 1554. Caxton's *Confessio* appears without much in the way of introductory commentary, but with an extensive table of contents. Berthelette's, on the other hand, includes a lengthy preface and makes typographic distinctions between the text's various parts and languages that Caxton's does not. Berthelette calls attention to his efforts to perfect the text so that it might be more accessible to readers – restoring parts that had been left out, correcting misreadings and the like. He writes that the defects of the earlier text "caused that this most pleasant and easy auctor coude not wel be perceyved" (A3v).[39] Throughout his editorial commentary, Berthelette presents Gower as a learned writer in whose poem the reader can find many kinds of profit – "who ever in redynge of this warke dothe consider it well shal fynde that it is plentifully stuffed and fournysshed with manyfolde eloquent reasons sharpe and quick arguments and examples of great auctorite perswadynge unto vertue" (aa ii r-v) – but also as an "auctor" whose work is pleasing and "easy." Gower thus appears as an accessible writer whose work unites pleasure and profit. Berthelette does stress the moral content of Gower's poem, but, unlike Greene, he does not focus on it as the primary justification for Gower's worth as poet.

Emphasis on the moral content of Gower would increase as the sixteenth century progressed. Derek Pearsall writes that "the availability of a good printed text, the praise of respected scholars, and the association with Chaucer, contribute to something of a Gower renaissance in the latter half of the fifteenth and the first half of the sixteenth century," pointing out how Gower receives praise as one of the first refiners of English into a poetic language (190). He points out that Gower begins to be more talked of than read, however, and that a somewhat impoverished image of "moral Gower" comes to dominate his portrayal in encomia of English literature.[40] This separation of Gower's reputation from his actual works makes his image increasingly susceptible to deployments like Greene's or Shakespeare's some years later.

When Shakespeare turns to Gower and puts him on stage in *Pericles*, he presents a Gower far more closely resembling the

---

38. See Siân Echard, "Gower in Print."
39. I am citing the copy held in the Folger Library's collection.
40. Pearsall suggests that Greene probably hadn't read Gower, since the version of Gower in the *Vision* does not resemble that of the poems.

Chaucer of *Greenes Vision* than Greene's Gower.⁴¹ Interestingly, Shakespeare's Gower diverges from Greene's and from the larger "Gower tradition," which depicts him fairly consistently as an increasingly dour moralist. Shakespeare appears to have been thinking about Greene around the time he composed *Pericles* (with *The Winter's Tale* about two years later), and a reading of the *Vision* could have inspired Gower-as-character. He was also producing plays with unconventional narrative structures that span vast ranges of time and space in a way characteristic of medieval (and renaissance) narrative romance.⁴² And, like Greene, he uses the figure of Gower to authorize a particular adaptation of the *Confessio Amantis*' medieval version of the Apollonius narrative. This particular intervention is unlike Shakespeare's other romances, which do not resort to an authorial chorus.⁴³

Rather than presenting the audience with the grave and sober Gower of *Greene's Vision*, Shakespeare's *Pericles* offers a Gower whose work is meant as a pleasing restorative:

> If you, born in these latter times
> When wit's more ripe, accept my rhymes,
> And that to hear an old man sing
> May to your wishes pleasure bring,
> I life would wish, and that I might
> Waste it for you like taper light. (1.0.11–16)⁴⁴

Gower wishes to provide pleasure and enlightenment – *solaas* and *sentence* – in a way that the "moral Gower" Greene imagines would reject. Shakespeare's Gower asserts that the latter times' wit is "more ripe," but still produces a recognizably Gowerian version of the story, which undercuts his downplaying of his own wit. Gower's ironic self-deprecation fits in with other such moments in Shakespearean choruses – the chorus of *Henry V* being an immediate example – and does not suggest that his mode is any less valid or sophisticated than that of the riper time of the play's production.

---

41. On the intersection between Greene's and Shakespeare's Gowers, see Helen Cooper, "*Pericles* and other Gowers, 1592–1640."
42. We can productively see the tale of Apollonius of Tyre as a travel narrative.
43. Time's role in *The Winter's Tale* resembles that of Gower's in *Pericles*, but Gower's role is vastly larger than Time's.
44. All quotations from this play are from the Arden Shakespeare 3rd Series, edited by Suzanne Gossett, and are cited parenthetically in the body of the text.

Nevertheless, critics have often taken Gower's comments as a disparagement of the play's reliance on medieval romance. F. David Hoeniger has argued that Shakespeare turned to Gower in this play as a way to experiment with new forms as he turned "to works of an entirely new kind, the romances" (478). Depicting *Pericles* as a precursor to *Cymbeline, The Winter's Tale,* and *The Tempest,* Hoeniger states that:

> [Shakespeare] decided as he set out that it was desirable to begin by imitating the very manner of early storytellers and plays and even, though of course only partway, their lack of sophistication and crudity of devices and writing. So he revived Gower and his tale, and had him retell it for a while largely in his own manner before making his own presence and art felt. Then, in the plays which follow *Pericles*, Shakespeare step by step discovered the ways of creating a new art entirely his own. (479)

This position downplays the structural and narrative experimentation Shakespeare was already engaging in around the turn of the century, and it depicts medieval narrative as encumbered by a "lack of sophistication and crudity of devices" that is difficult to reconcile with a reading of Gower or of Chaucer – especially the works Shakespeare was looking to as sources.

As Hoeniger argues, *Pericles* needs to be understood in the context of the later Shakespeare's experimentation with form, but I argue that his experimentation does not oppose modern sophistication to medieval crudity – an opposition which automatically downgrades earlier romance to a lower position. Instead, Shakespeare is redeploying strategies from verse romance into dramatic form in order to enable alternative forms of dramatic narrative. The Gower he resurrects enables a dramatic romance that combines the resources of the capacious medieval narrative signified by Gower as well as those of Shakespeare's contemporary stage, bringing the "lords and ladies" of the courtly romance's audience into contact with the more diverse audience of the amphitheater.

Francis Beaumont's *Knight of the Burning Pestle* documents the taste that contemporary audiences had for both narrative and dramatic romance as well as presenting a "sophisticated" acting company's antipathy towards that mode. A good deal of the comedy in Beaumont's play depends on the conflict between the Citizen's taste for romance and the Prologue Boy's distaste for it. The play marks this disdain as class-related: the Boy asserts that the gentlemen will not like the intrusion of Rafe's chivalric romance into the play, while the Citizen insists on keeping the grocer-errant a part of the action. As in Shakespeare's experiments in *Pericles*, an idea about romance enables Beaumont to produce a play that intervenes in the early modern genre system. In addition, *The Knight of the Burning Pestle* serves as a useful reminder that a dramatic romance tradition did exist before Shakespeare's romances (themselves only labeled as such much later) and that we must take the influence of that tradition on Shakespeare's plays as seriously as the influence of narrative romance.[45]

Shakespeare, in contrast to Beaumont's parodic use of romance conventions linked explicitly to prose romances like *Amadis de Gaul*, uses the figure of Gower to manage the expectations set up by a play based on a well-known tale. Instead of producing parodic comedy out of medieval materials, Shakespeare produces a dramatic version of that narrative by using a medieval author to present and manage the tale. Gower locates the tale in his own tradition in the first chorus, citing authorities for his own narrative, much as Shakespeare does in personifying Gower in the play. Gower states,

> I tell you what mine authors say:
> This king unto him took a fere,
> Who died and left a female heir
> So buxom, blithe and full of face
> As heaven had lent her all her grace,
> With whom the father liking took
> And her to incest did provoke. (1.0.20–6)

Disavowing sole responsibility for the story of Antiochus' incest, Gower introduces the plot and turns judgment over to his audience, much as a more conventional dramatic chorus would. Throughout the play, Gower operates in this way: introducing shifts in scene, discoursing on the role of Fortune in the geographic shifts associated with Pericles' changing situation, citing the textual authorities for the story, and referring the play to the audience's judgment. These choruses mobilize an idea of Gower's narrative to organize a retelling of the tale in a new form. Thus Shakespeare, like Greene, makes use of conventional associations with authors like Gower to enable his

---

45. Christopher Cobb's *The Staging of Romance in Late Shakespeare* (2007) provides a useful discussion of the earlier tradition of specifically dramatic romance from 1570 to 1610. Shakespeare's version of romance, in Cobb's view, follows a sudden decline in dramatic romances after 1600 and represents a re-engagement with the form.

own work, and, Shakespeare, like Beaumont, makes use of deprecating devices to deal with the kinds of narrative problems created by dramatic romance. Where Beaumont turns to parody, however, Shakespeare uses Gower's commentary to provide cohesion, retaining and finally validating his source narrative's loose, episodic structure.

Pericles, probably first performed in 1607–8 and printed for the first time in the same year as the *Troilus and Cressida* quarto, was a success on stage and in print.[46] We can infer that the play was successful from Ben Jonson's complaints about its popularity in his 1629 "Ode: To Himself," occasioned by the failure of his *New Inn*. *Pericles* is, in many ways, a less coherent play than *Troilus and Cressida* and has very clear links to the romance tradition but still found audiences. Of course, *Pericles*, unlike *Troilus and Cressida*, does end "happily," without disturbing bequests, and it is tempting to speculate that this difference (among others) between the plays contributed to its more positive reception. However, that difference seems inadequate as an explanation, particularly when the play remains both confusing and unsettling. In the next chapter, I will consider ways that the explicitly "medieval" presentation of the play may have contributed to its popularity, but it is worth pointing out that the five or six years between what we think was the first appearance of *Troilus and Cressida* and the first performances of *Pericles* saw the appearance of plays like Marston's *The Malcontent* (1604), and Fletcher's *Faithful Shepherdess* (1608) was performed roughly contemporaneously with *Pericles*.

The first quarto of Fletcher's play includes a variety of paratextual material, including a dedicatory poem to Walter Aston, knight of the Bath, and a letter to the reader.[47] The dedication asks for Aston's patience before stating that:

This play was never liked, unlesse by few
That brought their judgements with vm, for or late
First the infection, then the common prate
Of common people, have such customes got
Either to silence plays, or like them not (par. 1r)

---

46. Two quartos appeared in 1609, another in 1611. Pavier included it in his three-play collection in 1619, and two more quartos appeared in 1630 and 1635.
47. We believe the quarto was printed in 1610. It was printed by Edward Allde for Richard Bonian and Henry Walley. Three more quartos followed in 1629, 1634, and 1656. It appeared in the second Beaumont and Fletcher folio in 1679.

The poem goes on to state that the play would have been "falne for ever prest downe by the rude" had not "the saving sence of better men / Redeem'd it from corruption" (par. 1r). The poem positions the play in a position not unlike that of Shakespeare's *Troilus and Cressida* or *The Knight of the Burning Pestle* – rescued from the scorn of ignorant masses by the intervention of someone wiser – and, like both plays, flatters readers by addressing them as among the wise as well.

Fletcher's much better-known address to the reader calls attention to the unfamiliarity of the form, specifying the "anger" of the rude referenced in the dedicatory poem before turning to more proper definition of its tragicomic genre. Fletcher opens the letter acknowledging that readers might not know precisely what kind of "poem" they have picked up:

> If you be not reasonably assured of your knowledge in this kind of Poem, lay down the book or read this, which I would wish had been the prologue. It is a pastoral Tragic-comedy, which the people seeing when it was played, having ever had a singular gift in defining, concluded to be a play of country hired Shepherds, in gray cloaks, with curtailed dogs in strings, sometimes laughing together, and sometimes killing one another: And missing whitsun ales, cream, wassail and morris-dances, began to be angry.

Fletcher gives his readers a choice not offered in the theatre: of either going no further or reading his explanation of the play. As he writes, had the letter been the prologue, the play might have been better received. Instead, the "people" with their gift of defining, decided it was a play of shepherds "sometimes laughing together, sometimes killing one another" and grew angry at a lack of other rural pleasures. From the perspective of historical genre theory, this definition leaves something to be desired since it says nothing about traditional categories, even if it responds to a represented desire on the part of the audience. Fletcher depicts the "people" as being given to defining but not particularly skilled or informed in their definitions. Turning to his readers, Fletcher instructs them in better definitions:

> In their error I would not have you fall, lest you incur their censure. Understand therefore a pastoral to be a representation of shepherds and shepherdesses, with their actions and passions, which must be such as may agree with their natures at least not exceeding former fictions, and vulgar traditions: they are not to be adorned with any art, but such improper ones as nature is said to bestow, as singing and poetry, or such as experience may teach them, as the virtues of herbs,

and fountains: the ordinary course of the Sun, moon, and stars, and
such like. But you are ever to remember Shepherds to be such, as all
the ancient Poets and modern of understanding have received them:
that is, the owners of flocks and not hirelings.

This is a fairly traditional definition of pastoral and adheres to ideas
of social decorum, in that the shepherds and shepherdesses should
only do and feel things in accord with their natures and literary precedent. Fletcher's appeal to tradition – "former fictions, and vulgar
traditions" – places the play in that tradition, carving out a place for
it in the field. In addition, in his version of pastoral, all the shepherds
are owners, not hirelings. This social distinction separates proper
pastoral shepherds from mere hired men: the shepherds come from
a (however slightly) higher class than a hireling, which in turn justifies the leisure they display in their "singing and poetry."[48] It also
indicates that these shepherds and shepherdesses are fit images for a
discerning audience.

Fletcher goes on to the sentence that English scholars most-often
quote and treat like a maxim in much criticism that takes up the
reception of tragicomedy:

> A tragi-comedy is not so called in respect of mirth and killing, but in
> respect it wants deaths, which is enough to make it no tragedy, yet
> brings some near it, which is enough to make it no comedy: which
> must be a representation of familiar people, with such kind of trouble
> as no life be questioned, so that a God is as lawful in this as in a tragedy, and mean people as in a comedy. This much I hope will serve to
> justify my Poem, and make you understand it, to teach you more for
> nothing, I do not know that I am in conscience bound.

This definition of "tragi-comedy" distances it from the "sometimes
laughing, sometimes killing" definition Fletcher treats as mistaken
at the start of his letter by invoking definitions of other genres.[49] He
defines his tragicomedy by what it is not: it is not tragedy because
no one dies, it is not comedy because characters are brought near

48. Virgil's first eclogue stages a conversation between Tityrus, an owner, and
    Meliboeus, a dispossessed wanderer whose fate is not to play the flute and sing
    while overseeing his flocks. The social distinction Fletcher points to features in
    some of the earliest versions of pastoral.
49. Part of what is fascinating about this letter is the way that Fletcher moves to
    dismiss a definition of "pastoral tragicomedy" based on more or less on content
    – a play with shepherds laughing and killing – with one that appeals to literary
    tradition and classical precedent.

to death. It must, instead, be "a representation of familiar people, with such kind of trouble as no life be questioned." In other words, imperfect tragedy and imperfect comedy become tragicomedy. In an almost direct response to Sidney's worries about inappropriate mixing in his *Defence of Poetry,* Fletcher justifies the appearance of gods and mean people in his play based on the "representation of familiar people," which makes the appearance of "a God" and "mean people" lawful. This defensive definition of a relatively new genre of stage play makes a claim for value and distinction intended to change the structure of audience expectation and thus the shape of the field.[50]

V

It has a noble breeder and a pure,
A learned, and a poet never went
More famous yet 'twixt Po and silver Trent.
Chaucer, of all admired, the story gives;
There, constant to eternity it lives.
If we let fall the nobleness of this,
And the first sound this child hear be a hiss,
How will it shake the bones of that good man,
And make him cry from under ground, 'O fan
From me the witless chaff of such a writer,
That blasts my bays and my famed works makes lighter
Than Robin Hood?' This is the fear we bring,
For to say truth, it were an endless thing
And too ambitious to aspire to him,
Weak as we are, and almost breathless
Swim in this deep water . . .

        Shakespeare and Fletcher, *The Two Noble Kinsmen* Prologue[51]

50. The Oxford English Dictionary lists Sidney's "mongrel tragicomedy" (1586) as the first use of the term in English. The earliest surviving printed playbook using the term is Samuel Brandon's 1598 closet drama *The Virtuous Octavia* (printed by Edward Allde for William Ponsonby). Samuel Daniel's *The Queene's Arcadia* (performed at Oxford in 1605, printed 1606, 1607, 1611, and 1623 in several different formats) is the first surviving printed play to label itself a "pastoral tragicomedy").
51. The prologue appears to have been written by Fletcher, but matters of authorship are less important to my argument than the appearance of Chaucer in the prologue.

Fletcher and Shakespeare's play begins with a prologue that closes with the assertion that the play "hath a noble breeder and a pure" in Chaucer and with the hope that he will not be displeased at its reception. Many critics have noted that while the play avers its debt to Chaucer and takes its plot from *The Knight's Tale*, it treats the narrative quite differently.[52] Ann Thompson writes, "In *Troilus* Shakespeare's overtly satirical approach transformed the material, whereas in telling the story of Palamon and Arcite it is Chaucer who takes the more comic approach, mocking and deflating his subject-matter, and forcing the reader to see it with detached irony, while Shakespeare treats it seriously" (166). Calling the play "most distressing," Donaldson writes "It's not that it is a bad play . . . but that it is a very unpleasant one in which the dark side that Shakespeare saw in the *Knight's Tale* when he was writing *A Midsummer Night's Dream* is fulsomely reexpressed" (50). The play is far bleaker than the Chaucerian original, and its characters seem like cruel automata in their inability to engage in the kind of self-reflection that might produce an at least somewhat less dark tone. Given this deliberate and pervasive departure from the mood of their source, in this final section of the chapter, I will speculate what the voiced anxiety about Chaucer's reaction to the play might signify.

A sense of anxiety infuses the whole of the prologue, which opens by stating that new plays and "maidenheads" are "near akin" because both draw attention and money if they "stand and sound well" (1–3).[53] Fletcher and Shakespeare immediately introduce the audience into a world that links artistic production, sexuality, and commerce into an uneasily unified whole. The linkage offers a kind of echo of *Troilus and Cressida*'s debunking of the title characters' love story (not to mention that of Paris and Helen), and it suggests a similar kind of disposition to the play's source in medieval romance.[54] The prologue then hopes that play might be like a wife "that after holy

---

52. There has, until fairly recently, been a striking lack of critical interest in the play. Whether that is because of the play's disturbing content or its collaborative nature or both is difficult to say, of course, but these are some of the reasons offered by those critics who do actually engage with it.
53. This anxiety might be disingenuous as it is a common feature of inductions to plays; even so, the explicit reference to worry about what the source-poet might think is interesting and distinctive. All subsequent citations of the play are to Greenblatt's 2008 edition and will be cited parenthetically.
54. The blushing uncertainty attributed to the play (gendered male) is also interestingly akin to Troilus' uncertainty in the moments before Pandarus brings him to Cressida.

tie and first night's stir / Yet still is modesty, and still retains / More of the maid than husband's pains" (6–8) and alleges that it should be so because it "hath a noble breeder and a pure" (10). Why the play should remain (or ever be) modest when it derives from such a noble and famous "breeder" is not immediately clear. Unlike the presenter-prologue Gower in *Pericles*, the prologue says nothing about the content of the play, instead preferring to talk about its lineage and the playwrights' worry about Chaucer's reaction. That worry and the hope that the play will retain its maiden modesty derive from the same source: anxiety about the incapacity of the play to measure up to its noble progenitor.

When the prologue imagines Chaucer to speak, it is to utter a complaint about the failure of the "writer" to measure up to his reputation. However, it is *not* Chaucer speaking in his own person, and the ventriloquized speech represents the putative fear of the playwright and acting company:

> O fan
> From me the witless chaff of such a writer,
> That blasts my bays and my famed works makes lighter
> Than Robin Hood. (Prol. 18–21)

The prologue's imaginary Chaucer worries that the play will be "witless chaff" that will cloud his reputation, the reputation of a writer the prologue also describes as "all admired." The prologue goes on to further explain that:

> This is the fear we bring,
> For to say truth, it were an endless thing
> And too ambitious to aspire to him,
> Weak as we are. (Prol. 21–4)

The prologue expresses consistent doubt about the play's capabilities to present the noble and pure product of such a famous writer. This discourse of incapacity runs throughout the prologue and extends to the epilogue, which expresses great anxiety about the play's reception while waiting for applause or hisses. The worries are, as is usual with such expressions, belied by the confidence with which Shakespeare and Fletcher adapt Chaucer's poem into their play.

The Chorus to *Henry V* serves as a useful point of comparison, as that Chorus also consistently offers disclaimers about the incapacity of the theatre to present the "swelling scene" properly: there are no "princes to act," no "muse of fire," that would enable Shakespeare's company to do the story justice (Prol.1–4).⁵⁵ All the company has is the "rough and all-unable pen" of the "bending author" who has:

> pursu'd the story,
> In little room confining mighty men,
> Mangling by starts the full course of their glory. (Epil. 2–5)

Like the doubt of *Troilus and Cressida*'s prologue in the "author's pen" (24*)*, *Henry V*'s Chorus expresses a consistent doubt in the ability of the author's work to live up to his great model in history. At the same time, of course, the play demonstrates very little actual worry about what it is doing – depicting history on stage, intervening in the telling of history, and finding solutions to dramatic problems – and presents the story of Henry V and Agincourt with great confidence and authority.⁵⁶ In *Henry V*, history functions like Chaucer does in *The Two Noble Kinsmen*: as a powerful and authorizing precedent but one that can be adapted once the gesture of apology is made.

One significant adaptation in *Two Noble Kinsmen* is the play's intense deflation of the claims of chivalry to have some kind of transcendent value or even moral dignity. Chaucer's tale has elements of this, but the play is more thorough in its exploration and debunking of chivalric values. As only one example, Shakespeare and Fletcher foreground the brutality and arbitrariness of the code in Theseus' staging of the combat for Emilia's love, which imposes death on all of the losers. Critics have regularly noted this feature of the play, and this deflation has alternately produced sympathetic and unsympathetic readings of the play. I would suggest that Shakespeare and Fletcher's critical presentation of chivalry in the play is both an engaged qualification of Chaucer's tale and a redeployment of Chaucer's own questioning of chivalry that is nevertheless presented as new (a "new play" which might falter) and thus a source of anxiety for the playwrights.⁵⁷ The prologue cites Chaucer

---

55. All subsequent citations of the play are from the *Riverside* second edition and are noted parenthetically in the body of the text.
56. The history plays represent another kind of look back to medieval narratives or, better, narratives about the late Middle Ages.
57. I am convinced that this questioning also has much to do with the death of Prince Henry. For a thorough justification of this claim, see Peter C. Herman's "'Is this winning? Prince Henry's Death and the Problem of Chivalry in *Two Noble Kinsmen*" (1997). Herman's article locates the play in the context of the death of Price Henry and sees its questioning of chivalry as a response to the loss of the most important exemplar of Jacobean chivalry. He argues that Shakespeare and Fletcher's use of Chaucer is innovative because before the play

both as authorization and as a disclaimer. With characteristic irony, the disposition of the play is, in some ways at least, fairly close to that of its "noble breeder."

According to the prologue, Chaucer's story lives "there, constant to eternity," and that "there" appears to refer to Chaucer's works.[58] Of course, early modern versions of Chaucer's works are anything but "constant to eternity," a fact of which either Shakespeare or Fletcher may have been aware (even the Speght editions of 1598 and 1602 differ in content: the 1602 edition adds another poem to the corpus), and the play itself is not precisely constant to the Chaucerian original. Thus "constancy" might be a moving target that affords the playwrights the latitude to retool the material into a play whose tone is different than that of Chaucer's tale. The prologue's "Chaucer of all admired" works as a flexible authorizing figure whose works are both capacious and mutable enough to accommodate such children as *Two Noble Kinsmen*. Chaucer thus appears in this play as both narrative source and as "auctor"/"auctorite." When the chorus wishes "sweet sleep" (29) to Chaucer's bones, it is tempting to think of the unquiet rest of the Chaucerian corpus in early modern England. Because of the unstable nature of his text, Chaucer is a usefully flexible "auctorite," enabling all kinds of adaptation and tonal revision. Like the Gower of *Pericles*, he may have also offered a narrative model that was useful in producing this play as well as others.

VI

This chapter has argued that Chaucer and medieval narrative more generally operate as sources and models for the later Shakespeare. Other scholars have argued the specifics of textual and thematic borrowings, and the succeeding chapter points at additional ways that romance inflects Shakespeare's dramatic project in the early seventeenth century.[59] To return to the Bakhtinian ideas that subtend much of this book, the work-utterances of Shakespeare and his contemporaries are engaged in a complex and multiply-layered dialogue

> "virtually nobody considered Chaucer subversive or contestatory" (1). This is a claim I would qualify: earlier uses of Chaucerian antecedents seem to me to be both, which seems in keeping with Chaucer's own characteristic irony. The questioning disposition Herman identifies, then, has a longer history in Shakespeare's work than his essay allows.

58. Eugene Waith's Oxford edition (1989) suggests this reading for "there."
59. See especially Donaldson's *The Swan at the Well*.

with the literary past, a dialogue that operates at the level of emulation and revision as well as that of structure and form. The level of structure and form relates in turn to matters of generic innovation. All three of the plays here are to a greater or lesser extent generically innovative: *Troilus and Cressida* represents a radical revision of the Troy story and an unsettled and unsettling dramatic experiment, *Pericles*' venture in to dramatic romance experiments with the possibilities of staging narratives that range far in time and space and uses the figure of Gower to accomplish that movement, and *Two Noble Kinsmen* adapts Chaucer and presents a bleaker and starker picture of human nature than the *Knight's Tale* in a play that ends with a curiously dispassionate attitude towards the workings of fate. All three look back to medieval literature, I argue, for more than incident or language. The following chapter shows ways that Shakespeare's later plays make use of the kinds of romance narrative structures used by Spenser's *Faerie Queene* to produce plays that refuse simple closure, invite doubt, and trouble any kind of confidence in the authority and reliability of narrative. This chapter and the next are companion pieces whose arguments, I hope, converge to offer an account of some of the generic innovations of these plays that locates them in a broadly construed field of cultural production.

Chapter 2

"Mirrours more then one": Spenser, Shakespeare and Generic Change

> It is thus possible to distinguish, very roughly, *classical periods*, in which a style reaches its own perfection and which the creators exploit to the point of achieving and perhaps exhausting the possibilities provided by an inherited art of inventing and *periods of rupture*, in which a new art of inventing is invented, in which a new generative grammar of forms is engendered, out of joint with the aesthetic traditions of a time or an environment.
>
> Pierre Bourdieu, "Outline of a
> Sociological Theory of Art Perception"

My goal in this chapter, as in the previous chapter on the appropriation of a specifically medieval tradition, is to examine generic innovation in the later Shakespeare (post-1600) as responses, reconsiderations, or revisions of earlier generic experiments. If *Winter's Tale* looks back to Greene's *Pandosto* as a source of narrative *material*, might Shakespeare not also look back to Spenser's *Faerie Queene* as a source for narrative *form*? Spenser's shifting and non-unified narrative in Book III of the *Faerie Queene* bears a suggestive resemblance to Shakespeare's narrative technique in the tragedies and the romances. In this chapter, the innovation I am interested in operates across kinds, altering the way that *Hamlet* presents revenge tragedy and producing the unsettled and unsettling treatment of Troy in the roughly contemporaneous *Troilus and Cressida*. Both plays approach their central stories from deliberately complicated and multiple perspectives, and this proliferation represents their intervention in the generic system. While both Spenser and Shakespeare respond to and revise tradition, neither writer can or desires to break completely with the past. Their interventions in the field are better and more easily understood as position-takings in the field of cultural production. The shape of the field enables and constrains the breaks from tradition. As demonstrated by the history of the two plays this chapter focuses on, some innovations find audiences more readily than others. In the case of *Hamlet,* Shakespeare's innovation was successful and popular, while *Troilus and Cressida*'s reception appears to have been rather less enthusiastic.[1]

This chapter and its companion on medieval legacies are Shakespeare-centric in a way that other chapters in this book are not. There are several reasons for this focus, the first being rooted in the history of criticism. The so-called romances, like the history plays, exist in part as a critical construct, and Shakespeare serves as the central, defining, writer for these "genres," despite their being in many cases collaborations. Another reason for this focus is more practical: considerations of space encourage choosing a bounded sample with which to work, and since several of the plays designated as romances have the added virtue of being collaborations, they are more representative of the field than a series of plays by a single playwright. The blurriness of the critical categories typically used to describe these plays also makes them useful research objects in a book about generic innovations.

The relation of romance to the theatre has been of critical interest at least since Edward Dowden's description of some of Shakespeare's plays as "romance" in his *Shakespeare, A Critical Study of His Mind and Art.* Today, *Pericles, Cymbeline, The Winter's Tale, The Tempest,* and *The Two Noble Kinsmen* are the usual plays gathered together under this rubric, though others conceivably fit as well (including *Henry VIII*). This chapter demonstrates ways the narrative practices of verse romance serve as a resource for Shakespeare in his post-1600 plays. Neither the specifics of this discussion of romance or the actual existence of such a dramatic genre will be the central topic of this chapter; instead, it will discuss the practical impact of verse romance on the drama.[2] Helen Cooper's *The English Romance in Time* (2004) points to the pervasiveness of romance narrative in early modern England and argues that critics lose some sense of what is happening

1. The play was not printed until 1609 and was only ever reprinted in the Folios. The seeming failure of *Troilus and Cressida* offers a potentially useful way to think about the generic experiment represented by the play.
2. The existence and nature of romance are not unimportant, and I will not ignore them, but my emphasis will be elsewhere. The distinction between "romance" and comedy or tragicomedy remains unclear, and as with the "history play," it may obscure more about the dramatic field than it reveals. *The Winter's Tale* has distinctive effects, but I suggest that we do not necessarily need a special generic category to explain it.

in the plays when we lose sight how romance works and what it meant for the period (2–3). As one example, Cooper describes how Shakespeare exploits the association of bears and romance in *The Winter's Tale*, arguing that the famous stage direction, "exit, pursued by a bear" refers to a whole tradition.[3] That tradition matters to later writers not only, and not even primarily, as a source of events or plot, but in terms of structure. She writes:

> The greatest influence of the French Arthurian prose romances on later romance was in terms of structure more than of material. The earlier verse romances had traced the adventures of a single hero (or at most two protagonists, or a hero and a heroine); the prose romances decisively broke with that model. The Lancelot-Grail cycle, the prose Tristan, and the Perceforest substituted a structure in which a large number of stories could be pursued in parallel. (*English Romance* 39)

English verse romance takes up this paratactic narrative structure, one example being Book III of *The Faerie Queene,* as a way to make stories more capacious and to present multiple perspectives on some more general theme. Cooper treats aspects of romance as memes – ideas that replicate in a culture and transmit more than their literal content – that carry both content and structures of thought. Part of the argument of this chapter is that Spenser's multiplied, sometimes contradictory narratives in verse function similarly for drama and for Shakespeare in particular: these memes of romance transmit more than plot and engage audiences in questions about form. Cooper's argument is general and offers an overview of the medieval tradition into the early modern period, but later romances had similarly powerful roles in the cultural field. Focused on one central example, Lori Humphrey Newcomb's *Reading Popular Romance in Early Modern England* (2001) shows just how popular and pervasive Robert Greene's *Pandosto* was in early modern England. Her work serves as an important reminder of the enduring popularity of forms sometimes considered to be out of fashion, played out, or otherwise passé. Greene's work looks back, and his contemporaries deployed it to move forward. Both Cooper and Newcomb show that romance functioned as a resource for writers in multiple ways – and not only as a source of plots.

---

3. She grounds this claim about bears and romance in the popularity of *Valentine and Orson*, a romance that readers constantly encountered and writers constantly referenced throughout the period.

One way these texts served as a resource is in the way they create spaces for reader engagement, for the staging of debates. As Cooper writes, "Romances could provide a secular forum analogous to academic debate. Their audiences expected to respond actively to them, and the writers encouraged such a response" (*English Romance* 13). Provocations to response range from obvious direct invitations, like those where the poet pauses the narrative to ask questions, to more subtle stagings of scenes of debate or judgment within the poems that invite readers to participate in the debate, if only as a silent and late interlocutor. Theatre, by virtue of being live performance, naturally affords more opportunity for this kind of response, and early English drama famously includes moments of direct address, apology, and "explanations" of the action that often only provoke more questions. What I am interested in in this chapter is what I take to be a more subtle phenomenon that operates not at the level of explicit address or even content, but in the structure of narrative in certain of Shakespeare's plays after 1600. Shakespeare turns to romance as a sophisticated reader who wants to avoid other audiences receiving that turn as parodic.[4] *Hamlet*, *Troilus and Cressida*, *Pericles*, and all the "dramatic romances" work to mark themselves off from being simple retellings of romance materials by only using romance structures or by implying affiliations to other genres (like revenge tragedy or epic). Even when these plays do retell earlier stories – as in *Troilus and Cressida* – those stories distance themselves from their sources. These careful moves indicate changes in the audience that are important to an understanding of the theatrical field.[5] *Hamlet*'s reflections of and on revenge work as a kind of invitation to consider the nature and implications of vengeance in a way that echoes Spenser's invitations to consider the many virtues represented in his poem. Likewise, reading *Troilus and Cressida* as a meditation on faithlessness of all kinds asks its audiences in quite explicit and disconcerting ways to think about war, honor, and love through the mirror of faithlessness. In what follows, I discuss the narrative structure of Spenser's Book of Chastity before turning to what I see as Shakespeare's appropriation of that structure and its romance associations in his post-1600 plays.

4. The overt parody in a play like Beaumont's *Knight of the Burning Pestle* is alien to the plays commonly called "romances" in Shakespeare's canon, for example.
5. These changes are, however, a bit trickier to ground, since we lack the kind of documentary evidence provided by Henslowe's *Diary*. Publication information, while rich and useful, stands at a remove from production and tracks a somewhat different audience.

I

> Ne let his fairest Cynthia refuse,
> In mirrours more then one her selfe to see,
> But either Gloriana let her chuse,
> Or in Belphoebe fashioned to bee:
> In th'one her rule, in th'other her rare chastitee.
>
> Edmund Spenser, The Faerie Queene

Spenser announces Book III of the *Faerie Queene* to be the Book of Chastity, containing the "Legend of Britomartis or Of Chastitie." However, as we well know, the book spends a great deal of time following the adventures of a host of other characters as they engage in their many ways with the book's central virtue. The book's narrative structure is thus multiple, often nonlinear, and refractive.[6] Spenser's intent appears to be to present readers with a choice analogous to that offered to Cynthia in the passage above: to see the virtue of chastity in different figures, as seems fit to the reader. While Spenser encourages Cynthia to choose one or another mirror of herself or more than one, he also urges the readers to seek for representations of chastity in "mirrours more then one." Spenser's narrative form in this book – a peculiarly decentered and deliberately dilatory mode of storytelling – is linked to developments in early modern dramaturgy that draw on the resources of romance.[7]

The question of Spenser's influence on Shakespeare has been, as J. B. Lethbridge writes, "a niche subject" because "there has been a conviction that there is not much to say on the matter" (3). Like this chapter, the essays collected in *Shakespeare and Spenser* (2008) argue the opposite position. Even if Shakespeare does not make explicit allusion to Spenser, it is clear that he was deeply familiar with not only *The Faerie Queene* but also much of Spenser's other work.[8]

---

6. *The Faerie Queene* as a whole comprises a broad range of narrative structures from the relatively clear lines of Books I and II to the looser and more recursive structures of the later books. Varying modes seems a Spenserian habit.
7. My own students find Book III to be much more challenging than Book I, mostly because there is no single narrative to follow through the cantos.
8. The bibliography of Lethbridge's collection offers an illuminating look at this tradition of scholarship. His introduction makes the important point that much of this work assumes a kind of one-way transaction between Spenser and Shakespeare and that Shakespeare's use of Spenser's work functions almost entirely at the word or phrase level. Lethbridge attributes this critical assumption to perceived differences between Spenser's romance-inflected epic verse and

A. Kent Hieatt argues that Bellay's *Ruins of Time* (through Spenser's translation) influenced Shakespeare's writing in the Sonnets; and many others have contributed to this body of scholarship. Much of this model depends on thinking about source and influence in terms of an "iterative" model of source study, where verbal echoes or appropriation serve as the marker of influence. My goal, as elsewhere in this book, is to further characterize the field in which these plays and poems were produced and either found or did not find audiences. Rather than dismissing direct influences on plot and language, I emphasize other, perhaps less obvious, but still important shaping elements.

Scholars routinely describe (and praise) Shakespeare as an innovator in terms of his dramaturgy, his role in the theatre, as a poet, and his productivity in diverse genres.[9] Acknowledging Shakespeare's inventiveness is both true and unhelpful in an effort to account for that innovation; that is to say, it is one thing to recognize innovation and quite another to account for it. Often the recognition goes only so far as to point out innovations, which these scholars then attribute to Shakespeare being Shakespeare. Shakespeare's later plays – whether designated "romances," "problem plays," or any of the other terms attached to them – represent responsive reactions to the genre system and innovate within that context.[10] The argument of this chapter is that one aspect of the formal and thematic innovation of the later Shakespeare lies in his deployment of narrative resources from Spenser's epic poem.

Bourdieu's call for a structural history and Bakhtin's more general ideas about the workings of genre, which I discussed in the introduction, are particularly helpful in working through connections between Spenser and Shakespeare – two writers who, as is oft-noted, exerted considerable influence over the shape of the early modern lit-

---

Shakespeare's "dramatic poetry" (15). I would add that it participates in the historical focus on Shakespeare, a focus that sometimes obscures more complex relations between texts and writers. The collection represents an important corrective to earlier scholarship.

9. From the grandiose claims about "inventing the human" made by writers like Harold Bloom to more restrained claims about the representation of subjectivity in books like Katherine Maus's *Inwardness and Theatre* (1995), arguments about Shakespeare's distinctive innovativeness are everywhere in the scholarship.

10. I recognize that even *late* is somewhat problematic as a label, since the plays can only be called late in retrospect. Gordon McMullan's *Shakespeare and the Idea of Late Writing* (2007) offers an enlightening discussion of the usefulness and problems of "late Shakespeare" as a label.

erary field.[11] The broad meta-conversation that Bakhtin sees as characteristic of literary production (and language more generally) helps characterize the interactions between Spenser and Shakespeare's works at a higher level of generality than verbal echoes or direct borrowings. Placing both writers in the field of cultural production clarifies the structure within which both writers took overt or subtly claimed positions.[12] At the turn of the century, Shakespeare was engaged in producing plays that challenged and transformed more or less established boundaries of genre, blending epic, history, tragedy, and comedy in a play like *Troilus and Cressida*. In this process, he may have looked to *The Faerie Queene* as a similarly blended and hybrid text. Spenser's *Faerie Queene*, itself a kind of digest of and response to the verse romance tradition, seems a likely place for Shakespeare to have looked given that Spenser's work, despite differences in form and medium, engages in a similar project.

The question of structural influence from Spenser's poem to the drama is, of course, complicated by differences between the two mediums, and my account here attends to these complications. Iterative notions about source are, in some ways, simpler to work from – one finds verbal links and pursues the implications, and those verbal links are fairly readily apparent – while thinking in terms of structures of narrative is necessarily more abstract. Too, the problem of moving from Spenser's romantic epic to the stage involves the loss of an explicit narrator, as Lethbridge points out, though plays like *Pericles* work around that problem. Nevertheless, as I hope to show, Shakespeare seems have been influenced by Spenser's narrative practice, if not always by his vocabulary or the details of his poem's plot. Spenser's highly reflexive narrative, with its shifting and multiple points of view, offered a useful model for composing plays that offer similarly diverse voices and narrative positions.[13] Shakespeare is far from averse to drawing on nondramatic materials as sources, and part of his intervention in these plays is to draw on narrative poetry for narrative models, not only plot.

11. Though, as Lethbridge's collection notes, scholars name the connection more often than thoroughly analyze it.
12. From the beginning of his career, Spenser's position-takings are consistently more overt than Shakespeare's, whose "signature" (to borrow Patrick Cheney's term) is typically more subtle. See Cheney's *Shakespeare's Literary Authorship* (2008).
13. Ovid's *Metamorphoses* offers similar formal resources, as I argue in "'materia conveniente modis': Ovid and Drama" (2020). Shakespeare seems to be looking to a range of classical and vernacular resources in producing these plays.

In a 1977 essay, Paul Alpers takes issue with ideas about Spenser's narrator and narration that derive from what he terms a dramatistic way of thinking about the narrating voice in the poem.[14] Alpers opens his essay by commenting on how recent criticism had shown "that *The Faerie Queene* is a profoundly undramatic poem" (20). This position seems contingent on a particular idea about drama, an idea that downplays the prominent role, for example, of long rhetorical set pieces in early modern plays. He goes on to discuss the opening stanza of the poem as evidence that thinking about the narrator in dramatic terms presents problems – chiefly that a narrator conceived in terms of a dramatic character implies a kind of consistency of narrative voice that the poem itself does not demonstrate. In addition, readings of the poem that treat the narrative as somehow independent of the narrator are, for Alpers, contradictory: how, he asks, can the narrating voice be a character within the narrative it presents? Alpers rightly points out the fruitlessness of this kind of inward-looking approach to narrative, but, as later writers point out, his essay throws out the baby of reflexivity with the bathwater of straightforwardly dramatic notions of the "narrator." Spenser's narrative is enormously self-conscious, and if it isn't logical to separate the narrator from the narrative, it is equally illogical to underestimate the degree of reflexive critique in that narrative.

In Harry Berger's essay "Narrative as Rhetoric in *The Faerie Queene*," he argues that Alpers's position misdescribes Spenser's project as being fundamentally transactional – interested more in content than in form. Alpers, according to Berger, sees the narrator of the poem as confident in both his ability to speak and in the truths he speaks: "The rhetorical transaction Alpers commends includes a poet who trusts the universe and a reader who trusts the verse" ("Narrative" 181). This description is problematic because it assumes a kind of substance in the transaction: "Alpers misdescribes the transaction as an empirical one" when it is better conceived as a "virtual or fictive transaction" (182). For Berger, instead of being the voice of some kind of more or less straightforward truth,

> The narrator, in short, is the voice of the literary traditions that the poem puts in play by imitation, allusion, parody, and conspicuous

---

14. Berger's comments on this essay form an important part of his "Narrative as Rhetoric" in *Situated Utterances: Texts, Bodies, and Cultural Representation* (2005). Berger's essay has been important in my thinking.

revision. The values embedded in those traditions are placed in question by a variety of strategies, of which the poet's arch mimicry of the moralizing voice is only one. (182)

The poem puts multiple traditions into play which opens the contents of those traditions to question – and this play of traditions both illustrates and questions the central virtues of each book. Discussing the work of Lauren Silberman and David Lee Miller, Berger goes on to write that:

> Silberman and Miller direct attention to the aesthetic reflexivity of the critique – that is, to the ways in which the poem places in question the narrative strategies, allegorical translations, and episodic visualizations that seem most vividly to get the message of that ideology across. (204)

Shakespeare's plays engage in a similar kind of reflexive questioning of literary traditions and modes of representation. Spenser's narrative in Book III represents one model for this reflexive narrative style, a model that the later Shakespeare, I argue, found both congenial and, as always, subject to question.

It is critical orthodoxy to recognize that Shakespeare's metadramatic interests offer, at least in part, a meditation on how dramatic representation works, and it is equally orthodox to note that Spenser demonstrates the same kind of attention to his version of metanarrative. Self-consciousness about representation has an important structuring role for both Shakespeare and Spenser.[15] In effect, I am asking a question related to Berger's:

> The question is, does it make a difference if, instead of merely reading the poem as a piece of storytelling, we approach it as a poem that represents storytelling, and does so in a manner that isn't innocent, a manner that interrogates the values and motives, the politics and ideology, embedded in the structures of storytelling? (173)[16]

Does it make a difference to approach a play like *Hamlet* or *Troilus and Cressida* in view of this question and with the energy of the

---

15. As Jonathan Goldberg argued thirty years ago in his book *Voice Terminal Echo: Postmodernism and English Renaissance Texts* (1986), there are good reasons to link early modern texts to postmodern ones, including the self-consciousness of writers like Spenser.
16. Shakespeare and Spenser approach storytelling in this interrogative mode most of the time.

question directed not only at the narrative in the play but the manner in which that narrative is constructed? Both plays question the "politics and ideology" implicit in both acts of storytelling and in stories themselves. In both cases, it seems to me that questions like Berger's do make a difference. Some answers come from thinking through Shakespeare's appropriation and adaptation of narrative structures from Spenser specifically and from romance more generally.

II

> It falles me here to write of Chastity,
> That fairest virtue, farre above the rest;
> For which what needs me fetch from Faery
> Forreine ensamples, it to have exprest?
> Sith it is shrined in my Soveraines brest,
> And formed so lively in each perfect part,
> That to all Ladies, which have it profest,
> Need but behold the pourtraict of her hart,
> If pourtrayd it might be by any living art.
>
> Spenser, *The Faerie Queene*

The poet's task in Book III is to offer an account of Chastity – the fairest of virtues – and he introduces the book with this address to the Queen, protesting that all he really needs to do, were it possible, would be to show a picture of her "hart" and that would do all the necessary work. But this is not possible for painters or even for "Poets wit, that passeth Painter farre / In picturing the parts of beautie daint" (Proem 2.6–7) which is in danger of marring the excellence of the Queen's virtue.[17] As he writes:

> But liuing Art may not least Part express,
> Nor Life-resembling Pencill it can paint,
> All were it Zeuxis or Praxiteles;
> His Daedale Hand would fail, and greatly faint,
> And her Perfections with his Error taint;
> Ne Poet's Wit, that passeth Painter far
> In picturing the Parts of Beauty daint,
> So hard a Workmanship adventure dare,
> For fear, thro want of Words, her Excellence to mar. (Proem 2.1–9)

---

17. Puttenham speaks to a similar distinction in his *Art of English Poesie*.

All attempts at representation are doomed to fail because "her excellence" is a kind of Platonic ideal to which even the highest forms of art – poetry in Spenser's view – can only approach and mar in that approach. Spenser offers a series of approaches to an idea, and no single one of them is capable of producing a perfect representation. His mention of various media in this passage underscores the need for multiple kinds of representation, no one of which will reach to "her Perfections" but can approximate or shadow it. The protestations of incapacity lead to Spenser's introducing of his own, apparently doomed, attempt to picture "the parts of Beauty daint":

> How then shall I, Apprentice of the Skill,
> That whilom in divinest Wits did reign,
> Presume so high to stretch mine humble Quill?
> Yet now my lucklesse lot doth me constraine
> Hereto perforce. But O! dread Sovereign,
> Thus far forth pardon, sith that choicest Wit
> Cannot your glorious Pourtraict figure plain,
> That I in coloured Shows may shadow it,
> And antique Praises unto present Persons fit. (Proem 3.1–9)

With some false humility, Spenser apologizes for his lack of skill as a mere "Apprentice." His request for pardon is justified since his "lucklesse lot doth [him] constraine" to attempt to write about Chastity. His solution is not to attempt to produce a "glorious pourtraict," but instead to "shadow" her and to fit "antique praises unto present persons."[18] His allegorical approach allows him sufficient leeway for error and excuses any failure to adequately represent the Queen, the caster of the shadows. Spenser presents his "colour Shows," the multiple stories and varied mirrors to come in Book III, as both the only and the best way to develop the impossible portrait of his "dread Sovereign." After referring to the superior excellence of Raleigh's poem as praise of the Queen, Spenser finally moves into his own project by asking leave for his rustic muse to sing of Chastity in the varied mirrors that his book goes on to present:

> But let that same delitious Poet lend
> A little leave unto a rusticke Muse
> To sing his mistresse prayse, and let him mend,
> If ought amis her liking may abuse. (Proem 5.1–4)

18. He seems to be both managing expectations in these lines and offering instruction about how to read Book III. The lines here refer indirectly to the "Letter to Ralegh" about the cloudy, shadowy wrappings of allegory.

Addressing Raleigh, "that same delitious poet" whose poem Spenser describes as a far better representation of Elizabeth than any other, Spenser begs leave for his rustic muse to contribute to the praise of his Cynthia in a pastoral vein, or at least with the assistance of a pastoral muse. Spenser's muse in the *Faerie Queene* may not be exactly or consistently "rusticke," but his poem does subsume that mode, embracing and deploying the poetic and representational resources of elegy and a whole range of other forms.[19] The work of the book, like that of the whole poem, appears to require this kind of syncretic and multimodal approach.

I have dwelt on these introductory stanzas because they describe Spenser's project as refractory, in all senses of the word, from the start of the book. He first dismisses visual art as a way to present "ensamples" of virtue before arguing that poetry is better, even though all his work can do is present what he calls "coulour Shows." His dismissal of visual art in the proem offers an interesting contrast to the many examples of ekphrasis in the book that follows – from the description of the tapestries at Malecasta's castle to the decorations of the House of Busyrane – where the poem offers a poetic version of the visual art he begins the book by dismissing. Spenser's claim is that all he can do is offer multiple partial images of the glorious image of Elizabeth that might, if taken together, resolve into an approximation of her embodied virtues. The only way that he can see to write of chastity is to offer many partial images – "mirrours more then one."

Spenser explains his method in Book III in terms of mirrors – reflecting and refracting images of one of the central virtues of the Queen – and images of all sorts run through the whole of the book. When Spenser writes of "mirrours more then one" in the proem to the book he radically understates the variety and number of mirrors that Book of Chastity will contain. Unlike the relatively straightforward structures of Book I and II, which (more or less) stick with central characters and keep a focus on a (more or less) clear narrative thread, Book III is composed of a proliferating network of subnarratives, all of which have some role in illustrating the value and proper definition of chastity.[20] Not all of these mirrors prof-

19. Arthur's lament in Canto IV partakes of elegy as do the various lovers' complaints in Book III. And, of course, Spenser's own *Shepheard's Calendar* (1579) represents his own version of the mode (and is part of his Virgilian cursus towards epic).
20. This narrative multiplication may look forward to the even more complex structure of Book IV. The later books intensify the degree of interlacement in the narrative, pushing this element of romance quite far.

fer images of chaste and proper behavior: some present examples to be avoided, others trouble unitary versions of what Chastity means, and so forth. The subnarrative mirrors here are often more distorting than clear, and this complexity too seems to be part of Spenser's argument since they require readers to exercise the faculty of judgment. As he writes in the proem, his "Cynthia" can choose various images of herself: "But either Gloriana let her chuse, / Or in Belphoebe fashioned to bee: / In th'one her rule, in th'other her rare chastitee" (Book III.Proem 5). The poet here offers two options in Gloriana and Belphoebe, but only Belphoebe actually appears in the poem, and, curiously, he fails to mention Britomart, the Knight of Chastity. Belphoebe – the huntress sister of Amoret raised by Diana – serves as the image of Elizabeth's chastity and the absent Gloriana as an image of rule.[21] Gloriana's absence preserves from the poet's incapacity and leaves her image in the mind of the reader, rather than on the page. Britomart's active virtue and her story's direction towards marriage makes her less of an example of Elizabeth's virtues than of some more general and worldly notion of Chastity. Spenser's project multiplies reflections in the interest of a more complete and complicated picture rather than making any effort at presenting a kind of unitary image and by extension any unitary message about the meaning of chastity.

Early modern writers frequently used *mirror* or *looking glass* as part of titles, and there is an interesting and diverse scholarship on both the literary and material meanings and deployments of mirrors.[22] In most of these works, the mirror is intended to model behavior, to offer examples, and, most generally, to teach. Indebted to the medieval *speculum* tradition, writers on poetry like George

---

21. See the entry on Belphoebe in the *Spenser Encyclopedia* for a discussion of her ambiguous status as an image of Elizabeth – her chastity may be unassailable, but, unlike Britomart's, it's also sterile. Gloriana is a mirror only visible in her absence, never appearing in the poem except in report or dream.
22. A cursory search of titles using the word *mirror* between 1473 and 1603 in Early English Books Online returns 122 titles, ranging from treatises on manners to technical handbooks. The most well-known of these, *A Mirror for Magistrates*, in its collected poems functions as a combination of conduct manual and handbook on statecraft. Most of these figurative mirrors are not operating as simple reflectors but as active shapers of images and guides to action. They rarely merely "hold a mirror up to nature." There is an extensive scholarship on both literal and figurative mirrors in the period. For example, Rayna Kalas's essay, "The Technology of Reflection: Renaissance Mirrors of Steel and Glass" (2002), makes an argument linking developments in mirror technology to texts like Gascoigne's *Steel Glas*.

Puttenham link the "fantasy" or imagination to mirrors as well. Puttenham writes:

> This fantasy may be resembled to a glass, as hath been said, whereof there be many tempers and manner of markings, as the perspectives do acknowledge, for some be false glasses and show things otherwise than they be indeed, and others right as they be indeed, neither fairer nor fouler, nor greater nor smaller. There be again of these glasses that show things exceeding fair and comely, others that show figures very monstrous and ill-favored. Even so is the fantastical part of man (if it be not disordered) a representer of the best, most comely, and beautiful images of things to the soul and according to their very truth. If otherwise, then doth it breed chimeras and monsters in man's imaginations, and not only in his imaginations, but also in all his ordinary actions and life which ensues. (110)

Mirrors, in Puttenham, are not simple objects that return clear and undistorted images back to the viewer; instead, they shape those images according to the nature of their "tempers." By analogy, the "fantastical part of man" operates similarly and produces all manner of images in accord with the nature of the producer. Unlike Spenser, Puttenham does not see room for good uses of "chimeras and monsters." Indeed, Spenser's poem is as full of monsters and chimeras as it is of the comely and the beautiful. Disordered fantasies, like Hellenore's in canto 9, take the stories they hear and transform them into "worlds of fancies" that lead her into error (3.9.52.4). Puttenham's discussion of "fantasy" in terms of mirrors assumes that representation has force: the mirror of fantasy can breed, to use his words, either good or bad behavior. Spenser describes his work in similar terms and the artworks within the poem work in similar ways – either good or bad.[23] In Book III, as elsewhere in the poem, he makes use of all the various possible products of his glass in his efforts to fashion gentlemen. All these images are busy doing work for their in-poem creators, for their viewers, and for the poet, and the diversity of images is itself what generates the larger image of "Chastity."

---

23. For example, the art in the House of Busirane seems designed to produce concupiscence in its viewers.

III

> But she to none of them her love did cast,
> Save to the noble knight Sir Scudamore,
> To whom her loving hart she linked fast
> In faithfull love, t'abide for evermore,
> And for his dearest sake endured sore,
> Sore trouble of an hainous enimy;
> Who her would forced have to have forlore
> Her former love, and stedfast loyalty,
> As ye may elsewhere read that ruefull history.
>
> But well I weene, ye first desire to learne,
> What end unto that fearefull Damozell,
> Which fled so fast from that same foster stearne,
> Whom with his brethren Timias slew, befell:
> That was to weet, the goodly Florimell;
> Who wandring for to seeke her lover deare,
> Her lover deare, her dearest Marinell,
> Into misfortune fell, as ye did heare,
> And from Prince Arthur fled with wings of idle feare.
>
> Spenser, *Faerie Queene*

These two stanzas, appearing at the end of the sixth canto of Book III, present readers with part of the backstory of Amoret and Scudamour, a story whose proper telling is deferred until cantos eleven and twelve.[24] Amoret, we are told, endures "sore, / Sore trouble of an hainous enimy" (III.vi.53.5–6), which seems calculated to prompt the curiosity of a reader about the nature of that trouble. Despite this narrative prompt, the poem postpones relating the "ruefull history" of Amoret and Scudamour, in many ways the heart of the story of Book III, for four cantos. Instead, the narrator here tells us that he knows that readers really want to hear the rest of the Florimell and Marinell story, itself a story that has already been repeatedly interrupted. Spenser's narrator reminds readers that we have heard about the wanderings of Florimell and her fearful flight from Arthur – calling attention to the broken-up nature of the story

---

24. Indeed, the story does not conclude even there in the 1596 edition, which defers their reunion to another place so the Poet can catch his breath. In the 1590 text, Amoret and Scudamour have an emotional reunion that almost provokes envy in Britomart, who is still seeking her mirror-induced beloved Artegall.

and indicating (however vaguely) where an interested reader might go to be reminded of the story so far.

Spenser's epic often makes narrative itself a topic of its narrative: the poem is full of stories that are variously interrupted, disjointed, or inadequate to the events narrated. This interest in narrative is at least in part due to the meta-influence of Ovid's *Metamorphoses* on Spenser's poetics. Ovid's poem is as much about the project of narrative as it is about any of the individual stories he tells in the poem. Shakespeare learned much from Ovid as well, and it seems to me that Spenser and Ovid's "examples" (for lack of a better term) converge in the later Shakespeare. Book III of the *Faerie Queene* repeatedly pauses, switches focus, and insistently calls attention to its multiple perspectives on its central virtue – defining and exemplifying it from a multitude of directions. The book's trajectory is thus organized around a need to offer as many possible views and examples of chastity in action rather than to show some sort of developmental narrative as in Book I. Instead of presenting a unified narrative that might simplify or reduce the virtue of chastity to a unitary definition, Book III provides a more full and nuanced exploration of the problem of determining what chastity is and what it means to practice it. For example, by contrasting Belphoebe's Diana-like celibate chastity to the marriage and progeny-oriented chastity of Britomart, Spenser is able to present alternative models that expand rather than contract the possibilities inherent in this multivalent virtue. As everywhere in the poem, the allegory is anything but simple and straightforward. Book III stresses the value and importance of representing a central theme from a variety of angles – giving readers a range of images with which to work and develop a picture of Chastity, a never-complete and always changing picture. While Britomart may be the Knight of Chastity, the virtue is not unitary and, more importantly, exists in practice not theory.

From the very start of the Book proper, Spenser indicates that it will not be quite as straightforward as either of the first two books. The canto opens with Guyon and Arthur departing the Castle of Alma, despite the urgings of Alma to stay longer. They encounter Britomart and without explanation (at least initially) Guyon charges her and is unhorsed.[25] After the usual exchanges of courtesies (once

---

25. The explanation, of course, comes through an appropriation of Ariosto when Spenser explains that such combat is a "goodly usage of those antique times" (3.1.13) designed only for the gaining of praise, not deriving from malice. Even here, though, the picture is complicated. Guyon has to be dissuaded from

Guyon calms down), Spenser introduces the first of many forks in the narrative: Florimell, here unnamed, bursts from a thicket pursued by the Foster, a kind of incarnation of "beastly lust" (3.1.17). The male knights and Timias immediately pursue:

> Which outrage when those gentle knights did see,
> Full of great envie and fell gealousy,
> They stayd not to avise, who first should bee,
> But all spurd after fast, as they mote fly,
> To reskew her from shamefull villany.
> The Prince and Guyon equally bylive
> Her selfe pursewd, in hope to win thereby
> Most goodly meede, the fairest Dame alive:
> But after the foule foster Timias did strive. (3.1.18)

Book III's initial fork thus results from responses to a display of lust on the part of the Foster and from desire to win "the fairest Dame alive," itself a species of lust. Guyon and Arthur pursue Florimell seeking, the lines suggest, the "goodly meede" that she embodies, a desire that troubles the ideal of chastity from the start of the book. Timias, in contrast, pursues the pursuer in an effort to protect Florimell or to punish the Foster. The reader can attribute his motives to either a social decorum that places Florimell beyond his reach or a moral distinction suggesting that he is more interested in pursuing a criminal than in courtly love. Britomart remains, not driven by the pursuit of "beauties chace" and uninterested in "Ladies Love" (3.1.19). She waits for a while before heading off on her own way. The narrative splits into a series of stories following the separate pursuits of these characters, which in turn contribute to the developing picture of Chastity.

Significantly, the sight of the Foster's outrageous pursuit fills the knights with "great envie and fell gealousy," neither of which are typically qualities of gentle knights.[26] Unsurprisingly, Florimell continues to flee, having apparently merely substituted one pursuer for two rather better-equipped ones. Their angry desire makes Arthur and Guyon into more civilized versions of the "griesly Foster," brighter mirrors of his bad desire. Timias, on the other hand, goes in chase of

---

"revenging rage" by Arthur and Britomart's victory is explained by her magic spear.

26. This is only one of many examples of such seemingly inappropriate reactions in this book (and the rest of the poem). Guyon's violence in his opening encounter with Britomart in Book III is another.

the "foule foster," pursuing the pursuer not the pursued, and his own chase produces a sub-fork in this first fork. Such breaks and shifts in focus will characterize the whole of Book III. Breaks and shifts of this kind also characterize Shakespeare's plays after 1600 – narratives fragment in ways distinct from the structures of plays of the 1590s – especially those we have come to call the romances. While it is difficult to be sure that the Spenserian influence is the dominant one, it is clear that Spenser was an influence and that his poem is a powerful example of this disposition towards narrative.

IV

> I could a tale unfold whose lightest word
> Would harrow up thy soul, freeze thy young blood,
> Make thy two eyes like stars start from their spheres,
> Thy knotted and combined locks to part,
> And each particular hair to stand on end
> Like quills upon the fretful porpentine.
> But this eternal blazon must not be
> To ears of flesh and blood.
>
> Shakespeare, Hamlet

Tellings and retellings of a central story represent the core of *Hamlet*: if there is a "thing itself" in the play, it lies in these tales. Even before the Ghost appears to offer its story, the play provides multiple explanatory narratives to auditors both onstage and in the theatre. That that core is at least partly inaccessible – an "eternal blazon" that cannot be uttered – has been an object of commentary since Freud's comments on Hamlet in *The Interpretation of Dreams* (1900), an argument taken up and expanded in Ernest Jones's 1949 *Hamlet and Oedipus*. This section, like much of this book, has a double object. It examines specific innovations in Shakespeare's dramatic practice around 1600, and it situates those innovations in the context of the field of cultural production. I have argued that the play is an intervention in the field; now I turn to examining what manner of intervention is it. To answer this question, rather than attempting to pluck out the heart of *Hamlet*'s mystery once again, I want to focus my attention on the ways that these tellings (and refusals to tell) contribute to a broader picture of revenge, among other things, in the play. We cannot ever get to the heart of the play, in part due to the proliferation of story that makes up the play. The obscurity or inscrutability of the mirrored image serves a range of purposes, from enhancing the illusion of depth to underscoring the ambiguous status of exhortations to revenge. While refractions of a central story in drama do not function in exactly the same way as in romance, nevertheless the multiplication of versions does offer mirrors more than one. *Hamlet* offers, in a sense, Shakespeare's Book of Revenge, and the narrative multiplies versions of and motives for vengeance in a way that resonates with Spenser's depictions of Chastity in Book III of the *Faerie Queene*.

Aside from the play's undeniable connections to the genre of revenge tragedy – whether as successor to plays like Kyd's *Spanish Tragedy* or as an originator – it speaks overtly and covertly to a range of other literary and dramatic antecedents. Much of the play's intertextuality is well-known in the scholarship and needs little justification, but my interest in the play's invocation of romance requires some more discussion. Following Helen Cooper's argument that a bear in a stage direction serves as a marker of romance enables us to read plot elements like Hamlet's weirdly under-discussed adventures with the pirates mark a similar affiliation, linking *Hamlet* to another tradition with distinct representational tools. I want, in other words, to think about the play in relation to the so-called romances, plays employing similar narrative strategies.

Hamlet is notoriously complicated in terms of its poetics, its thematics, and its philosophical ramifications in all sorts of areas from theology to phenomenology to hermeneutics. Some of this richness and complexity derives from the play's refusal to present definitive and unambiguous evidence about the status of the Ghost, of Claudius' crime, of Hamlet's sanity or madness, and so forth. Shakespeare achieves this fundamental ambiguity by having what evidence there is in the play take the form of inset narratives, narratives whose perspectives are often questionable and whose content is difficult to judge. The quotation above from the Ghost's initial speech to Hamlet in 1.5 is an example of an authorizing narrative than never gets started because its telling is banned – "forbid" – by the otherworldly authorities the Ghost must obey.[27] The "eternal blazon" of this harrowing tale "must not be / To ears of flesh and blood" (1.5.21–2). Instead, Hamlet hears a different, perhaps just as harrowing and certainly destructive, tale that explains (more or less) how his

---

27. Ironically, the banning of the narrative gives the Ghost some measure of authority, indicating the paradoxical nature of both narrative and authority. I cite from Harold Jenkins's Arden edition of the play.

father's spirit came to walk the night. This story, itself problematic because of its echoes of Hamlet's own "prophetic" thoughts in 1.2, provides an explanation of what is rotten in the state of Denmark, a program to fix it, and multiple exhortations not to forget about it. Rather than present this account as definitively true, Shakespeare chooses to make it doubtful, problematic, and, to Hamlet at least, in need of verification. Unlike Hieronimo or Andrea, whose course of revenge is clear and unambiguous despite the destruction that it entails, Hamlet's is complicated by a lack of evidence, by his own reflection on consequences, and, however latently, his sense of his position as prince.[28] Hamlet needs another mirror to reflect the truth of the Ghost's account, to verify his already-present suspicions, and to justify his choice of action.

Narrative and the always-fraught interpretation of narrative are almost constantly at issue in the play, and the play's remarkably fitful forward movement seems to be a result of its obsession with narration and the analysis of narrative. In the process of narrating, stories proliferate and come towards but rarely reach a central object or subject. Even at the close of the play when an audience might expect something resembling clarity and resolution, the play concludes with promises of retellings – retellings that are not and cannot be adequate to the play just witnessed by the theatrical audience. Like Spenser's work, the story turns back on itself, breaking images into fragments that coalesce and dissolve as they work towards a more complete picture of the events. That that picture is only available to audiences – whether theatrical or reading – seems a large part of the point. Like Spenser's poem, *Hamlet* demands its audiences' judgment.

Conventionally, Laertes' desire to avenge his father serves as a foil to the main plot of Hamlet's revenge, contrasting his certainty to Hamlet's doubt. The term "foil" in reference to a character is commonly associated with a jeweler's use of a "thin leaf of some metal placed under a precious stone to increase its brilliancy or under some transparent substance to give it the appearance of a precious

---

28. Hieronimo may, briefly, doubt the veracity of Bel-Imperia's note written in blood, but once events confirm its contents, he is committed. Even when Hamlet gets "proof," he deliberates. The outcome of Hieronimo's revenge in *The Spanish Tragedy* may be unclear – especially given the strangeness of the disposition of the dead at the end of the play – but the direction of the plot and the need for the wild justice of revenge is clear. Later plays, like *The Revenger's Tragedy* or *Women Beware Women*, push the violence and lack of questioning towards the absurd. See chapter six below.

stone."²⁹ This usage is problematic here since Laertes' actions (and his clarity of purpose) do not necessarily increase the brilliancy of the stone it sets off in Hamlet. Laertes' focus clarifies and justifies Hamlet's doubts about the pursuit of his revenge but does not in any simple way increase Hamlet's "brilliancy." The sense of foil as the backing of a mirror (fourth listed in the *Oxford English Dictionary* entry) makes a good deal more sense here, particularly when "mirror" also functions as a sort of generic label.³⁰ Laertes functions in the play far more like a mirror than a "foil," a mirror that reflects one model for how to be a revenger.³¹ The same argument applies to Fortinbras, who represents what might be the most successful version of the revenger in the play. Speaking of Fortinbras and his army's march to Poland, Hamlet's "all occasions" soliloquy suggests that such foils make him less than brilliant. The foils here are the kind that multiply images – not the kind that show a central precious stone off to advantage. This section develops an account of the multiplicity of mirrors in the play in relation to Spenser's strategy in Book III of the *Faerie Queene*. Representing a central thematic from a range of perspectives and characters is not unique to either Spenser or Shakespeare, of course, as the history of allegorical drama amply demonstrates. However, the complications and dilation of the plot in *Hamlet* seem distinctive, particularly when compared with the relatively straightforward plots of morality or cycle plays (or, for that matter, of many other revenge plays). One distinctive feature of the mirroring here lies in the indirectness of the reflections: they do not function simply or as straightforward representations of a theme or idea. They are refractions whose splintered images are well suited to Hamlet's revenge. Hamlet's infamous delay echoes the kinds of delay Spenser deploys to amplify and expand his mirror pictures of Chastity.

Mirrors actual and figurative do, of course, figure in the play: Hamlet instructs the players not to hold up a distorting mirror to nature, Gertrude sees a tainted image in the glass of Hamlet's accusations, and productions have a long history of using mirrors in scenes

---

29. *Oxford English Dictionary*. This usage of foil is the fifth heading of the definition. OED cites Marlowe's *Jew of Malta* (1592) as its first example of this sense of the word.
30. For this use in reference to mirrors, *OED* cites a technical text by William Bourne on the properties of glass from 1583.
31. One could very easily see Hamlet as Laertes' foil (and with more technical, if not literary, accuracy).

throughout the play.³² In his instructions to the Players, Hamlet wishes for a theatrical, discursive, mirror that reflects an undistorted version of the world:

> suit the action to the word, the word to the action; with this special o'erstep not the modesty of nature: for any thing so overdone is from the purpose of playing, whose end, both at the first and now, was and is, to hold, as 'twere, the mirror up to nature; to show virtue her own feature, scorn her own image, and the very age and body of the time his form and pressure. (3.2.16–22)

He wants a singular mirror here, not one that offers a series of images of the world, all of which might be true but all also slightly different as in Spenser's poem. This profoundly restrictive notion of dramatic (or representational) decorum holds that the shaping power of playing comes from it being a perfect reflection of the world. Hamlet's own effort at dramatic representation in the play within the play fails to meet this standard and instead produces a response precisely from not being a good mirror. He is disappointed in this hope, and the desire for a clear and unambiguous signification that undergirds this passage is consistently frustrated over the course of the play.³³ Against Hamlet's wish for an authoritative and controlled kind of representation, the play provides versions of "the age and body of the time" not the thing itself.³⁴ Shakespeare, the acting company, and the audience well knew just how impossible getting a simple, singular mirror was in the theatre.³⁵ Hamlet's program for the theatre – at

---

32. In one memorably strange production at Suffolk University in the 1990s, Hamlet leaps through a looking-glass, in an effort to suggest that the play had shifted into some kind of parallel universe (an effort "supported" by the unexplained and inexplicable presence of Malvolio as a kind of momentary chorus). Other, better, productions use mirrors in various contexts: the DVD cover of the RSC's 2009 film with David Tennant is an image of Hamlet in a fractured mirror, and Branagh's film stages Hamlet's confrontation with Ophelia in a mirrored room in a "real" Elsinore.
33. Shakespeare rarely offers clear and unambiguous meaning anyway, preferring a provocative and productive ambiguity.
34. The versioning of stories in the play extends far beyond the revenge narratives. One example can be found in the story of Old Hamlet's fight with Old Fortinbras, which Horatio, Claudius, and the Grave-digger all tell or allude to. Each figure treats it in a slightly different way, both clarifying and obscuring the story's meaning.
35. Discussions of the failure of theatre to represent accurately appear repeatedly in the plays; the oft-discussed Chorus to *Henry V* is only the most thorough of them.

least his wish that it reflect nature without overdone gesture or language – contradicts much of what we know about actual theatrical practice, and, more importantly, its implications deny how much of representation itself works through refraction.

From the first scene of the play, the plot circles around central events, narrating them from a variety of perspectives in order to call attention to the elusive nature of proof, knowledge, and evidence. Skepticism about story appears even before a story does as Marcellus describes Horatio's doubt:

> Horatio says 'tis but our fantasy,
> And will not let belief take hold of him
> Touching this dreaded sight twice seen of us.
> Therefore I have entreated him along
> With us to watch the minutes of this night,
> That if again this apparition come
> He may approve our eyes and speak to it. (1.1.21–7)

According to Marcellus, Horatio dismisses the story of the ghost as "fantasy," and therefore not valid.[36] His ears, "fortified against our story" (1.1.30), are overwhelmed by his eyes when the ghost appears at precisely the time Barnardo and Marcellus report it did in its other appearances. As he says, "before my God, I might not this believe / Without the sensible and true avouch / Of mine own eyes" (1.1.54–6). The play stresses here strangeness of the apparition as well as the mystery of what it means: Horatio does not know "in what particular thought to work" but thinks, correctly in outline if not in detail, that it "bodes some strange eruption to our state" (1.1.66, 68). Like any number of other events and images in the play, the ghost demands reading at the same time that it frustrates certainty. Like a mirror, it reflects images from the viewer's preoccupations. Horatio's questions when it reappears are an example of this effect:

> Stay, illusion.
> If thou hast any sound or use of voice,
> Speak to me.
> If there be any good thing to be done
> That may to thee do ease and grace to me,
> Speak to me.
> If thou art privy to thy country's fate
> Which happily foreknowing may avoid,

---

36. Puttenham uses the same term in his discussion of mirrors and the imagination – Horatio seems to think that Marcellus' fantasy is of the disordered kind.

> O speak!
> Or if thou hast uphoarded in thy life
> Extorted treasure in the womb of earth –
> For which, they say, you spirits oft walk in death –
> Speak of it, stay and speak. (1.1.108–120)

The ghost's appearance could mean any number of things all of which seem equally likely, none of which are confirmed or denied by the ghost, and only parts of which are even possibly true.[37]

Elsewhere in the scene, Horatio claims to be someone who "knows" and can report truths or at least accurate analyses of events. In his treatment of the Old Hamlet-Old Fortinbras backstory, the most expansive of the versions we see, Horatio tells it as part of his explanation for the apparently unusually stringent watch set by the King and considers the ghost's appearance to be necessarily related to the preparations for war.[38] When Marcellus asks "who is't can inform me" of the significance of the strict watch, Horatio responds:

> That can I;
> At least, the whisper goes so. Our last king,
> Whose image even but now appear'd to us,
> Was, as you know, by Fortinbras of Norway,
> Thereto prick'd on by a most emulate pride,
> Dared to the combat; in which our valiant Hamlet—
> For so this side of our known world esteem'd him—
> Did slay this Fortinbras; who by a seal'd compact,
> Well ratified by law and heraldry,
> Did forfeit, with his life, all those his lands
> Which he stood seized of, to the conqueror.
> Against the which, a moiety competent
> Was gaged by our king; which had return'd
> To the inheritance of Fortinbras,
> Had he been vanquisher; as, by the same covenant,
> And carriage of the article design'd,
> His fell to Hamlet. (1.1.79–95)

---

37. While the Ghost has no extorted treasure, it does have a voice and some knowledge about its country's fate, but, perhaps, foreknowing will not avoid that fate. There is something to be done to ease the Ghost, but not by Horatio, and it brings Hamlet no grace.
38. This scene, like many others in the play, a scene of interpretation. Horatio works from data – his knowledge of the past – but his interpretation of the Ghost's appearance is incorrect because he lacks crucial pieces of information. Only the Ghost can offer a "true" explanation for its presence.

Horatio conflates his knowledge of the "whisper" of rumor with a true report and uses the appearance of the Ghost as a kind of illustration of the story (the Ghost appears in the very armor Old Hamlet wore when he fought Old Fortinbras, but the play never addresses the source of Horatio's knowledge) that explains the current (as yet unnamed) king's setting of an extra watch. As Horatio continues, he fleshes out the first of the play's many-layered father-son stories:

> Now, sir, young Fortinbras,
> Of unimproved mettle hot and full,
> Hath in the skirts of Norway here and there
> Shark'd up a list of lawless resolutes,
> For food and diet, to some enterprise
> That hath a stomach in't; which is no other—
> As it doth well appear unto our state—
> But to recover of us, by strong hand
> And terms compulsatory, those foresaid lands
> So by his father lost: and this, I take it,
> Is the main motive of our preparations,
> The source of this our watch and the chief head
> Of this post-haste and rummage in the land. (1.1.95–107)

The "hot and full" Fortinbras seeks to retrieve the lands lost by his father. More importantly, Horatio couches this explanatory narrative in the language of evidential judgment. He looks at the evidence of Fortinbras' activities and based on what he thinks it imports to "our state" offers an analysis of motive: "this, I take it, is the main motive" for the watch. Events more and less significant consistently appear this way in the play, leaving audiences in the position Horatio claims for himself (if usually less certain about the accuracy of interpretation).

Horatio's narrative, however accurate it may be, does not fully explain the ghost's presence. Or, perhaps better, it offers only a partial explanation that indicates something about the ramifying revenges in the play, but it does not speak to the central reason the ghost has come. In the first scene, we get the first of many readings of events, none of which are complete on their own, but which when combined offer a more adequate picture of the events of the play.[39] This mode of representation appears again and again in the play: events are described and redescribed from different perspectives, in full or

---

39. That picture is only accessible to the audience. As in *The Faerie Queene*, only the viewer outside the text can hold the mirror.

in part, and no character, with the possible exception of Hamlet, gains a full picture of them. Even the audience, occupying a privileged position of knowledge, can only produce partial explanations or understandings of the play's events.[40]

One of those mirrors, *The Mousetrap*, purports to confirm the Ghost's story and thus "catch the conscience of the King," but, of course, there are problems with the reflection and thus with the nature of the confirmation. Rather than holding up a clear image of the crime, Hamlet's play distorts the image by making the murderer a nephew rather than a brother, and this revision provokes the King, but this performance does not go far as verification of the Ghost's tale. Hamlet believes it, but audiences onstage and off might (and do – Horatio's response is notably muted) view it differently. Still more versions of the story appear in the play: Claudius' unheard confession, Hamlet's own retelling of the tale to Gertrude, and, we imagine, Horatio's tale of murder promised at the end. This central tale appears in multiple iterations and so do other important narratives, and the fractured narrative backtracks and revises stories as the plot proceeds, shedding light on the central matter from multiple directions.[41]

Hamlet's trip to England represents a break in the narrative that removes Hamlet from Denmark and thus accommodates a shift in attention to Ophelia's madness and death and Laertes' return as revenger. Turning to the story of Polonius' family, the play offers more images of grief for a murdered father. Laertes returns as a revenger unencumbered by the kinds of scruples and doubt that characterize Hamlet and thus is a partial image of Hamlet – of the Hamlet who claims to be able to "drink hot blood."[42] Ophelia's grief-induced madness reflects Hamlet's own grief – a grief that in both cases exceeds the capacity of signification – and offers yet another way of looking at the central narrative. Against Hamlet's place as the central

---

40. Even the history of criticism of the play points to this failure: the mystery is never solved.
41. It is almost too convenient that the play text itself presents in multiple, refractory, versions. *Hamlet* has its own mirrors that editors have traditionally attempted to focus into one image. The recent decomposition of the composite text foregrounds the plurality of the play (not to mention parodies, adaptation and so on). One would like to imagine that the *Ur-Hamlet* had a more straightforward narrative, and the "Hamlet, revenge!" tag at least points in that direction.
42. His willingness to cut Hamlet's throat in a church is one example of this similarity.

figure in the play, Laertes and Ophelia represent distinct fragments of his image, produced by the prism of the subplot.

The events that take place offstage during this break – Hamlet's adventures with the pirates, his return from England, and the deaths of Rosencrantz and Guildenstern, all events important to the unfolding of the play – only appear on stage in the form of a letter and Hamlet's own report. Aside from the obvious interest of pirates, this series of episodes marks the oft-discussed transition from the more manic Hamlet of the earlier parts of the play to the more stoic one of the final action. It is surprising just how little critical attention scholars have given to the pirates. This oversight is probably mostly due to the fact that the play keeps the action off stage and gives us only Hamlet's brief and tantalizing account, but there also seems to be some resistance to this episode as, perhaps, less than serious enough for this play in particular. Martin Stevens's "Hamlet and the Pirates: A Critical Reconsideration" serves as an example of the kind of criticism that does exist regarding this episode. Stevens's essay discusses earlier takes on the pirates, which tend to emphasize chance and dismiss them as contrary to the text.[43] He writes:

> ... a close reading of the text will not permit this interpretation and that, indeed, the intervention of the pirates has been carefully prepared for by Shakespeare as part of the subterranean (and offstage) counterplotting by Hamlet which transpired during Act III. (276)

He argues this position strenuously, if finally not convincingly in my reading, through the rest of his essay. Stevens's argument works to assimilate the pirate episode into a larger tragic pattern in the play in which "the sea adventure is the last link in a chain of self-willed events" (284). Like many other readers of the play, Stevens wants to maintain a sense of order to the events, making the play easier to fit into a notion of tragic seriousness that excludes randomness, sea adventures with pirates, or other plot elements seemingly not in keeping with "tragedy." More recently, Tom Rutter's "*Hamlet, Pirates, and Purgatory*" (2015) considers how the pirate episode may also draw on a sermon by a Swiss theologian that likens Purgatory to "being captured by pirates and robbers" while on a journey instead of going straight to either Heaven or Hell (125–6). Rutter links this idea to Old Hamlet's own interrupted journey and suggests another way Shakespeare "uses the contested idea of purgatory to achieve

---

43. He takes H.D.F. Kitto's 1944 *PMLA* essay on providence in *Hamlet* as his exemplar.

uncanny effects within the play (139). The travel narrative has links to romance but can work to multiple ends, like much in the play.

Rather than attempt to place the pirates into a tragic scheme in an effort that requires an elaborate scaffolding of conjecture, I see the pirates as a kind of intrusion from another genre – romance – and as a signal of the play's however attenuated connections to that genre. Alongside bears, Cooper demonstrates how romance enthusiastically adopts the sea voyage (especially one not controlled by the traveler) as a motif or meme, and *Hamlet*'s most explicitly romance moment is the sea voyage and his encounter with the "thieves of kindness."[44] In romance narratives, "pollution, guilt, and fate of nations" are linked to ocean travel:

> The link lies in the threat inhering in patrilineal societies, such as can turn blood relationship, small babies, or pregnant women into a political danger. Victims of casting adrift who are regarded as a threat to the state are sometimes the subject of a prophecy that they will cause the death of the King; or they may simply have *too much legitimacy*. A linear claim, like ritual pollution, inheres in the potential heir: if you have a right to the throne, or have a certain future predicted for you, there is no more that you can do to free yourself from that right or that prophecy than you can free yourself from bastardy or incest. (Cooper, *English Romance* 113, original emphasis)

Hamlet's run-in with the pirates works as a kind of reworking of this romance meme.[45] Claudius is not so much exposing him at sea as sending him for execution, but instead of dying Hamlet is rescued by pirates and redeemed somehow by this sea voyage. He then returns to his homeland, like Romulus and Remus, to kill a wicked uncle, but rather than founding a dynasty, his action ends one. Hamlet also has the problem of an excess of legitimacy: a son who did not inherit, a son with a murdered father, and, as we find out in the play, an heir whose cause is at least feared to be popular. In romance, these would be good reasons to be cast adrift, and when the cast out returns "their return is likely to be dangerous for those who set them adrift in the first place" (Cooper, *English Romance* 115). As Cooper notes,

---

44. Cooper's discussion of the memetic aspect of romance is fascinating and suggestive. It works around some of the difficulties of iterative modes of source study and makes it easier to think about the dispositions and associations that come with particular romance memes.
45. His laments about being born to set things right, while appropriate to revenge tragedy, also fit into romance notions of an inescapable future, as Cooper describes them.

boats are often providential, and if not all are fatal, all of them are fateful. It is also tempting to see Hamlet's stoical disposition upon returning as an effect of the providence that structures romance in Cooper's view.

The story of Hamlet's sea voyage appears in fragments, is susceptible to multiple interpretations, and as so often in the play, Horatio stands in, if not as an interpreter, as an auditor of the tale. When Hamlet finally does describe the events at sea, Horatio's responses are characteristically muted and ambiguous. Hamlet tells Horatio the details of how he forged a new letter condemning Rosencrantz and Guildenstern to death:

> HAMLET: Being thus benetted round with villainies—
> Ere I could make a prologue to my brains,
> They had begun the play—I sat me down,
> Devised a new commission, wrote it fair.
> . . .
> Wilt thou know
> The effect of what I wrote?
> HORATIO: Ay, good my lord.
> HAMLET: An earnest conjuration from the King,
> As England was his faithful tributary.
> As love between them like the palm should flourish,
> As peace should still her wheaten garland wear . . .
> He should the bearers put to sudden death,
> Not shriving time allowed.
> HORATIO: How was this sealed?
> HAMLET: Why, even in this was heaven ordinant.
> I had my father's signet in my purse . . .
> HORATIO: So Guildenstern and Rosencrantz, go to't.
> HAMLET: Why, man, they did make love to this employment.
> They are not near my conscience. Their defeat
> Doth by their own insinuation grow.
> 'Tis dangerous for the baser nature comes
> Between the pass and fell incensed points
> Of mighty opposites.
> HORATIO: Why, what a king is this! (*Hamlet* 5.2.30–63).[46]

---

46. A side question here has to do with why it is that we tend to take Hamlet at his word about the events. There's no positive reason not to do so, of course, but neither is there any reason not to doubt his account. The self-justifying lines here could readily be taken as protesting too much, and it is not as if Hamlet has not set up stories in ways that guarantee the "right" result elsewhere in the play.

Horatio asks questions that draw out details throughout the early going of Hamlet's tale. His reaction to the news of Rosencrantz and Guildenstern's deaths is muted in a way that could indicate sadness or judgment, and even "Why, what a king is this!" could mean several things. At the close of Hamlet's report, Horatio's final comment is a practical one referring to the short time it will take for the news to arrive from England, and he either reserves or defers offering a judgment. Like many other moments in the play, this scene of report invites audience response and, especially, judgment in a way that echoes that of the romances Helen Cooper discusses.

To take a final example before turning to *Troilus and Cressida*, Horatio's promised account of the preceding action in 5.2 intends to present an explanation of the dismal sight that confronts Fortinbras and the English ambassadors and to fulfill his promise to tell Hamlet's story "aright." Taking control of the stage at the end of the play, he asks to be permitted to speak:

> . . . since so jump upon this bloody question
> You from the Polack wars, and you from England,
> Are here arrived, give order that these bodies
> High on a stage be placed to the view;
> And let me speak to th'yet unknowing world
> How these things came about. So shall you hear
> Of carnal, bloody, and unnatural acts,
> Of accidental judgments, casual slaughters,
> Of deaths put on by cunning and forc'd cause,
> And in this upshot, purpose mistook
> Fall'n on th'inventors heads. All this can I
> Truly deliver. (*Hamlet* 5.2.319–29)[47]

The tale Horatio promises to deliver, of "carnal, bloody and unnatural acts," represents the events of the play as a series of killings belonging more to older versions of revenge tragedy than to the more measured, contemplative and slow play the audience would just have witnessed. Horatio's mirror, then, offers yet another perspective on the action, but, like the others, it is partial, distorting, and in need of evaluation. Rather than conclude with a definitive statement about

---

47. Horatio takes command of the moment, in however deferential a way, ordering the stage and claiming, as he often does in the play, to be in a privileged position of knowledge. The Bastard in the earlier *King John* does much the same at the close of that play, ordering the succession and delivering the final patriotic speech. Unlike Horatio, the Bastard speaks from a position inside the court and does not promise explanation.

the meaning of the events, Shakespeare leaves the audience in an odd kind of suspense, between accounts, between images of Hamlet and his revenge that is not unlike the kind of suspension in which readers of Book III of the *Faerie Queene* often find themselves. Where Spenser seems to have intended to offer a kind of prismatic definition of Chastity, Shakespeare uses these multiple narrative mirrors to make definitions or certainty about revenge or justice or meaning itself ever more difficult to attain. Shakespeare's awareness of such limits and his efforts to push against them appear throughout his plays; offering a never-to-be-told story as he does here is only one strategy designed to make the end of a play less a conclusion than a provocation. In *Othello*, a play that depends on multiple plausible but contradictory narratives, Iago's refusal to speak at the end ("what you know, you know") leaves his story hanging, even as the audience does know much more than the characters onstage. The end of Kyd's *Spanish Tragedy* has characters demanding more stories even when all the explanations have been given and the person being asked to speak has bitten his own tongue out. Shakespeare extends the action of the play beyond the confines of the theatre and thus finds a way to get around the problem Berowne identifies in *Love's Labours Lost* of a tale being "too long for a play."

V

And hither am I come,
A Prologue armed, but not in confidence
Of author's pen or actor's voice, but suited
In like conditions as our argument,
To tell you, fair beholders, that our play
Leaps o'er the vaunt and firstlings of those broils,
Beginning in the middle, starting thence away
To what may be digested in a play.
Like or find fault; do as your pleasures are;
Now good or bad, 'tis but the chance of war.

Shakespeare, *Troilus and Cressida* Prologue

In *Troilus and Cressida*, Shakespeare turns to a very oft-told tale and another one "too long for a play" (if not quite "mouldy") and proceeds to present a curiously inconclusive, partial, and disconcerting story of the Trojan War. Spenser's poem, drawn by the remarkable gravitational force of the Troy story, contains his own version of the fall of the city and "the chance of war." By giving us descendants of two Trojan lines in Paridell and Britomart, his version also has disconcertingly multiplying effects. Most of my attention will be on the Shakespeare play's refusal to resolve the romance narrative of Troilus and Cressida and its cursory attention to other events related to the matter of Troy.[48] The section from the prologue cited above suggests that the play will concern itself with war: the prologue's armor is "like the argument," but the play begins with Troilus divesting himself of his armor and complaining about love. This immediate disjunction prefigures others in the play, setting up narrative expectations and consistently disappointing them. I would like to suggest that what Shakespeare does here is offer a series of problematizing perspectives on the Trojan story, reflecting on it with mirrors more than one, in order to raise questions of the sort raised by *Hamlet*. The combatants in the play look noble and honorable from one perspective and base and treacherous from another, the lovers partake of both the high poetics of courtly love and elaborate bawdry, and the war itself appears as both an occasion to demonstrate heroic virtue and a tragic waste.[49] Reading *Hamlet* as Shakespeare's Book of Revenge enables us to read *Troilus and Cressida* as his book of Faithlessness, faithlessness writ very large.[50]

Shakespeare's play transforms the tragedy of, for example, Chaucer's version of the story into a troubling series of problematic and disappointing versions of the story of Troy. I discuss the impact of satire on the play more fully in chapter one and explore the historical aspects of the play in chapter five. Here, I consider the use of the multiple mirrors of romance narrative as well as its occasional deliberate refusal of closure as a resource deployed by Shakespeare in his Trojan story. As noted above, the central narrative of Book III of the *Faerie Queene* remains unresolved at the end of the book – Britomart's quest to find Artegall is unfulfilled – which leaves the central, titular, realization of Chastity to be imagined or expected. Spenser removes the union between Amoret and Scudamour, movingly described in the 1590 *Faerie Queene*, in 1596, making their reunion *possible* but not actual. Keeping these conclusions in the realm of possibility but

---

48. See chapter one for a discussion of the play's generative relation to the medieval literary tradition.
49. In Spenser's poem, Britomart and Paridell's conflicting versions of the Trojan story serve similar purposes as discussed below.
50. While Cressida's putative falseness has drawn much attention, it's as easily argued that almost every character functions as a figure for Faithlessness, wittingly or not.

removed from certainty ensures that the reader must continue the work of reading and thus continue being fashioned into the discipline Spenser describes in the prefatory material. The unfinished quality of the narrative also suggests what in another context Spenser terms the endless work of the poem's project and those of the characters: Britomart must always be *achieving*, not having achieved. In *Troilus and Cressida*, the whole plot is unresolved (the only major story with a firm conclusion is Hector's, and that only because he is dead), and narrative threads remain hanging in a twisted mirror image of the closure of Spenser's Book of Chastity.

The matter of Troy appears in Spenser's poem as an authorizing story for the version of Britain represented by figures like Red Crosse and Britomart. It functions in different ways in different locations, sometimes to lend support to value claims, but at other times it calls characters into question. In Canto 9 of Book III, Spenser relates the Paridell-Hellenore-Malbecco story, a tale that resembles the Troy story in its trajectory and has a character of Trojan ancestry as a protagonist. The canto opens with a return to questions and worries about representation and its effects:

> Redoubted knights, and honorable Dames,
> To whom I level all my labours end,
> Right sore I feare, least with unworthy blames
> This odious argument my rimes should shend,
> Or ought your goodly patience offend,
> Whiles of a wanton Lady I do write,
> Which with her loose incontinence doth blend
> The shyning glory of your soveraigne light,
> And knighthood fowle defaced by a faithlesse knight.
>
> But never let th'ensample of the bad
> Offend the good: for good by paragone
> Of evil, may more notably be rad,
> As white seems fairer, matcht with black attone;
> For lo in heaven, whereas all goodnesse is,
> Emongst the Angels, a whole legione
> Of wicked Sprights did fall from happy blis;
> What wonder then, if one of women all did mis? (3.9.1–2)

Spenser claims to be worried about the potential criticism he will get from readers of the "odious argument" of this canto, which might obscure the "shyning glory" of the book's crowning virtue with the "loose incontinence" of both Hellenore and Paridell. To counter criticism, he reminds readers that it is possible to encourage virtue by contrasting it to its opposite: "for good by paragone / Of evil, may more notably be rad, / As white seems fairer, matcht with black attone." To this end, Spenser produces another, diminished Paris and Helen in Paridell and Hellenore. Both Britomart and Paridell are of Trojan descent, but Britomart's ancestors were "noble Britons sprong from Trojans bold" (3.9.38.8), while Paridell descends from Paris and proves true to his lineage in being led by desire.

Paridell's retelling of the fall of Troy presents his ancestor in a positive light, passing over any questions about the legitimacy of his seizure of Helen. Paridell calls him the "most famous Worthy of the world, by whome / That warre was kindled, which Troy did inflame" (3.9.34.1–3).[51] Helen becomes the "meed of worthiness," not a kind of bribe in a contest designed by Ate whose result is years of war and certainly not the figure staged in Shakespeare's play. In Paridell's account, Paris "through great prowess and bold hardinesse, / From Lacedaemon fetcht the fairest Dame, / That ever Greece did boast, or knight possesse" (3.9.34.6–8). Rather than a stealthy seducer, Paris is the doer of unspecified heroic deeds when he "fetcht" Helen from Greece. Moreover, his version of the tale blames the Greeks rather than Paris' kidnapping of Helen for the fall of Troy.[52] It is a different mirror of the central narrative of the *Iliad* as well as on Chastity. Indeed, as critics have noted, Paridell and Hellenore's story is a version of the epic narrative about Helen, Menelaus, and Paris. While no city falls here, Malbecco abandons his castle and is transformed into the spirit of jealousy.

The refraction of historical narrative into literature is part of the subject of Heather Dubrow's 1990 essay "The Arraignment of Paridell: Tudor Historiography in *The Faerie Queene,* III.ix." Dubrow points out that:

> Spenser's rendition of the Troy legend plays several narratives against each other, and a study of that rendition invites us, in effect to do the same: to understand the treatment of Trojan and British history in

---

51. Of course, Paris is not one of the Worthies, nor is causing the flames that burned Troy necessarily a marker of worthiness. From his introduction, Paridell displays inaccurate perceptions and engages in various kinds of deception.
52. Spenser himself gives a different version of the story at 2.7.55.4–9. There "partiall Paris" awards the apple to Venus and "had of her, faire Helen for his meed, / That many noble Greekes and Trojan made to bleed." No heroic fetching in Book II. In Shakespeare's play, the Trojans blame the Greeks for the war in the debate scene, arguing that the kidnapping of Helen responds to a prior kidnapping: "for an old aunt whom the Greeks held captive, / He brought a Grecian queen" (2.2.77–78).

III.ix, we need to place this episode in the context of contemporary controversies about historiography that occurred both in England and on the continent during the Renaissance. The overarching issue in this discussion is the reliability and objectivity of history, or, to put it another way, is Rumor, not Clio, really its Muse? (313)

The question Dubrow raises about whether Rumor or Clio is the Muse of history is one taken up in the plays I discuss in Chapter Four and remains unsettled. For my purposes in this chapter, Dubrow's essay highlights the way that Spenser's poem, by virtue of presenting competing and not always reliable stories, puts readers in the position of having to evaluate them in the process of interpreting. The importance of the Troy story as a foundational myth – despite being questioned by contemporary antiquarians – was still high, and representing it as unstable problematizes those narratives. As Dubrow writes, the Troy story related in Book III "unsettles and unravels, calling into question issues that had seemed more straightforward and uncovering problems that had seemed more straightforward or at least concealed earlier" (315). This description of the effect of the stories told fits both Spenser's poem and plays like *Hamlet* and *Troilus and Cressida*.

The version the Troy story Paridell presents, as much as his own flaws, evokes a darker and less heroic version of the Trojan story – a story that, as Britomart's own continuation of the story underlines, serves as an origin story for Britain. Both Paridell and Britomart describe the founding of London by "Trojan Brute" (3.9.46). Interestingly, Paridell reports that Brutus killed his father Sylvius with an errant arrow and

> fled for feare of that he had misdonne,
> Or else for shame, so fowle reproch to shonne,
> And with him led to sea an youthly trayne,
> Where wearie wandring they long time did wonne,
> And great adventures found, that now were long to sayne.
>   (3.9.48.4–9)

Brutus flees the consequences of killing his father, even if by mistake, and thus begins the British story with a stain even before reaching the island where he will fight giants and found both London and Lincoln. Spenser contrasts the filial piety that characterizes the founder of Rome with Brutus' killing of Sylvius. In addition, he tells Britomart that Brutus' adventures, while "great" are too long to tell at the moment, deferring the story to a time that never comes, much as characters in *Hamlet* do.[53] His darker version of the Troy and Troynavaunt story has a suggestive relationship with Shakespeare's own telling of part of the Troy story. These mirrors produce varied images of this mythic past, versions of the story that trouble simple identifications with putatively historical legitimation of, say, Britain's distinction and worth.

Paridell's story has the more immediate effect of drawing Hellenore's "vigilant regard, and dew attent" (3.9.52.3), and she hangs on his story. Guided by or prompted by his words, she listens "fashioning worlds of fancie evermore / In her fraile wit, that now her quite forlore" (3.9.52.4–5). This is an example of the bad effects of a distorted fantasy that Puttenham writes of, warning that it can produce monsters, chimeras and bad behavior.[54] The tale of Paridell and Hellenore presents a dark mirror that highlights the value of Chastity by showing readers consequences of its failure. Paridell abandons Hellenore: "having filcht her bels, her up he cast / To the wide world, and let her fly alone, / He nould be clogd. So had he served many one" (3.10.35.7–9). The abandoned Hellenore wanders the wood until Satyrs find her. They take her "with them as housewife ever to abide, / To milk their gotes, and make them cheese and bred, / And everyone as commune good her handeled" (3.10.36.7–9). When Malbecco comes to try to rescue her, he witnesses a scene that resembles Cressida's being kissed in general when she arrives in the Greek camp, although without the coercive overtones of that scene. Before the Satyrs pack up their pipes and gather their flocks, they "first did give a busse / To Hellenore: so busses did abound" (3.10.46.3–4). Malbecco, like Troilus in another scene in Shakespeare's play, spies on Hellenore, observing her voyeuristically and only daring to approach her once the satyr is asleep.[55] Despite his pleading, she chooses to stay among the Satyrs, and this rejection drives him to his transformation into Gealosie. The poem is curiously reticent about judging Hellenore's actions: it does not praise her but neither does it explicitly condemn her in this moment. Malbecco is transformed into Gealousie, but Hellenore, as far as the

53. And it seems that both hark back to Ovid. Paridell, in particular, has been linked to an Ovidian tradition where Britomart is more Virgilian.
54. See discussion of Puttenham above. Hellenore represents a female version of Paridell's disordered fantasy.
55. Both characters change through their spying: Malbecco goes further on his way towards his transformation into Gealousie, and Troilus at least attempts to not be himself ("I will not be myself, nor have cognition / Of what I feel" (5.2.65–6).

poem tells us, lives contentedly among the Satyrs. There is no Ulysses to read the "language in her eye, her cheek, her lip" and to discern how "her wanton spirits look out / At every joint and motive of her body" (*Troilus and Cressida* 4.5.56–7). Like this episode in Book III, Shakespeare's Trojan play depicts a troubling version of Troy and a love story that goes awry, calling some of the conventions of both kinds of stories into question.

Shakespeare's Helen and Paris have more in common with Spenser's Hellenore and Paridell than with their classical antecedents or, for that matter, Spenser's own barely-described Paris and Helen. In their one scene in the play, Helen and Paris indulge themselves in bawdy song, puns, and jokes about Troilus' "exploits." The constant repetition of "queen" cannot help but pun with "quean" – here, *prostitute* – and further undercut the Paris-Helen love story. They appear trivial rather than tragic, and even Troilus' peculiarly fearful love seems deeper and more valid than what little we see of Paris and Helen. Thersites' description of the war as being for a placket underscores the play's trivializing of the war's cause and aligns him with Pandarus' curse at the end of the play. Instead of populating his Trojan play with admirable figures who exemplify the chivalric values that the Troilus and Cressida story at least nominally evokes, Shakespeare produces a play characterized by satire and a dismissive attitude to the values supposedly represented by the too-famous characters in the play.[56]

To take only a few examples, the courtship – for lack of a better term – of Troilus and Cressida is a thorough undermining of a courtly love narrative. Troilus languishes like a courtly lover, but his love is as a knife wound or an open ulcer on his heart before its consummation. When Troilus asks Apollo for an image to describe his love, the image Apollo comes up with is mercantile, akin to Pandarus' language about the hold-door trade in his epilogue though Troilus speaks in a higher register:

Tell me, Apollo, for thy Daphne's love,
What Cressid is, what Pandar, and what we?
Her bed is India; there she lies, a pearl.
Between our Ilium and where she resides,
Let it be called the wild and wand'ring flood,
Ourself the merchant, and this sailing Pandar
Our doubtful hope, our convoy and our bark. (1.1.94–100)

56. See Charnes's *Notorious Identity* on the effects of being too well-known on the characters.

Troilus envisions his love-object not only as an object but uses a metaphor that implies that she is an object-to-be-traded rather than kept. He is, after all, the merchant in this description. This metaphor, as many readers of the play have noted, is not exactly the language of a courtly lover.[57] Nor, for that matter, does Troilus sound like a conventionally eager lover in the scene where he finally makes his way to the pearl. His descriptions of his state of mind as he stands outside Cressida's house reflect both erotic anticipation and the expectation that satisfying his desires might kill him.[58] As he lurks in the street, Troilus tells Pandarus, "I stalk about her door / Like a strange soul upon the Stygian banks / Staying for waftage" (3.2.7–10). He is far from Romeo in the garden waiting to see Juliet at her window. Later in the same scene, after Pandarus has gone in to fetch Cressida, Troilus describes his mental and emotional state:

> I am giddy; expectation whirls me round.
> The imaginary relish is so sweet
> That it enchants my sense. What will it be,
> When that the wat'ry palates taste indeed
> Love's thrice-repured nectar? Death, I fear me,
> Swooning destruction, or some joy too fine,
> Too subtle-potent, tuned too sharp in sweetness,
> For the capacity of my ruder powers.
> I fear it much; and I do fear besides
> That I shall lose distinction in my joys,
> As doth a battle, when they charge on heaps,
> The enemy flying. (3.2.16–27)

His giddy expectation is a source of anxiety rather than joy. The "imaginary relish" will be too much for him and, tellingly, he glosses his state as being like the confusion of battle, and battle in this play is far from noble or even respectable.[59] Shakespeare's undercutting of Troilus and Cressida is only one element of the play's undermining

---

57. See, for example, Carolyn Asp's "Th' Expense of Spirit in a Waste of Shame" (1971). Asp's essay's focus on the play's satire of courtly love conventions is useful, but the essay treats Troilus more as a victim of the debasement of the tradition than as complicit in that debasement. Kris Davis-Brown's "Shakespeare's Use of Chaucer in *Troilus and Cressida*: 'That the Will is Infinite, and Execution Confined"' (1988) emphasizes the ways that Shakespeare's play "inverts" Chaucer's poem's love story (31).
58. He conflates the little and the big death, and fear colors his anticipation. He fears the "loss of distinction" in his joys (3.2.25).
59. In the wedding scene, Romeo is as enchanted by "imagined happiness" (2.6.28) as Troilus is, but his happiness is not tempered by a fear of death. Romeo

of the whole Troy story: the play depicts both Greeks and Trojans in ways that contradict, question, and demystify these authorizing figures.

The armed prologue of *Troilus and Cressida* may then be armed not only to suit the argument but also to ward off the kinds of charges about "odious argument" Spenser worries about in Book 9.[60] As it says, "like or find fault, do as your pleasures are; / Now good or bad, 'tis but the chance of war" (Prol. 30–1). That the prologue's protection was only marginally successful emerges in the relatively poor fortunes of the play in its moment of production. What little we know about it suggests that the play was not a success in its earliest performances – the two versions of the title page of the 1609 quarto make contradictory claims – and it is not reprinted until its inclusion in the 1623 Folio. The February 7, 1603 entry to James Roberts in the *Stationer's Register* asserts that the play was performed: "when he hath gotten sufficient aucthority for yt. The booke of Troilus and Cresseda as yt is acted by my lo: Chamberlens Men."[61] But, Qb asserts that the play has never been "clapper-clawed" by the vulgar multitude and deploys that assertion as a source of distinction.[62] The play's corrosive aesthetic and its devaluing of all the players in the Trojan War may have been caviar to the millions, or its lack of anything like conventionally satisfying closure might have been off-putting in the theatre.[63] Unlike Beaumont's *Knight of The Burning Pestle*, *Troilus and Cressida* appears not to have found a theatrical audience in the seventeenth century, despite the apparent vogue for "satirical drama" in that century's first decade or so.

> never expresses worry about losing distinction in his joys, nor does Juliet. Too, "relish" is not the same as happiness.
> 60. The long tradition of situating this speech in the context of the Poet's War might serve as a sort of evidence for this claim. Jonson's version of an armed prologue in his *Poetaster* defends itself against the attack of Envy who submits to the mailed foot of the prologue.
> 61. See records in the *DEEP* database. Why he didn't print the play in 1603 and waited to transfer it for six years is an unanswerable question. The printer's preface's mention of the resistance of the "grand possessors" of the play is both suggestive and unhelpful in this regard. See also Wiggins and Richardson 4: 372–77.
> 62. Lesser has written about the publisher's preface to *Knight of the Burning Pestle* as a kind of publishing strategy.
> 63. There is a long tradition of arguing that this line from Hamlet's description of the play from which the Hecuba speech comes refers indirectly to *Troilus and Cressida*, even though no similar speech appears in that play.

As David Bevington's introduction to his Arden edition notes, the play's experimental nature is thematically related to others of Shakespeare's plays produced between 1599 and 1603 (5). Bevington asserts that the play, if it was staged, would have found a receptive audience whether in the Inns of Court or on the public stage, but it is unclear if it was staged and its reception is quite uncertain especially given the delay between what we think is the play's date of composition and its appearance in print. If the reprint rate of plays is a measure of popularity, *Troilus and Cressida* lagged behind other plays first performed in the years Bevington uses. The most reprinted plays in this sample are Heywood's *How a Man May Choose a Good Wife from a Bad* (1601–2, Q 1602) and the anonymous *Wily Beguiled* (1601–2, Q 1602). Both had seven editions before 1660. Even with the assertion that the play had been performed by the "Kings majesties servants at the Globe" in Qa and the pleas of the Never Writer of the publisher's preface Qb, the play was not printed again until Shakespeare's 1623 Folio and never again in quarto. In contrast, *Pericles,* surely as play experimental as *Troilus and Cressida* in its way, saw five quartos by 1635.

While it is tempting to speculate about reasons the play was relatively less well received than its contemporary *Hamlet*, there is no way to be certain. The available evidence suggests that the play was not a success, but that suggestion could be wrong, since a stationer thought it worth printing. *Troilus and Cressida*'s approach to its plot – fragmentary, inconclusive, uncertain – resembles that of later plays like *Pericles* or *Timon of Athens* and is akin to the way *Hamlet* proliferates and complicates narratives rather than resolving them. *Hamlet*'s engagement with the revenge plot structure refracts earlier plays and structures such later plays as Middleton's *Revenger's Tragedy*. If *Hamlet* found an immediate and enduring audience and *Troilus and Cressida* did not, both still had an impact on the dramatic field. As position-takings in the cultural field, both *Hamlet* and *Troilus and Cressida* represent engagements with a set of representational techniques, generic structures, and traditions from a broad swath of the literary field.

Chapter 3

"King Cambyses' vein": Generic Change in the 1580s and 1590s

> Well, and the fire of grace be not quite out of thee, now shalt thou be mov'd. Give me a cup of sack to make my eyes look red, that it may be thought I have wept, for I must speak in passion, and I will do it in King Cambyses' vein.
>
> Shakespeare, 1 Henry IV

At the outset of the play extempore, Falstaff describes his characterization of Hal's father with a reference to Thomas Preston's by then decades-old play *Cambises*. "King Cambyses' vein" describes a whole dramatic tradition that Shakespeare and his contemporaries increasingly represent as passé and unfashionable.[1] These references have helped shape narratives about the development of early modern drama that see the cruder, gorier, and less competent works of the 1560s and 1570s develop into the great theater of the 1590s and after. The idea that there was an upward movement from crude to sophisticated, from "plodding" fourteeners to the mighty line, is fundamental to most of these narratives. The apotheosis of this movement is typically found in Shakespeare and, to a lesser extent, in the work of contemporaries like Marlowe or Jonson.[2] Developmental narratives like these distort ways that later playwrights respond to Tudor drama, which as Howard B. Norland notes in *Drama in Early*

---

1. Other more overtly slighting references to this vein are in *Midsummer Night's Dream* and in Jonson's *Devil Is an Ass*.
2. See Jeremy Lopez's *Constructing the Canon of Early Modern Drama* (2014) on this issue. The *Oxford Handbook of Tudor Drama* (2012) represents another important contribution to questioning this orthodoxy. Andy Kesson's *John Lyly and Early Modern Authorship* (2014) argues for the formative influence of Lyly on later plays and playwrights. I am in sympathy with *Before Shakespeare* project's focus on Tudor drama *as* Tudor drama. See especially the "About" section. The Project Team is Kesson, Callan Davies, and Lucy Munro.

Tudor Britain, 1485–1558, extended "to all corners of the commonwealth and to every level of society" (xvii).

This chapter begins with a discussion of Thomas Preston's *Cambises, King of Persia*. First printed in 1569 and likely in performance well before that, the play is generically hybrid, drawing on both a native allegorical tradition and on Senecan drama, which was then associated with the universities. It was also, as Falstaff's comment indicates, well remembered into the 1590s and after. I use this discussion both to characterize the field and to call attention to continuities between early Tudor drama and later plays. Preston's play, like those of later playwrights, drew on classical and neoclassical drama. The chapter's next section looks at connections between university tragedy and Thomas Kyd's *The Spanish Tragedy*. Kyd's play represents a crucially important intervention in the generic system and the discursive repertoire of English drama. It is one of the first blank verse plays to appear on the public stage and, in structure as much as in content, it is also one of the more innovative plays of the period.[3] The impact of *The Spanish Tragedy* is pervasive throughout the period; playwrights and commentators refer to elements from it directly three decades later, and the play was revived (and added to) repeatedly.[4] Kyd was deeply influenced by the classical tradition, and his deployment of Senecan motifs in *The Spanish Tragedy* exerted an immediate and durable effect on playwriting, recognized both by contemporary playwrights and later scholarship. The chapter closes with a discussion of *Arden of Faversham* as a case study of innovation in the early 1590s, a particular moment of transition in the dramatic field. The play is both an early example of domestic tragedy and a historical drama drawing on the same sources as Shakespeare's historical plays.

I

Preston's *Cambises, King of Persia* appears to have been a popular success in the 1570s and 1580s and is a hybrid drama that mingles historical and allegorical characters within the same narrative. The

3. *Gorboduc* (1565), usually described as the first blank-verse play performed in England, was performed at the Inns of Court. Its impact and popularity are of a different kind than that of *The Spanish Tragedy*.
4. Lukas Erne's *Beyond* The Spanish Tragedy: *A Study of the Works of Thomas Kyd* (2001) offers a detailed and convincing discussion of the impact of Kyd's work as well as its durability.

play was printed in multiple editions and later references to it, like Falstaff's in this chapter's epigraph, indicate both the play's presence in theatrical memory and its association with a particular mode of stage rhetoric.[5] The tragic main plot about the fall of the Persian king alternates with comic episodes centered on a vice figure named Ambidexter. Often held up as an example of the kind of play that the early Shakespeare was reacting against, the play sounds odd to our ears (the fourteeners in particular sound like nursery rhyme or doggerel to an ear habituated to the blank dramatic verse of Kyd, Marlowe, and Shakespeare). The anachronism of this response is itself important to recognize: the play only sounds strange in retrospect. It is also worth noting that the play does use other meters and is not quite so mechanically dominated by the fourteener as it sometimes appears to be from critical discussions. For example, Ambidexter moves back and forth between a fourteen-foot line and a ten-foot one. Additionally, translators like Jasper Heywood used the fourteener in translations of Seneca at the same time that Preston was likely composing his play, which suggests that the fourteener was not automatically marked as either high or low. Critics like Fraser and Rabkin have criticized the play for its mingle-mangle gallimaufry, but that may have been what made it interesting to audiences.[6] Certain elements of the play appear to derive from a set of dramaturgical practices that later playwrights used. Those practices include the mixing of comic and tragic moments, the deployment of allegorical figures in historical or realistic plots, and staging in an emblematic mode.[7] As James Siemon notes in his introduction to the play in the *Routledge Anthology of Early Modern Drama*, the play's "treatment of genre, action, spectacle, language, and even moral complexity was also a resource for the great Elizabethan tragic dramatists" (5). Despite the play's usefulness to later playwrights and its evident popularity, scholars have often overlooked and dismissed the play as crude and tasteless.

5. Martin Wiggins and Catherine Richardson date the play to 1569 in their *British Drama 1533–1642* (2012). They list three early quartos: Q1 c. 1569, Q2 1584–8 (only two leaves survive), and Q3 after 1593 (2: 45–48).
6. As I discussed in the introduction, these are Lyly's terms and he uses them in his prologue to *Midas* in a positive or, at the very least, an accepting way. This disposition seems more characteristic of practicing playwrights in the period than the disdain seen in Fraser and Rabkin's edition or, more immediately, in Jones's preface to *Tamburlaine* or parts of Sidney's *Defence*.
7. See Scott McMillin and Sally Beth MacLean's *The Queen's Men and Their Plays* (1998) for a discussion of these practices in the Queen's Men's repertory in the 1580s and 1590s.

The introduction to the play in the Fraser and Rabkin *Drama of the English Renaissance* (1976) asserts that the "most intriguing mystery may well be not the details of date and authorship but that a work so patently atrocious warranted two editions and deserves inclusion in a collection of drama from one of the great theaters in the world's history" (1: 59).[8] Rabkin's comments are worth some discussion because they represent ways that a presumption that "all roads lead to Shakespeare" obscures more about the dramatic field than it reveals. First, the collection presents the plays in terms of their relation to the emerging "great theater" of the post-1580s professional stage.[9] This narrative projects a direction on the plays that would have been impossible for the writers, players, and audiences to anticipate. Second, it deploys categories of judgment constructed by a later state of the field in a context to which they do not belong. Burton Fishman's 1976 article on the theatrical iconography of the play recognizes that "since *Cambises* may have held the stage until Shakespeare could have seen it, the play struck a resonant chord in the theatre-going populace," but he attributes its popularity to its "urgent and violent realism" because it otherwise offers little in the way of "poetic or dramatic pleasures" (203). It is difficult to see how a play offering few dramatic pleasures could be popular, regardless of any urgent and violent realism the play might display.[10]

The "mystery" of *Cambises*' popularity is less confusing if we place the play more carefully (and with less retrospective judgment)

8. Rabkin wrote the introduction to this play. There appear actually to have been three editions (see Wiggins and Richardson).
9. Fraser and Rabkin's collection is, of course, dated, and I do not mean to treat them as straw men. Their collection remains important as a classroom text focused on the non-Shakespearean drama of the English Renaissance. The introduction I am discussing is only a brief introduction to a play in an anthology. Like many of us, my first reading of the play, despite the best efforts of my teachers, was more in line with Rabkin's position than not, and I have been guilty of using parts of the play as illustrations of what Kyd, Marlowe, and Shakespeare leave behind. The depiction of the play and its place in a developmental narrative remains representative of the kind of readings that the play and other "specimens of the pre-Shakespearean drama" (to quote the title of Manly's 1897 collection) have typically received. In fact, most recent collections of Renaissance drama participate in this narrative by virtue of mostly excluding plays before Kyd's *Spanish Tragedy*. Arthur Kinney's Blackwell anthology is an exception, but for understandable reasons of space, the selection of plays before 1580 is slim. Again, see Lopez's *Constructing the Canon* for another take on the canon of early modern drama.
10. There's no little irony in the similarity of this line of criticism to responses to Shakespeare's *Titus Andronicus*.

in the context of the theatres and printing houses of the period. Indeed, even Rabkin's introduction indicates ways to solve the mystery. He writes that the "naïve mixture of genres" in the play "points much more directly than anything in the far more artful and respectable GORBODUC, at a characteristic mingling of comedy and tragedy that was as natural to Shakespeare as writing plays" (1:59).[11] Eugene D. Hill's essay, "The First Elizabethan Tragedy: A Contextual Reading of *Cambises*," is in agreement with this position and remains one of very few accounts of the play that take the play as anything other than a feeble precursor to Shakespeare or a worthy object of parody.[12] His argument places the play in the context of its composition and production and, if it does not thoroughly address the play's continued popularity into the 1590s, makes a convincing case for taking the play seriously. As he notes, though Sidney looked to *Gorboduc* as the ideal type for English drama, the theatre "would go another way —the way of resolute mingling of clowns and kings, the way of *Cambises*" (407).[13] Hill makes a case for Preston's play as a sophisticated engagement in the political and religious discourse of the 1560s. The bad example of Cambises serves to warn the new Queen not to take the path of tyranny (that her father took) and at the same time not to engage in half-hearted measures to reform the English Church.[14] Hill's essay is valuable in that it makes a compelling claim for taking the play seriously and understands it not as an object of caricature but as a sophisticated engagement in theatrical, religious, and political debates in the early years of Elizabeth's reign.

11. Fraser and Rabkin's capitals; they capitalize titles of plays throughout their edition.
12. Hill's essay spends far more time situating the play and playwright in their contexts than reading the play, but it does argue that the play, in his words, "stands up" to "the elegant text of *Gorboduc*" in "boldness of implication and elegance of design" (432). He also makes the point that the play is almost always used in the classroom as a humorous example of the theatre later playwrights transform.
13. Hill's position, though far more sympathetic to the play than Rabkin's, resembles it in that both see *Cambises* as a better indicator of the direction of literary history than *Gorboduc*.
14. See Hill 430: the play was a "warning to Elizabeth not to repeat the errors of her father." Hill also notes that Latimer preached a sermon for Edward VI in 1549 that links the Cambises story to an admonition not to make "a mingle-mangle and hotch-potch" of Reform (421, quoting Latimer). It is interesting that the language of mixture appears here: these terms get applied to the mingle-mangle of the mixed forms of the drama. Indeed, Lyly uses this language to refer to his own work.

The play appears to have been in print by the 1570s and was reprinted in 1585 and 1595.[15] The quartos appear with a detailed doubling scheme that would allow a relatively small acting company to present all the many speaking parts required by the play text.[16] The three editions of the play point to the play's durability and the printer's sense that it would sell. The existence of multiple editions points to the strong possibility that the play was in the general dramatic repertory at roughly the same time that Kyd, Marlowe, Greene, and Shakespeare were beginning their dramatic careers.[17] Recollections of it on stage like Falstaff's give support to this idea, despite the absence of records of performance. Far from being obscure and dated, it was a contemporary play and remained current enough for later playwrights reference it. While the language gets left behind (and later becomes the object of parody), we can read the gallimaufry of the play alongside more critically favored plays as an indicator of the kind of generic change that becomes more and more apparent in the

15. Drawing on the resources of DEEP: The play was entered in the *Stationer's Register* in 1569 to John Allde: "an enterlude a lamentable Tragedy full of pleasaunt myrth." The undated first quarto was printed perhaps as early as 1570 and was followed by two other quartos (c. 1585 and c. 1595). John Allde, the father of Edward Allde, printed Q2 and Q3. Significantly, the Alldes printed Kyd's *Spanish Tragedy*, Marlowe's *Massacre at Paris* (1593), and (for John Perrin as part of a collection with Lydgate's *Serpent of Division*) *Gorboduc*. He was printing the "atrocious" *Cambises* around the same time that he was also printing Kyd and Marlowe, suggesting that he saw a place for both in his business. Edward Allde's wife, Elizabeth, took over the business after his death and printed (among other things) editions of Robert Greene's *Friar Bacon and Friar Bungay* (1594), *Arden of Faversham*, and Dekker's *Honest Whore, Part 2* (1630) and some tragicomedies. As a group, the family was responsible for quite a few important editions of drama. In addition, Anthony Munday, the dramatist, served an apprenticeship under John Allde before embarking on his writing career (Edward Allde printed two of his civic pageants: the pageants of 1610 and 1614). See also Wiggins and Richardson, *British Drama* 2: 45–48. As I note above, they date the texts slightly differently.
16. The printed division of the parts calls for eight actors. This scheme appears in Q3 as well, suggesting that it was also part of Q2 though, according to DEEP, that edition only survives as two leaves.
17. To my knowledge, we have no solid evidence about the play's performance history beyond later references to it by characters in other plays. It is not printed with any playing company attribution. Identifying *Cambises* with a lost play known as *Huff, Ruff, and Suff*, Bevington argues that it was performed by Dudley's Men (later Leicester's) at court in 1560–1, but there is little confirming evidence in the extant records (*Tudor Drama and Politics* 158; cited in Hill 405). Wiggins sees "no good reason to identify this play with *Huff, Ruff, and Suff*" (Wiggins and Richardson 2: 45).

1590s.[18] Specifically, the combination of comic, historical, and tragic elements closely resembles the basic form of, for example, Marlowe's *Faustus* (1604) with its combination of Faustus' tragedy with the homologous but comic clown subplot or the combination of forms and styles in Greene's *James IV*. Marlowe and Greene may leave the fourteener behind, but allegorical habits of staging and a willingness to deploy both representational and presentational modes of staging are threads connecting plays like Preston's to later works.

Taking one example, *Cambises* is partly populated with allegorical figures representing the voice of the people. In scene 4, Commons' Cry, Commons' Complaint, Proof, and Trial enter to present grievances:

> Common's Complaint I represent, with thrall of doleful state.
> By urgent cause erected forth my grief to dilate.
> Unto the King I will prepare my misery to tell,
> To have relief of this my grief and fettered feet so fell.
> Redoubted prince and mighty King, myself I prostrate here.
> Vouchsafe, O King, with me to bear for this that I appear.
> With humble suit I pardon crave of your most royal grace
> To give me leave to break before you in this place. (V.21–8)[19]

"Common's Complaint" appears as both a character of the same name and the representative of those complaints – the doubleness of the figure seems part of the point – and his "I represent" also necessarily refers to the actor playing this part. Layered self-reference appears throughout the play (even in Cambises' infamous death scene, which moves back and forth between presentational and representational strategies). Cambises agrees to hear the plea and proceeds to punish the corrupt Sisamnes for his oppression of the common people.[20]

18. Lyly's court plays of the 1580s combine forms in a highly self-conscious way (see the *Midas* prologue I discuss in the introduction as an example). Many other examples of both popular and elite drama do the same thing. Robert Miola has convincingly argued that classical tragedy and classical comedy pervasively influenced early modern drama and that these influences often operated in the same play (see *Shakespeare and Classical Tragedy* [1992] and *Shakespeare and Classical Comedy* [1994]). Kent Cartwright, in *Theatre and Humanism* (1999), has shown that humanist drama (like that of Lyly or Wager) merits closer examination than its usual dismissive treatment as a mode to be transcended by Marlowe and Shakespeare.
19. I cite from James Siemon's edition in *The Routledge Anthology of Early Modern Drama*.
20. Rabkin alludes to this moment in his introduction as an "augury" of the future greatness of the English theatre since it points at an awareness of the complexity

This moment is less interesting as a scene of judgment and execution (however spectacular) than as an example of the play's easy mingling of allegorical and historical figures, a mingling designed to illustrate the bad state of Cambises' kingdom.[21] The play is densely populated with such allegorical figures – most famously by the Vice Ambidexter – and they interact easily with non-allegorical figures. Commons' Complaint here gives Cambises a chance to demonstrate good kingship by punishing Sisamnes' corruption while at the same time showing Cambises engaging in capricious and excessive violence. The allegorical figure allows the play make this point efficiently. A later playwright like Robert Greene uses a similar tactic in *James IV* to illustrate the problems following that play's misruling king.

Late in *James IV*, there is a long dialogue between a Merchant, a Lawyer, and a Divine that touches on the destructive side-effects of James' being led by flatterers and desire. Unlike *Cambises*, where these figures interact directly with the (more or less) historical figures of play's plot, these three figures appear in their own scene, late in the action and have almost no explicit connection to the plot beyond their choric function.[22] Greene's play presents itself as a demonstration of the corruption of the world, justifying its presenter's retreat from the world, and to do so makes use of a broad range of dramatic resources. I have argued elsewhere that Greene's dramaturgy depends as much on an awareness of the craft traditions of theatre as on a literary (for lack of a better term) tradition.[23] Greene's deployment of semi-allegorical figures, dumbshows, and vice figures (like the not-very-talented stage Machiavel Ateukin in *James IV*) represents his borrowings from dramatic precursors like *Cambises*. While Preston's play might be more heavy-handed in its allegorizing, Greene makes use of these traditions to produce a new or at least different kind of play. *James IV* uses a broad range of theatrical conventions drawn from court and popular drama in order to stage a debate over the proper ends of drama. The debate at the same time tests the various means to those ends – theatrical spectacle, didactic allegory, dumbshow, among others – and in so doing it produces a play that in some

> of theatrical representation. Sisamnes is killed by a sword blow to the neck and then flayed "with a false skin."
> 21. This kind of unremarked appearance of allegorical figures is characteristic of the plays of the Queen's Men.
> 22. In what seems almost like an afterthought, Greene has them remember that warring armies are about to pass through the area and they'd best be on their way.
> 23. See my *Representing the Professions*.

ways prefigures what we have come to call "romance." This effort makes sense coming from Greene, who was a prolific writer of prose romance. It is also consistent with his other work for the Queen's Men and their repertory more generally, which is characterized by allegory and is sometimes discussed as increasingly out of date. Such borrowings from craft and literary traditions are a product of and produce the kinds of shifts in genre observable in the course of the 1590s, like the emergence of what we have come to call Elizabethan tragedy. Like Preston, Greene draws on theatrical resources drawn from the liturgical and popular drama of the late middle ages.

Preston's play is also an example of one way that the neoclassical drama associated with the two universities comes to be a resource for the professional theatre. It makes use of Senecan style but not Senecan matter, stages the violence that Seneca only describes, and surrounds its Senecan elements with elements drawn from the vernacular tradition. Cambridge, Preston's institution, and Oxford produced translations of Seneca, and, as Norland notes in *Neoclassical Tragedy in Elizabethan England* (2009), those translations were important because of "inspiration they gave to the popular dramatic tradition manifested first in such works as *Cambises* and culminating in the tragedies of Kyd, Marlowe, and Shakespeare" (68). *Cambises'* combination of materials provided its own inspiration and represents one important connection between university and professional drama in the period. The influence of the Latin drama referenced here – both translations and new work like that of William Gager – was considerable and, as the next section argues, helped shape innovations in the tragedy of later 1580s and 1590s.

II

That classical literature was an important influence on the dramatic literature of the sixteenth century is a critical commonplace, and there is a substantial literature on, for example, the influence of Ovid on writers like Marlowe and Shakespeare.[24] The role of neo-Latin drama is less-often noted, partly because much of what survives remains untranslated. Many early modern playwrights became familiar with that tradition at the universities or in the Inns of Court and drew on that exposure in their dramatic careers. Interactions

---

24. See, for example, Jonathan Bate's *Shakespeare and Ovid* (1986) and Michael Stapleton's *Marlowe's Ovid: The Elegies in the Marlowe Canon* (2014).

between the tradition of neo-Latin drama at Oxford and Cambridge and the professional stage in London in the later sixteenth century were important to the shape of the dramatic field. There was a long and vigorous tradition of Latin drama at the universities and grammar schools, and early educators looked to classical drama for teaching materials. Professional playwrights also looked to classical antecedents for subject matter and technique. Shakespeare, for example, makes extensive use of Latin comedy in plays like *Comedy of Errors* (1595) which draws on two plays by Plautus – the *Menaechmi* and *Amphitruo*, both of which draw on Greek originals – for structure and incident. Marlowe's *Dido, Queen of Carthage* (1594) draws on both Virgil and Ovid, and he possibly wrote it while he was at Cambridge. Shakespeare returns to Ovid repeatedly throughout his career – whether in tragedy, like *Titus Andronicus* (1594), or in comedy, as in *Midsummer Night's Dream* (1600).[25] Less direct appropriations of classical drama abound as well. Scholars often describe Thomas Kyd's *Spanish Tragedy* as the first Senecan tragedy on the early modern stage because of style and technique, not because of the play's content.

The Records of Early English Drama volumes for Cambridge and Oxford demonstrate the frequency of performances of classical and neo-Latin plays at Oxford and Cambridge.[26] Both institutions mandated that Latin plays be performed each year, and many critics and historians have noted the importance of Latin dramatic texts in humanist pedagogy. Bruce Smith's 1988 *Ancient Scripts and Modern Experience on the English Stage* discusses performances of classical plays between 1500 and 1700 and very usefully documents the prevalence of such performances. Gordon Braden's book *Renaissance Tragedy and the Senecan Tradition* (1985) remains the landmark study of the influence of Seneca on English drama; in the sections on English tragedy, he focuses on the legacy of what he terms a Senecan selfhood on conceptions of character in plays like Marlowe's *Tamburlaine* and Kyd's *Spanish Tragedy*.[27] In his 2009 essay, "The

---

25. Magisterial works, such as Bullough's *Narrative and Dramatic Sources of Shakespeare* and others, have commented on and extensively documented these facts.
26. See Alan H. Nelson's edited *Cambridge* (1989) and John R Elliott, Jr., Alan H. Nelson, Alexandra F. Johnston, and Diana Wyatt's edited *Oxford* (2004).
27. Braden does discuss style but, curiously, passes over the Latin Senecan drama performed at Cambridge and Oxford, except for some passing references to Thomas Legge's *Ricardus Tertius*. He discusses continental Senecanism far more fully.

University and the Inns of Court," Alan Nelson argues that the universities "produced plays mostly – but not entirely – for internal consumption" and that some of those plays "may have influenced professional playwrights over the years" (291, 286). Norland's 2009 *Neoclassical Tragedy in Elizabeth England* offers a thorough examination of the neoclassical dramatic tradition at Oxford, Cambridge, and the Inns of Court in an effort to demonstrate the importance of this tradition to the vernacular drama of the 1580s and later.

Critics have understandably given a great deal of critical attention to particular "Senecan" elements of later tragedy – especially revenge tragedy – such as the presence of ghosts, a declamatory mode on the part of the revenger, long speeches of lament, and in some cases (though not in all, and not as much in Shakespeare as in others) the use of stichomythia to construct stage dialogue.[28] These elements have a clear connection to the tradition of Latin tragedy, and early modern English playwrights are clearly adapting those elements. Kyd's *Spanish Tragedy* is a responsive reaction to classical tragedy that operates at the level of technique and intellectual content as much as it does by way of direct reference.[29]

Seneca was available to early modern readers in Latin, though a collection of English translations appeared in print in 1581. *Seneca: His Tenne Tragedies* contains English translations of *Hercules Furens, Thyestes, Thebais, Hippolytus, Oedipus, Troas, Medea, Agamemnon, Octavia,* and *Hercules Oetaeus.* Jasper Heywood, the son of John Heywood (himself an important playwright in the 1530s and 1540s), translated three of the plays. Heywood's translations put Seneca's plays into common early modern English dramatic form, and, as Norland argues, his translations "established the model for Senecan translation that his younger contemporaries emulated and adapted but never bettered" (*Neoclassical Tragedy* 46).[30] The translators also add and alter parts of the plays to "perfect" them for the English stage; this free disposition towards the classical text is an

---

28. There remains some debate about how directly such elements come from Seneca's plays: many later plays seem to get their Senecan elements at second or third hand, constituting an English Senecan tradition that is at some remove from the classical "source." Critics have long remarked on stichomythia as an important technical legacy of classical drama.
29. When Hieronimo says "*Vindicta mihi*" in Act 3, his utterance ironically layers references to the Bible and to Seneca in a single phrase.
30. Norland characterizes Heywood as one of the most accurate of Seneca's early translators into English (*Neoclassical Tragedy* 48), but at the same time, it is striking how much he relies on native dramatic traditions.

important feature of early modern dramatic practice. An example of this mode of translation lies in *Hercules Furens* (translated in 1561), as Juno describes her plans:

> Let now Megara bring to sight, and with her mournful hand
> For burning rage bring out of hell a huge and direful brand.
> Do this, require your vengeance due, and pains of hell his spoil.
> Strike through his breast, let fiercer flame, with his bosom boil
> Than which in Aetna furnace beats, so furiously to see.
> That mad of mind and witless may Alcides driven be
> With fury great through pierced quite, myself must first of all
> Be mad. Wherefore doth Juno yet not into raging fall? (b2r)[31]

Plays of the 1560s and 1570s characteristically use this meter, and the classically learned poet-playwright Ben Jonson later caricatured this mode in his 1616 play *The Devil Is an Ass*. Heywood (and other translators) make no effort to echo the prosody or structure of the Latin verse; instead, the play deploys the rhyming couplets of Tudor interludes. He distorts the syntax of the lines in the interest of meter and rhyme, and it sounds highly artificial to an ear more accustomed to plays from the 1580s and later. Technical features like stichomythia do appear in the play, but the verse is assimilated to the model of the early drama, and the play is Senecan only in the sense that it presents an accurate translation of the content of Seneca's play – but in an already established native form.

Other writers in the period treat this Senecan legacy differently and write original plays in Latin on classical subjects rather than translating or adapting the plays into vernacular drama. William Gager (1555–1622) was a canon lawyer, poet, and playwright whose Latin plays were produced at Oxford in the 1580s and 1590s. His 1582 play, *Meleager*, was performed in 1585 for an audience including Sir Philip Sidney and the Earls of Leicester and Pembroke (both of whom were patrons of acting companies), and his plays were among those performed for the Queen when she visited Oxford in 1592.[32] Contemporary commentary widely praised him, including Francis Meres' *Palladis Tamia* (1598), which listed him as among those who were "best for comedy":

---

31. I have modernized the spelling.
32. *Meleager* was printed at Oxford in 1593 in a volume that included his additions to Seneca's *Hippolytus*, his prologue to a 1592 revival of *Rivales* (1582), and his prologue and epilogue to *Bellum grammaticale* (1581). See Wiggins and Richardson (2: 291–294).

the best for comedy amongst us be *Edward* Earl of Oxford, Doctor *Gager* of Oxford, Master *Rowley*, once a rare scholar of learned Pembroke Hall in Cambridge, Master *Edwards*, one of her Majesty's Chapel, eloquent and witty *John Lilly, Lodge, Gascoyne, Greene, Shakespeare, Thomas Nash, Thomas Heywood, Anthony Mundye,* our best plotter, *Chapman, Porter, Wilson, Hathway,* and *Henry Chettle*. (Oo3v)

Meres begins his listings by stating who were the best writers in each genre in Greek and Latin and then lists English writers who follow those classical precedents. He appears to list writers more or less in terms of rank, placing Oxford first followed by Gager and other scholars. Gager's one comedy, *Rivales*, does not survive, nor do any of Oxford's plays, making it difficult to assess Meres' rankings. As Norland notes in *Neoclassical Tragedy*, Meres demonstrates a preference for academic drama, praising Oxford and Cambridge writers first. However, Gager's name appears in a list that includes non-academic writers like Shakespeare and suggests that in Meres' eyes there was a fair amount of literary (for lack of a better term) contact among these writers. From mentions such as this one, it is clear that Gager's work exerted an influence over academic drama (and that professional dramatists were involved in bringing some of his plays to press). *Meleager* takes up the story of Meleager as chronicled in Ovid's *Metamorphoses*, but it converts the Ovidian narrative into a Senecan tragedy and is Gager's invention. The play opens with a lengthy speech delivered by Megaera which sets out the plot. Echoing the opening of Seneca's *Thyestes*, the play chronicles the destruction of Meleager, his mother Althaea, and his father Oeneus to satisfy Diana's anger over Oeneus' failure to sacrifice to her.[33] Megaera's first lines read:

Vastam relinquens noctis aeternae plaga
Silentis Erebi, et manium tristes domos,
Megaera superas extuli ad sedes gradum.

33. *Thyestes* opens with Tantalus speaking: "Quis inferorum sede ab infausta extrahit / auido fugaces ore captantem cibos? / quis male deorum Tantalo visas domos / ostendit iterum? peius inuentum est siti / arente in undis aliquid et peius fame / hiante semper?" ["Who from the unfortunate dwellings of underworld draws me forth, snatching at food which ever flies from my hungry lips? Which of the gods shows suffering Tantalus again the houses of the living? Has something worse been found than parching thirst midst water, worse than ever-gaping hunger?"]

En fervet odio pectus, exundat furor,
Maior q[ue] rabies crescit aspectus loci. (A8v)[34]

[Leaving the vast region of eternal night, home of silent Erebus and the sad shades, I, Megaera, have come forth to the step of the upper regions. Behold, my breast boils with hate, rage floods out, and my madness grows greater at the sight of this place.]

Not only does the content of these lines echo that of *Thyestes,* Gager adopts the meter of Seneca's play. This is worth noting because when his peers translate Seneca, they produce a very different kind of verse. Frederick Boas writes of the play that:

He uses, as a matter of course, the Senecan machinery and technique, and he observes the unities strictly. But it is only a superficial view that would dismiss the play as merely imitative and unoriginal. Gager ... shows genuine inventiveness and dexterity in his management of the plot, fusing into an attractive whole episodes of his own devising with those of which Ovid was the direct source. (175)

Gager wrote other original plays – his comedy *Rivales* and the "tragoedia nova" of *Ulysses Redux* – that display this "inventiveness and dexterity" and that demonstrate the usefulness and power of Senecan dramaturgy for non-Senecan plays. According to Howard Norland, Gager's drama "reduced the static qualities and elevated style of Seneca and his sixteenth-century imitators in order to accommodate the stage practice of the popular theater" (*Neoclassical Tragedy* 192). It is this innovation that Kyd's drama builds on.

Meres' description of tragedy in England is equally as illuminating. Just before he turns to listing the best for comedy, he offers a list of tragic writers:

these are our best for tragedy, the Lord *Buckhurst,* Doctor *Leg* of Cambridge, Doctor *Edes* of Oxford, Master *Edward Ferris,* the author of the *Mirrour for Magistrates, Marlow, Peele, Watson, Kid, Shakespeare, Drayton, Chapman, Decker,* and *Beniamin Iohnson* ... As M. *Anneus Lucanus* writ two excellent tragedies, one called *Medea,* the other *de Incendio Troiae cum Priami calamitate,* so Doctor *Leg* hath penned two famous tragedies, the one of *Richard the 3.* The other of the destruction of *Jerusalem.* (Oo3r)

---

34. The Folger Shakespeare Library copy that I consulted is a small, pocket-sized octavo. Dana Sutton's digital edition of Gager's works has been enormously valuable as well.

The list, as with the list for comedy, begins with a nobleman and then turns to academic writers like Thomas Legge, whose *Ricardus Tertius* was an influential play, before turning to professional playwrights including Kyd. Kyd's work then figures as part of a perceived group of those English writers "best for tragedy" (vernacular or not).

Thomas Kyd was born in 1558 and was educated at the Merchant Taylors' School in London, recently founded by Richard Mulcaster, one of the most prominent Tudor educators. Kyd would have become very familiar with Latin at the School and would also have learned some Greek. Like many educational institutions of the period, the Merchant Taylors' School put on plays, both as part of its pedagogical program and for exhibition before the Queen. Kyd was writing plays for the Queen's Men – one of the leading acting companies of the time – by 1585 and was close to other writers such as Christopher Marlowe and Thomas Lodge. *The Spanish Tragedy*, the play he is best known for, dates to around 1590 and was an immediate and enduring success on the early modern stage. In his *Diary,* the only surviving account book from the public theatres, Philip Henslowe records twenty-nine performances of the play between 1591 and 1597, as well as payments to Ben Jonson for additions to the play in 1601-2.[35] The play remained a consistent part of the repertory throughout the period, and other playwrights constantly refer to it.[36] It has no single major source; instead, Kyd develops a story about justice and revenge using Senecan tools without reference to some specific antecedent. In this lies his response to the practice of playing classical drama in early modern England – his is a creative response to the resources made available by these plays. Kyd's *The Spanish Tragedy*, scholars often say, inaugurates the tradition of revenge tragedy on the public stage in England, and that tradition is one of

---

35. According to Henslowe's *Diary*, Jonson received 40s in September 1601 for additions and ten pounds "in earneste of A Boocke called Richard Crookbacke & for new adicyons for Jeronymo" (182, 203). Henslowe often refers to the play as "Jeronymo."
36. Ben Jonson, the best example, makes remarkably frequent reference to the play – often to critique what he wants to characterize as a particular kind of theatrical bad taste (i.e., a taste for the old, rather than the new). For example, in *Bartholomew Fair,* Jonson describes playgoers who thirty years later still say that "*Jeronimo* or *Andronicus* are the best plays" as people whose "judgement shows it is constant and hath stood still, these five and twenty or thirty years" (Ind. 94–96, cited from Ben Jonson, *Five Plays* [492]). For more on Kyd's reception, see Emma Smith's "Hieronimo's Afterlives" in her edition of the play. *The Spanish Tragedy* Arden edition (2013) offers helpful commentary on the play's popularity and its sources.

the more important components of early modern drama more generally.[37]

As my introduction argues, Bakhtin's notion of works as utterances engaged in a kind of literary dialogue represents a productive way to avoid the impasses of the iteration and tradition models of source study, and it allows for a more dynamic account of generic change. Bakhtin argues that all utterances are necessarily responsive reactions to other utterances and therefore contain, in various ways, the utterances to which they are responding and that these reactions do not always take the form of citations or importations:

> one's responsive reaction to them can be reflected only in the expression of one's own speech—in the selection of language means and intonations that are determined not by the topic of one's own speech but by the other's utterances concerning the same topic ... very frequently the expression of our utterance is determined not only—and sometimes not so much—by the referentially semantic content of this utterance, but also by others' utterances on the same topic to which we are responding or with which we are polemicizing. ("Problem of Speech Genres" 91).

Plays are often directly engaged in such polemicizing – making claims for the value of the work-utterance at hand, denigrating other works, or pointing to the inadequacies of other's appropriations of a particular genre or topic. The early seventeenth century Poet's War between Ben Jonson, John Marston, and Thomas Dekker is only the most obvious example of this kind of contention. Any period appropriation of Senecan material is necessarily engaged in the kind of dialogue Bakhtin is describing here, and Kyd's is no exception.[38]

Kyd's dramatization of Hieronimo's dramatic writing offers an interesting point of access into this dialogue: Hieronimo, like Kyd, is

---

37. Kyd, of course, was only one of a number of playwrights working with this classical material. The university drama in Latin was deeply engaged with it and exerted an influence on writers like Marlowe. Jonson's epistle in the 1623 Shakespeare First Folio lists "Sporting Kyd" in the same breath as Marlowe's "mighty line," attesting to the force of his work. The play's immediate and enduring success speaks both to the undeniable power of the play and indicates that its innovations spoke to audiences.
38. The literary and social stakes in such appropriations are high, and part of what is at stake in complaints – like those in *Greenes Groatsworth of Wit* – has to do with the legitimacy of writers' claims to this material. Nashe's comment in his preface to Greene's *Menaphon* that Kyd thrusts Elysium into a Hell where it does not belong could be construed as a comment on Kyd's learning.

a playwright capable of working in multiple modes. His dumbshows on matters of state represent one kind of dramaturgy (a mode also seen in Sackville and Norton's Seneca-influenced play *Gorboduc*), while the infamous play in sundry languages is another. Moreover, the use of the play-within-the-play as a method of revenge represents another version of dramatic writing. Siemon has discussed the play's representations of social contention in his article "Sporting Kyd," and that contention extends beyond represented struggles for status within the play towards a claim for the play's status as a whole. The literary field is, like any other field, structured by competition for distinction, and that competition is played out, at least in part, through the interventions made by plays like Kyd's, which stake out new positions in the field. At the same time, these literary position-takings represent claims for social distinction. Like Marlowe, Kyd's background was humble, and he lacked the distinction a university education granted to Marlowe. His appropriations of classical materials and his translations of continental works function both as claims of poetic distinction and as bids for a social place distinct from his origins.[39] Kyd's play demonstrates a deep awareness of the arbitrary and often unjustified power of social status, and that awareness gets articulated in part through the specific way Kyd appropriates the classical tradition as well as the sonnet tradition. Moreover, his central revenger (unlike many other revengers) is a professional (a lawyer and judge), not an aristocrat. Hieronimo both voices a critique of hierarchy and embodies it.

Kyd's response to classical drama is as much discursive as it is thematic. Kyd appropriates structures from the tradition of Latin drama, repurposes them and fills them with other kinds of language. At the same time, *The Spanish Tragedy* embraces the ethical problems of justice and revenge, problems that Seneca's plays explore, and that at least some neo-Latin adaptations paper over or simply leave out of consideration.[40] Kyd's innovations are part of a complex historical dynamic, and a survey of the field is necessary to a more adequate characterization of his work. Later plays, like Shakespeare's *Titus Andronicus* or other revenge tragedies that take at least some of its inspiration from *The Spanish Tragedy*, are among the texts that

39. Pierre Bourdieu's *Distinction* (1987) offers an extended discussion of these strategies, strategies he calls the "reconversion" of cultural into social or economic capital.
40. See Norland's *Neoclassical Tragedy* for an extended discussion of early modern efforts to simplify and reduce the complexities of Seneca's plots to fit various kinds of didactic purposes.

respond to Kyd's work and expand on it in what Bakhtin calls the chain of speech communion.[41]

Kyd's play participates in a broad dialogue with other plays and is responding as much to the content of earlier texts as to their reception. Writing about William Gager's additions to an earlier stage version of Seneca's *Hippolytus*, Bruce Smith argues that Gager "rather confuses things morally" by making Hippolytus both an innocent victim and a "culpable, hard-hearted lady-killer" (215). As Smith suggests, the additions derive from a morality tradition that spoke to Gager's audience's love for debate regardless of whether those debates actually resolve problems.

> The only difficulty is that Seneca's ethical assumptions and Gager's polemical program work at cross purposes. Gager evinces the same easy moral self-assurance as Nowell and Neville, the same assumption that one can make a simple moral judgment about the tragic protagonists and the complicated situations in which those characters find themselves. (215)

Smith attributes this assumption to the context of the play's production – the school or college – and the audience's unwillingness to question the values of those institutions. Kyd makes no such assumption about judgment or about institutions. His refusal to represent judgment as simple constitutes one of the most distinctive features of his response to the deployment of Senecan practices in early modern drama. Kyd's play depends crucially on the ambiguities and problems of revenge, of a stoic response to injustice, and it makes no effort to ignore, sidestep, or simplify them. By refusing to offer a singular moral gloss on the events on stage, Kyd's play denies the possibility of simple moral judgments. That denial is an important part of many later English tragedies.

Kyd, then, does not translate the matter of Senecan tragedy so much as its forms and structures in writing what is often described as the first English revenge tragedy. His response is not a rejection or a criticism but a deployment and development of earlier work-utterances. Rather than choosing classical matter like Gager's plays that draw from stories in Ovid or Homer, Kyd's play chronicles a series of

---

41. See the discussion of Bakhtin's "Speech Genres" essay in the Introduction. In that essay, the "chain of speech communion" refers most generally to what Bakhtin sees as the centrality of communication to all discourse and also characterizes the literary field as a chain of interacting utterances in dynamic dialogue.

interlocking revenges that derive from Balthazar, Prince of Portugal, unchivalrously killing Don Andrea, a Spanish gentleman, and end with the deaths of most of the Spanish court as well as the Portuguese prince. The play begins with the ghost of Don Andrea describing his death at the hands of Balthazar and his desire for revenge. The Ghost of Revenge, of course, promises that that desire will be satisfied. Andrea and Revenge remain onstage throughout the play to watch the eventual satisfaction of that desire. The primary revenger is Hieronimo, a court official, whose son Balthazar and Lorenzo, a Spanish nobleman, have murdered. That murder drives a proliferation of revenge plots that culminate in a murderous play-within-the-play and Hieronimo's suicide in the final act. Andrea only achieves vengeance as a side-effect of Hieronimo's revenge. Specific moments in the play, such as the long introductory speeches from Don Andrea and the Spanish General, appear to be responding to English neo-Senecan drama.

In the play, Kyd adopts something of the philosophical disposition of Seneca's plays in his use of what Braden terms "Senecan selfhood" in characterizing his main revenger. Influences in terms of style are an elusive object of study – especially in translation or adaptation – however, the tone of Kyd's play clearly owes a great deal to Seneca and his English inheritors. Kyd translated the French playwright Robert Garnier's *Cornelie* (printed in 1595, likely translated earlier), and his work demonstrates an engagement with this dramatic tradition. In the first scene of the play, the ghost of Don Andrea and Revenge enter (they never leave the stage), and Andrea reports his condition to the audience. The declamatory mode of this speech and the whole of the play make it difficult to excerpt only brief quotations, so I will quote the speech at length:

> When this eternal substance of my soul
> Did live imprisoned in my wanton flesh,
> Each in their function serving other's need,
> I was a courtier in the Spanish court.
> My name was Don Andrea; my descent,
> Though not ignoble, yet inferior far
> To gracious fortunes of my tender youth.
> In secret I possessed a worthy dame
> Which hight Bel-Imperia by name.
> But in the harvest of my summer joys
> Death nipped the blossoms of my bliss,
> Forcing divorce between my love and me.
> For in the late conflict with the Portingale
> My valor drew me into danger's mouth,

> Till life to death made passage through my wounds.
> When I was slain, my soul descended straight
> To pass the flowing stream of Acheron;
> But churlish Charon, only boatman there,
> Said my rights of burial not performed,
> I might not sit amongst his passengers. (1.1.1–22)[42]

The speech goes on for some eighty-five lines altogether. Andrea describes his passage through the underworld – which is purely classical – and chronicles the various deferrals of judgment of where he should be lodged until Proserpine requests the right to decide. She whispers instructions to Revenge, who conveys Andrea to stage where they watch the action of the play which will show "the author of [his] death, / Don Balthazar, the prince of Portingale, / Deprived of life by Bel-Imperia" (Ind. 87–9). Seneca clearly deeply influences the choric induction here, while at the same time Kyd transforms this material in a response to plays which either follow the pattern very closely, as in Heywood's translation, or treat Senecan technique as a resource but only in Latin. Kyd's specific intervention in the dialogue is to use these technical resources in the vernacular and for an audience not composed of scholars or students. This shift represents what Bakhtin terms a responsive reaction to the tradition within which the play takes shape.

Kyd uses patterns of construction from Senecan drama to build his play, and later in the play he stages a stichomythic courtship scene between Horatio, Andrea's friend, and Bel-Imperia that Balthazar (who desires her) and Lorenzo (her brother) overhear:

> *Bel-Imperia.* Why stands Horatio speechless all this while?
> *Horatio.* The less I speak, the more I meditate.
> *Bel-Imperia.* But whereon dost thou chiefly meditate?
> *Horatio.* On dangers past, and pleasures to ensue.
> *Balthazar.* On pleasures past, and dangers to ensue.
> *Bel-Imperia.* What dangers and what pleasures dost thou mean?
> *Horatio.* Dangers of war, and pleasures of our love.
> *Lorenzo.* Dangers of death, but pleasures none at all. (2.2.24–31)

Instead of a conversation between two people, Kyd gives us a conversation overheard and commented on by two other interlocutors,

42. All further citations of the play are from Mulryne's edition. Beaumont parodies this speech in *The Knight of The Burning Pestle* decades later. In her 2007 article, Rebekah Owens argues that parodies like Beaumont's tell us that the play was "at some point, new. That it was an impressive play; and that it was *very* difficult to ignore" (35).

and both overlapping conversations are stichomythic. The lovers turn each other's phrases, playing on dangers and pleasures, while the eavesdropping villains play on the same phrases in a dialogue of threat that only they can hear. The dialogue here is not deliberative or directly confrontational (as in many other uses of this mode) but instead is both playful and threatening at the same time. The effect derives from the overlaid dialogue in which multiple voices speak at the same time but are not heard at the same time, except by the audience. These overlaid and competing dialogues represent an example of the kind of heteroglot, many-voiced language that Bakhtin sees as characteristic of literature (and language more generally). Moreover, this doubling and overlaying represents a response to and deployment of elements of classical drama that Kyd uses here to remarkable dramatic effect.

Elsewhere in the play, he uses this same structure in a conversation between Lorenzo and Balthazar in which they trade lines of sonnets in order to lament the woes of the lover. The exchange combines classical technique and contemporary verse forms. Lorenzo, son of the Duke of Castile (the King's brother) and heir presumptive to the Spanish crown, is attempting to comfort his friend (and prisoner) Balthazar, son of the Portuguese viceroy who is in love with Bel-Imperia, Lorenzo's sister:

> LORENZO: My lord, though Bel-Imperia seem thus coy,
>   Let reason hold you in your wonted joy:
>   "In time the savage bull sustains the yoke,
>   In time all haggard hawks stoop to lure,
>   In time small wedges cleave the hardest oak,
>   In time the flint is pierced with softest shower"—
>   And she in time will fall from her disdain,
>   And rue the sufferance of your friendly pain.
> BALTHAZAR: "No, she is wilder, and more hard withal,
>   Than beast, or bird, or tree or stony wall." (2.1.1–10)

The lines marked with quotation marks here are quotations from a collection of sonnets by Thomas Watson called *Hekatompathia, or Passionate Century of Love, Divided into two parts: whereof, the first expresseth the Authours sufferance in Love: the latter, his long farewell to Love and all his tyrannie* which was published in London in 1582.[43] Thomas Watson is an interesting figure in his

---

43. Printed by John Wolfe for Gabriel Cowood. Wolfe had also printed Watson's Latin version of Sophocles' *Antigone* in 1581.

own right: bridging the academic and professional population of writers, he worked as a dramatist and had personal connections to Marlowe and Kyd.[44] Extensive headnotes explaining the rhetorical situation, the condition of the speaker, the source for the poem and such preface all of the sonnets, and Kyd was likely familiar with the quoted sonnet due to his personal connection to Watson. He may have chosen this sonnet because of the way the headnote describes a reader who, like, say, Balthazar attempts to profit from the poem. That Balthazar cannot move from mere imitation to creative appropriation – he cannot, to use Bakhtin's phrase, react responsively – helps to show how he becomes Lorenzo's dupe. Moreover, the scene, in keeping with Kyd's overall aesthetic, parodically undercuts this performance of aristocratic sprezzatura by having Balthazar interminably mimic Watson's lines even as Lorenzo pleads with him to stop. The Prince of Portugal demonstrates that he is worse than "no great Clarke," by showing his inability to profit from the poem. Kyd, here as elsewhere, is deploying the resources offered by the poem in service of both the scene and an argument about cultural production. The lines, which neither character remembers exactly, are from Watson's sonnet 58. This particular sonnet has a lengthy preface, worth quoting at length:

> This passion conteineth a relation through out from line to line; as, from every line of the first staffe as it standeth in order, unto every line of the second staffe: and from the second staffe unto the third. The oftener it is read of him that is no great Clarke, the more pleasure he shall have in it. And this posie a scholler set down over this Sonnet, when he had well considered of it: *Tam causa, quam arte et industria*. (F4v)[45]

---

44. Watson was involved in a brawl between William Bradley and Marlowe, eventually killing Bradley, and being imprisoned for it. He knew Lyly and Peele, and in Dekker's *A Knight's Conjuring* is lodged in heaven near Kyd. His plays are lost, but he was well known as a writer of Latin and vernacular verse. Michael J. Hirrel has recently argued that he "was the most important playwright in English none of whose plays survive" (187). He sees Kyd and Watson in the vanguard of what he calls "modern drama," a drama that leaves the medley style of the 1570s behind in favor of the blank verse form associated with Kyd, Marlowe, and Shakespeare. For biographical details, see Albert Chatterley; Hirrel also cites Ibrahim Alhiyari's "Thomas Watson: New Birth Year and Privileged Ancestry" for additional information about Watson's biography.
45. The Latin roughly translates to "for so great a cause, as much art and zeal." The headnotes offer a kind of preemptive gloss of the content of the poems as well as a guide to reading (and using) them.

The two characters here demonstrate their cultural capital and familiarity with recent lyric poetry. They appear to be acting in accord with the prescriptions of courtesy handbooks like Castiglione's *Book of the Courtier* which require the courtier to demonstrate familiarity and facility with the work of the best wits of the period. Lorenzo shows his ability to repurpose literary language from one mode into another. The irony, at least for an audience familiar with Watson's text, is that the preface instructs repeated reading by "him that is no great Clarke" in order to gain the full measure of enjoyment from the complicated repetitions of motifs from stanza to stanza. Such artfulness is lost on Balthazar, who proceeds to offer more poetry in his own words but poetry that merely repeats itself without the structural articulation of the sonnet. Kyd draws from the stichomythic dialogue of Senecan tragedy to stage this exchange and at the same time from the discourse of lyric poetry and combines them to characterize his speakers here. This innovation is, more famously, used by Shakespeare in *Romeo and Juliet*, which uses sonnet language throughout the play to heighten the tragic affect of the plot.

In a different voice, Hieronimo's declamatory mode responds to the Senecan tradition. He even appears onstage carrying a book of Seneca's tragedies. He cites three plays: *Agamemnon*, *Troades*, and *Oedipus*. The speech quotes lines from those plays in what looks like an effort to convince himself to pursue private revenge in the face of the failure of more sanctioned forms of justice. However, as Scott McMillin has noted in "The Book of Seneca in *The Spanish Tragedy*," he has already resolved on revenge and chooses passages that do not have anything specifically to do with revenge. For example, although Hieronimo quotes "per scelera semper sceleribus tutum est iter" [the safe way through crime is by (further) crimes] from *Agamemnon*, those lines do not refer to revenge: they come from a speech in which Clytemnestra is deciding that after ten years of crime she can only secure her "safety" by killing Agamemnon. At this point in the play, Hieronimo has committed no crimes, but Lorenzo and Balthazar have and Hieronimo's use of Seneca's lines points to his expectation that they will commit further crimes to secure their safety. His turn to violence ("strike and strike home where wrong is offered thee" (3.13.7)) is both revenge and an effort to secure his own safety. The other citations likewise are not immediately about revenge but about its consequences. McMillin concludes that Hieronimo's reading of Seneca here "finds significance in the situations of language rather than in the literalism of words" and sees this mode of reading as a pattern in Hieronimo's speech and action through the rest of the play

(207). I would add that this disposition to the Senecan inspiration is precisely Kyd's in composing the whole of the play. It is not just Hieronimo who looks at the book of Seneca (and by extension at books influenced by Seneca) and finds more significance in situations of language than in literal meanings. Kyd looks to Seneca in the same way. This mode of response represents a dialogue with playwrights who focus more on the literal meaning of the Senecan "original." Kyd's intervention in the broad ideological colloquy of the literary field is this contribution to the development of a disposition toward the Senecan legacy that enables creative adaptations instead of varieties of duplication: it is not imitation or translation but engagement. Where Gager translates and writes new plays that hew fairly closely to the Senecan material, Kyd treats it as a resource in a way unlike other appropriators of Seneca.

Kyd's play explores problems of justice, the state, and private revenge and uses elements and techniques from Senecan and neo-Senecan drama to conduct this exploration. The declamatory mode of lament, the stichomythic dialogue of complaint and courtship, and the spectacular violence of the play all draw on earlier plays, and Kyd's deployment of these elements in his revenge tragedy constitutes a response to earlier drama – a response that exerts a profound influence over later works. Moreover, he synthesizes other modes into a particularly English version of Senecan tragedy: he cites the language of the sonnet, and he parallels the main plot with an almost parodic subplot but one that keeps the language of Senecan tragedy. This synthesis appears to have been quite productive, and we can see it as an influence on other transformations of the genre in plays like Shakespeare's *Titus Andronicus* or *Romeo and Juliet*. *The Spanish Tragedy*'s responsive reaction to an earlier tradition changed the shape of what Bakhtin and Voloshinov term the large ideological colloquy of utterance and in doing so changed the shape and purview of the genre of tragedy generally, and revenge tragedy more narrowly.

III

Kyd's play was first published in 1592, and this section turns to the dramatic field in that year. That year offers a useful glimpse at the state of the field of dramatic production because we can put the records of dramatic performance in Henslowe's *Diary* in relation to the surviving publications of dramatic texts in the same year. The printed plays are as follows:

1. William Gager, *Ulysses Redux*
2. John Lyly, *Gallathea*
3. John Lyly, *Midas*
4. Anon., *Arden of Faversham*
5. Anon., *Soliman and Perseda*
6. Thomas Kyd, *The Spanish Tragedy*
7. Mary Herbert (translator), Robert Garnier, *Antonius*
8. Anonymous, The Entertainment at Bisham
9. Anonymous, The Entertainment at Sudeley
10. Anonymous, The Entertainment at Rycote

One of Gager's Latin plays was printed in Oxford (*Ulysses Redux*), two of Lyly's court plays (*Midas* and *Gallathea*) were published in London (for Joan Broome, by two different printers), and William Ponsonby published a translation of Garnier's *Antonius* by Mary Herbert, Countess of Pembroke. Lyly's plays are court plays for the Children of Paul's – both comedies – and were printed with statements about their performance for the Queen and were also performed at the playhouse at Paul's. *Arden of Faversham*, *Soliman and Perseda* (often attributed to Kyd) and Kyd's *Spanish Tragedy* were all published in London for Edward White, by Edward Allde. *The Spanish Tragedy* appears to have been a second edition of the play which had been entered to Abel Jeffes, though Jeffes' early edition is no longer extant.[46] The quartos of *Arden of Faversham*, *Soliman and Perseda*, and *The Spanish Tragedy* offer no information about performance, but Henslowe's *Diary* makes clear that *The Spanish Tragedy* was a solid performer in the repertory in the period his records cover, February 1591 to November 1597. As discussed above, references to the popularity of the play appear for decades. Also in 1592, Jeffes printed an edition of *Arden* as part of what looks like a series of retaliatory publications. Jeffes' edition was later ordered suppressed by the Stationers' Company. According to the Stationers' Court Book:

> Whereas Edward white and abell Ieffes haue eche of them offendyd. viz Edw White in havinge printed the spanish tragedie belonging to Abell Ieffes / and Abell Ieffes in having printed the tragedie of arden of kent belonginge to Edw White. yt is agreed that all the bookes of eche ympression shalbe as confiscated and forfayted, according to thordonnances, disposed to thuse of the poore of the companye / for

---

46. Jeffes printed the 1594 second quarto of the play for Edward White, in a mysterious turn of events.

that eche of them hath seuerally transgressed the ordonnances of the seid impressions (B, fol. 456b).[47]

Lacking other context, it is difficult to establish the sequence of events here, but regardless of which man "offendyd" first, White and Jeffes seem have seen the two plays as equivalents in the exchange of dueling editions. This conflict over the two plays is as significant an index of the state of the market as the other plays published in this year.[48] Kyd's tragedy had the broader and more long-lasting impact of the two – appearing in ten quartos to *Arden*'s three – and it has a well-attested performance history lacking for *Arden*.

However, these futures would have been hard to see in 1592.[49] What the contending editions indicate is that both plays seemed a good risk to printers and publishers, as did those by Lyly.[50] Indeed, the plays printed in 1592 are in a range of genres – Lyly's *Midas* famously stresses its mixed nature in a prologue that argues such mixture is the current natural state of the drama – and appear to suggest an audience for plays with diverse tastes. That *The Spanish Tragedy* was a good investment is demonstrated by its long publication history and its success on the stage. Stage success preceded the 1592 edition. The play was registered only in October of that year, and Henslowe records performances before that month. Despite differences over how profitable playbooks were to stationers, it remains clear that plays like *The Spanish Tragedy* were important players in the field, whether onstage or off.[51]

47. See *DEEP* and see Arber. *DEEP* reproduces excerpts of both the Register and the Court Books where relevant to the printing of plays.
48. I draw on information from the *DEEP* database. By comparison, *DEEP's* records for 1591 show eleven playbooks: four were royal entertainments, two closet dramas, one Inns of Court play, one Children of Paul's play, and two or three public theatre plays (depending on how the *Troublesome Reign of John* is counted). *The Fair Em* is placed in 1591, but there is some question about the date. Despite being the year of *Tamburlaine*'s first publication, 1590 saw still fewer playbooks. Only two playbooks appear in DEEP for 1593. The year 1594 was something of a boom year – with twenty playbooks, including two plays first performed in 1592.
49. For a discussion of one playwright's shaping of that future, see Kesson's *John Lyly and Early Modern Authorship* (2014).
50. Gager's plays were printed in Oxford in Latin and most likely for an academic audience. *Ulysses Redux*, for example, opens with prologues for a "critic" and for "academics." Both prologues justify the way the play mixes comedy and tragedy.
51. For an important article addressing both the relative unprofitability of playbooks as well as the mechanics of the publishing business in early modern

Henslowe's *Diary* offers another, if still incomplete, glimpse at the shape of the field in 1592 and at dramatic taste. The payment records for performances begin with Lord Strange's Men in 1592 and early 1593.[52] *The Spanish Tragedy* appeared sixteen times between 19 February 1592 and 30 January 1593, a span of time in which Henslowe records 134 performances of twenty-seven plays, only seven of which are marked "ne."[53] Only one other play in this first set of records was performed more often: *Henry VI* is listed seventeen times.[54] The first recorded performance in the *Diary* is of Greene's *Friar Bacon and Friar Bungay*, followed by "Muly Mullocco" (spelled variously), "The Spanish Comedy of Don Horatio," "Sir John Mandeville," "Henry of Cornwall," and *The Jew of Malta* in the first full week. The second week sees "Clorys and Orgasto," another performance of "Muly Mullorco," "Pope Joan," "Machiavel," *Henry VI* (marked as "ne," or new), and "Bendo and Richardo."[55] Most of these plays are lost, but the titles do give some evidence of the shape of the repertory of one acting company. Marlowe's *Jew of Malta* was staged fourteen times, *Henry VI* seventeen times, *Friar Bacon and Friar Bungay* five times, "Muly Mullocco" twelve times, "Titus and Vespasian" ("ne") ten times, the "Spanish Comedy of Don Horatio" seven times, *A Knack to Know a Knave* ("ne") seven times, and "Sir

London, see Peter W. M. Blayney, "The Publication of Playbooks." Farmer and Lesser's "The Popularity of Playbooks Revisited" questions Blayney's conclusions and argues that playbooks were significantly more important to the book trade than Blayney allows. Blayney's response, in "The Alleged Popularity of Playbooks," counters these arguments.

52. For the sake of both manageability and consistency, I stop at a performance of *The Jew of Malta* on 1 February 1593, since that date closes the first set of records for Strange's Men. This data, of course, offers only a small window on the field since there was a great deal of other theatrical activity in London, but the *Diary* offers the most detail of any of the surviving records. The company performed more or less continuously from February to June of 1592 and then resumed playing from December 1592 to February 1593.

53. I am counting only performances with the title "Jeronymo" (or variants), and I exclude "the Comodye of Jeronymo" (see 10 April 1591–2, for example) since that seems to refer to *Don Horatio*. This play, the forepiece to *The Spanish Tragedy*, appears multiple times as well.

54. This record, as the critical consensus holds, most likely to refer to Shakespeare's *1 Henry VI*. Henslowe's typical practice is to mention the part of a multi-part play only beginning with the second, and the dates are consistent with Nashe's reference to Talbot in *Pierce Pennilesse*.

55. "Muly Mullorco" may be Peele's *The Battle of Alcazar*, but there is no consensus. See Charles Edelman, "*The Battle of Alcazar*, *Muly Molocco*, and Shakespeare's *2* and *3 Henry VI*."

John Mandeville" eight performances; the other plays all received less than five performances, and nine of them appeared on stage only once, giving some sense of the relative popularity of each play.[56] Only eight of the twenty-seven plays in this run survive in print, and those eight plays account for slightly more than half (sixty-eight) of the performances recorded in the *Diary*. However, the lost "Muly Molocco" and "Titus and Vespasian" were performed more often than *Friar Bacon and Friar Bungay* or *Knack to Know a Knave*, suggesting that frequent staging did not necessarily correlate with attractiveness to printers.

While Henslowe is not particularly interested in noting the plays' genres, they do seem to display a striking diversity in subject matter and kind (see Table 3.1).[57] The broad range of plays combined with the patterns of repetition show the Lord Strange's Men's sense of the desires of their audience. The plays demonstrate a clear emphasis on exotic settings and on plays treating the past (whether historical, romantic, or classical). That only six titles are "ne" indicates a certain aversion to risk and preference for proven "old" plays like Kyd's or the lost "Muly Mollucco" – but of those seven "ne" titles three got many repeat performances based, most likely, on their initial financial success. Kyd, Marlowe, and Shakespeare were popular on the stage. The diversity of genres and subject matter in this list of plays indicates something about audience interests in a broad range of historical materials as well as in comedy. Because few of these plays survive, any generalizations about innovation or audience tastes must be tentative. As David McInnis has recently argued in *Shakespeare and Lost Plays* (2021), Henslowe's records for Strange's Men in 1592 indicate that the lost plays in their repertory "provided demonstrable financial value to their playing companies," and we must take that value into account in considering the shape of the dramatic field (41). Working from the admittedly speculative generic attributions in the *Annals*, the majority (fifty-one) of the 134 performances were of "histories," with comedies being the second most common genre

---

56. Marlowe's *Massacre at Paris* was only performed once, but that was at the end of the run; the play took in £3 14s, which is consistent with the first day takes of plays that Strange's company played multiple times.
57. For most of the plays, any attempt at assigning a genre would be an exercise in conjecture based on the content suggested by the title. Content-driven generic definitions problematically bracket questions of form, or what Fowler's *Kinds of Literature* calls "historical genre," in ways foreign to the period. *Four Plays in One*, for example, was called a Moral by Harbage, though there is no evidence to confirm the designation.

Table 3.1 Plays performed by Lord Strange's Men, February 1592–February 1593[a]

Title[b]	Performances	Printed	Genre	
			Annals	Wiggins
Friar Bacon	8	1594	Comedy	Comedy
"Muly Molocco"	12	Lost	Foreign History	Tragedy (?)[c]
Orlando	1	1594	Romantic Comedy	Romance
Spanish Comedy of Don Horatio	7	Lost	Comedy	Comedy
Sir John Mandevill	8	Lost	Romantic Comedy	Romance
Harry of Cornwall	4	Lost	History	History
Jew of Malta	14	1633	Tragedy	Tragedy
Clorys and Orgasto	1	Lost	Pastoral (?)	Pastoral (?)
Pope Joan	1	Lost	Foreign Pseudo-History	History
Machiavell	3	Lost	Foreign History (?)	Not defined
ne- *Henry VI*	17	1623	History (*1 Henry VI*)	History
Bendo and Richardo	3	Lost	Comedy	Romance
Four plays in one	1	Lost	Moral	Anthology
Looking Glass	4	1594	Biblical Moral	Biblical Moral
Zenobia	1	Lost	Classical History	Romance
Jeronymo (*The Spanish Tragedy*)	16	1592	Tragedy	Tragedy
Constantine	2	Lost	Classical or English History	History (?)
Brandymer	2	Lost	Romantic Comedy (?)	Romance
Jerusalem	2	Lost	Heroical Romance	Romance
ne-*Titus and Vespasian*	10	Lost	Classical or British History	History
ne-*Second Part of Tamber Cam*	2	Lost	Heroical Romance	Tragedy
ne-*Tanner of Denmark*	1	Lost	History (?)	Not defined
Tambercam	4	Lost	Heroical Romance	Tragedy
ne-*Knack to Know a Knave*	7	1594	Comedy	Moral
ne-*Gelyous Comedy*	1	Lost	Comedy	Comedy
Cossmo	2	Lost	Comedy	Comedy
Tragedy of the Guise (*Massacre at Paris*)	1	1594	Foreign History	Tragedy

[a] Drawn from Henslowe's *Diary*, *Annals of English Drama, 975–1700*, and Wiggins and Richardson.
[b] Titles are listed in the order in which they appear in Henslowe's *Diary*.
[c] Titles with a question mark following their genre are lost, and the ascription cannot be assessed.

(thirty-nine). Tragedies comprised thirty of the performances, "heroical romance" (eight), "moral" (five), and "pastoral" (one) rounding out the total. Wiggins and Richardson's generic labels are less elaborate and less speculative, but with some signal exceptions (they call *Massacre at Paris* a tragedy, while the *Annals* call it a foreign history) they are largely consistent with the *Annals*.[58] Of the eight plays for which we have printed texts, only one (Greene and Lodge's *A Looking Glass for London and England* [1594]) clearly looks back to an earlier tradition. Greene's *Friar Bacon and Friar Bungay* and *Orlando*, Shakespeare's *1 Henry VI*, Kyd's *The Spanish Tragedy*, and Marlowe's *Massacre at Paris* innovate in terms of structure, content, and language. As Knutson has argued, the diversity of titles points to the broad nature of the repertory of acting companies in the period.[59] The company hedged its bets with a good deal of breadth while at the same time returning to reliable performers like *The Spanish Tragedy, The Jew of Malta, Henry VI, Friar Bacon*, "Muly Molocco," and "Titus and Vespasian" for more than half of the total performances.

The next section of this chapter turns to a discussion of the anonymous play, *Arden of Faversham*, whose text survives while no records of performance do. I include the play, in spite of this fact, because it represents an early example of what scholars have come to call "domestic tragedy" and because it increasingly appears to have been collaboratively written by professional playwrights. The play makes a series of formal and topical interventions that are both distinctive and influential.

IV

Gentlemen, we hope you'll pardon this naked tragedy,
Wherein no filéd points are foisted in
To make it gracious to the ear or eye;
For simple truth is gracious enough,
And needs no other points of glozing stuff.

Anon., *Arden of Faversham* Epilogue

---

58. Wiggins and Richardson describe their approach as "avoiding Polonian over-elaboration," an overelaboration not avoided by the *Annals* (1: xxiv).
59. See Knutson, *Playing Companies and Commerce in Shakespeare's Time* (2001) as well as her *The Repertory of Shakespeare's Company* (1991). For a discussion of repertory strategies, see *Playing Companies and Commerce* (56–63).

Arden of Faversham, probably first performed between 1588 and 1592 and printed in 1592, represents arguably the earliest example of what we have come to call domestic tragedy. None of the three editions of the play (1592, 1599, and 1633) make any reference to the play's performances, but the existence of three editions at least suggests stage success.[60] Another indication that the play was influential lies in the fact that a number of other similarly topical plays based on real events were performed in the years after its appearance. Vivian Comensoli notes that "between c. 1590 and 1610 approximately twenty domestic tragedies, most of them murder plays, were written, only five of which survive" (173 n6). The four plays other than *Arden of Faversham* are *A Warning for Fair Women* (Q 1599), *Two Lamentable Tragedies* (Q 1601), *A Woman Killed with Kindness* (Q 1607, Q2 1617), and *The Yorkshire Tragedy* (Q 1608, Q2 1619). While I am not willing to make more confident pronouncements about *Arden* being, in Ros King's words, a "very popular play" in the absence of better (or any) evidence, it did have success in the bookstalls, provided an example for a series of later plays, and has a strong legacy of performance after the seventeenth century (635). Primary evidence of its popularity in the seventeenth century derives from it having been printed in several editions, which does point to success in the bookstalls, which is sometimes preceded by (or followed by) stage success. In her Arden edition of the play, Catherine Richardson argues that the appearance of the three quartos "may well indicate moments of revived stage popularity" and points to evidence of performances of the play in the eighteenth century by professional traveling companies playing "the circuit of east Kent theatres, fairs and races ... and sometimes back through west Kent" (66).[61] Recent scholarship into the play's authorship, while not by any means settled, points to it being the product of collaboration between professional playwrights.[62] Its title page calls it:

The lamentable and true tragedie of M. Arden of Feuersham in Kent
Who was most wickedlye murdered, by the meanes of his disloyall

---

60. Wiggins and Richardson date the play's composition to somewhere between 1587 and 1592 (3: 9–12). In addition to the three quartos, excerpts from the play appear in John Bodenham's *Belvedere, or The Garden of the Muses* (1600).
61. I cite this text parenthetically. Richardson discusses a tradition of marionette versions of the story performed into the nineteenth century. *Arden*'s story appeared in many kinds of media.
62. Richardson's introduction offers an excellent overview of these questions. See 33–61.

> and wanton wyfe, who for the loue she bare to one Mosbie, hyred two deseperat ruffins Blackwill and Shakbag, to kill him.
>
> VVherin is shewed the great malice and discimulation of a wicked woman, the vnsatiable desire of filthie lust and the shamefull end of all murderers.

The play is a "lamentable and true" tragedy, taken from the pages of Holinshed's chronicles, and represents not the more conventional elite subjects of tragedy but a story of lust, betrayal, and murder in the provinces. Holinshed's text asserts that the horrible nature of the crime justifies the inclusion of what "may seeme to be but a private matter, and therefore as it were impertinent to this history" (qtd in Richardson 290).[63] The play's persistence and engagement with contemporary issues about, for example, the structure of the household in a period of change, underscore the story's pertinence. The title page also avows its exemplary nature: the malefactors' crimes are revealed, and they are all punished. Critics have discussed the play's action in terms of its engagement in a range of social and political ideas.[64] The play's tragic form as much as its content encourages the critical turn to politics in readings of the play. In other words, the play's concerns rise to seriousness in part with help from the associations of the tragic genre, and elevating domestic concerns to tragedy is one of the play's innovations.

Because of its emphasis on the murder and its punishment, it is tempting to label it a "true crime" play – based as it is on a sensational murder case not, perhaps, ripped from the headlines, but certainly taken from the *Chronicles*. All of these post-facto labels imply certain frames of interpretation that, while suggested by the play and its title page, also cut against the terms the play itself uses. The play's epilogue, spoken by Franklin, a character who serves as a kind of detective in the play, calls it a "naked tragedy" without extra "glozing stuff" foisted in to supplement its "simple truth."[65] That he uses the verb "foist" – usually in the period associated with

---

63. Many recent editions of the play include Holinshed's narrative. The full account appears in his *Chronicles* (1587) (fol. 1062–6).
64. Catherine Belsey's essay, "Alice Arden's Crime," remains one of the best-known readings of the play, discussing it in the context of gender politics and debates about marriage. Richard Helgerson's essay "Murder in Faversham" discusses many of the ways the story of Arden's murder has been valued by historians and critics.
65. Franklin is a character standing on the border of allegory: his name is both simply a name and a marker of a particular social status and place. That he

deception of one kind or another – is especially significant given the various efforts of the murderers to foist their accusers off with lies. Why he feels compelled to offer this apology is an interesting question: if simple truth is sufficient, then why apologize for a lack that doesn't require one? And, after all, the play is a fiction – its truths couched in, if not lies, at least something other than "simple truth."[66] Moreover, as critics have noted, the play *does* contain "filéd points" of rhetoric even if we grant it is not filled out with "glozing stuff."[67] Probably the most obvious example of filéd points is how frequently characters employ language that echoes that of Kyd and Marlowe if from a different social location. Part of its interest to critics lies in its development of a tragic mode for representing the middling sort, a social grouping theoretically inappropriate for tragedy – many period and classical theorists argue that tragedy ought to concern the great and comedy the less great. As Emma Whipday writes, "domestic tragedies demonstrate that the domestic sphere is worthy of the dramatic reach of tragedy" (232). Treating the lives of the middling sort as tragic is a position-taking in the field: the play claims a new kind of subject matter for tragedy, another of its signal innovations.

The play has drawn attention from critics due to the way it depicts the social order and the domestic sphere. The pertinence of the play, to invoke Holinshed, lies with both its content and the particularities of its dramatic form. The play's exploration of large questions of public import, whether about the nature of marriage or treason (petty or otherwise), is connected to the play's generic form – its mingle-mangle nature, to use Lyly's term from the prologue in the 1592 text of his play, *Midas*. To offer one example, the hapless hired murderers Shakebag and Black Will's constant failures to kill Arden draw on comic archetypes in a play that culminates in gory death. They shift from comic bumblers to effective murderers in the final scene as part of the play's movement towards its tragic conclusion. That hybridity also has much to do with its intervention in the field, deploying chronicle material to both make an implicit claim about

> delivers this epilogue only underscores his place between character and type: he quite literally stands between the play and its audience.
> 66. Chapter four discusses the role of fiction in the historical drama in more depth.
> 67. Eugene Hill discusses the play's rhetoric and topical references to Mary, Queen of Scots in "Parody and History in *Arden of Feversham* (1592)" as well as its connection to contemporary events. James Forse discusses the play's form in "*Arden of Faversham* and *Romeo and Juliet*: Two Elizabethan Experiments in the Genre of 'Comedy-Suspense.'" Richardson's edition of the play makes a strong case for the power and sophistication of the play in the introduction.

the scope of tragedy and to engage in these debates. Moreover, we can productively think of *Arden* as a chronicle play, drawn as it is from a section of Holinshed's work treating events during the reign of Edward VI. Chronicle plays are themselves a generic hybrid, like *Arden,* and they share common sources and forms. At the same time "the English history play," usually defined through an interest in dynastic questions, excludes plays like *Arden* simply because it is not directly connected to these questions, the questions that, say, Shakespeare's history plays engage with.[68] *Arden*'s claim that the events it depicts merit tragic treatment extends to historical drama. Of the presentation of the Arden story in Holinshed's *Chronicles,* Helgerson writes:

> Where most of Holinshed's other murder stories get no more than a sentence or two, the Arden account goes on for a full seven tightly printed folio columns, nearly five thousand words, considerably more than he gives many events of state. (133)

Holinshed's explanation for this difference of scale lies in the "horribleness" of the murder, a horribleness that makes sense of his choice "to set it forth somewhat at large" (fol. 1062). Holinshed is not specific about exactly what that horribleness consists of, leaving it an open question for later writers. The long-form title of the play asserts horror lies with what it calls the wicked murder of Arden, which in turn demonstrates the wickedness of Alice, the destructive effects of lust, and the just end of murderers. In contrast to the play's title's focus on murder and punishment, Belsey's essay, "Alice Arden's Crime" argues that the "horribleness" has less to do with the details of the murder than with Alice's challenge to marriage as an institution, and she locates the play in the context of an intensifying debate over marriage in the 1590s (83–4). Frances Dolan's "The Subordinate('s) Plot: Petty Treason and the Forms of Domestic Rebellion" links the play's treatment of Arden's murder to the offence of petty treason and argues that the play "moves outside of the genres that give shape to experience and questions the social order and dramatic forms that achieve cohesion by excluding or subordinating the story of petty treason" (333). Dolan's argument about the centrality of petty trea-

---

68. "The chronicle play" defines a genre purely by its source and is almost always used to talk about plays included under what seems to be the broader category of the "history play." That *Arden* is not typically called a chronicle play points out the limitations of such generic definitions. The next chapter takes up the definitional issue of the "history play" in much more detail.

son to the play recognizes how the play expands and questions the boundaries of tragedy. As both Belsey and Dolan show, contemporary society saw the household as the state in little, and the play's literal conflicts – while confined to the provinces and to the middling sort and lacking the dynastic or international implications of historical drama focused on the doings of monarchs – are necessarily related to similarly substantial ideological questions about the state, questions within the purview of the history play.

Appealing to the truth of the story to legitimate its telling, Holinshed states that the "instructions," the information, about this event was "delivered to me by them that used some diligence to gather the true understanding of the circumstances" (fol.1062). This emphasis on the truth of the narrative is echoed by Franklin's epilogue and seems to be one of the distinctive features of both Holinshed's narrative and its dramatic representation, both of which focus on ferreting out of the truth of Arden's murder. In fact, Franklin's speech echoes Holinshed's apology in the way he asserts the play is one of "simple truth," a truth as valid as those in the events of state more commonly found in Holinshed's pages. The *Chronicles,* as Annabel Patterson has shown, demonstrate a commitment to the presentation of "instructions" – evidence – to readers who could then judge what they read. The "naked tragedy" Franklin invokes at the close of the play is another way to say "true tragedy," a representation of an unvarnished true story.[69]

As Lorna Hutson and others have argued, the play also represents the dramatic reception of particular kinds of legal and oratorical practice, a reception that helps create reality effects distinct from plays less imbued with the forensic tradition.[70] Legal practices like evidence gathering in criminal procedure provided playwrights with new methods for constructing plots. These new methods in turn offer opportunities for generic innovation, as here with domestic tragedy

---

69. "True Tragedy" appears on the title pages of the Queen's Men *Richard III* play (Q1594) and Shakespeare's *3 Henry VI* (*The True Tragedy of Richard Duke of York and the Good King Henry the Sixth,* Q1595). The "Lamentable and True" locution also appears in the title page of Middleton's *A Yorkshire Tragedy* (Q1608).
70. See Lorna Hutson, *The Invention of Suspicion: Law and Mimesis in Shakespeare and Renaissance Drama* (2007). Hutson also discusses the deployment of forensic oratory in Kyd's *Spanish Tragedy,* among other plays. See also Cheryl Dudgeon, "Forensic Performances: Evidentiary Narrative in *Arden of Faversham*" (2009). The historical dramas I discuss in the next chapter evince similar effects.

or elsewhere with other new forms. One durable legacy of both Kyd's play and *Arden* is in this use of discursive patterns from the law to create plots that are, as Hutson argues, probable in the way that courtroom narratives are probable. In *Arden,* Franklin functions as a detective, constructing a probable (and accurate) narrative of the events of Arden's murder from a variety of clues (rushes in Arden's shoe, bloodstains on the floor, and the discovery of the murder weapon) that guarantees the punishment of the perpetrators. The investigation provides proofs and verifies an account of the events. In Hutson's view, these techniques also produce a sense of interiority that is different than in other plays: the play invites audience members to consider motive through emerging legal categories that attempt to discern motive through acts of interpretation.[71]

Questions about the play's genre offer insight into the field at the point of the play's composition and first performances as much as they do about how critics have received the play and may suggest reasons why the Arden playwright thought it would be wise to produce such a play in around 1588–90. Holinshed's role as a direct source of event for plays about dynastic history is well known and is part of the subject of the next chapter, but for the Arden playwrights, writing shortly after the publication of the 1587 edition of the *Chronicles,* the book appears to have also made sense as a source for a different kind of plot – a kind of plot that later plays offer to audiences with and without specific historical antecedents. By the time Thomas Heywood writes his *Apology for Actors* in 1608, tragedy is peopled by characters from all status groups without the need for any apologetical gestures.

The next chapter turns to other plays based on historical narratives – most famously from Holinshed, the source for the story of Arden's murder. These plays emplot historical events in diverse modes and, like *Arden of Faversham,* intervene and shape later thought on genre and innovation.

---

71. *Hamlet* and *Othello* both turn on efforts to secure proofs, and the title characters' search for those proofs contributes to a sense of their interiority.

Chapter 4

"Lies like truth": History, Fiction, Genre, Innovation

... In that Empire, the Art of Cartography attained such Perfection that the map of a single Province occupied the entirety of a City, and the map of the Empire, the entirety of a Province. In time, those Unconscionable Maps no longer satisfied, and the Cartographers Guilds struck a Map of the Empire whose size was that of the Empire, and which coincided point for point with it. The following Generations, who were not so fond of the Study of Cartography as their Forebears had been, saw that that vast Map was Useless, and not without some Pitilessness was it, that they delivered it up to the Inclemencies of Sun and Winters. In the Deserts of the West, still today, there are Tattered Ruins of that Map, inhabited by Animals and Beggars; in all the Land there is no other Relic of the Disciplines of Geography.

Suárez Miranda, *Viajes de varones prudentes*,
Libro IV, Cap. XLV, Lérida, 1658
Jorge Luis Borges, "On Exactitude in Science"

Borges' one-paragraph short story imagines an empire so committed to accuracy in mapping that the maps came to match the territory mapped exactly, making both map and geography useless. Work on the history plays sometimes falls to the same temptation as scholars add layers of qualifying adjectives to what purports to be the thing itself, a temptation we are led to by early modern title practice and its characteristic offers of a range of putative subgenres of "history" ("true," "chronicle," "famous" and so on).[1] While not, perhaps, as

---

1. Herbert Lindenberger's *Historical Drama: The Relation of Literature and Reality* (1975) offers many examples of this kind of critical habit. Most of his labels (like the "conspiracy play") are defined more by content than by some other kind of marker of generic difference, and they bear little resemblance to labels used by early modern printers. "Reality" is much less a concern in the book than "literature."

useless as the map in Borges' story, the development of this array of sub-genres obscures central questions about what the "history plays" actually are in terms of genre and how they give the impression that they offer some kind of historicity to audiences in the past and in the present. This chapter will argue that if there is a specific innovation in these plays it lies in the representational tools they use to create the touch of the real: a little touch of history in the theatre.

Where the previous chapter offered a description of a dramatic field in ferment by examining a range of plays and placing them in the context of theatre history, print culture, and literary history, this chapter turns to one of the most discussed of early modern genres: the history play of the 1580s and 1590s. Questions about what a "history play" is go back at least as far the Catalogue at the start of the 1623 Folio of Shakespeare's plays, and efforts at definition are a recurrent feature of the scholarship on the plays gathered under that rubric. Shakespeare's plays about English history typically represent these plays. I am most interested in two key questions: first, what *are* these plays? second, how do they create a sense of historicity?

Further obscuring a full picture of the "history play," the label often refers to the ten plays by Shakespeare that the Folio designates as "Histories," thus excluding a whole range of plays on historical subjects from consideration as part of the genre. This critical habit also makes Shakespeare's plays the standard against which other historical plays are measured and usually found wanting. Shakespeare-centric definitions have the effect of distorting the field and reinforcing a restrictive notion of the form. A focus on specifically English history becomes a defining quality, which, as I will argue below, has made it difficult to see plays like *Troilus and Cressida* as invested in an historical project. Paulina Kewes has recently offered a detailed and persuasive account of many of these attempts at definition in her essay "The History Play: A True Genre?" in the History Plays volume of *A Companion to Shakespeare* (2003). Her conclusion is that the "Elizabethan history play is not a 'true' genre if by that is meant a dramatic form clearly distinguishable from the Elizabethan tragedy or the Elizabethan comedy" (188). We cannot nor should not, she says, abandon the term (it is pragmatically useful) but it "should not be mistaken for a theory of dramatic genres" (189). The term has the virtue of describing a group of plays that (in many cases at least) share an interest in staging the history of dynastic struggle in the long period of strife preceding the accession of Henry VII. At the same time, it itself has a history with considerable and often overlooked weight, guiding interpretation not least because of the assumption that the "genre" is a real thing. Heminges and Condell and the other compilers of the First Folio may have seen value in associating these plays, but that fact does not necessarily make them a genre and still less does it mean that the "history play" means "plays written by Shakespeare on the events surrounding the Wars of the Roses."

In agreement with Kewes, I will argue that to assume that there is such as thing as a genre called the "history play" is a problem because definitions rooted in that assumption conceal more about real innovations than they reveal. If there is something new or distinctive in these plays on historical subjects, we have to think about that novelty less in terms of definite substances and more in terms what the plays *do* that is distinctive. How, in other words, do these plays give the impression that they are "historical" rather than tragic or comic (and to who)? The plays' success in representing history has everything to do with their success as fictions. In fact, their most distinctive features and the ones that produce reality effects, the lies like truths of the chapter title, tend to be almost entirely fictional, and this use of fiction is one the features of these plays that make them distinctive.[2] For example, in historical drama, many of the most memorable and enduring characters are non-historical. Falstaff is only the most discussed of such characters. Middleton's historical play *Hengist, King of Kent* was known as "The Mayor of Queenborough" in both manuscript and early printed texts, taking its title from the comic subplot, rather than the historical main plot. Traditional definitions of the history play obscure the durability and popularity of these plays since they often imply that the history play is over as a "living" genre by around 1600. The existence of plays like Middleton's *Hengist, King of Kent* or Ford's *Perkin Warbeck* (1634) – not to mention the plays that Judith Spikes calls "Jacobean history plays" – contradicts this claim as does the continued popularity of Shakespeare's histories on stage and in the printing house throughout the period. These later plays are the focus of the next chapter.

Thus, rather than add still more to a Borgesian map of the genre, this chapter discusses ways that these plays offer representations of history – focusing on their deep reliance on figures and plots from other genres – and explores more concrete changes that contributed to the happy coincidence between producer and consumer that

---

2. The extensive literature on the theory of history – see Hayden White's *The Content of the Form* (1990) or Frank Ankersmit's *Historical Representation* (2002) for examples – attests to the central importance of questions of representation to historical writing.

Bourdieu argues subtends literary innovation. The emergence and persistence of plays engaged in historical representation depends on this coincidence, as does the ability of later critics to name the "history play." The current chapter discusses Marlowe's *Edward II* and Shakespeare's *2 Henry IV* as instances of the "early" historical drama.[3] I have chosen these plays partly because they stand in a liminal position with regard to the conventional boundaries of the genre. Marlowe's play stands between tragedy and "history," much like Shakespeare's *Richard II* (1597) or *Richard III* (1597). Formally distinct among Shakespeare's plays on English history, *2 Henry IV* defers the appearance of both Henry IV and Hal until relatively late in the play because a substantial part of its power as "history" derives from the purely fictional elements of the play's comic plot, perhaps best signaled by Rumour's role as presenter. Historians and poets spent considerable energy thinking about the proper writing of history – as truth or rumor – and their work was an important part of the context in which early modern plays on historical subjects emerged. The next section offers a consideration of some of that work.

I

> A great many things keep happening, some of them good, some of them bad. The inhabitants of different countries keep quarrelling fiercely with each other and kings go on losing their temper in the most furious way ... However, no writer has come to the fore who has been sufficiently skilled in setting things down in an orderly fashion to be able to describe these events in prose or verse.
>
> Gregory of Tours, *The History of the Franks*

Gregory of Tours, writing in the sixth century, describes the problem of writing history in terms that remain familiar. Events keep succeeding events – some good, some not – and writers struggle both to keep up with them and to put them into some kind of order. Saint Gregory's *History of The Franks* represents an attempt to produce

---

3. There are many other extant plays on historical subjects. Based on the ascriptions in Harbage's *Annals* (themselves open to question), there are 137 extant "history" plays printed before 1642 (11 percent of the 1240 records in *DEEP*, to 1642). Playbook attributions as "history" are fewer – only eighty-nine – and problematic because the term is so multivalent. As Kewes notes, the "history" in "history play" cannot be restricted to England. Classical history, for example, was a common subject across the whole of the period.

an orderly account of events so that later readers might both remember and understand them. His work combines features of religiously inflected universal history (it begins with the Creation before moving quickly towards his own times) with a chronicle history of the deeds of the Franks up to about 591. Despite his achievement, the problem of representation that motivates his lament about there being no writer able to present these events "in an orderly fashion in prose or verse" remains an important part of theoretical debates about history.[4] As historians and literary critics well know, the debate takes on increased resonance in the early modern period with the advent of an historical humanism, and both historians and poets across Europe feel its impact.

Philip Sidney engages in these questions about historical representation in his *Defence for Poesy*. Discussing the debt historians owe to poets, he states that historians, with truth written on their foreheads, gain "fashion" and "weight" from the work of the poet:

> And even historiographers, although their lips sound of things done, and verity be written in their foreheads, have been glad to borrow both fashion and perchance weight of the poets: so Herodotus entitled the books of his history by the names of the nine Muses; and both he, and all the rest that followed him, either stole or usurped of poetry, their passionate describing of passions, the many particularities of battles which no man could affirm; or, if that be denied me, long orations, put in the mouths of great kings and captains, which, it is certain, they never pronounced.
>
> So that, truly, neither Philosopher, nor Historiographer, could, at the first, have entered into the gates of popular judgments, if they had not taken a great disport of poetry; which in all nations, at this day, where learning flourished not, is plain to be seen: in all which, they have some feeling of Poetry. (20)[5]

Fashion here refers as much to style as to structure – historiographers borrow fashion from poets to make their work more readable – and order is as important to the writer of history as it is to the poet. Herodotus and all his followers "either stole or usurped of poetry" to write their accounts of events in the past – making use of the tools

---

4. The problem of orderly description is one of the central questions in the philosophy of history. See, for example, Arthur Danto's *Narration and Knowledge* (1985), which includes his 1968 *Analytical Philosophy of History*, or much of Paul Ricoeur's work.
5. Sidney goes on to give examples of places where learning might be lacking but poets are still important.

of the poet to create their narratives. Fiction is an essential aspect of historical writing. Writing from the position of the poet in a debate over the relative value of various kinds of writing, Sidney thinks of the poet as superior to the historian in terms of didactic effectiveness but nonetheless sees poesy and history as complementary, rather than opposed.[6] Poetry's superiority derives from its deployment of form and structure that makes it possible to put its imagined events into a coherent shape. History borrows this formal structuring, in Sidney's scheme, to make sense of the "things done" which are its object. In this way, poesy contributes to intelligibility, and that in turn makes the work of the historiographer useful. His assertion about how historians make use of the tools of the poet points to both the connection between these kinds of writers and underscores the importance of considerations about representation in the writing of history.

Edmund Spenser, naming himself a "poet historical" in the "Letter to Ralegh" that accompanies *The Faerie Queene*, addresses questions of method in differentiating the practices of poets and historiographers:

> For the methode of a poet historical is not such as of an historiographer. For an historiographer discourseth of affayres orderly as they were donne, accounting as well the times as the actions; but a poet thrusteth into the middest, even where it most concerneth him, and there recoursing to the things forepaste, and divining of things to come, maketh a pleasing analysis of all. (3)

Spenser's attention to the recursiveness of the work of the poet historical links his poetry not only to history but to forms like epic, which range more freely backwards and forwards in time. The poet does not write of "affayres orderly as they were done," like the writer of chronicles, but instead structures the work to make "a pleasing analysis of all." In this view, the meaning of history (what it is for) takes a central place. Spenser sees his historiographer as a chronicler – writing events as they happen without "recoursing" – and his description of the poet historical is a better description of historical writing.[7] Spenser's discussion of how his poet historical "thrusteth

---

6. His comments on the limits placed on historians by the need to be true to events return to this point: the poet is better than other writers because of the freedom of the imagination.
7. White's work on the distinction between chronicle and history emphasizes the importance of judgment in distinguishing chronicle from historical writing proper. See *The Content of the Form*.

into the middest, even where it most concerneth him" assimilates poesy historical to epic and at the same time underscores the importance of selection and analysis to the poet's project. The "Letter to Ralegh" demonstrates that the question of time and the structure of historical writing are as crucial to Spenser as they are to historiographers, even if his "historiographers" are chroniclers. These questions are as important to dramatists as they are to narrative poets.[8]

At roughly the same time as Spenser is writing the *Faerie Queene*, George Puttenham's *Art of English Poesy*, echoing and synthesizing other thinkers, spends some time discussing what he calls "poesy historical" as part of its overall project of describing and systematizing English poetry. Discussing the purpose of "poesy historical," he writes:

> ... the poesy historical is of all other—next the divine—most honorable and worthy, as well for the common benefit as for the special comfort every man receiveth by it, no one thing in the world with more delectation reviving our spirits than to behold as it were in a glass the lively image of our dear forefathers, their noble and virtuous manner, which, because we are not able otherwise to attain to the knowledge by any of our senses, we apprehend them by memory, whereas the present time and things so swiftly pass away, as they give us no leisure almost to look into them, and much less to know and consider of them thoroughly. (129)

For Puttenham, historical poetry holds second place in his hierarchy of kinds because of the benefits it confers on its audiences. Stories of our "dear forefathers" have a reviving effect and, more importantly, we "apprehend them by memory" which affords the chance to "know and consider of them thoroughly." This careful consideration is very important to the "special comfort" that history provides. As Puttenham says, the present moves too quickly to consider carefully as it passes, but the past, being fixed in memory, can be looked at in depth. At the same time that history offers us access to the truths of the past, Puttenham argues that feigning – one of the central features of poesy in Sidney's account – is an important part of what "historical men" do:

> These historical men nevertheless used not the matter so precisely to wish that all they wrote should be accounted true, for that was

---

8. See, for example, the way that the Chorus introduces Shakespeare's *Henry V* or how the prologue describes the play to come in *Troilus and Cressida*.

> not needful nor expedient to the purpose, namely to be used either for example or for pleasure, considering that many times it is seen as a feigned matter or altogether fabulous—besides which it maketh more mirth than the most true and veritable, but oftentimes more, because the poet hath the handling of them to fashion at his pleasure, but not so of the other which must go according to their verity and none otherwise without the writer's great blame. Again, as ye know, more and more excellent examples may be feigned in one day by a good wit, than many ages through man's frailty are able to put in ure, which made the learned and witty men of those times to devise many historical matters of no verity at all, but with purpose to do good and no hurt, as using them for a manner of discipline and precedent of commendable life. (129)

They "used not the matter so precisely to wish that all they wrote should be accounted true" because the more important consideration was "example" or "pleasure." Puttenham here appears to be blending Sidney's positions on history and poesy, approvingly writing of the "learned and witty men" of the past who produced "many historical matters of no verity at all, but with purpose to do good and no hurt" as a way of providing examples of good action.

In a similar vein, Thomas Nashe and later playwrights like Thomas Heywood pick up this emphasis on the usefulness of history in defensive commentary on drama. In these oft-quoted lines from *Pierce Penniless*, Nashe asks:

> What if I prove plays to be no extreme, but a rare exercise of virtue? First, for the subject of them, (for the most part) it is borrowed out of our English chronicles, wherein our forefathers' valiant acts (that have lain long buried in rusty brass and worm-eaten books) are revived, and they themselves raised from the grave of oblivion, and brought to plead their aged honors in open presence; than which, what can be a sharper reproof to these degenerate effeminate days of ours? How would it have joyed brave Talbot, the terror of the French, to think that after he had lain two hundred years in his tomb, he should triumph again on the stage, and have his bones new embalmed with the tears of ten thousand spectators at least (at several times) who in the tragedian that represents his person imagine they behold him fresh bleeding. (1010)

The ideas in this passage recall Puttenham's on the memory of great ancestors published three years earlier: Talbot's embodiment on the stage functions as an example, a reproof to "these degenerate effeminate days of ours," and, more importantly, brings his (and other heroic figures) out of the "rusty brass and worm-eaten books" where they have lain forgotten. This attention to purposes – didactic in the defenses, more commercial in the theatres – is an important aspect of the plays and one that exerts a great deal of influence on their form. All three writers stress the power and usefulness of the poetic or dramatic representation of historical events and figures.

Writing specifically of Spenser's work but making a general case, Bart Van Es argues that it is "the choice of form that determined and expressed a writer's historiographic perspective—if not always regarding the ultimate facts of history, then certainly the way in which those facts were approached" (11). In the theatre, the shape of the dramatic field and the writer's sense of audience also necessarily influence (if not wholly determine) that choice. When Shakespeare (or Marlowe, or Middleton, or anyone else) chooses to include figures more at home in comic fictions in an historical drama, he expresses a specific disposition towards history and towards what its representation entails as much as he responds to the taste of his audience. Comic fiction, attractive to early modern audiences, can become a tool to in producing effective and accessible representations of history while at the same time responding to the demonstrated tastes of theatre audiences. Innovations like those in the Elizabethan historical drama depend on the success of the writer's efforts to respond to an audience and to shape the response of that audience.

Like the poets, philosophers were interested in what Spenser calls "methode" in the writing of history. Period thinkers' theoretical work on history influenced developments in historical fiction, particularly as they are invested in ideas about the uses of history, an interest shared by poets like Spenser. Peter Burke describes the fitful emergence of a "sense of the past" with Italian humanists like Petrarch, who in Burke's account "reveres the ancients—as men, not as magicians; and is acutely aware of the difference between their age and his own" (21). D. R. Woolf has shown the importance of historical thinking in the period, and my discussion is especially indebted to his body of work. Woolf's work in particular has been vital in developing an account of changes in what he calls the "historical culture" of early modern England. His essay "From Hystories to the Historical: Five Transitions in Thinking about the Past, 1500–1700," describes five changes that, in his argument, led to what amounts to a modern historical consciousness by 1700:

1. The articulation of a sense of period and the acquisition, among a greater proportion of the population than previously, of a historical mental map.

2. The emergence of a sense of the past as continuous process and the establishment of the primacy of causal relationships between diachronically contiguous or proximate events over exemplary and analogical relationships between temporally remote and disconnected ones.
3. The development of a visual sense of the past.
4. A growing understanding of formal boundaries between genres but also of the liquidity of historical matter and its capacity to transcend such boundaries.
5. A more confident sense of the "real" and the "probable," together with a willingness to concede the existence of the unknowable rather than attempt to "fill in the blanks." (38)[9]

Item four is of particular importance to the writing of historical drama, but most of these developments occur in the drama of the period. None of these transitions operated in isolation, and they formed part of the intellectual background for more literary writers who could see past events not, for example, as unconnected to the present except as abstract exempla, but as ways of understanding the present.

Thomas Blundeville, a prolific writer and translator, translated two Italian works of historical theory as his *True Order and Methode of Writing and Reading Hystories* (1574), a work that can serve as an exemplar of the kind of historical ideas put forward by humanist theories of history.[10] Blundeville's dedication to Leicester indicates the disposition he means to inculcate with his work:

---

9. Woolf's earlier essay, "Genre into Artifact: The Decline of the English Chronicle in the Sixteenth Century," argues that the chronicle fades as a genre due to competition from other forms of historical writing, including the history play, which transform the chronicle from history into a source for histories. Hayden White's work on the key role of narrative and emplotment in historical writing is likewise crucial to my thinking. See for example, the essays in *The Content of the Form*.
10. The two Italian writers were Francisco Patrizi and Jacob Acontius. Blundeville drew from Patrizi's dialogues on history but dropped the dialogue form. Acontius' work appears to have been a treatise given to Leicester some years earlier – probably on history or method in research. Blundeville was also interested in practical sciences like surveying, and his interest in history is an expression of that interest. Blundeville was an important figure in the period's intellectual history, and his work was influential in a range of fields. For example, Henry Turner's *English Renaissance Stage* (2006) discusses the relation between the surveying that Blundeville discusses and developments in the spatial poetics of the period's drama.

> Knowing that youre Honor amongst other your good delyghtes, to delight most in reading of Hystories, the true Image and portraiture of Mans lyfe, and that not as many doe, to passe the tyme, but to gather thereof such judgement and knowledge as you may therby be the more able, as well to direct your private actions, as to give Counsell lyke a most prudent Counseller in publyke causes, be it matters of warre, or peace. (A.ii.r)

History, in language that anticipates Hamlet's description of the theatre as the image of nature, serves as the best image of "Mans lyfe" and should be a sound guide to good practices whether public or private. Leicester, in the dedication, reads histories properly and for the practical purpose of being better able to direct his actions. The reading of history, then, in good humanist fashion, shapes its reader into a "most prudent Counseller." Blundeville's book proceeds to lay out a method for writing histories that is almost astonishingly structured. He presents an approach to history based in explanation: historians can and must understand events in terms of their causes as much as in their effects. They must, in turn, break down causes into smaller units so they too can be better understood. Blundeville and his sources have faith in the potential for histories to make sense of past events and to serve as guides to current practice. For example, in talking about war, it is necessary that the writer carefully describe all the relevant aspects of the war, from the levy and pay of the soldiery to details of logistics: "all which things are very necessary to be knowne, for to avoid all evill happes that may hereafter chaunce in like cases" (C.i.recto). Blundeville assumes that history is not a random flux of incommensurable events, instead seeing it as both patterned and comprehensible. Because of this instructive potential, the work of the historiographer is, or ought to be, directed at use.

Blundeville's interest in fact, or, better, truth extends to his treatment of rhetoric in the production of historical texts.[11] For the historiographer's work to be useful, it must be as accurate a reporting of what actually happened as possible. Thus, the writer of history

---

11. "Truth" and "fact" have a complicated relationship in period thought. Barbara Shapiro's *A Culture of Fact: England, 1550–1720* (2003) discusses the shifting meanings and uses of "fact" in the period and its relationship to "truth." One consistent concern throughout Blundeville's text is that the work of the historian be accurate, and many of his references to truth seem to be about accuracy. Questions and problems regarding "truth" have a long history. See Richard Firth Green's *A Crisis of Truth: Literature and Law in Ricardian England* (1999).

works best when offering a bare narration, not embellished with unattested oratory:

> Of those that make anye thyng, some doe make much of nothing, as God dyd in creating the World of naught, and as Poets in some respect also doe, whilest they faine fables and make thereof theyr poesies and poetical Hystories: some agayne of more doe make lesse, as kervers and gravers of Images, and other suchlike artificers, some of little doe make much, and of muche little, as the Oratours whylest sometime abase great things. And some do make of so much asmuch, as true Philosophers and Hystoriographers, whose office is to tell things as they were done without either augmenting or diminishing them, or swarvying one iote from the truth. Whereby it appeareth that the historiographers ought not to fayne anye Orations nor any other thing, but truly to reporte every such speech, and deede, even as it was spoken, or done. (E.iv.r-v)

Those who make things of any kind are divided into subgroups here – poets make "much of nothing" when they "faine fables" and make their "poesies and poetical Hystories," for example – and each has their own set of practices. Making here includes all kinds of artistic production, not just writing. Historians and philosophers ought to "tell things as they were done without either augmenting or diminishing them, or swarvying one iote from the truth" because, unlike God or poets, they must be faithful to what actually happened. He specifically forbids the introduction of speeches not fully attested by other historical accounts, ruling out much of the practice of classical historians. This stricture would, of course, also rule out drama as a vehicle for history of this kind – fiction has no place in Blundeville's *True Order* – and fiction is essential to the power of drama about history.

Brian Walsh's *Shakespeare, the Queen's Men, and the Elizabethan Performance of History* (2009) focuses not on definitions but on representation: on how the past is, to use his term, performed. As he writes:

> The history plays by Shakespeare, and the history plays by others who influence Shakespeare, which I examine in this study contribute to Elizabethan historical culture their cultivation of a historical consciousness that centers on a key dialectic: they enact historicity as a sense of discontinuity and all the while reflect on the strategies through which historical representation, particularly corporeal representation, addresses that discontinuity. (20)

The question is not one of *genre* but of *representation*, which is one of the questions I will address below in terms of ways the play's fictions work to support their ability to produce the appearance of historicity. Walsh argues:

> History plays, through their very existence as works that unfold in the performative present, highlight and help to inculcate a sense of historicity, or, to use T. S. Eliot's useful phrase, of the "pastness of the past." Dramatic histories thereby reflect on, even "theorize," the concept of history itself. This theorization is driven by the very "liveness" that defines theater as a form. Puttenham saw the desire for the past as a longing to encounter "the lively image of our deare forefathers." Theater traffics precisely in the "lively image," for liveness is the ontological condition of theater. (21)

Historicity thus is an effect of the representation and, as I hope to show, is linked to the fictiveness that characterizes these plays. Many of the "lively images" in the plays under discussion are fictional, but their effects are as durable (if not more in some cases) than the real ones. Walsh consistently points to the diversity of kinds that engaged in the representation of history and refuses to reduce that diversity into anything resembling a unified formal definition.

In part about the use and reuse of historical narratives, Patterson's *Reading Holinshed's Chronicles* (1994) offers a compelling case for reading Holinshed from the dual perspective of a literary scholar and a cultural historian, and it offers a way to think about both what the writers of the *Chronicles* were doing and what writers appropriating materials from them were actually appropriating. Part of Patterson's argument is that a specific attitude towards history and the writing of history comes out of the *Chronicles*. Her injunction to read the *Chronicles* from the perspectives of cultural historian and literary scholar also makes sense as an approach to the plays. The *Chronicles* deploy techniques from fiction as they produce history just as the plays deploy techniques from history as they produce fictions of history. This overlap does not mean that distinctions between history and its representation blur into insignificance. As Patterson writes: "Reading the *Chronicles* with a literary intelligence may alert us to the mobile boundaries between 'facts' and fictionality, or between documents and stories, but it does not require us to deny their existence, not, at least, if we also try to read as cultural historians" (55). The extensive recent literature on cultural memory and history underscores this shifting boundary as well as highlights the often substantial stakes of defining it.[12] England, like many European countries, saw its history extending quite far into the past, and the "facts" of history include stories we now think of as myths – from the Arthurian legends to the "history" of Troy. A focus on Shakespeare's plays on the Wars of the Roses as representative of the "English history play" obscures these other narratives and even overshadows plays on other aspects of English history, like Marlowe's *Edward II* or later plays I take up in the next chapter like *Perkin Warbeck* or *Hengist, King of Kent*.

Scholars often cite the extended induction of *A Warning for Fair Women* (1597?, Q 1599) as evidence for the existence of the three genres of comedy, history, and tragedy well before the First Folio's defining them by example. I discuss the paratexts in Chapter Six as exemplifying a practical rather than restrictive disposition towards generic kinds, while here I am interested in how the play intervenes in the theatrical field. In this play, Tragedy comes to preside over a play whose plot draws from an historical murder. Like *Arden of Faversham*, the play is about a notorious murder. This one was committed in 1573. Arthur Golding, the translator, wrote an account of the crime in a pamphlet published in 1573 and republished in 1577. An account of the murder also appears in Holinshed. We could thus argue that the story appears under the sign of history. The text on the title page of *Warning* bears a close resemblance to that on Arden's in its specificity and emphasis on the lamentable nature of the crime and the ends of the conspirators. In another likeness to Arden, it is printed in blackletter, further associating it with its historical sources. In the prologue, History enters with a drum and ensign, associating itself with plays about English history, while Comedy enters apparently carrying a fiddle, and Tragedy has a whip in one hand and a knife in the other. Tragedy claims the stage from both History and Comedy, whipping them off saying:

> Thus with your loose and idle similes,
> You have abused me: but I'll whip you hence.
> I'll scourge and lash you both from off the stage!
> 'Tis you have kept the theaters so long,

12. Paul Ricouer's work in both *Time and Narrative* (1984–8) and *Memory, History, Forgetting* (2005); Derrida's *Spectres of Marx* (1993) and *Archive Fever* (1995); and Frank Ankersmit's interventions in historical theory all engage with the importance of this definitional contest. Shakespeare's plays on English history have a major effect on how events like the Battle of Bosworth Field were remembered – "memories" that, for example, color our reception of the recent discovery and investigation of Richard III's skeleton.

Painted in playbills, upon every post,
That I am scorned of the multitude,
My name profaned; but now I'll reign as Queen
In great Apollo's name and all the Muses,
By virtue of whose Godhead, I am sent,
I charge you to be gone and leave this place. (Ind. 75–83)[13]

That Tragedy is being "scorned" or "profaned" around 1597 is hard to believe, given how many plays with tragedy or tragical content and titles were being performed and printed (including, of course, *Warning*).[14] Instead, Tragedy (like History or Comedy) is making a claim for its authority and importance by comparing itself to other modes and by claiming it is under attack – a position-taking, in Bourdieu's sense – and the truth of the claim is less important than the way that it positions the play as being different and novel compared to the plays that have "kept the theaters so long." She clears the stage and makes way for the play that follows, preparing the audience. Both Comedy and History recognize this dismissal, if belatedly, when they see the black draperies of the stage.

While these allegorical figures do appear to represent something about these genres, it is hard to take them as representations of a fully realized theory of genre since they do not articulate any detailed arguments. Instead, these figures give a sense of a competitive theatrical field in which the value of plays is the object of competition. As Comedy and History depart, they promise that they'll be back "tomorrow" to make the audience "laugh with mirthfull jeasts" and to "domineere" respectively. Like *Arden,* this play claims a place for itself by bringing the murder of a citizen into the purview of Tragedy and drawing on the resources of history to do so.[15] As Tragedy says:

My scene is London, native and your own,
I sigh to think, my subject too well known.
I am not fained: many now in this round
Once to behold me in sad tears were drowned,

---

13. I am citing Ann C. Christensen's recent edition of the play (2021).
14. The unlikeliness of tragedy being scorned means that the idea that these figures represent something like authoritative versions of their kinds needs to be taken with a measure of skepticism: if Tragedy misrepresents its relative position, the same is likely true of Comedy and History.
15. The play makes use of dumbshows and allegorical characters like Justice (and Mercy and Diligence), all of which associate it with older modes of tragic drama and make an implicit claim for a kind of distinction.

Yet what I am, I will not let you know,
Until my next ensuing scene shall show. (Prol. 7–12)

London, familiar to the audience, and a subject "not fained" will bring the audience to tears. If not the naked tragedy of *Arden*, this tragedy is native and well known. After the play's conclusion, Tragedy enters as epilogue and underscores precisely what it is the play has attempted to do in language reminiscent of Franklin's speech at *Arden*'s close:

> Here are the launces that have sluiced forth sin,
> And ripped the venomed ulcer of foul lust,
> Which, being by due vengeance qualified,
> Here, Tragedy of force must needs conclude.
> Perhaps it may seem strange unto you all,
> That one hath not revenged another's death,
> After the observation of such course.
> The reason is, that now of truth I sing,
> And should I add, or else diminish aught,
> Many of these spectators then could say,
> I have committed error in my play.
> Bear with this true and home-borne Tragedy,
> Yielding so slender an argument and scope,
> To build a matter of importance on,
> And in such form as haply you expected.
> What now hath failed, tomorrow you shall see,
> Performed by History or Comedy. (Epil. 4–22)

Tragedy begs pardon for the "strange" ending of the play where "one hath not revenged another's death," appealing to "truth" which demands that tragedy not add or diminish anything in the story. Conventions about revenge thus must bend to the force of historical truth, and this accounts for what Tragedy describes as a peculiar ending to the play. Moreover, she asks us to bear with the "true and home-borne Tragedy" she has just presented, suggesting that despite the slender argument the play has presented a "matter of importance." Comedy and History will appear to correct or supplement "what now hath failed," a promise that undercuts the kinds of firm distinctions between these kinds that might otherwise be suggested by the three presenters. The play's translation of a native and familiar tale from England's history into the register of tragedy represents its specific innovation and it is this sort of novelty that the next section of this chapter turns to.

II

> ... were he here, detested as he is,
> How easily might some base slave be suborned
> To greet his lordship with a poniard,
> And none so much as blame the murderer,
> But rather praise him for that brave attempt,
> And in the chronicle, enrol his name
> For purging of the realm of such a plague.
>
> Marlowe, *Edward II*

Christopher Marlowe's play about English history, titled in the early printed texts *The Troublesome Raigne and Lamentable Death of Edward the second, King of England: with the tragicall fall of proud Mortimer*, was first printed in 1594, having been entered in the *Stationer's Register* on July 6, 1593. Marlowe's play shares the "Troublesome Raigne" label with the anonymous *Troublesome Raigne of John, King of England* and no other surviving plays of the period. We can think of *Massacre at Paris* as a history play, as well as *Tamburlaine*, *Dido*, and even *Dr Faustus*. Other generic labels have more force, but Marlowe's turn to historical source materials is a common feature of much of his drama. Marlowe's insistent turn to history for the materials of his plots is as typical of early modern drama as the diversity of his plays' genres. The relative lack of attention to this aspect of Marlowe's work seems to be partly an effect of the close association between Shakespeare and the "history play." The usual narrative about *Edward II*'s publication is that Pembroke's Men, having fallen on hard times, were compelled to sell some of their playbooks to publishers. The other plays associated with Pembroke's Men printed in 1594 are *Titus Andronicus* (attributed to Pembroke's, Derby's, and Sussex's Men), *Taming of a Shrew*, and *2 Henry VI* (though this play was printed without any company attribution).[16] Shakespeare's *3 Henry VI* appeared in 1595 with an attribution to Pembroke's Men. We can confirm no other plays to be in their repertory around the time *Edward II* was written and

---

16. *Titus*' place in Pembroke's repertory seems dubious given that Henslowe does not associate it with Pembroke's (its first appearance as a "ne" play is in Sussex's Men's run, on 23 January 1594). The title page attribution to Derby's, Pembroke's, and Sussex's Men may reflect that it was acted by combined companies or that there was a sequence of ownership, but we lack any confirming evidence for this.

first performed, though there must have been, given the shape of the other repertories we are aware of.[17] The hardship narrative is largely based on brief comments in a letter from Henslowe to Alleyn:

> as for my lorde a Penbrockes wch you desire to knowe wheare they be they are all at home and hauffe ben t<his> v or sixe weackes for they cane not saue ther carges <w>th trauell as I heare & weare fayne to pane the<r> parell for ther carge. (280)

The other evidence adduced is that they appear to have sold some plays, but the reasons for this sale are not clear, particularly based on their known plays.[18] Like other scholars, I cannot contribute anything but speculation to the debate on the reasons for their inability to "save their charges," and I am more interested in what this information suggests about the market for plays and the players' projections of what would be profitable in both the theatrical and the print market.

Based on the evidence of these four Pembroke's plays, Marlowe's work was performed in a repertory with a two-part history play and a comedy successful enough to prompt a later Shakespearean adaptation. As Knutson notes, the plays compare favorably to those in Strange's repertory especially since all three of the plays on historical subjects "expand the definition of the generic chronicle play" ("Pembroke's Men" 131). Marlowe's play in particular extends, if it does not transcend, the more or less established conventions of historically-themed drama. In *The English History Play in the Age of Shakespeare* (1957), Ribner argues that "we have in *Edward II*, perhaps for the first time in Elizabethan drama, a tragedy of character in which a potentially good man comes to destruction because of inherent weaknesses which makes him incapable of coping with a crisis which he himself has helped to create" (123–4). Ribner sees the play as important to the development of "the history play," deploying the familiar image of Marlowe as the opening of the way for Shakespeare.[19] While this teleological argument is both compelling

17. See Andrew Gurr's *The Shakespearian Acting Companies* (1996) for extended, if sometimes unavoidably speculative, discussions of the repertories and personnel of Pembroke's and other acting companies.
18. See Knutson's "Pembroke's Men in 1592–3, Their Repertory and Touring Schedule" for a discussion of their repertory. Based on the plays we know were Pembroke's plays, Knutson makes a convincing case that their repertory cannot be the reason for their hardship, whatever it was. The thinness of the evidence makes it difficult to discern what the trouble was with any precision.
19. See for example: "In many respects Marlowe prepared the way for Shakespeare's

and might even be true if only in hindsight, the end point was by no means clear in the early 1590s when Marlowe's play was composed and performed. The question of the relation between the tragic form of the play that Ribner recognizes and its historical content still needs addressing.

Indeed, the playing of history in this and other plays raises the question of the relationship between "fact" and "fiction," a question kept implicit in Marlowe's work compared to say, the Chorus' stress on it in Shakespeare's *Henry V*. Marlowe's play engages with the emergent category of the "history play" in the moment of its production and I will consider the play as an intervention *at that moment* rather than in light of later "developments." Based on what is admittedly a small sample of Pembroke's Men's plays, it appears that their repertory resembles that of other successful companies and that they thought that plays on historical themes were a good investment. One reason for this investment – at least with regard to Marlowe's play about Edward II – is what appears to be a more general interest in the reigns of Edward I and Edward II. A number of texts – dramatic and nondramatic – take up the history of this period, and if they are not quite so plentiful or well-known as works on the Wars of the Roses, they still occupy a significant place in the cultural world of early modern England.

One of these texts, Michael Drayton's poem *Peirs Gaveston* (sic), was published in a stand-alone edition in 1595 and revised as part of a larger book of historical poetry in 1596. The poem takes up Gaveston and Edward II's story from Gaveston's perspective.[20] The poem appears to date to 1593 and almost certainly could not have been a source for Marlowe's play, but it could represent a response to the play or, more likely, an indicator of broad interest in Gaveston and Edward's story. Questions of priority are not especially relevant to my argument here; the mere fact that both play and poem are contemporary is more interesting than the likely pointless effort to determine which text came first. Kelly Quinn's "Mastering Complaint: Michael Drayton's *Peirs Gaveston* and the Royal Mistress

---

great historical tragedy of *Richard II*, and not least in that he gave a new tragic significance to the *de casibus* theme of rise and fall which we have already seen in the *Henry VI* plays and *Richard III*" (Ribner 126).

20. The 1596 edition appears with a dedication to Lucy, Countess of Bedford, also the dedicatee of the 1596 *Mortimeriados*. The Countess of Bedford was a noted patron, a member of the Sidney circle, and Drayton's dedications suggest that he believed work on these figures would find favor, which in turn we can take as another signal of a broader interest in this material in the early 1590s.

Complaints" locates the poem in a genre Quinn calls the "royal mistress complaint" and argues that Drayton's poem is "modeled on poems such as Thomas Churchyard's *Shores Wife* and Samuel Daniel's *Complaint of Rosamond*, which combine elements of *de casibus* complaint (through the *Mirror for Magistrates*) with female complaint traditions to tell the woes of the lovers of English kings" (439). Quinn takes pains to distance Drayton's poem from Marlowe's play, arguing that the poem does not simply "retell" Marlowe's play and that the "play is not even the primary model Drayton responds to in his poem" (440). What she does concede is that Edward II's reign seemed a likely topic for such a poem and later in the essay shows how Drayton's work fits into a tradition with its own set of familiar conventions. Pointing to critical confusion about a reference to Idea, a figure from Drayton's sonnet sequence, she writes that:

> Drayton seems to expect that his readers, familiar with the convention of the listening beloved, do not need the frame to be fleshed out—as if, that is, if we know the genre, the frame goes without saying. Gaveston is discussing Idea because Drayton assumes we expect him to do so. (442)

The argument regarding how Drayton's poem intervenes in this genre – a male plainant instead of a female, for example – depends on there being an audience that would recognize the poem as an engagement in a tradition. That structure of expectation helps to explain both the formal choices that Drayton makes and his choice of subject matter. Marlowe's play takes up the same narrative, and his choice of subject matter seems a response to a sense of an audience receptive to artistic treatments of the reign of Edward II.

Quinn's essay places the poem in the complaint tradition, but Drayton's work also shows clear links to stage tragedy and, more specifically, to plays like Kyd's *Spanish Tragedy*. The poem opens with Gaveston's ghost arriving, as he says:

> From gloomy shadow of eternall night,
> Where cole-black darknes keeps his lothsom cel,
> And from those ghosts, whose eyes abhor ye light,
> From thence I come, a wofull tale to tell:
> Prepare the Stage, I meane to act my part,
> Sighing the Scenes from my tormented hart. (K4r)[21]

---

21. I quote from the 1596 edition (STC 7232) printed by James Roberts for Nicholas Ling, which Drayton calls a corrected edition. EEBO associates an earlier edition with Abel Jeffes, the printer of *The Spanish Tragedy* (STC 7214.5).

Gaveston's ghost takes this metaphorical stage, sighing forth the scenes in a kind of variation on Kyd's Andrea or Revenge in *The Spanish Tragedy*. Gaveston is less confused about what is happening than Don Andrea is, but that is more a function of the tale than any formal consideration. Gaveston simply knows more about the significance of his death than Andrea does. The poem thus opens in the Senecan territory described in neo-Latin plays like Gager's *Meleager* or Kyd's work.[22] Drayton frames the poem in terms of the tragic stage, a framing that the opening stanzas insist on:

> Wing-footed Fame nowe summons me from death,
> In Fortunes triumph to advance my glory,
> The blessed Heauens againe doe lend me breath,
> Whilst I report this dolefull Tragicke storie:
> That soule & body, which death once did sunder
> Now meet together, to report a wonder. (K3v)[23]

His glory lies in the doleful nature of his story that he has been given time to tell. Gaveston goes on to invoke the "mournful Maidens of the sacred nine," the Destinies, who dwell in "the shades beneath," desiring them "with sable pens of direfull Ebonie, / To pen the processe of [his] tragedie" (K3v). After this plea, Gaveston's ghost makes explicit allusion to Kyd's work in a stanza structured like Hieronimo's lament but in a joyful vein. Describing the days of his youth, when Edward I was king, he says:

> O daies, no daies, but little worlds of mirth,
> O yeeres, no yeeres, time sliding with a trice;
> O world, no world, a very heauen on earth,
> O earth, no earth, a verie Paradice:
> A King, a man, nay more then this was hee,
> If earthly man, more then a man might be. (K5r)

This is, of course, not an uncommon rhetorical pattern, but the lines echo and play on specific parts of Hieronimo's speech ("O world" and "O earth"). His imitation (or emulation) of Kyd's combination of anaphora and correctio is another signal of connections between

---

22. The biographical narrative of the poem has some resonance with Andrea's self-presentation in the opening chorus of *The Spanish Tragedy*. These links to Kyd and to the neo-Latin tradition indicate the deep roots of the poem and how far the influence of this tradition goes.
23. What this "wonder" actually might be is likewise unclear – that Gaveston's speaking after his death? The whole story?

this poem and the dramatic tradition.[24] Drayton saw dramatic rhetoric as useful in writing narrative poetry, which in turn indexes the influence of dramatic forms on the writing of other modes of history.

The poem's 302 stanzas cover Gaveston's life from his youth to his death and burial, including a long lament by Edward II about the loss of his favorite. Gaveston depicts himself as a paragon, almost an icon of beauty, who uses that beauty as a hook to fish for the Prince's love. The Prince, Gaveston tells us, would have been a great king were it not for his lust and Gaveston's "lascivious will":

> *Edward* surnam'd *Carnauan* by his birth,
> Who in his youth it seem'd that Nature chose,
> To make the like, whose like was not on earth,
> Had not his lust, and my lasciuious will,
> Made him and me the instruments of ill. (K8r)

The "ill" to come is Edward's bad kingship and the civil dissension that results from Gaveston's taking revenge on the barons who were instrumental in his exile. The self-castigation Gaveston voices is entirely absent in Marlowe's play, which reserves criticism of Gaveston to the barons.[25] Drayton's poem relates his whole life, far too long for a play, and ends with a lament by Edward and a description of Gaveston's interment. The poem does not deal with the remainder of Edward's reign or the revenges promised (again in terms recognizable from the theatre) in Edward's lament:

> You damned Furies, break your Stigian Cell,
> You wandring spirits, in water, earth, and ayre,
> Lead-boyled Ghosts which live in lowest hell,
> Gods, deuils, men, vnto mine ayde repayre,
>   Come all at once, conioyne you all in one,
>   Revenge the death of my sweet *Gaveston*.
>
> Eyes neuer sleepe, vntill you see reuenge,
> Head, neuer rest, vntill thou plot reuenge,
> Hart, neuer think, but tending to reuenge,
> Hands, neuer act, but acting deepe reuenge.
>   Just-dooming heauens, reuenge me frome aboue,
>   That men vnborne may wonder at my Loue. (P2r)

---

24. The early stanzas are filled with references that at least have an affinity to Kyd's version of a classical underworld.
25. Also absent from Marlowe's play is any sense that Gaveston laments the passing of the days of Edward I, quite the opposite.

Echoing Hieronimo again, Edward calls on the rhetorical and mythological resources of revenge plays in his invocations of the Furies and in his blazon-style exhortation to himself regarding his revenge. An imagined stage never seems far away in Drayton's historical poems.

Published in 1596, Drayton's *Mortimeriados* continues the narrative of Edward II's reign and the bad effects of his indulgence of favorites and continues to deploy theatrical language as part of its rhetorical strategy. The poem focuses on Mortimer who is, as Jean Brink writes in *Michael Drayton Revisited*, depicted as an heroic figure despite the fact of his treasonous ambitions and his adulterous relationship with Queen Isabel (35). This poem, like *Peirs Gaveston*, deploys theatrical language: the poem describes Mortimer's entry into the factional disputes as "the gastly prologue to thys tragick act" (B4r). As in the earlier poem, Drayton employs the resources of both Ovidian and Senecan lament in his verse tragedy of Mortimer and uses references to stage tragedy as a way to orient readers to the text. Taken together, the two poems mark an interest in the history of the period before the Wars of the Roses, and both emplot that history in tragic terms.

George Peele's *Edward I* also takes the history of this period as its subject.[26] Its 1593 title page called the play a "famous chronicle" with the "life of Lleuellen rebell in Wales" and "the sinking of Queene Elinor, who sunck at Charingcross, and rose againe at Pottershith, now named Queenehith." Scholars since at least Ribner have noted that Peele's play bears the mark of *Tamburlaine*'s influence and appears to have been popular on the public stage. It is loosely episodic – as the compendious title suggests – and takes significant liberties with the history it recounts. The loose structure and episodic nature of the play contrasts Marlowe's more focused version of

---

26. The traditional identification of this play with the "Longshankes" in Henslowe's *Diary* has come into at least some question in recent decades. In her 1984 article "Play Identifications: *The Wise Man of West Chester* and *John a Kent and John a Cumber*; *Longshanks* and *Edward I*," Knutson argues that a plausible case can be made that *Longshanks* is not the same play as even a revised version of Peele's *Edward I*. If Knutson is right, it is an indication of an even broader interest in the history of Plantagenet England, an interest that even a play far from "actual" history like Greene's *James IV* responds to. *Thomas of Woodstock* might also be included, despite the difficulties of assigning dates to the play and the lack of evidence of performance. The text of Peele's *Edward I* is notoriously poor, and the only modern edition (1974) edits it pretty freely in order to produce a "retroform" that the editor thinks the play probably looked like.

Edward II's story. Peele's play was registered to Abel Jeffes in October of 1593 and printed sometime later that year. Jeffes, as discussed in chapter three, was also the printer of Kyd's *Spanish Tragedy* and a suppressed edition of *Arden of Faversham*. Jeffes' interest in plays in this, for lack of a better term, Marlovian mold seems consistent across the few plays he printed.[27]

Another Plantagenet play, the anonymous *Edward III*, takes up the heir where Peele's takes up the father of Edward II. *Edward III* appears to have been a collaboration and bears signs that point to Shakespeare as having a hand in it as a writer or a reviser. As the Arden editors argue, *Edward III* has deep connections to the theatrical field of the early 1590s in terms of its approach to sources and general dramaturgy. After a discussion of the play's links to *The Famous Victories of Henry V* and Marlowe's plays, Proudfoot and Bennett write "*Edward III* can be seen as growing from the same soil as Shakespeare's earliest histories" (49). They suggest *Edward III* responds to Marlowe's *Edward II* by showcasing Edward III's triumphs in contrast to the many humiliations of Edward II in the earlier play. That playwrights and theatre companies produced these plays speaks to both a perceived demand for Plantagenet history and for plays that sounded like Marlowe and Kyd. One sign of that interest is in other treatments of figures in Marlowe's play like Drayton's poems, Peele's play, *Edward III* and the chronicles. Marlowe's play is linked to the dramatic field at its moment of production in both its tragic structure and its historical content.

The play begins with Gaveston's reading of a letter from Edward on the death of Edward's father, and Marlowe's *Edward II* immediately signals both its engagement with and distance from contemporary plays on historical subjects. Opening with the announcement that a king has died and that a new king has succeeded – if not exactly a convention – is a feature of several historical plays.[28] Gaveston, like Edward, rejoices in the death of the old King and sees it as a promise of great "bliss":

> "My father is deceased; come, Gaveston
> And share the kingdom with thy dearest friend."
> Ah, words that make me surfeit with delight!

---

27. Lesser's work suggests that stationers did specialize at least to a degree, and it is at least possible that Jeffes was engaging in a kind of marketing strategy though the small body of texts makes the argument difficult.
28. The obvious example is the reference to the funeral of Henry V at the beginning of Shakespeare's *Henry VI* plays.

What greater bliss can hap to Gaveston,
Than live and be the favourite of a king? (1.1–5)[29]

Gaveston's opening lines perform some choric functions, such as informing us that the old king has died and that the new king has sent for his favorite. The speech also, as it continues, signals that this is a Marlovian treatment of history since it deploys habits of speech we have come to see as typical of his plays, like the classical allusion and the focus on a central object of desire:

Sweet prince, I come; these, these thy amorous lines
Might have enforced me to have swum from France,
And, like Leander, gasped upon the sand,
So thou wouldst smile and take me in thy arms.
The sight of London to my exiled eyes
Is as Elysium to a new-come soul;
Not that I love the city or the men,
But that it harbours him that I hold so dear,
The King, upon whose bosom let me die,
And with the world be still at enmity. (1.6–15)

Gaveston's allusion to the Hero and Leander story suggests Marlowe's own treatment of the story, placing the King in Hero's role.[30] Conflating London and Elysium refracts Faustus' confounding of Hell with Elysium, and the "surfeit" of delight likewise resonates with Faustus' search for the ever-expanding delights promised by magic. In lines reminiscent of Aaron's speech on his ascent to the heights of Fortune in *Titus Andronicus* and of Tamburlaine's farewell to his shepherd's weeds, he goes on to bid farewell to a servile status: "Farewell, base stooping to the lordly peers; / My knee shall bow to none but the King" (1.17–18).[31] This opening signals the play's interest in the dynamics of the king-favorite relationship and Gaveston's interest in both the King and the status his association with Edward

29. I cite from the New Mermaids edition, edited by Martin Wiggins and Robert Lindsey (1997).
30. Wiggins and Lindsey's note to line 8 dates Marlowe's poem "Hero and Leander" to "c. 1593," but it was not printed until 1598. How clear an allusion to the poem this was remains obscure. It does, however, indicate connections between the play and the poem that serve as a sort of signature.
31. *Titus Andronicus* appears as "ne" in Henslowe's *Diary* in January of 1594, but scholars have advanced arguments for earlier productions that coincide with conjectural productions of Marlowe's play. Regardless, both plays appear to have been produced within the same few years and priority is less important than that rough contemporaneity.

will bring him, but the play gives relatively little attention to the dynastic and political concerns introduced at the outset of, for example, *2 Henry VI*.[32]

Underscoring this distinction, after dismissing his first set of suitors, Gaveston discourses on the kind of men he does want to attend him. The speech is often discussed as evidence of Edward's weakness, of a shared interest in theatre, and the homosociality of Gaveston's (and implicitly Edward's) imagination. It also echoes descriptive passages in, for example, *Doctor Faustus*. The masques Gaveston imagines in this speech never actually appear on stage, but the details and richness of Gaveston's imagination of the masques produce images as vivid as any in other plays of the period, historical or not:

> I must have wanton poets, pleasant wits,
> Musicians, that which touching of a string
> May draw the pliant King which way I please.
> Music and dancing is his delight;
> Therefore I'll have Italian masques by night,
> Sweet speeches, comedies, and pleasing shows;
> And in the day when he shall walk abroad,
> Like sylvan nymphs my pages shall be clad,
> My men like satyrs grazing on the lawns
> Shall with their goat-feet dance an antic hay;
> Sometime a lovely boy in Dian's shape,
> With hair that gilds the water as it glides,
> Crownets of pearl about his naked arms,
> And in his sportful hands an olive tree
> To hide those parts which men delight to see,
> Shall bathe him in a spring; and there hard by,
> One like Actaeon peeping through the grove,
> Shall by the angry goddess be transformed,
> And running in the likeness of an hart,
> By yelping hounds pulled down, and seem to die.
> Such things as these best please his majesty. (1.49–70)

Gaveston displays none of Richard III's contempt for this kind of display, a contempt typical of the warrior ethos of many historical plays, and these luxuriant theatrical displays are linked to wasteful

32. Shakespeare's play opens in court with Suffolk presenting the betrothed-by-proxy Margaret to the King in a scene foregrounding the linked political and dynastic nature of the marriage. By contrast, *3 Henry VI* opens on the battlefield with Richard of Gloucester carrying Somerset's severed head. Marlowe's play, at least to start, is in a quite different place.

kings like Richard II.[33] The speech marks a certain distance from other plays on history, which typically eschew positive descriptions of such displays, while at the same time presenting images of more properly "chivalric" ones. That none of these shows actually appear in the play is also characteristic of Marlowe's dramaturgy – Faustus' promises of great works also only appear as promises – and suggests that Gaveston and Edward's satisfactions lie mostly in the imagination.[34] The world of politics is alien to them, and Edward makes the same political errors repeatedly in the play. Instead of Gaveston's spectacles, the play gives the audience repeated glimpses at faction, at the aristocrats' disdain for the base-born Gaveston, and at a botched usurpation. The play sets up and then disappoints one set of expectations (for sylvan nymphs) while fulfilling another (seeing Edward II's fall), representing the same process in historiography, which – while it cannot give us the vasty fields of France – works on our imaginary forces and does give us a version of history. The actions of the rebellious barons participate in this sort of separation of expectation and result: their grievances are at least rhetorically rooted in a desire for good government, but mask other motives that are more akin in content and trajectory to Gaveston's than any of Mortimer's faction would want to admit.[35]

Characters in the play come recognize that their trajectories are tragic – displaying a degree of self-consciousness, if only too late – and their use of the vocabulary of tragedy is consistent with both stage tragedy and poems like Drayton's whose speakers consistently invoke "tragic muses." The vocabulary also represents a common way to emplot history as seen in the *de casibus* tradition. When Edward sees Lightborne in scene 24, he can read the meaning of his appearance: "These looks of thine can harbour nought but death. / I see my tragedy written in thy brows" (24.72–3). In the following scene, Isabella recognizes the turn to tragedy when her son enters knowing of his father's murder:

---

33. The barons do express disdain for the shows and weakness of Edward's military – especially Mortimer.
34. It is worth noting that such spectacles were at least possible on stage in the 1590s, making Gaveston's description an even more explicitly unfulfilled promise.
35. Mortimer's adulterous desire for the Queen is one example. The nobles' jealousy over the favorites is about as close to topicality as the play gets and may contribute to some of its printings in the seventeenth century.

> Ay, ay, but he tears his hair and wrings his hands,
> And vows to be revenged upon us both.
> Into the council chamber he is gone
> To crave the aid and succour of his peers.
> *Enter the King, with the LORDS*
> Ay me, see where he comes, and they with him.
> Now, Mortimer, begins our tragedy. (25.18–23)

In both scenes, Edward and Isabella recognize the onset of tragedy and associate it with the arrival of the figure who will enact it. The tragedy written in Lightborne's brow is personal, physical, and if not private, is concealed. The tragedy Isabella recognizes will take place in public.

Edward II conflates historical tragedy with domestic, dramatizing at one level the problems that attend on a king who confuses the private and the public. Whatever metaphoric links to questions about treason there are in *Arden of Faversham*, Arden's tragedy remains, more or less, within his household, Edward's necessarily involves the state. Even Edward's moment of recognition, if we can call it that, is couched in personal terms:

> The wren may strive against the lion's strength,
> But all in vain; so vainly do I strive
> To seek for mercy at a tyrant's hand.
> Immortal powers, that knows the painful cares
> That waits upon my poor distressed soul,
> O level all your looks upon these daring men,
> That wrongs their liege and sovereign, England's King.
> O Gaveston, it is for thee that I am wronged;
> For me, both thou and both the Spencers died,
> And for your sakes a thousand wrongs I'll take.
> The Spencers' ghosts, wherever they remain,
> Wish well to mine; then tush, for them I'll die. (22.34–45)

The speech invites comparison to Richard II's prison speeches in Shakespeare's later play, but this is a prison speech with a difference. The "cares" that wait on Edward's "distressed soul" are left unspecified but echo language from Thomas Lodge's classical history *The Wounds of Civil War*.[36] The lines in Lodge's play read:

> Immortall powers that know the painfull cares,
> That waight vpon my poore distressed hart,

---

36. Lodge's play is set during the wars between Marius and Sulla.

> O bend your browes and leuill all your looks
> Of dreadfull awe upon these daring men. (G4r)[37]

Antonius, an orator and opponent of the ascendant Marius, goes on to invoke divine inspiration for his speech as he reminds his murderers of the service his speeches have rendered to Rome. Like Clarence's words in *Richard III*, his speech all but persuades them not to kill him before a soldier enters and stabs him. The difference, of course, is that while Antonius' speech laments that he is to be killed only for serving Rome, Edward's version turns the explicitly public and political concerns to personal ones, and he sees his fate as related only to Gaveston and the Spencers. This distinction would have been clear to those familiar with Lodge's play. While Wiggins is right to point out that the play's concerns are political in his introduction to the New Mermaids edition of the play, for Edward, those concerns are almost always refracted through the lens of his personal life and affections. Marlowe's is a version of history that turns history personal – the King's affair with Gaveston explains his fall – and seems less interested in providing the kind of teaching that writers like Blundeville demand from history than in presenting Edward's tragedy, a tragedy that is secondarily a matter of state. The play conflates Edward's domestic tragedy with that of the kingdom because the characters do. When Edward III takes the throne at the close of the play, he orders Mortimer's execution and his mother's imprisonment in the Tower, acts that in effect banish the domestic from the play and demonstrate that he will be a far more politic monarch than his father.

In an important 1999 essay, Joan Parks discusses the play's distinctive deployment of fictional resources in its historical project, bringing together the play's dual engagement in drama and history. Parks discusses how Marlowe takes chronicle material and turns it into tragedy while at the same time recognizing how essential artifice is to history:

> Denying his own artifice while aggressively reworking the chronicle account in the elevated style of classical tragedy, Marlowe identifies artifice and fiction as fundamental principles governing not only the writing of history but also historical action itself. (290)

Her essay is more focused on the play's engagement with the historiographic tradition – its fictionalization of historical writing – and that

---

37. I cite from the copy reproduced in EEBO (STC 16678, printed by John Danter). The play was printed in 1594 but was first performed in around 1588.

approach complements my interest in the way the plays on historical subjects work in the other direction at the same time. The plays make fiction historical: they make the fiction lie like truth, rather than making the truth lie like fiction. Lying like truth is the equivocation of the theatre, and Macbeth's response to the coming-true of the Weird Sisters' prophecies seems appropriate here, not least because *Macbeth* is an historical fiction. The "fiend" of representation – prophecy, history, drama – produces belief but also demands questioning. In the following section, I turn to Shakespeare's *2 Henry IV*, which appears under the sign of Rumour – a figure whose words partake of an unstable and unknowable mixture of truth and lies like history itself.

III

> RUMOUR: ... not a man of them brings other news
> Than they have learn'd of me: from Rumour's tongues
> They bring smooth comforts false, worse than
> true wrongs.
>
> Shakespeare, *2 Henry IV*

2 Henry IV, like its immediate predecessor and like many of the history plays, is a play obsessively concerned with report. These reports take many forms and are of varying reliability, the one common feature being that they come on "many tongues" and are accessible to everyone. In this, as Rumour points out, report is like the theatre. Rumour offers a description of *2 Henry IV*'s intervention into the writing and representation of "history." Rumour's many tongues are the voices of history: many-voiced, contradictory, and in need of judgment.[38] When Rumour asks what need it has to anatomize itself before its "household," it seems to be referring specifically to the theatre in which the play is being performed. At the same time, that household includes the whole of the country since Rumour's reach extends to anywhere there are people. Rumour links history and theatre in explicit and implicit terms, and the play goes on to show the inevitability of this connection in the production of "history." The

---

38. Patterson's *Reading Holinshed's Chronicles* describes the chronicles as presenting an array of voices, accounts of events and so on, so that the reader can evaluate them. Turning the making of historical meaning over to the reader has many similarities to what happens in the theatre.

History, Fiction, Genre, Innovation   185

play, unlike *Edward II* or some of the more clearly tragic plays on history, does not promise a single story focused on a character's fate or even that of the Crown; instead, it is a tissue of smaller stories, only some of which function as "true" in the way that Renaissance historiography would recognize.

Scholars have long discussed reasons why the play has been less popular than *1 Henry IV*, and one reason commonly adduced for this different reception lies in differences in the two plays' representational strategies.[39] Where the first part saw nine quartos before 1642, *2 Henry IV* was only printed once in a stand-alone edition. Both parts were printed for Andrew Wise but were not entered in the *Stationer's Register* at the same time and were first printed together in the First and Second Folios.[40] The play's relative lack of popularity, at least in print, is somewhat surprising given the many editions of the first part and what appears to have been the popularity of Falstaff as a character. When Falstaff appears in *Merry Wives of Windsor*, it is in a setting not far off from the Gloucestershire scenes in *2 Henry IV*, and that play had two printed quartos before the First Folio and one after.[41] The play's peculiar structure – the title character and Prince Hal do not appear until relatively late – and its insistent focus on characters whose historical status is marginal help explain the play's critical and theatrical fortunes.

In the induction, Rumour introduces itself and, before turning to introducing the matter of the play, addresses the audience as its household:

But what need I thus
My well-known body to anatomize
Among my household? Why is Rumour here? (Ind. 20–2)

In the 2004 Shakespeare Theatre production of *2 Henry IV*, Rumour was represented – not by a single figure wearing a cloak covered

---

39. See James Bulman's introduction (1–16) to *King Henry IV, Part 2* (2016) for a discussion of the play's critical history. I cite this text hereafter unless I note otherwise.
40. *1 Henry IV* was entered on 25 February 1598 and printed for the first time in that year, but *2 Henry IV* was not entered until 23 August 1600 and appeared in print that same year. Why they were never printed together in a two-play collection remains an interesting question. *Henry V* was printed in three quartos before the First Folio – more than *2 Henry IV* but far less than *1 Henry IV*.
41. Falstaff is joined by Bardolph, Pistol, Nym and Mistress Quickly, all of whom cross over from the "historical" world of Eastcheap into a comic landscape.

in tongues, nor by a group of actors in stage – but by a group of actors seated at a long table who divided the speech among themselves in a strange kind of table conversation. Staging Rumour as a conversation made its project explicitly a social interaction and underscored ways that history, here if not everywhere, depends on both conversational transmission of stories and the sifting of those stories for truth content. Literally polyglot, Rumour thus became presenter and presented, a visibly present "wav'ring multitude," literalizing the position of self-address it speaks to in the lines cited above. Rumour speaks with many tongues, embodying the heteroglot nature of speech and of history. Full of conflicting accents, this figure is an icon for Bakhtin and Voloshinov's ideas about language. Rumour is here, of course, to introduce a play that spends far more time with report, reminiscence, and memory than actual action, but at the same time it is the wholly appropriate presenter for a play whose effect as history depends at least in part on its status as theatrical fiction.[42] Rumour's household, its addressee here, was comprised of the theatrical audience as well as the acting company acting as Rumour's tongues. In addition, Rumour's words circulate throughout the play's England:

> through the peasant towns
> Between that royal field of Shrewsbury
> And this worm-eaten hold of rotten stone,
> Where Hotspur's father, old Northumberland,
> Lies crafty-sick. The posts come tiring on,
> And not a man of them brings other news
> Than that they have learnt of me. (Ind. 33–8)

The household thus extends wherever speech extends, and Rumour's work infiltrates any effort at reporting events: all news comes through Rumour, true or not. The social and spatial inclusivity of Rumour and its household is striking here, ranging from royal field to peasant town to worm-eaten castle. At the same time, the speech continually alludes to the theatrical framework within which this particu-

---

42. Rumour's gender has been the subject of much debate in the critical history of the play; see Frederick Kiefer's "Rumor Fame and Slander in *2 Henry IV*," and Harry Berger's "Sneak's Noise or Rumor and Detextualization in *2 Henry IV*." Rumour's connection to Fama makes a female gender plausible at the same time that Rumour's general unreliability makes any particular identification difficult. I prefer the neuter pronoun to point to what seem to me its abstract and collective nature.

lar set of rumors is being communicated.⁴³ Loren Blinde argues that Rumour represents a "signal" of Shakespeare's engagement in questions of historiography. Specifically, "by embodying the conflict between narrative and display, Rumour transcends the split between aural and visual epistemologies in order for Shakespeare to argue that history is fundamentally imaginative" (35).⁴⁴ To take this a step further, Rumour, like the Chorus of *Henry V*, argues that history is also fundamentally theatrical.⁴⁵

Rumour opens the play commanding its audience to listen and then immediately asserts that that command is unnecessary because it cannot imagine any ears that would not open to its speech:

> Open your ears; for which of you will stop
> The vent of hearing when loud Rumour speaks?
> I, from the Orient to the drooping West,
> Making the wind my post-horse, still unfold
> The acts commenced on this ball of earth.
> Upon my tongues continual slanders ride,
> The which in every language I pronounce,
> Stuffing the ears of men with false reports. (Ind. 1–8)⁴⁶

A. R. Humphries's Arden edition of the play references John Dover Wilson's note to Rumour's unfolding "the acts commenced" as being in "the theatrical sense," and the whole of the speech engages with theatrical representation. When Rumour asks this opening question, it is assured of obedience not only because everyone listens to rumors but also because it is speaking as the prologue to a play whose audience has come to hear it. It can assume that it will get a hearing because it is in its house – the theatre. Theatre commands the hearing of its audience at the same time that it fills the ears of the audience

---

43. Rumour references the previous play's events and, as it describes Northumberland's castle as "worm-eaten," reminds us of the fate of Hotspur. It also reminds audience members of Northumberland's characterization in *1 Henry IV* as a politic figure even as it suggests a new reading of Northumberland's illness in *1 Henry IV*. Much of the speech makes such overt and covert allusion to either *1 Henry IV* or to theatre more generally.
44. Blinde's essay is very provocative, and the attention it gives to the role of imagination in history has been enormously helpful in my thinking about the role of theatrical allusion in the play.
45. Rumour is, however, both more confident than the *Henry V* chorus and less committed to a more or less unified narrative. Rumour's lies operate in the ears of the audience, in contrast to *Henry V*'s choric invocation of "imaginary forces" in the minds of its hearers.
46. I quote here from the Arden text edited by A. R. Humphries (1966).

with "continual slanders" and "false reports" – both descriptions of theatrical fiction.[47]

When Rumour describes its project here, it does not merely offer an account of its audience's desire for its reports; it delivers that description in language that derives from the drama it introduces, analogizing historical report with theatrical fiction.

> I speak of peace, while covert enmity
> Under the smile of safety wounds the world.
> And who but Rumour, who but only I,
> Make fearful musters, and prepared defence,
> Whiles the big year, swoll'n by some other grief,
> Is thought with child by the stern tyrant War?
> And no such matter. Rumour is a pipe
> Blown by surmises, Jealousy's conjectures. (Ind. 8–16)

Rumour speaks of deceitful smiles of safety that hide enmity, like those of Richard of Gloucester or any number of theatrical villains, and of the way imagined threats produce real reactions, like the responses that Hamlet will expect from his theatrical threat. Rumour's surmises, the suppositions of jealous or fearful imaginations, are thus the stuff of both theatre and history, and the play suggests that the effect of historical drama derives precisely from this combination. In this induction, Rumour mixes true and false report about the outcome of the Battle of Shrewsbury, mimicking the confused nature of historical report, which strives to sift fact from fiction but inevitably confuses them.[48]

Rumour runs before historical truth, carrying tales that Henry IV "hath beaten down young Hotspur and his troops," reporting this fact before returning to its office of noising the false story "abroad that Harry Monmouth fell / Under the wrath of noble Hotspur's rage" (Ind. 24, 29–30). The many-voiced nature of Rumour's reports resembles that of a theatre purporting to present "real" events but only ever produces a series of simulacra. Responding to this problem, the Chorus in *Henry V* explicitly addresses the failure of a theatre to

---

47. As one example, the change of name from Oldcastle to Falstaff derives from perceptions of slander, a slander retailed by the theatre that falsely reported him to be the fat knight dismissed in this play. Anti-theatre polemic uses these terms as well.
48. Blundeville, like other writers of *ars historica*, talks about this problem but has more faith in the sifting than Rumour does. Shakespeare repeatedly returns to scenes dramatizing the sifting of conflicting reports; *Hamlet* and *Othello* are only two well-known examples of this interest.

present adequately the events it strives to put forth. The inadequacy of the "wooden O" requires the imagination and forbearance of the audience to supplement the sketch offered by the action onstage. In *2 Henry IV*, Rumour seems unworried about this problem. Instead, it relies on what it suggests are the natural effects of rumor to fill in gaps and do the work of *Henry V*'s "imaginary forces."[49] The first scene of the play enacts this process as Northumberland sifts through the conflicting reports that come to him regarding the disaster at Shrewsbury. Asking Lord Bardolph for news, Northumberland shows the effect of Rumour's tongues:

> Every minute now
> Should be the father of some stratagem;
> The times are wild; contention, like a horse
> Full of high feeding, madly hath broke loose,
> And bears down before him. (1.1.7–11)

The times, like Rumour's post-horses, prompt wild ideas and stratagems based on the unsettled nature of events. "Contention," Northumberland says, bears down all before it in much the same manner that Rumour outpaces true report. As many critics have noticed, this speech and many others in the play show a deep awareness of time and its vicissitudes. In addition, the play suggests that Time, Rumour, and History are all linked and, moreover, that all three are inflected by the specifically theatrical mode that Rumour represents.

Later in the scene Northumberland makes the theatrical connections more explicit. When Morton enters, Northumberland addresses him saying "Yea, this man's brow, like to a title-leaf, / Foretells the nature of a tragic volume" (1.1.60–1), using the same kind of language as characters in *Edward II*.[50] He may also allude to Hieronimo's lamentations in one of the additional scenes in Kyd's *Spanish Tragedy* when he refers to Priam's hearing about Troy's burning:

> How doth my son and brother?
> Thou tremblest, and the whiteness in thy cheek
> Is apter than thy tongue to tell thy errand.

---

49. By conflating Rumour with the acting company, the 2004 production referenced above underscores this reliance.
50. This sort of language also links Northumberland to historical poetry like Drayton's, which makes use of the same imagery of writing for the stage.

> Even such a man, so faint, so spiritless,
> So dull, so dead in look, so woe-begone,
> Drew Priam's curtain in the dead of night,
> And would have told him half his Troy was burnt:
> But Priam found the fire ere he his tongue,
> And I my Percy's death ere thou report'st it.
> This thou wouldst say, "Your son did thus and thus;
> Your brother thus: so fought the noble Douglas"—
> Stopping my greedy ear with their bold deeds:
> But in the end, to stop my ear indeed,
> Thou hast a sigh to blow away this praise,
> Ending with "Brother, son, and all are dead." (1.1.67–81)[51]

The context of this scene in *The Spanish Tragedy* is suggestive here in terms of theatrical reference and indicating the usefulness of a specific variety of stage rhetoric in creating representations of grief. In the scene added to Kyd's play, Hieronimo is speaking to the painter, Bazardo, who also has a murdered son. As part of the conversation, Hieronimo asks if Bazardo can "draw a murderer" (Addition 4, 130). He goes on to imagine a painting of his entry in 2.5, quoting 2.5.4 and describing a possible staging of that scene. The likelihood that Shakespeare's scene refers to this scene seems to me to be strengthened by Northumberland's turn to the kind of ranting grief that is repeatedly displayed in *2 Henry IV* (and in similar sequence). In Addition 4, after Hieronimo refers to Priam, the Painter asks "is this the end?" – prompting Hieronimo to complain, "O no, there is no end: the end is death and madness!" (l. 159). When Northumberland shifts into a mode of loud lament that closes with a wish that "the rude scene may end" with darkness and death, he thus resembles both Hieronimo in the added scene and the Portuguese Viceroy. His "strained passion" (1.1.161), as Lord Bardolph calls it, is in the vein of a certain kind of theatre. While Lord Bardolph attempts to steer Northumberland away from what he thinks of as unproductive and self-indulgent "passion," this vocabulary nevertheless links Northumberland to the other mem-

---

51. The scene with the Painter appears in the 1602 quarto and was probably on the stage in early 1597. Humphries argues that the *Jeronimo* that Henslowe records as "ne" on January 7, 1597 was probably this version of Kyd's play ("renovated with editions" [11]). If we can accept that Northumberland's lines refer to *The Spanish Tragedy*, they suggest how Shakespeare draws on a distinct dramatic tradition in order to enhance the effect of his play and to characterize Northumberland by linking him to a tradition of rhetorical bombast (to which Hotspur is also connected).

bers of Rumour's Household, to whom I will turn in the next section.

Characters in the subplot belong to what Rumour calls "the blunt monster with uncounted heads, the still-discordant wavering multitude" that comprise its household. Pistol comes out of this multitude, and his speeches are built out of a particular mode of theatre that helps define the outlines of Rumour's household. The kind of history produced in the play likewise depends on the same kind of theatre. Specifically, a significant portion of Pistol's speech draws on the dramatic language of other playwrights, and while he is a fiction his career through the second tetralogy is tied to Shakespeare's historiographic project. Pistol is introduced as a "swaggerer" and enters speaking a language that lifts from the bombast of *Tamburlaine* and imitators of Marlowe's play. These are theatrical allusions, and they also refer to plays with ostensibly historical subjects. To take one example, in 2.4, Pistol speaks in a mixture of quotations from plays, familiar proverbial tags, and speeches from Eliot's *Ortho-epia Gallica* (1593):

> These be good humours indeed! Shall pack-horses,
> And hollow pamper'd jades of Asia,
> Which cannot go but thirty mile a day,
> Compare with Caesars and with Cannibals,
> And Troyant Greeks? Nay rather damn them with
> King Cerberus, and let the welkin roar. (2.4.160–5)

Beyond his reference to "humours," Pistol's whole speech is laden with dramatic allusion. When Pistol talks about "Caesar," "Cannibals," and "Troyant Greeks," he is making historical references that are at the same time theatrical. Pistol's misquotation of Marlowe's "pamper'd jades of Asia" passage – getting the mileage wrong – attempts to associate himself with Tamburlaine's grandeur and is in keeping with his *miles gloriosus* antecedents. *Tamburlaine*, though not generally acknowledged to be a "history play" in the way that *2 Henry IV* is, still offers a dramatic representation of putatively historical events.[52] Like Shakespeare's history plays, several of the other plays Pistol alludes to (Peele's *Battle of Alcazar*, and so on) equally retailed "history" to their audiences, offering a mixture of truth and fiction in much the same way as Rumour does.

---

52. See Kewes's "The Elizabethan History Play: A True Genre?" As part of her argument about the problematic boundaries of the "genre," she discusses a number of plays about "foreign" history, including several alluded to by Pistol.

Pistol's allusions also participate in the kind of "passionate" theatrical discourse deployed by figures like Northumberland when preemptively lamenting the death of his son in 1.1. Arguing with Doll Tearsheet, Pistol characteristically uses language far in excess of the concrete situation he is:

> To Pluto's damned lake, by this hand, to th'infernal deep, with Erebus and tortures vile also! Hold, hook and line, say I! Down, down, dogs! Down, faitors! Have we not Hiren here? (2.4.153–7)

Commentators have suggested many specific sources for the references here – from Peele's *Battle of Alcazar* to Kyd's *Spanish Tragedy* – but they all partake in what the Arden editor terms the "dramatic rant of the early 1590s" (73).[53] The plays Humphries sees Pistol referring to include Greene's *Alphonsus of Aragon* (1589, Q1594), Peele's *Battle of Alcazar* (1589?, Q1594), Kyd's *Spanish Tragedy*, *Locrine* (1594?, Q1595), and the lost *Turkish Mahomet and Hiren the Fair Greek* (1589?). Notably, most of these plays deal with historical or pseudohistorical events and deploy the tools of a more or less Marlovian dramaturgy. Pistol's irrepressible rant attests to the memorable nature of this stage language, and it is this quality of the speech that makes Pistol (and other Eastcheap figures) stand out, regardless of their lack of historical "reality." Humphries' "dramatic rant" is also the language of Northumberland's lamentation and, significantly, of the dead Hotspur in the early scenes of *1 Henry IV*. Rather than being restricted to the Eastcheap population, the stage rhetoric of these plays provides much of the language of Rumour's household, and its speakers are from across the whole spectrum of rank.[54]

As Giorgio Melchiori notes in his New Cambridge edition of the play, *2 Henry IV* participates at least tangentially in the comedy of humors most closely associated with Ben Jonson (18–19). The early title pages of both *1* and *2 Henry IV* describe the plays as containing "humours" (the "humourous conceits" of Falstaff alone in the 1598 quarto of *1 Henry IV* and the "humours" of Falstaff and "swaggering" Pistol in the *2 Henry IV* quarto of 1600). Scholars have long recognized the links to humors comedy and city comedy more generally, but we have less considered the relation of such comedy and

---

53. It is also worth considering how this speech resembles parodic versions of Hotspur's "drowned honor" speech in *1 Henry IV*, which itself has this kind of theatrical and literary antecedents.
54. If these speakers have anything in common, it is that they are marginal figures, either historically (being on the losing side) or socially.

such dramatic language to Rumour's household and to the kind of history Shakespeare's play is working to produce. The tavern scenes in both parts of *Henry IV* occupy a social space more akin to that of the later city comedy than the courts of princes or the battlefields where the plays of the first tetralogy tend to take place. Pistol's kinship to other *miles gloriosus* figures in plays like the roughly contemporary *Every Man in His Humour* seems clear, and he and Bobadill occupy a very similar social space – that of the tavern, the ordinary, and the street.[55] Jonson's Bobabill offers comic color and a certain kind of realism to both versions of *Every Man in His Humor*.[56] Pistol and other members of the fast-eroding tavern world perform a similar function in the *Henry IV* plays.

A final set of references and allusions to theatre demonstrate the pervasiveness of the language (and material) of Rumour. Shallow's household is populated by figures with various kinds of theatrical ancestry – whether from the morality tradition or, again, from what would come to be called city comedy. Falstaff calls Shallow a "Vice's dagger" when he describes Shallow's falsification of his personal history, and Shallow himself alludes to a previous career as an actor when he was a student at the Inns of Chancery. Even more specifically, Falstaff makes a joke that, while making immediate fun of Wart's ragged appearance, refers to the carpentry upon which the actors themselves stand: "the whole frame stands on pins" (3.2.143). Not only Wart's clothes but the whole edifice of the play stands on pins and, following Falstaff's joke, ought not be pressed too hard or made to serve too hard a purpose.[57] Allusions to the linguistic and physical fabric of the theatre are everywhere in the play and constantly call attention to the specifically theatrical kind of history the play presents to its audiences.

Like the tavern scenes in *1 Henry IV*, the London scenes and the Gloucestershire scenes serve as a kind of temporal or historical bridge between the imagined past of the play and the lived present of the audience. Their historical anachronisms – like the specific allusions to plays produced centuries later than the stage action – serve twin

---

55. I am not arguing for some kind of direct influence, tempting as it would be to do so, but to indicate that the representational work of characters like Pistol (or Falstaff) crosses genres.
56. This realism is of course clearer in the Folio *Every Man in His Humour*, but the plausibility of the play world in both versions depends to some extent on the presence of Bobadill (and his fellow gulls).
57. It appears that Falstaff passes over Wart in his recruitment drive: he has been "pricked" enough and won't bear any more.

representational agendas. First, they make the image of the past "lively," to quote Nashe, by evoking recognizable and vibrant figures to populate the past imagined in the play. Second, that same vibrancy carries over to other to characters whose representation is less free from the demands of historical accuracy, making them appear more real by association with the fiction. The lie of the representation – its anachronism and patent theatricality – thus both creates the impression of historicity that accounts for the plays' status as "history" and at the same time points to the necessary distance between the reality of the past and its representation.

V

> FALSTAFF: I do see the bottom of Justice Shallow. Lord, Lord, how subject we old men are to this vice of lying! This same starved justice hath done nothing but prate to me of the wildness of his youth and the feats he hath done about Turnbull Street and every third word a lie, duer paid to the hearer than the Turk's tribute.
>
> Shakespeare, *2 Henry IV*

Like city comedy, the tavern scenes and the Gloucester scenes offer an image of "everyday life" to the audience – an image conspicuously lacking in Shakespeare's other history plays – but the apparent realism of these scenes in both parts of the play is constantly undercut by their insistence on their status as fiction. Falstaff's statement that "every third word" of Shallow's tales of his youth is a "lie" at the end of 3.2 can just as easily apply to Falstaff himself (as he acknowledges) and to the play as a whole. "We old men" are subject to the vice of lying, audience members enjoy the consumption of these lies, and the theatre is in the business of generating them. Shallow's lies about his connections to John of Gaunt as well as his youthful amorous adventures (themselves as much Falstaff's manufacture as Shallow's) are rumors, rumors subject to assessment and revision, much as any of the rest of the events and information in the play. Even Falstaff's own status is in the border space between history and fiction. The epilogue to *2 Henry IV* evokes a desire for the next play and addresses the Falstaff-Oldcastle identification:

> One word more, I beseech you. If you be not too much cloyed with fat meat, our humble author will continue the story, with Sir John in it, and make you merry with fair Katharine of France: where, for any

thing I know, Falstaff shall die of a sweat, unless already a' be killed with your hard opinions; for Oldcastle died a martyr, and this is not the man. (Epil. 26–34)

Falstaff is here both identified with and distanced from Oldcastle – placing him both inside and outside of actual history since this seems like to have been delivered with a wink and a nudge. The story does continue, of course, but Falstaff is all but absent from *Henry V*; his actual reappearance is delayed until *Merry Wives*, and that play takes place in a fictive, comic world whose connection to the historical lies only in the characters it shares with *1* and *2 Henry IV*. Depending on the tavern and Gloucestershire scenes and on this epilogue to attest to its historicity, *2 Henry IV*'s presents history very much under the sign of Rumour.[58]

Both the tavern scenes and the Gloucestershire scenes develop a particular kind of historicity, one that depends on reminiscence, allusion, and the representation of what we might call daily life. At the same time, the play shows those reminiscences to be lies, the allusions are to bombastic and theatrically distorted versions of exotic history, and the figures who populate both locations find themselves increasingly marginalized as the play moves towards its end. The extra- or para- historical quality of figures like Pistol or Shallow includes them pretty unambiguously in Rumour's household, as they are fictions and retailers of fictions. At the same time, however, characters in the main and more ostensibly historical plot of the play use the same kind of theatrical language and, at times, offer the words of Rumour as truths. This shared vocabulary indicates that characters of high status (and who have "real" past existences) belong as much to Rumour's household as a figure like Pistol does. To answer Rumour's question from the prologue, Rumour is here because it is the proper presenter of a play that necessarily mingles the true and the false, the fictional and the real, the theatrical and the historical. As it tells us, "the posts come tiring on, / And not a man of them brings other news / Than they learnt of me" (Ind. 36–9). That news is history – the product of Rumour's household. The careful deployment of fiction to support the "reality" of the history presented in these plays is one of the central innovations of these plays and continues to be deployed in the later plays on historical subjects, to which I turn in the next chapter.

---

58. Critical associations of Falstaff with Rumour derive from a recognition of this tie. See, for example, David Bergeron's "Shakespeare Makes History: *2 Henry IV*."

Chapter 5

"What's aught but as 'tis valued": "History," Truth, and Fiction

Quha wait gif all yt Chaucer wrait was trew.
                      Robert Henryson, *The Testament of Cresseid*

Such as give
Their money out of hope they may believe
May here find truth, too.
                      Shakespeare and Fletcher, *Henry VIII* Prologue

Among the greater wants in our Ancient Authors are the wants of Art and Style, which, as they add to the lustre of the Works and Delights of the Reader, yet add they nothing to the Truth; which they so esteemed, as they seem to have regarded nothing else. For without Truth, Art and Style come into the Nature of Crimes by Imposture. It is the act of high Wisdom, and not of Eloquence only, to write the History of so great and noble a People as the *English*.
                      Edmund Bolton, *Hypercritica: or, A Rule of Judgement, for writing or reading our History's* (c. 1618)

Where the preceding chapter looked at the "history play" at its putative moment of emergence, this chapter examines "late" examples of historical drama – from after the "genre" had supposedly met its end and transformed into romance in Shakespeare and Fletcher's *Henry VIII*. From at least the publication of Ribner's *English History Play*, the "English History Play" has been closely – almost exclusively – associated with Shakespeare and especially with his plays of the 1590s. Ribner writes that "Following the accession of James I the history play passes into a period of rapid decline, with only a momentary rise at the very end of the great age of the English drama in the *Perkin Warbeck* of John Ford" (266).¹ Ribner offers a series of reasons for this decline – the rise of romance, that all the history had been staged, that the "history play" lost its didactic purpose somehow around 1600 and so on – but the existence of a whole range of historical plays contradicts the decline narrative; only reference to a restrictive notion of what counts as a "history play" sustains it.² Because of the dominance of the decline narrative, scholars typically describe the historical drama of the early seventeenth century as out of place, unusual, untypical, or not historical at all. In taking a range of "late" plays seriously as historical, this chapter is questioning traditional ideas about what constitutes a "history play."

Truth is, naturally, frequently associated with historical narratives. Many of the plays I will discuss in this chapter share an interest (marked in titles or choric introductions) in truth and knowledge. The epigraphs above (to which could be added many more) underscore this association and at the same time index concern about how doubtful the "truth" retailed in history actually is. Henryson's introductory lines to the *Testament of Cresseid* immediately raise doubts about Chaucer's veracity and about the testament that he himself is producing (or pretending to transcribe). Countering the truth-claim of the poem's title, Henryson thematizes the potential unreliability of "authoresit" narratives. The choric introduction of Shakespeare and Fletcher's *Henry VIII* finds truth in the belief of the play's audience and in the title's assertion that "all is true." Bolton's *Hypercritica* insists on truth as the most important aspect of history. Art and style might be desirable (and are, in his view, lacking in "our Ancient Authors," whose commitment to truth outweighed any interest in ornament) but only as "lustre" to their works and the delight of the reader. Bolton's clear line between Truth and what he describes as the pleasant, but unnecessary, adjuncts of style is consistently blurred in

1. As I noted in chapter four, this kind of thinking runs through much of the criticism on these plays. Ivo Kamps's *Historiography and Ideology in Stuart Drama* (1996) sees Ford's *Perkin Warbeck* (1633) as the last meaningful history play. Benjamin Griffin's *Playing the Past: Approaches to English Historical Drama, 1385–1600* (2001) is as committed to an early-seventeenth century end for the history as Ribner was in 1957.
2. The proliferation of explanations suggests a lack of certainty about any one of them. Together with the continued, if slower, production of new historical plays and the consistent popularity of historical drama in print, it is difficult to see anything like a definitive decline. The decline narrative owes a great deal to stories about Shakespeare's career that see him turning away from history after 1599.

early modern historical writing. Indeed, much of that writing and especially the staging of history is almost inevitably guilty of the "Crimes by Imposture" Bolton complains of above. Truth, fiction, art, style, authority: all come into play in the production of history whether staged, poetic, or presented in prose. This chapter turns to plays whose fictions insist on their historicity so that I can further pursue questions about genre and innovation often obscured in more narrowly construed accounts of the "history play."

This chapter begins with a discussion of Shakespeare's response to the Troy tradition before turning to a series of plays about the reign of Henry VIII either written or reissued around the time of the death of Prince Henry, and it concludes with readings of Middleton's *Hengist, King of Kent* and John Ford's *Perkin Warbeck*. *Troilus and Cressida,* while not as unambiguously historical as Shakespeare's plays on classical history, raises questions about genre and about historical representation from the very first words spoken on stage (whether those words belong to the Chorus or to Troilus). All of these plays in their various ways trade on the supposed truth of their subject matter, while at the same time many can and have raised doubts about that truth – even the plays themselves. If "All is true" in Shakespeare and Fletcher's *Henry VIII*, what kind of truth are we seeing? What is "strange" about the truth of John Ford's *Perkin Warbeck*? How is a play as distant from even a minimal adherence to historical sequence as Rowley's *When You See Me, You Know Me* to be considered a "chronicle history"? Old plays on history remained popular, and new plays on history were still being written and performed throughout the period, indicating continued interest in both history and historical drama.

I

Go, litel bok, go, litel myn tragedye
Ther God thi makere yet, er that he dye,
So sende myght to make in som comedye!
                    Geoffrey Chaucer, *Troilus and Criseyde*

Quha wait gif all yt Chaucer wrait was trew
Nor I wait nocht gif this narratioun
Be authoresit or fenyeit of the new
Be som Poeit, throw his Inventioun
Maid to report the Lamentatioun

And wofill end of this lustie Cresseid,
And what distress scho thoillit, and quahat deid.
                    Robert Henryson, *The Testament of Cresseid* (1593)[3]

As we well know, Troy serves as a mythic origin for Britain through Brutus, a descendant of Aeneas, who supposedly founds London as New Troy. This mythical version of English history links the English to the founders of Rome and served as a legitimating fiction for the authority of English crown, and claiming Trojan precedent was a common feature of legitimating narratives across Europe. As Sylvia Federico writes, "scores of European states and their rulers claimed Trojan precedent in efforts to achieve, consolidate, and maintain their power in relation to other states and often in relation to their own fractious constituencies" (xii). These precedents, were, as C. David Benson has argued in *The History of Troy in Middle English Literature* (1980), taken seriously as historical and the writing of the Troy story was in large part historiographic and directed towards these political and dynastic uses. Poems like *The Destruction of Troy*, *The Laud Troy Book*, and Lydgate's *Troy Book*, despite their different styles and programs, all treat the history of Troy as just that: a narrative of events that actually occurred and that need to be transmitted as accurately as possible to succeeding time.[4]

The Chaucerian version of the narrative, however, is far more skeptical about the story's meaning and use (and transmissibility). Lee Patterson argues that Chaucer's *Troilus* is deeply engaged in questioning the contradictory nature of writing history. "For Chaucer," he writes, "the story of Troilus and Criseyde was a definitive moment in the founding myth of Western history in the middle ages, the myth

---

3. In the 1598 Speght edition of Chaucer's works, the Scots of this passage is anglicized and reads: "Who wote if al that Chaucer wrate was trew / Nor I wote nat if this narracion / Be authorized, or forged of new / Of some Poete by his invencion /Made to report the lamentacion / And woful end of this lusty Creseide / And what distresse she was in or she deide" (fol. 164 v, Do ii v). Henryson's poem appears immediately after the end of the fifth book of the *Troilus*, without any signal of authorship.
4. Heather James's book *Shakespeare's Troy: Drama, Politics, and the Translation of Empire* (1999) offers a discussion of Shakespeare's response to the Troy tradition that has been influential in my thinking. Bevington's Arden edition of *Troilus and Cressida* discusses what he calls "a seeming vogue of plays on the subject around 1596–1601" (394), pointing to a play known as *Troy*, produced by Henslowe in 1596; a *Troilus and Cressida* written by Chettle and Dekker, which only survives as a damaged plot in Henslowe's papers; and Thomas Heywood's *1* and *2 Iron Age* (1612, printed 1632 by Nicholas Okes).

of Trojan origins. And as a poem of origins, the *Troilus* was by definition available to a meditation on the nature of history per se" (84). Patterson goes on to argue that as Chaucer proceeded with his "essay into the philosophy of history," he encountered a series of contradictions. These contradictions (between secular and religious history, between genres and others) lead him to produce a poem whose "deepest message is not about the failure of any particular historical moment but about the failure of history, and of historical understanding, per se" (163). This description of Chaucer's poem points towards the disposition towards history that Shakespeare develops in his play: historical figures cannot sustain the burden of meaning placed on them, pointing to the problematic nature of any narrative of origins.[5] Along similar lines, Sylvia Federico's book *New Troy* (2003) argues that the more celebratory version of this founding narrative gives way to a more troubled one that stresses the flawed nature of the Trojan founders of Britain in the late fourteenth and early fifteenth centuries, particularly at problematic moments in English history. The flaws and moral failings of Troy – not to mention actual fall of the city – become important as ways to explain contemporary contradictions, not necessarily to resolve them or to justify solutions. Both of these readings of medieval literature resonate with Shakespeare's own version of the Troy story, which presents the history of Troilus and Cressida in its own skeptical, morally unsure, and corrosive way.

Chaucer's address to his "little book," cited above, calls it a tragedy, but this naming only appears at the end of a very long poem that rarely is presented with such a label. In the beginning of the poem, Chaucer writes that he will not tell of the fall of the city because

> it were a long digression
> Fro my matere, and you to long to dwelle.
> But the Troian gestes, as they felle,
> In Omer, or Dares, or in Dite,
> Whoso that can may rede him as they write. (1.143–7)

Chaucer's "matere" may be more limited than that of Homer or Dares or Dictys, but he does not deny that he is writing on historical material, and, as commentators have shown, he goes out of his way to align his story with earlier versions of the Troilus and Criseyde narrative. His is a historiographic project but one that reads history as

---

5. See Charnes, *Notorious Identity*.

tragedy, not comedy or chronicle. Henryson's *Testament of Cresseid* opens with a description of a reading of Chaucer's poem that raises profound doubts about the veracity (and verifiability) of the events narrated in that poem – "quha wait gif all yt Chaucer wrait was trew" – and then raises doubts about the contents of the poem to come as well. As Henryson writes: "Nor I wait nocht gif this narratioun / Be authoresit or fenyeit of the new / Be som Poeit." History becomes a dubious project, one fraught with questions rather than sanctioned by authorities and whose use is hard to discern. Both Chaucer and Henryson take up the historical matter of Troy, but they present that matter in a more skeptical, questioning, and contradictory way than many of their immediate predecessors.[6]

For these writers, Troy was a highly productive narrative locus for thinking about history, the project of historical writing, and for experimentation with genre. It was also a privileged narrative of origins for England, giving it an imperial history predating that of Rome, one that English monarchs had been interested in at least since Chaucer's time. It was also a narrative of failure, of treasons (political, personal, ethical) that poets turned to at moments of crisis. If the eight plays of the Henriad in some ways respond to an actual or imaginary consolidation of Englishness under the Tudors, the uncertainty of the turn of the century and the prospect of an unsettled succession make the turn to Trojan material understandable in terms of both the logic of the field and Shakespeare's pattern of practice.[7] For all these reasons, it should be no surprise that Shakespeare might have considered it fit material for a play about a kind of history.

What happens if we take the Quarto title page of *Troilus and Cressida*'s designation of the play as a "history" seriously as a description of the play? Despite the efforts of historians and antiquarians to

6. Despite common readings and representations of Henryson's *Testament* as a kind of effort to produce closure and judgment for Cresseid, it is very hard for me to read the poem as doing anything nearly that simple. The poem seems to me to be doing something much more akin to Shakespeare's project in *Troilus and Cressida* than is often allowed. See Holly Crocker's "'As false as Cressid': Virtue Trouble from Chaucer to Shakespeare" for a discussion of the complexities that make it all but impossible to read Cressida's position in any kind of singular way.
7. If we accept a late date for the writing of *Troilus and Cressida*, then its composition was in the midst of the Essex Rebellion – a moment of crisis centering around traditional claims to legitimacy but an abortive one. In her book *New Troy*, Federico argues that Gower's turn to the Troy story is at least in part an effect of late fourteenth century crises of legitimacy and that this is case for other literary versions of the fall of Troy. Shakespeare may be no different.

relegate the Trojan origins of Britain to rumor or myth, stories about the Trojan War had a particular kind of historical interest for the English, and a retelling of this oft-told tale was necessarily part of an historical project, a project connected to an ongoing figuring and refiguring of Englishness. Chaucer's contemporaries clearly saw the Troy story this way – Lydgate's *Troy Book* was labeled as history – and Lee Patterson argues that Chaucer's Troy poem is itself an engagement in the philosophy of history.[8] Most of early printed texts of the *Troilus* do not give it a generic label, but Wynkyn de Worde's 1517 edition calls it "The Noble and Amerous ancyent history of Troylus and Cresyde in the time of the Syege of Troye." Despite the famous difficulties of assigning Shakespeare's play an appropriate generic label, "history" seems like a logical enough choice given the history of the source story's reception and its importance in thinking about England. In 1600, Shakespeare had recently finished an extended engagement with historical questions and with the origins of the current Tudor monarchy, and it should not be surprising that he would turn to another, earlier origin story – one as contradictory and difficult as that represented in the two Henriads.[9]

II

... our play
Leaps o'er the vaunt and firstlings of those broils,
Beginning in the middle; starting thence away,
To what may be digested in a play.
Like or find fault; do as your pleasures are;
Now good or bad, 'tis but the chance of war.

Shakespeare, *Troilus and Cressida* Prologue

This prologue, which only appears in the First Folio, locates the play in the generic territory of epic – "beginning in the middle," but only because that is what may be "digested in a play."[10] It demonstrates

8. I will return to Patterson's discussion below. The "history of Troy" is a recurrent topic in medieval poetry. Lydgate's poem was first printed in 1513 under the title *The Hystorye, sege, and dystruccyon of Troy*. A 1555 edition calls it *The auncient history and onely trewe and syncere chronicle of the warres betwixte the Grecians and the Troyans*.
9. Indeed, both *King Lear* and *Cymbeline* turn to the ancient history of Britain, albeit under different generic labels.
10. The Folio prints the play among the tragedies, though close to the histories in at

certain aspects of epic – a highly compressed version of an epic catalogue (the reference to the sixty and nine kings with their "crownets" and ships and the mini-ekphrasis on the gates of Troy) and an emphasis on war – but undercuts that epic invocation at almost every turn, sometimes in favor of theatrical reference, sometimes to reduce the scope of the epic. For example, the "quarrel," as many commentators have noted, is reduced to its most basic level – Helen "with wanton Paris sleeps" – bracketing claims of honor or duty or national offense in favor of the sexual. If we are watching epic (itself an odd project in the traditional economy of genres), we are watching epic of a singularly peculiar sort, one that all but forgoes the broils that are the chances of war in favor of narrating a failed love story and debases the larger epic story itself.[11] This prologue only appears in print in the Folio – neither early printing of the play has this introduction – and both quartos are presented as belonging to slightly different genres.

Both states of the Quarto describe the story of Troilus and Cressida as simple "history" (Qa) and "famous history" (Qb). Billing the play as a "history" locates the play in one theatrical mode, leaving the generic weirdness of the play to be discovered in the process of reading.[12] Labelling the play a "famous history" and stressing its excellence as comedy in Qb's publisher's preface points to the play's generic difficulties before a reading of the play properly begins, and those difficulties are only complicated by the play's appearance in the Folio, a text that stresses both questions of kind and the importance of reading. Because of these peculiarities, we can easily ask Troilus' question about Helen in the council scene about the play.

In both quarto editions of the play, *Troilus and Cressida* begins with Troilus unarming himself, exchanging the external struggle of the battlefield beyond the walls of Troy for what he terms the "cruel battle" he finds inside the city. He abandons the public and historical narrative of the play for one of private romance. Troilus depicts himself as weak, foolish, and "skilless" in comparison to the Greeks

least some copies. The copy digitized for EEBO (STC 22273 (Reel 774:11) from the Folger's collections) places *Troilus and Cressida* between *Henry VIII* and *Coriolanus* – right between the histories and the tragedies. Only the one quarto edition – in two states – was printed.

11. For a useful exploration of this question see David Hillman, "The Gastric Epic: *Troilus and Cressida*."
12. That the play presents itself for reading is also worth consideration: the play places itself in an unusual cultural location for a dramatic text, since many printed plays complain about being printed when they are meant to be spoken. It at least raises the question of use, of what the play is for.

who are "strong and skilful to their strength" (1.1.7–8). He strives to present this abandonment as a principled decision about the foolishness of the war, but he immediately turns back to his love for Cressida. Troilus goes on to characterize the back and forth between Pandarus, Cressida, and himself in mercantile terms before changing his mind again and joining Aeneas on the way out to the fighting. As Bevington's note indicates, "the young lover is mercurial of mood."[13] This introduction to a play, that in the terms of the later prologue is a kind of epic, represents a protagonist who seems, at least momentarily, uninterested in that epic conflict. Troilus rhetorically abandons the war as a "starved argument" and presents himself rather as a lover but a lover whose love (here and elsewhere) is likewise starved.[14] The first scene sets a pattern for a play which consistently baffles expectations of a play about the Trojan War or even about the familiar story of Troilus and Cressida.[15]

Troilus also shares some of the characteristics of late sixteenth and early seventeenth century satirical comedy, which question values and forms while still working within them. Thersites' snarling voice marks a way that the play stakes out a position in the dramatic field: signaling an investment in satirical drama, deploying the resources of satire in the midst of an epic narrative, and, at least potentially, engaging in the Poetomachia. Read as a kind of conclusion to Shakespeare's work on English history (projecting that history back to its earliest reaches), the play serves as a thorough evacuation of the kinds of legitimating narratives deployed in the more readily recognizable "history" plays.

Shakespeare's play ends with no real conclusion: it presents neither the end of the lovers' stories nor the war – and instead ends with Pandarus and his bequest of disease. The final speech, more importantly, specifically locates its target as the contemporary audience. The reference to Winchester geese places the play clearly in Southwark – moving it at the end from the source of London to its latter-day successor – and refuses to present any kind of closing comment on the action of the play beyond the suggestion that the diseases of Troy are to be visited on London. It would be hard to

13. Note to 1.1.111–12.
14. Troilus' pre-assignation speech, which likens the threshold of Cressida's house to the River Styx, added to his fears of the effects the actual encounter might have on him indicate that his love for Cressida is problematic from the start. In addition, neither of them discusses any specific future for their relationship, certainly not marriage.
15. I discuss this aspect of the play more fully in chapters one and two.

imagine Pandarus (or any other character) coming onstage to talk about how the survivors of Troy go on to found great European empires, but the absence of any kind of summation is striking. In this, the play is not only akin to *Hamlet*, which ends with a deeply problematic offer of an explanation of the events of the play, but also to the end of *Henry V*. That play does close with triumph, but, as the Chorus reminds the audience, it is a short-lived triumph and one that leads to the loss of France and the bleeding of England.[16] *Henry V* offers an historical narrative that acknowledges failure and signals that even triumphant moments can be tainted by succeeding disaster. These plays offer a refracted and refractory kind of historical narrative – troubled by conflicting report, by failure, by fiction. The compromised national history in *Henry V* (which contrasts starkly with the Bastard's patriotic speech at the close of *King John*) resonates with the compromised epic history in *Troilus and Cressida*.

To think about *Troilus and Cressida* as a history, then, allows it to be placed in relation to other history plays, plays that develop an ambivalent and doubtful disposition towards history. This ambivalence is consistent with versions of the story that appear in Shakespeare's sources and with the increasingly skeptical disposition towards the authority of narrative Shakespeare develops in the later tragedies and romances.[17] If Chaucer's poem is, in Lee Patterson's terms, an essay in the philosophy of history that represents the "failure of history and historical understanding," Shakespeare's play is working in the same tradition, and his play presents a similar narrative of failure and loss.[18] The case of *Troilus and Cressida* points to the arbitrary nature of the designation "history play" and shows how the traditional definition, based on a more or less narrowly defined idea of content, fails to describe the range of early modern plays on "historical" subjects.

---

16. Interestingly, the chorus in *Henry V* refers to the author's "all-unable" pen – the same lacking in confidence pen referred to in the Folio prologue to *Troilus*. The doubt expressed about representational adequacy runs through a number of Shakespeare's plays, not just those concerned with history.
17. I take up the specific legacy of romance and medieval narrative in chapter two, where *Troilus and Cressida* serves as a different kind of generic and narrative resource.
18. Failure and loss run through dramatic romance as well.

III

When Shakespeare and Fletcher's *All Is True* (aka *Henry VIII*) appeared on stage in 1613, it joined a number of recent plays about Tudor monarchs. W. S.'s *The True Chronicle History of the whole life and death of Thomas Lord Cromwell* (1600, Q1602, 1613), Thomas Dekker and John Webster's *Famous History of Sir Thomas Wyatt* (1602, Q1607 and 1612), Samuel Rowley's *When You See Me, You Know Me* (1604, Q1605 and 1613), Thomas Heywood's *The First Part of If You Know Not Me, You Know Nobody* (1604, Q1606, 1608, 1610, 1613), and *The Second Part of If You Know Not Me, You Know Nobody* (1605, Q1606, 1609) all stage aspects of the history of Tudor monarchs.[19] Elizabeth I only appeared on stage after her death, but even before 1603 there appears to have been interest in stage representation of this period of English history. This flurry of plays also belies arguments that the "history play" was in decline – debates about the relative quality of these works aside – and if they tend towards what we have come to call romance, that attests to writers' responsive reactions to shifts in the dramatic field (and bears a suggestive resemblance to the tragic form of a good many of the historical plays of the 1590s). All of them were reprinted around the same time that Shakespeare and Fletcher's *Henry VIII* was written and performed, further indicating an interest in this historical.

In his 1997 essay "What is the English History Play and Why are They Saying Such Terrible Things About It," Stephen Longstaffe argues Shakespeare's plays about English history have been taken to be exemplary instances of the "history play," and because of this collapse scholars have seen the historical drama written by his contemporaries more as deviations from or lesser versions of that Shakespearean norm. Writing about Robert Ornstein's *A Kingdom for a Stage*, Longstaffe says that Ornstein

> produces a literary history in which the genre depends upon the Bard, who is paradoxically constitutive of it, and transgressive of its (artistic) norms ... He also resembles the traditional picture of Marlowe, setting the pace for the London theatres by developing new kinds of possibly subversive theatricality, creating a whole genre, influencing, but never influenced. (par. 11)

---

19. I have noted editions up to 1613, but most of these plays had post-1613 printings as well. The two parts of *If You Know Not Me, You Know Nobody* were reprinted the most often of all these plays: a total of twelve editions of the two plays (eight of part one and four of part two).

In Longstaffe's view, with few exceptions this habit of thought has produced a body of scholarship on Shakespeare that has a difficult time discerning "the political and historiographical complexity of these histories" (par. 13). Though written in 1997, Longstaffe's description of the field is still more true than not, and this chapter turns towards historical drama in the early seventeenth century attending to both kinds of complexity to illuminate Shakespeare and Fletcher's project in *Henry VIII*.[20]

The first of these putatively late plays, *The True Chronicle History of the whole life and death of Thomas Lord Cromwell*, follows Cromwell from his youth to his death, tracking his career from obscurity to high office.[21] The play opens with Cromwell speaking, Faustus-like, of his frustrated ambition and love of learning:

> Good morrow morne, I doe salute thy brightnesse,
> The night seems tedious to my troubled soule:
> Whose black obscurity binds in my minde
> A thousand sundry cogitations:
> And now Aurora with a lively dye,
> Adds comfort to my spirit that mounts on high.
> Too high indeede, my state being so mean:
> My study like a minerall of gold,
> Makes my hart proude wherein my hope's inrowled,
> My books is all the wealth I doe possesse,
> And unto them I have ingaged my heart,
> O learning how devine thou seemes to me:
> Within whose armes is all felicity? (A2r-v)

Cromwell laments the limits placed on him by birth – his mounting spirit is aiming too high for his mean state – and sees learning as a consolation for those limitations. His melancholic night-thoughts as much as the brighter ones that come with the dawn express a feeling of oppression that would fit a scheming Machiavel. They

---

20. The whole idea of these seventeenth century plays as "late" depends on taking Shakespeare's plays of the 1590s as paradigmatic. A play like *When You See Me, You Know Me* is only "late" because it was produced after, say, *Henry V*.
21. The title pages of the two editions of the play link it to Shakespeare's company: the 1602 quarto states that the play was performed by the Lord Chamberlain's Men, and the 1613 edition names the King's Men. This linkage, in addition to the W. S. ascription, led to scholars attributing the play to Shakespeare. Both editions are well-printed (though the 1602 edition in the Folger's collection is incomplete), and the 1613 text gains more in the way of printer's ornaments. Thomas Drayton wrote an historical poem about Cromwell's fate in much the same vein as his poems about Gaveston and Mortimer.

speak to the kind of ambitions that run through Marlowe's plays, and Cromwell's exchanges with his father (and his career) underscore this common ground. Likewise, the young Cromwell's conflicts with his father echo struggles typical of the citizen comedies of playwrights like Thomas Dekker. For example, having been interrupted in his study by the sound of the smiths working in his father's shop, Cromwell offers to pay them not to work, and this "thriftlessness" angers Cromwell's father. Old Cromwell has put Thomas to school so that he might support his father in his age but now regrets it and wishes that Thomas had been bound "to some honest trade" which would have made him thrifty and hard-working (A3r). Like Marlowe's Faustus and other mounting spirits, the play's Cromwell puts his hopes in learning. His language echoes that of Marlowe's overreachers, and from the Faustus-like words of his first speech he jumps to Tamburlaine after being confronted by his father.

After a brief and acrimonious exchange with his father, Cromwell plans to leave the study behind:

> Why should my birth keepe downe my mounting spirit?
> Are not all creatures subject unto time?
> To time, who doth abuse the world,
> And filles it full of hodge-podge bastardy,
> There's legions now of beggars on the earth,
> That their original did spring from Kings:
> And many Monarkes now whose fathers were,
> The riffe-raffe of their age: for time and Fortune
> Weares out a noble traine to beggery,
> And from the dunghill minions doe advance,
> To state: and marke in this admiring world,
> This is but course, which in the name of Fate
> Is seene as often as it whirles about:
> The River Thames that by our doore doth passe,
> His first beginning is but small and shallow:
> Yet keeping on his course, growes to a sea.
> And likewise Wolsay, the wonder of our age,
> His birth as mean as mine, a Butchers sonne,
> Now who within this land a greater man?
> Then Cromwell cheere thee up, and tell thy soule,
> That thou maist live to flourish and controule. (A3r-v)

Cromwell aspires to "flourish and controule," citing as precedent the many kings whose fathers were "the riffe-raffe of their age" and, more appropriately given his future in King Henry's government, Cardinal Wolsey, the butcher's son. The speech has clear echoes of

Tamburlaine's "earthly crown" speech, if it follows a slower method, and Cromwell's mounting spirit finds a path to high position. Rather than switching shepherd's weeds for armor, Cromwell takes a position in a merchant house in Antwerp and, after a chorus conveys him and the audience across the Channel, next appears doing accounts in his Belgian study, averring that "It is not this same trash that I regard, / Experience is the jewell of my hart" (A4r). The "experience" that is his jewel leads him to a series of adventures in Europe before he returns to England and service to Wolsey and the Crown.[22] Moments like these transpose Marlovian aspiration to bureaucratic and administrative pursuits, and the play uses the tropes and rhetoric of Marlowe's plays to produce a "famous chronicle" about this bureaucrat.

The play's chorus, which appears part of the way into the action, links it to the current theatrical field. In its three appearances, the Chorus offers explanations of time lapses and of travel as a solution to the temporal problem of representing the whole life of Thomas Cromwell. It resembles the Chorus in Shakespeare's *Henry V* in enlisting the audience's imagination in moving through time and space. For example, after Cromwell departs the Low Countries for some adventures in Italy, the second chorus tells us about Cromwell's Italian sojourn, his visit to Spain, and his eventual return to England. Summing them up, the Chorus tells us:

> Now let your thoughts as swift as is the winde,
> Skip some few years, that Cromwell spend in travell,
> And now imagine him to be in England:
> Servant unto the Master of the Roules,
> Where in short time he there beganne to flourish,
> An hour shall show you what few years did cherish. (D1v–D2r)

Having rescued Bedford, Cromwell continues his tour of Europe seeking the experience he anticipates while in Antwerp, and the chorus tells us to let our "thoughts as swift as is the winde, / Skip some few years" so that we can see him begin his administrative career working for Wolsey and surviving his fall. Like Shakespeare's *Henry V*,

---

22. Cromwell and his servant Hodge have adventures in Italy, including the rescue of the Earl of Bedford from captivity and the threat of death by having the earl change clothes with Hodge and escape in company with a disguised Cromwell. Hodge – like Christopher Sly – enjoys the pretense and is set free by the Italians. Bedford, interestingly, talks about fighting in France using imagery that resembles some of the *Henry VI* plays, but there is no warfare in the play.

the speech stresses the temporal compression necessary to the play. Wolsey appears only briefly and the chorus apologizes for this, arguing that the play is more about Cromwell's death than Wolsey's:

> Now Cromwell's highest fortunes doth begin,
> Wolsay that lov'd him as he did his life,
> Committed all his treasure to his hands,
> Wolsey is dead, and Gardiner his man,
> Is now created Bishop of Winchester:
> Pardon if we omit all Wolsayes life,
> Because our play depends on Cromwells death,
> Now sit and see his highest state of all;
> His height of rysing: and his sodaine fall,
> Pardon the errors is all ready past,
> And live in hope that the best doth come at last:
> And looke to have your liking ere the end. (D3v)

Asking pardon for the omission of "all Wolsey's life," the Chorus directs the audience's attention to Cromwell's death. The audience is asked to excuse the errors in what has gone before and to hope that the best comes at the end, which appears to be a reference to Cromwell's death. The playwright keeps the focus on Cromwell – even to the extent of keeping the King entirely off stage – and the end of the play transitions into a bureaucratic version of *de casibus* tragedy.[23]

Thomas, Lord Cromwell's reluctance to put a Tudor monarch on stage is not shared by others among this cohort of plays. All the other plays listed above present Tudor kings and queens; even Dekker and Webster's *History of Sir Thomas Wyatt*, while it keeps Elizabeth off the stage, makes Mary I and Philip characters as well as Lady Jane Grey. The 1607 edition of the play was printed by Edward Allde for Thomas Archer, and Q2 (1612) was printed by Nicholas Okes for Archer. The play presents Lady Jane and her husband Guildford as sympathetic figures who are victims of parental ambition. Wyatt repeatedly refers to the memory of Henry VIII, invoking him as representing a lost golden age, and uses his memory to argue against, for example, Mary's desire to marry Philip of Spain. The play's action covers the period surrounding Edward VI's death and Mary I's succession to the throne and places Sir Thomas Wyatt the Younger at

---

23. As discussed below, Shakespeare and Fletcher's *Henry VIII* takes almost the opposite tack, placing both King and Cardinal on stage and limiting Cromwell's stage time.

the center of the action. In the play, Wyatt frames both his advocacy for Mary's succession rather than Jane Grey and his rebellion against Mary as acts of loyalty to England and to Henry VIII's will. In the early going, Wyatt confronts Northumberland and Suffolk who argue against Mary, who he calls rebels, lamenting the change since "Noble Henries daies":

> You have set your hands unto a will.
> A will you well may call it:
> So wils Northumberland:
> So wils great Suffolke. (A2v)[24]

Later in the play, Wyatt uses the same kind of argument to rationalize his own rebellion against Mary. Regarding Mary's marriage, he argues in favor of Henry VIII's desires – who had banned Spaniards from the land – and remains constant in his loyalty to his version of Henry's memory. He introduces his rising in terms of loyalty to England:

> O who so forward Wyat as thy selfe,
> To raise this troublesome Queene in this her Throane?
> Philip is a Spaniard, a proud Nation,
> Whome naturally our Countrie men abhorre.
> Assist me gratious heavens, and you shall see
> What hate I beare unto their slaverie.
> Ile into Kent, there muster up my friendes,
> To save this Countrie, and this Realme defend. (D2r)

The play offers a fairly straightforward chronicle of the succession, sentimentalizes the deaths of Jane Grey and her husband, and seems more concerned with Philip being a Spaniard than with his (and Mary's) Catholic faith.

As in many of these plays, Dekker and Webster have characters refer to their own fates in theatrical terms. When Jane and Guilford are in the Tower, they look out through their barred window to see a crowd gathering. Jane says:

---

24. Thomas Dekker and John Webster. *The Famous History of Sir Thomas Wyat. With the Coronation of Queen Mary, and the coming in of King Philip. As was plaied by the Queens Maiesties Servants.* London, printed by E[dward] A[llde] for Thomas Archer and are to be solde at his shop in the Popes-Head Pallace, nere the Royall Exchange. 1607. STC 6537.

> Out of this firme grate, you may perceive the Tower Hill
> Thronged with store of people,
> As if they gap'd for some strange Noveltie. (D2r)

In Jane's eyes, the crowd appears to be waiting for some kind of show, a novel kind of performance, and Guilford chimes in about how the crowd looks ready for a tragedy:

> And see you how the people stand in heapes,
> Each man sad, looking on his aposed object,
> As if a general passion possest them?
> Their eyes doe seeme, as dropping as the Moone,
> As if prepared for a Tragedie.
> For never swarmes of people there doe tread,
> But to rob life, and to inrich the dead,
> And shewe they wept. (D3r)

The play assimilates the historical spectacle of executions on Tower Hill to those of tragic drama. Like audiences at a play, the throng comes both to "rob life" by witnessing the execution and to "inrich the dead" with tears. They will also be able to "shewe they wept," claiming the distinction of being in the audience. When Jane and Guilford are finally taken to be executed, Guilford greets Winchester and Arundel as witnesses come to see "the blacke conclusion of our Tragedie" (F4v). Responding to Winchester's excusing them as merely doing their "office," Guilford stresses the roles played:

> Our office is to die, yours to looke on:
> We are beholding unto such beholders
> . . .
> Our office is to die, yours but to gaze. (F4v)

As in many other history plays, characters point to the theatricality of history itself as part of dramatic representation.

Wyatt's final speech alludes to a variety of earlier plays, echoing the kind of lament fallen leaders make in other historical drama as well as, more strangely, Titus' encomium of the tomb in *Titus Andronicus*:

> The sad aspect, this prison doth afford,
> Jumpes with the measure that my heart doth keepe:
> And this inclosure here, of naught but stone,
> Yeildes far more comfort then the stony hearts
> Of them that wrong'd their country, and their friend
> Heere is no periur'd Counsellors to sweare

> A sacred oath, and then forsweare the same,
> No innovators heere, doth harbor keepe,
> A stedfast silence, doth possesse the place,
> In this the Tower is noble being base. (F3r)

The Tower takes the place of the repose-filled and safe cell of Titus' family tomb – a place of "stedfast silence" empty of "periur'd Counsellors" and "innovators" – and is noble even if a prison. The repurposing of this motif bears a suggestive resemblance to the way that Marlowe adapts a speech from Lodge's *Wounds of Civil War* in *Edward II* (see the preceding chapter). It serves as a sign of Heywood's responsive reaction to earlier dramatic utterances. The layering of back-reference makes the speech seem familiar, which contributes to the play's aura of historicity. The history of the fiction helps produce the fiction of history. Dekker and Webster, like other writers of plays about history, make use of the current resources of the theatre both as tools of representation and as means of appealing to their audiences. If there are "innovators heere" in the Tower, they are the playwrights who have taken up this narrative and staged it in tragic form.

Thomas Heywood's two-part play *If You Know Not Me, You Know Nobody* (1604 and 1605) focuses on "the troubles of" Elizabeth in the first part before shifting its attention to Sir Thomas Gresham and the Royal Exchange in part two. Part one opens with a reference to Wyatt's rebellion and the deaths of Lady Jane, Guilford, and Wyatt, placing it as a kind of sequel to Dekker and Webster's play, but it quickly turns to portraying Elizabeth's persecution by agents of Queen Mary. Scholars have granted the second part more critical attention, largely because of the way that the play focuses on the city and especially on Gresham and commercial activity. The second part's affinity with citizen comedy appears to have obscured the first part's engagement with the group of historical plays around the turn of the century.

Part one, or "The Troubles of Queen Elizabeth," opens with Queen Mary ordering the punishment of Dodds, representing a group of "Suffolke men" who had been promised that they could "still enjoy [their] consciences, and use that faith / Which in king Edwards daies was held Canonicall" (A3r-v). The Cardinal of Winchester presents the petition as insolent and seditious because it would "tye [Mary] to conditions, and set lymits to [her] liking" (A3v). The play depicts Mary as disregarding her promise and assenting to Dodd's punishment, acting as the tyrant her sister Elizabeth later names her (if only in a soliloquy). Heywood has Sir Henry Beningfield [sic] take this opportunity to slander Elizabeth, which begins the "troubles" of the play's subtitle. Heywood follows Foxe's characterization of the historical Sir Henry Bedingfield as a villainous figure who, along with many others, persecutes Elizabeth throughout the play.[25] Elizabeth is summoned to court, despite being ill; is imprisoned in the Tower, forced to enter by the Traitors' Steps; and is generally ill-treated. As a result, the play presents Elizabeth consistently as an almost-martyr to her sister's zealotry and tyranny, making her forgiveness of the cruel Constable and her jailer Beningfield himself at the end of play an exemplary act of clemency and justice. The play consistently foregrounds religion as the crucial driver of the plot and, if it doesn't make actual theological arguments, presents a Foxean version of history.[26] This emphasis is in strong contrast to Dekker and Webster's play on Wyatt and to W. S.'s Cromwell play, in which religion figures very little.

Of these plays on Tudor history, scholars have perhaps discussed most Samuel Rowley's *When You See Me, You Know Me* (Q1 1605, Q2 1613) because it puts Henry on the stage and because the prologue to Shakespeare and Fletcher's *Henry VIII* seems to respond directly to the comic business on Rowley's play.[27] Rowley plays off the title of Heywood's play and puts Henry into a series of dramatic contexts familiar to audiences in the first years of the seventeenth century.[28] In Ribner's view, "Rowley's play is one of the last plays to carry on the dramatic traditions of the serious historical drama and it thus deserves an important place in any consideration of the subject" (283). This claim is an odd one for Ribner to make given the play's very loose commitment to the constraints of actual historical sequence and its exceedingly episodic structure, not to mention the comic business that seemed important to Shakespeare and Fletcher's response to the play. Rowley's play begins in 1537 with the birth of Prince Edward and the death of Jane Seymour, but it stages events

---

25. Foxe's account seems to distort the historical Bedingfield's conduct which appears to have been not much like what we see in the play.
26. Perhaps complicating the picture, in part one Philip consistently tries to moderate Mary's behavior towards her sister. The Spanish threat is far clearer in part two since it presents the defeat of the Armada.
27. The play appeared under the auspices of the Prince of Wales' Men (noted in all the early editions) and was printed for Nathaniel Butter by an array of printers from 1605 to 1632. Rowley is identified as "servant to the Prince," underscoring the play's connections to Prince Henry.
28. The King has a disguised-prince adventure that results in his being arrested for street brawling and sent to the Counter.

that occurred as early as 1514 and contains characters like Wolsey, who had been dead many years by that date. The end of the play shows the beginnings of Wolsey's fall and a wholly unhistorical meeting between Prince Edward and the Holy Roman Emperor. The play does not offer anything like even the kind of revised narratives typical of Shakespeare's historical plays, and it seems very deliberate in calling attention to its loose connection to the historical sequence of events. For example, in the wake of Prince Edward's birth and Jane Seymour's death, Wolsey talks with Gardiner about how he got Anne Boleyn executed as a way to protect England from Lutheranism:

> GARD. You saw how soone his Maiestie was wonne,
>   To scorne the Pope, and Romes religion,
>   When Queene Anne Bullen wore the diadem.
> WOOL. Gardner tis true, so was the rumor spread:
>   But Woolsie wrought such meanes she lost her head,
>   Tush feare not thou whilst Harries life doth stand,
> Hee shall be King, but we will rule the land. (C1r)

Speaking in the play's 1537, Wolsey describes his role in events that took place in 1536 – six years after his own death in 1530. Either Rowley expected his audience to ignore the impossibility of this sequence of events or, which seems unlikely, to be ignorant of it. Many other examples of this kind of deliberate violation of sequence occur in the play, making Rowley's disinterest in historical accuracy impossible to overlook.[29]

In service of both a political and representational agenda, Rowley's play stages a history that disregards dates and calls attention to how it brings characters back from the dead so they can interact with figures they could not have met. Teresa Grant argues that Rowley's "handling of history in *When You See Me* is an act with specific political purposes" linked to the accession of James, particularly to hopes that the Reformation "will be more thoroughgoing under James I" (148). The play manipulates the linear time of the stage to cover over the impossibilities of its sequence of events, and this strange temporality bears on both the staging of history and on

---

29. This loose to nonexistent connection to time extends throughout the whole of the play. Will Summers is said to be with "Doctor Skelton" (who died in 1529), the play puts Lady Mary's 1515 secret marriage with Charles Brandon on stage after the birth of Prince Edward, and Bonner and Gardiner blame Katherine Parr for the Dissolution of the Monasteries, which began well before she becomes Queen in 1543.

historicity more generally. The play puts chronology in service of a particular kind of political truth, and its representation of the past comments on the present moment. While Shakespeare and Fletcher's *Henry VIII* attends to the details of the historical record more carefully than Rowley does, Shakespeare also shapes the historical narrative to serve his particular purposes. As the Gordon McMullan notes in his Arden edition, where Rowley's play centers on Edward's birth and "vertous life," *Henry VIII* focuses on Elizabeth and is concerned to represent Elizabeth as the authorizing figure for the England to come that is described in Cranmer's prophecy.[30] This centering on Elizabeth works partly to secure the accuracy of his "prophecy" – because it reflects the actual history it predicts – and hedges dynastic claims in the wake of Prince Henry's death.

Shakespeare and Fletcher's collaborative historical drama has a complicated place in the scholarship about the "history play." Its deployment of pageant-like dream visions, elements reminiscent of tragicomedy, tonal and structural links to what we've come to call dramatic romance, as well as its date of composition have all contributed to critics' distancing the play from other historical drama. To take a seminal example, Ribner argues that *Henry VIII* fails "to embody an overall consistent philosophical scheme such as makes cohesive unities out of all of Shakespeare's earlier histories, including *King John*" (288). Ribner's idea that that the "history play" requires a unifying philosophical scheme or, better, philosophy of history works to exclude a whole range of plays.[31] Ribner's argument that *Henry VIII* is not really a history play runs strangely counter to his argument that Shakespeare "follows his sources with a greater fidelity than he had ever before observed in an English history play, but with a strange unawareness of the basic inconsistencies within his sources" (289).[32] Aside from it being difficult to see precisely what he means by this unawareness, the play's use of inconsistent sources is consistent with earlier plays and Shakespeare's willingness to alter events

30. Edward's absence makes historical sense, since Elizabeth was born before him, but Cranmer's prophecy wholly ignores both Edward and Mary. Mary is not named in the play at all. Instead, Cranmer hints at James and his legacy.
31. See chapter nine of *The English History Play*, "The History Play in Decline," for an extended discussion of how these plays are either signs of a decline or that they are not "history plays." He seems particularly exercised by the introduction of romance materials into the "serious" history play. For Ribner, "romance history" is not history at all.
32. For Ribner, the "history play" is essentially moribund as a genre by the time *Henry VIII* appears, and Ford's much later play only proves this.

for dramatic effect. It also can be argued to participate in the kind of historical writing that Annabel Patterson describes as typical of Holinshed – a mode where accounts are presented to the judgment of the reader/audience – and of the chronicle tradition more generally.[33]

When Shakespeare and Fletcher came to write *Henry VIII* or *All Is True* in 1613, they entered a field rich in representations of Tudor monarchs. The play sets out quite deliberately to distinguish itself from the others – especially those reprinted between 1611 and 1613 –but those claims for distinctiveness at the same time depend on tying it to earlier historical drama. That such claims are more or less conventional is true, and the Prologue's claims for the value of the play are likewise traditional, but the specifics of the prologue's tactics give insight into the play's efforts at defining the field. In a position-taking tied to the immediate conditions of the theatrical field, the playwrights stake a claim to seriousness, high-mindedness, and noble concerns:

> I come no more to make you laugh: things now
> That bear a weighty and a serious brow,
> Sad, high and working, full of state and woe,
> Such noble scenes as draw the eye to flow,
> We now present. (Prol. 1–5)

The prologue, in keeping with many others, differentiates the play from others and makes a claim for the special distinction of what it offers. Precisely what the comments about laughter refer to remains unclear, though the comic business of Rowley's play seems a logical object. Shakespeare and Fletcher's play is designed to produce tears, not laughter.

The prologue moves quickly to describing sections of the audience in terms of the affects and desires they bring to the theatre. The prologue divides the audience into several probably overlapping groups, all of whose expectations (save one) it will meet. The interests of the first two follow directly from the "weighty and serious" matter promised in the prologue's first lines:

> Those that can pity here
> May, if they think it well, let fall a tear:
> The subject will deserve it. Such as give
> Their money out of hope they may believe
> May here find truth too. (Prol. 5–9)

---

33. See Patterson's *Reading Holinshed's Chronicles*.

"History," Truth, and Fiction 219

The "working" parts of the play will permit those inclined to pity to weep, and the "state and woe" of the subject will speak to those looking for truth. Just what those truths might be is left open to question, and, not unlike *2 Henry IV*, some of the most arresting and memorable moments in the play (like, say, Queen Katherine's vision, or Cranmer's Virgil-inflected prophecy about the infant Elizabeth) are more matters of belief than they are truths. The chorus figures pity and truth as objects of potential audience interest – to be hoped for – rather than self-evident aspects of the play. Even such as only want "a show or two" will "see away their shilling / Richly in two short hours" (12–13). "Only they"

> That come to hear a merry, bawdy play,
> A noise of targets, or to see a fellow
> In a long motley coat guarded with yellow,
> Will be deceived. (Prol. 13–17)

These auditors, looking for noise and jokes, will be deceived by their expectations, expectations conventionally held to have been established by Rowley's play.[34] One of the distinctive features of the play is its distance from and revision of the "bluff King Harry" tradition that was important to the stage and remains a substantial part of how we remember Henry VIII – killing his wives or munching a turkey leg and drinking. The idea that Rowley's play is what the prologue refers to has a great deal to recommend it, but it also echoes claims of seriousness found in prologues at least as far back as Marlowe's *Tamburlaine*.[35] Typically, such choric claims represent efforts to locate the play they introduce in the dramatic field and to separate it from a less serious common run of theatre. *Henry VIII*'s opening is no different in its effort to locate the play in the field, but it makes claims about the play's particular kind of veracity that separate it from choric introductions to historical plays like *2 Henry IV* or *Henry V*.

34. See for example, the Arden edition's notes and introduction. McMullan does not, of course, argue for a certain identification but writes that "the play referred to is probably *When You See Me, You Know Me*, a comic history of Henry VIII's reign written in 1605 and revived in 1613; it is a loosely structured entertainment with a strong Protestant bias, and an emphasis on the role of Henry's fool, Will Summers" (note to Prol. 14).
35. Claims to seriousness are also found in the prefatory material to *Troilus and Cressida* and in John Ford's *Perkin Warbeck*. Prologues and commendatory verse demonstrate certain patterns of expression that make them recognizable as a genre. They are, to use Bakhtin's term, a speech genre.

The Chorus goes on in an almost Jonsonian vein as it appeals to the gentleness of the play's proper audience, telling auditors to

> know
> To rank our chosen truth with such a show
> As fool and fight is, beside forfeiting
> Our own brains and the opinion that we bring
> To make that only true we now intend,
> Will leave us never an understanding friend. (Prol. 18–22)

Opening with an emphasis on knowledge underscores that the play is concerned with truth. This "chosen truth" combines attention to the historical subject matter and a serious approach to that matter. The play's truth is connected to the "high and working" elements promised to the understanding audience and distinct from the implicitly lower kinds of pleasures that some in the audience might expect or prefer. The Chorus also deploys the language of distinction both to excuse the action and to assert its superiority to the "fool and fight" that the Chorus rejects as a debasement of truth, despite the expectations of ignorant and ungentle understanders. To set the "chosen truth" of the play with such plays would betray both the "brains" of the writers and the intention to make the play "only true." "Rank" plays on multiple senses of the word: the players will not line up "fool and fight" with the serious matter of their play, nor do they see the current work as having similar status to such a play.[36] Trading on and asserting the stature of the acting company presenting the play, whose work makes its hearers the "first and happiest hearers" (Prol. 24) of the town, encourages the audience to take what they are about to see seriously – to remember it. The "gentle hearers" are reminded that were the actors to lower themselves to "fool and fight," they would betray both their "own brains" and their reputation for presenting plays that are "true." Moreover, since the people in the theatre *are* the "first and happiest hearers," they ought to respond properly to the sad, high, and working truths that the play presents.

The final move the Chorus makes adds detail to what the audience is expected to do in language that ties the play closely to Shakespeare's *Henry V.* Repeated invitations to "think" deliberately echo the "suppose" of the earlier Chorus, who places much of the obligation for the play's success with the audience and its "imaginary

---

36. Rank could mean both "to arrange or draw up people" (*OED* "rank" v.3 1b) and "to give a certain position in a sequence, series, or hierarchy to (a person or thing)" (*OED* "rank" v.3 3b).

forces," but this Chorus seems more confident than its predecessor: "Think ye see / The very persons of our noble story / As they were living" (Prol. 25–8).[37] This Chorus is more hortatory than plaintive, better accustomed, perhaps, to command than request by this point. And this Chorus also makes explicit the play's connection to earlier plays about history even as it makes a claim for the play's distinction in the immediate theatrical context.

The epilogue recapitulates some of the positions taken in the prologue addressing the tastes and expectations of the audience and dismissing those who get it wrong and appealing to better understanders. Before detailing bad sorts of audience members, it tells us that "'Tis ten to one this play can never please / All that are here" (Epil. 1–2). The epilogue assumes that a substantial part of the audience will dislike, ignore, misunderstand, or be disappointed by the play that has just concluded. Those that who have come for a nap might be alarmed and woken up by the trumpets and so criticize the play, and others looking for anti-citizen plays will be disappointed, leaving only the "good women" of the audience to appreciate the toil of the actors. Critics have noted the appeal to female audience members and that such appeals are not uncommon, but we have paid less attention to how the epilogue, like the prologue, locates the play in relation to other kinds of drama.[38] It is not a play for the inattentive, which leads the epilogue to fear that "all the expected good" the company

> is like to hear
> For this play at this time is only in
> The merciful construction of good women
> For such as one we showed 'em. (Epil. 10–13)

The play will call forth the charity of "good women" because the play has represented a good woman as a kind of gesture of solidarity. The question of to which woman the prologue refers remains an open one. McMullan's edition calls this "probably a deliberately ambivalent reference to one or all of Katherine, Anne and Elizabeth, though generally taken to refer only to Katherine."[39] The salient point is that this good woman – whoever she is – was *shown* to the

---

37. Nashe's fresh-bleeding Talbot is in the background of phrasing.
38. On appeals to women in the theatre, see Richard Levin, "Women in the Renaissance Theatre Audience."
39. Note to line 11 of the epilogue in McMullan's edition.

audience, and their recollection of her representation is the key to the play's being appreciated.

The play marks Katherine and Elizabeth as "good women" through visions and prophecies that are substantially the stuff of theatrical fiction. Neither Katherine's vision nor Cranmer's prophecy about the upcoming Elizabethan Golden Age have clear "historical" sources. Instead, both draw on dramatic, poetic, and political traditions whose force (or truth) does not derive from historical fact. Katherine's vision may draw on a report in Holinshed of one of Anne Boleyn dreams and, as McMullan argues, may also refer to Princess Elizabeth's vision in Heywood's *If You Know Not Me, You Know Nobody*. This kind of repetition of theatrical fiction has at least a double effect: it associates Katherine with the other "good women" Elizabeth (and Anne), and it subtly points to a play about Tudor monarchs recently (1610 and 1613) reprinted (and possibly revived on stage). (This double invocation is akin to what Shakespeare does in *2 Henry IV*). Moments like these repetitions ready the ground for the epilogue's elision of the differences between Katherine, Anne, and Elizabeth and broaden the range of figures that the "good women" in the audience can see as making the play worth smiles and applause.

Cranmer's prophecy, though lacking authority from the chronicles, does have a series of sources that contribute to its power both as prophecy and as theatre. Cranmer prefaces his prophetic speech with a claim that no one should think his words "flattery, for they'll find 'em truth" (V.ii.16) before moving on to describing Elizabeth as a "pattern to all princes" (5.2.22). The speech is an instance of political prophecy that alludes to the Bible and to Virgil's fourth eclogue, which predicts a return to a pastoral golden age.[40] Cranmer tells his onstage audience that:

> she shall be—
> But few now living can behold that goodness—
> A pattern to all princes living with her,
> And all that shall succeed. (5.4.20–3)

Most of those hearing his prophecy onstage will not live to see its fulfillment, but the princess will become a pattern for both contemporary and later princes. The audience in the playhouse is in a position to remember her, and this fictional prophecy seems designed to create a kind of Elizabethan nostalgia and to place Elizabeth's

---

40. See McMullan's notes for the biblical references, and for the Virgilian echo see Heather James's *Shakespeare's Troy* (13).

reign into an historical succession from her father down to James. Cranmer's words fabricate a memory of Elizabeth's reign, a memory no less evocative or meaningful than the material derived from the chronicles despite it being fiction.

IV

> So in story what's now told
> That takes not part with days of old?
>
> Middleton, *Hengist, King of Kent*

An actor playing Raynulph Higden, author of the fourteenth-century history known as the *Polychronicon*, opens Middleton's history play with this statement about novelty and innovation, suggesting that "fashions now called new, / Have been worn by more than you." As with Shakespeare's turn to Chaucer, old stories keep being made new in the theatre. Middleton turns to an old narrative, first printed by Caxton in 1480 and dating in manuscript to the 1340s, for both incident and for an authorizing figure for the play.[41] Scholars have long considered Middleton an innovator in terms of form and dramatic genre, but this choric moment suggests that that innovation has a complicated relationship with the past it – at least supposedly – breaks from. Narratives of rupture have their place, of course, but ruptures (if they exist) also always exist in a context. *Hengist, King of Kent* helps in developing a description of the generic system of the drama that agrees with Higden's description of the new's relation to the old.

Critics have more or less neglected *Hengist, King of Kent*.[42] We can explain some of this oversight by the lack of texts: as for much

---

41. See also Shakespeare's *Pericles*, discussed in chapter one, which revives Gower to introduce and move the play along.
42. See for example, Samuel Schoenbaum's *Middleton's Tragedies* (1955). *Hengist* has a thin critical history. An MLA Bibliography title search turns up only twenty-one items, many concerned with questions of authorship rather than the play as play. For a discussion of *Hengist* and Middleton's historical writing, see Thomas Roebuck's "Middleton's Historical Imagination." Lucy Munro's "'Nemp your Sexes!' Anachronistic Aesthetics in *Hengist, King of Kent* and the Jacobean 'Anglo-Saxon' Play" and "Speaking History: Linguistic History and the Usable Past in the Early Modern History Play" discuss the play's use of archaisms and its relation to history. Lisa Hopkins's *From the Romans to the Normans on the English Renaissance Stage* (2017) also discusses the play.

of Middleton's canon, until the publication of the Oxford Middleton there were few edited editions of *Hengist* in collections and no standalone editions. Of *Hengist*, Margot Heinemann writes that the play is "one of his strangest works, at once powerful and inconsistent" and bears the marks of its composition in years of crisis (136). Schoenbaum describes *Hengist* as "the result of a divided artistic purpose. It is something of an anomaly—a curious union of psychological tragedy, pseudo-history, and comic buffoonery" (70). While Schoenbaum describes this mixture as an anomaly, many other plays on history display a similar mixture of elements (especially in mixing history and buffoonery). *Hengist*'s status as "anomaly" owes a good deal to the relative (and putative) paucity of new historical plays after about 1615, but it is not the case that history plays had vanished from the scene: multiple editions of Shakespeare's histories were printed between 1619 and 1622 as well as historical plays by other writers. Seen in context, the play tells us more about the theatrical field in the later part of James' reign than the usual discussion of it as an outlier or anomaly can.

Middleton's one foray into historical drama bears many marks that align it with plays of the 1590s – the choric presenter, the dumb shows, and the at times over-heated stage rhetoric – while also sharing those features with seventeenth century plays like Shakespeare's *Pericles*, which has a medieval writer as presenter and an episodic structure.[43] These marks, rather than serving as a sign of difference or discontinuity, place it into a longer context in the theatrical field. The play's representational strategies signal generic and thematic filiations as well as ways to approach the play. Nonetheless, with few exceptions, critics do not describe the play as a history play; instead, we talk about it under the rubrics of tragedy and tragicomedy.[44] As elsewhere in this chapter, my intention is less to claim the play for "history" than to place the play into a broader context of generic change in such way as to complicate ideas about "the history play" and to complicate narratives of discontinuity.

---

43. Even the dumbshows, occasionally cited as evidence of the play's old-fashionedness, have contemporary examples; see Middleton and Rowley's *The Changeling* and Webster's *The White Devil*).
44. See Julia Briggs, "*Hengist, King of Kent*: Middleton's Forgotten Tragedy," Schoenbaum's work cited above, and Swapan Chakravorty's *Society and Politics in the Plays of Thomas Middleton* (1996), among others. A. L. Kistner and M. K. Kistner in their essay, "What is Hengist, King of Kent?" offer one of the few discussions of the play as a history play.

Middleton's play begins with Raynulph Higden's choric prologue that makes clear the connections between "ancient stories" and "new ones" in a way that suggests the play's awareness of its location in a tradition:

> Ancient stories have been best:
> Fashions that are now called new
> Have been worn by more than you,
> Elder times have used the same
> Though these new ones get the name,
> So in story what's now told
> That takes not part with days of old?
> Then to prove time's mutual glory,
> Join new times' love to old times' story. (1.0.10–18).[45]

What story, Higden asks, does not partake of the past? New fashions of whatever kind are only new in "name." The play attempts to prove "time's mutual glory," the glory of past and present, by joining "new times' love to old times' story." "New times' love" is the mechanism for this project of linking past and present so both can be glorified as part of the long span of time. Through Higden's speech, Middleton locates the play in terms of both the historical past and the history of narrative, and new appears in its relation to the old.[46]

The play makes repeated reference to the literary past. The choruses and dumbshows of the main plot represent clear references to chronicle history (as well as the Shakespearean version of historical drama), and the comic plot points to comic tradition as much as it makes topical references to dearth and religious questions.[47] Late in the play, a group of "cheaters" pretending to be players visit Simon, the tanner mayor of Queenborough. Simon and the "cheaters" make extended reference to theatre and its effects on audiences.

---

45. I will cite all Middleton's work from the Oxford Middleton (2007).
46. Novelty, interestingly, lies not so much in the form or the story, but in the response to the old story. Middleton periodically calls attention to the importance of reception in the play: Vortiger's stratagems fail to achieve his desired effects, Simon talks about the effects of comic performances, and the dumbshows seem to require the glosses provided by Higden. This is typical of many of his plays; in *A Trick to Catch the Old One*, a character asked what kind of plot she's constructing answers in terms of effects: she's making a plot to "vex" her husband.
47. Margot Heinemann's *Puritanism and Theatre* (1980) and Bromham and Bruzzi's *The Changeling and the Years of Crisis, 1619–1624* (1990) point out the topical resonance of the play.

For instance, when Simon asks "are you comedians?" they introduce themselves in a kind of parody of Polonius' introduction of the players in *Hamlet*: "We are anything sir: comedians, tragedians, tragicomedians, comi-tragedians, pastoralists, humorists, clownists, and satirists" (5.1.71–5). The reference to *Hamlet*, while interesting in itself, is less significant than the repetition of the mixed categories for which Polonius' speech is best known. Even if the cheaters are not actually players, they are pretending to be, and this introduction supports that pretense. Players, then, ought to be capable of performing these hybrid forms and that in turn suggests the centrality of hybrid forms to the field. The metatheatrical allusions offer a glimpse of the contemporary field and help situate *Hengist* in that field.

The fake players offer a list of nonsense titles of plays they could perform, all of which appear to be comedies.[48] The scene itself is part of the comic subplot of the play and ends with one of the cheaters throwing meal in Simon's eyes so he can steal Simon's purse. Despite claiming to be skillful in all the modes of drama, they exclude history from their repertoire. This exclusion is especially interesting given that the play itself is "historical" and appears to have been received in its early performance more as comedy. We could take the cheaters' failure to mention history as evidence of their being more con-men than players, or it may be a more general point about the generic system: that "history" is not the name of a kind but only of a content, a content the play itself represents. Their list depicts their theatrical world as dominated by comic and satirical drama; even though they do mention tragedy, it appears more in combination with other forms than on its own. It is unclear whether we are meant to see them as being only con artists or as players who are also con artists. One of Simon's associates claims that they have just recently bought a playbook to use as a prop in their scam: "they only take the name of country comedians to abuse simple people, with a printed play or two they bought at Canterbury last week for sixpence, and which is worst, they speak but what they list of on't, and fribble out the rest" (5.1.359–63).[49] This reference to print helps to establish

---

48. *The Whirligig, The Whibble, Carwidgeon, Gull upon Gull,* and *Woodcock of our Side*. Grace Ioppolo's notes in the Oxford Middleton call these nonsense titles, and they have no attested existence. The one real play they reference is Fletcher's *Wild Goose Chase* (1621).
49. Significantly, part of the complaint has to do with the player/con-men being bad players: they only "speak what they list" from the play and make up or ignore the rest, a complaint that is especially pertinent to a playwright. Their lack of skill becomes evidence of their being criminals.

the play's place in the dramatic field; it is linked to new plays in the theatres and old ones from the booksellers. Situating the play in both theatre and bookshop helps clarify what is innovative: the synthetic disposition towards the resources of the theatre, a disposition that Middleton demonstrates throughout his career.

A further link to the contemporary field lies in 5.1, where Simon offers a long appreciation of theatrical clowns:

> O, the clowns I have seen in my time! The very peeping out of 'em would have made a young heir laugh if his father had lain a-dying. A man undone in law the day before, the saddest case that can be, might for his twopence have burst himself with laughing and ended all his miseries. Here was a merry world, my masters! Some talk about things of state, of puling stuff, there's nothing in a play to a clown's part, if he have the grace to hit on't, that's the thing indeed. The king shows well but he sets off the king.
> But not the King of Kent, I mean not so,
> The king I mean is the one I do not know. (5.1.124–36)

Understandably, as part of the comic subplot and a kind of clown himself, Simon is more interested in the clown's business than that of the kings in plays. The "clown's part" is the "thing indeed. The king shows well but he sets off the king" (5.1.133). He dismisses fictive kings and "puling" "things of state" as nothing compared to the clown's part, which outshines that of the king. There are multiple layers of reference: the metadramatic reference to elements of the theatre (Simon's dismissal of the puling stuff of staged "things of state"), a citation of one of Middleton's own plays ("a merry world, my masters"), and a careful distinction between his disdain for fictional kings and his relationship with the King of Kent. This last indicates an awareness of the potential problems of topical drama at a moment when the censor's pen was of especial concern.[50] Comedy may serve as a cover or step aside from the more dangerous genre of

---

50. Heinemann points to this as an explanation for the relative paucity of plays addressing political questions after about 1615. *Hengist*'s engagement in politics is less direct than, say, Shakespeare's *Richard II*. Despite what appears to be a reluctance to produce politically-relevant *new* plays, history plays were being reprinted throughout these years. Even this reluctance is arguable, as it depends on what one thinks qualifies as political relevance. DEEP lists 1619 printings of Shakespeare's *Henry V*; Wilson, Drayton, Munday, and Hathaway's *1 Sir John Oldcastle*, as well as 1622 printings of Marlowe's *Edward II* and Shakespeare's *Richard III* and *1 Henry IV*. It is hard to see *Edward II* not having some kind of resonance in the 1620s, for example.

history. Fredric Jameson's argument about romance in *The Political Unconscious* applies to the comic elements, which respond to questions about sovereignty and legitimacy but through a generic lens distinct from that of, say, plays of the 1590s. Despite the play's manifold engagements in politics, the comic plotline (and the distance of the historical plot) offer a kind of screen for those engagements that allow it some space to work.[51] *Hengist*, then, is a good deal more of its time than not, and its putative untimeliness may be a feature more of perspective than anything else. Plays printed in the years around 1621 (extant and lost) include a number of plays on historical subjects – enough to raise questions about the notion that the audience for plays on historical themes was small – as well as several tragicomedies and two quartos of *Mucedorus*. *Hengist* reflects and synthesizes elements from the variety of plays current in 1620–1 and in that is far more characteristic of the dramatic field than not. Its innovations appear in its efforts to be topical without being specific – avoiding the dangers of over-specific reference through historical distance – and may anticipate the tactics of the later *Game at Chess*.

V

> Studies have of this nature been of late
> So out of fashion, so unfollow'd, that
> It is become more justice to revive
> The antic follies of the times than strive
> To countenance wise industry.
>
> John Ford, *Perkins Warbeck* Prologue

Like *Hengist,* scholars almost universally think of the last play under discussion in this chapter in terms of untimeliness, of lateness, and even as the "end" of the history play. We have long discussed John Ford's *Perkin Warbeck, A Strange Truth* as the final history play of the pre-Civil War theatre in England.[52] Scholars thus picture it

---

51. That the play survives, at least initially, under the title "The Mayor of Queenborough" attests to the success of this tactic, even if that the tactic was too successful. If the play failed in some way, it's in that the comedy came to overshadow the play's other engagements.
52. Despite this being inaccurate at best and a willful distortion at worst. The subtitle aligns the play with Shakespeare and Fletcher's *Henry VIII*, which was known as *All is True* in its earliest stagings. The romance elements of the play – a "lost" prince recognized by his conduct, a love-story and similar tropes –

as a kind of curiosity in terms of genre, and its "latecomer" status appears as one of its more important characteristics. What I hope the foregoing discussion of Middleton has shown is that this idea of untimeliness or lateness is less a feature of plays themselves or of the dramatic field than it is an artifact of criticism. Much as is the case with the plays of the 1590s, these later plays are responses to the theatrical and literary field of their moment. Ford's play draws on historical material not unlike the chronicles in kind, despite common depictions of Francis Bacon's *History of The Reign of Henry VII* (1621) and Thomas Gainsford's *True and Wonderful History of Perkin Warbeck* (1618) as being a more advanced kind of history than Holinshed or Hall because they are more fully influenced by humanist theories about historiography.[53] Even discussions of its being unusual as a new history play in 1629 (or so) depend on definitions of the history play as focused on a fairly limited span of English history, definitions that seem needlessly narrow.[54] When scholars do discuss the play in terms of genre, they most often present it as late, unusual, or, in stronger forms, as evidence that the historical drama has played itself out.[55] Below, I offer a rereading of the play's paratexts as a way to suggest that the prevailing narrative about the play's lateness obscures more than it reveals about both the play and its place in the genre system.

Among the effects of the perceived belatedness of this play are misreadings of the play's prologue and other paratexts like the commendatory poems that take the play out of both its immediate contexts and the longer span of literary history. Miles Taylor's "The End of the English History Play in *Perkin Warbeck*" in some ways epitomizes the kinds of arguments I am questioning. Since the critical consensus holds that Ford's play is an outlier, a return of a dead form, and because this essay exemplifies that consensus, what follows will question both the premises and conclusions of Taylor's work. Taylor's essay usefully situates the play in Renaissance debates about how best to represent history, but it makes far too sweeping claims about playwrights ceding history to an emergent political

link it to other contemporary plays as well. A counter position akin to mine is Sarah Dewar-Watson's "Ford's *Perkin Warbeck* as Historical Tragedy"; she argues that the play is better seen as an experiment with historical drama than "confirming the end of the history play" (194).
53. Work like Annabel Patterson's on Holinshed questions this position on the chronicles.
54. See Judith Spikes's essay on the Jacobean history play, cited above.
55. This critical trend goes as far back as Ribner's *English History Play*.

science, suggesting a far smoother and more direct transition than seems actually to have occurred (399). In a representative summary of a discussion of Daniel, Puttenham, and Dekker, Taylor writes:

> The crucial observation we make, an observation shared both by Daniel, in his embrace of a new historiography characterized by prose, and by Puttenham and Dekker, in their defense of poetry, is that in early modern England the modes of historical writing and poetry were seen as increasingly antithetical. (396)

Aside from the significant differences in when these writers made the statements, it does not seem that a recognition that poets and historians work in different modes necessarily implies opposition between those modes, still less that they are antithetical. Puttenham's comments on historians and poets were first published in 1589, Dekker's *The Whore of Babylon* dates to 1606, and Taylor cites Daniel's 1609 preface to his *Civil Wars*.[56] Positions on the distinction between history and fiction were not consistent across the period, nor can I discern the kind of consensus about opposition between them that Taylor's essay uses as one of its premises.[57] Instead, the relationship of poetry and prose in the representation of history was always in productive flux. The chorus in Shakespeare's *Henry V* makes this dynamic relationship clear throughout the play when it requests the audience's help in piecing out the "history" written by the "all-unable pen" of the "bending author" with their imaginations. Bare truth, the goal of humanist historiography or scientific history, operates in conjunction with poetry and imagination in the theatre as much as it does in the historical writing set against it in Taylor's argument.[58]

Even if we grant that Ford's play is the last "Elizabethan English history play," it does not follow that anyone at the moment could have seen the play that way or that Ford wrote the play to reflect on the end of the genre (395). Ford and his contemporaries most likely

---

56. Puttenham's comments on historical poetry, discussed in the previous chapter, are more complicated than Taylor's quotations suggest. As with much of Puttenham's work, the argument develops over a longer period than scholars often quote, and the paragraphs taken together make a more nuanced and interesting case.
57. Nor is it easy to see straightforward lines of development in any one direction. This is another example of the distorting effects of developmental narratives.
58. Hayden White's work repeatedly makes this point: historical narrative depends on "literary" elements like plot for structure and meaning.

could or would not have known that the end had come.⁵⁹ Moreover, depending on one's definition of the form, "history plays" did appear after *Perkin Warbeck*, and they remained constantly in print throughout the period.⁶⁰ Ford appears to have thought that writing the play made sense and that the form still had both commercial and artistic possibilities.⁶¹ The commendatory poems do not take a valedictory position, instead they hold out the play as an example to be imitated. The playwright's "kinsman," John Ford, brags that

> Dramatic poets (as the times go) now
> Can hardly write what others will allow;
> The cynic snarls, the critic howls and barks,
> And ravens croak to drown the voice of larks.
> Scorn those stage-harpies! This I'll boldly say:
> Many may imitate, few match thy play. (1–5)⁶²

This poem, aside from characterizing audiences as filled with loud critics, can be read as a challenge to produce more of this kind of play – "many may imitate, few match thy play" – rather than suggesting that the play is in a dead or dying genre. Instead, it calls for imitations (even if those imitations cannot match the original). The question of why there were few of these imitators is a different question than asking why Ford would write such a play in the 1620s.⁶³

The one commendatory verse that names the play as a "Chronicle History" does so without any implication that the play is either unusual or belated. John Brograve offers an appreciation of the judgment of the author and of the play's verse:

> These are not to express thy wit,
> But to pronounce thy judgment fit

---

59. Moreover, it is worth asking what the "end" of the history play means in the first place.
60. Ben Jonson began a history play about Mortimer but died before he could complete it. It was published in 1641 and based on the explanatory note that "he dy'd and left it unfinished" it is at least possible that he was working on it in the 1620s or 1630s. Interestingly, it would have been another play about the times around the reign of Edward II.
61. Ribner's book talks about Ford's play as reviving a "dead dramatic genre" (298), which does not go far towards explaining why Ford (or an acting company) might have thought it was a good idea to produce the play.
62. I cite from Donald K. Anderson's edition (1965).
63. It is also, in my view, a much harder question to answer definitively. A number of historical plays did appear after *Perkin Warbeck*, and historical drama remained popular in the bookstalls throughout the period.

> In full-fil'd phrase those times to raise
> When Perkin ran his wily ways.
> Still, let the method of thy brain
> From error's touch and envy's stain
> Preserve thee free, that e'er thy quill
> Fair truth may wet, and fancy fill.
> Thus graces are with muses met,
> And practic critics on may fret.
> For here thou has produced a story
> Which shall eclipse their future glory. (1–11)

Like the other commendatory poems, Brograve's avers Ford's skill and judgment in writing the play and asserts that the play revives Perkin and his times.[64] This poem mounts a kind of defense of Ford's project by expressing hope that "the method of [his] brain" will preserve him from error and envy and that he may continue to write with a quill dipped in truth. Notably, it does not make any reference to the play being old-fashioned, which is true of all five of the poems. All of them point to the skill of Ford's pen and four of them single out the vividness of Perkin's character – "rediviv'd" in the word of George Crymes. Taken as a whole, they are typical of commendatory verse.

The prologue, which appears to have been written for the printed play since it appears without stage directions or other usual signs of having been performed, likewise focuses on the matter of the play more than its form.[65] Critics traditionally read it as stating that the form Ford writes in is out of fashion, and I want to argue against this prevailing critical opinion. The prologue's author writes:

> Studies have of this nature been of late
> So out of fashion, so unfollow'd, that
> It is become more justice to revive
> The antic follies of the times than strive
> To countenance wise industry. (Prol. 1–5)

---

64. These poems make no mention of Ford's reviving *Henry VII*, only Perkin, which does indicate the relative theatrical power of the two characters. The pretender is a more "stagy" figure than the actual monarch. It is not unlike earlier plays on historical subjects where usurping or otherwise less than legitimate monarchs are arresting characters. Richard III is only the most obvious example.
65. That Ford is referred to in the third person – "this author's silence," "he shows a history couched in a play" and so on – supports the idea that this prologue was composed separately from the play.

The question is what the prologue means by "studies of this nature": is this a reference to the "history play" or something else? What has been unfollowed of late are plays that "countenance wise industry" rather than "the antic follies of the time."[66] "Studies" does not seem necessarily to be a reference to the history play, and moreover it is difficult to see how the play that follows countenances wise industry since the most memorable figure in it is a failed and not especially industrious pretender to the throne. More reasonably, the prologue is setting up a distinction between plays on serious matter and those that are not – a distinction familiar in theatrical prologues at least from Marlowe's plays onwards. This mistaking of the prologue's meaning is of a piece with the general habit of treating the content of plays on historical topics as defining a genre. Our critical habit of reading this way works to distort the texts and obscures important features of the literary field.[67]

In a similar way, the rest of the prologue is more focused on content than form and offers the play to audiences of "clearer judgments" than those of writers or readers who are characterized by "want of truth" (13, 7):

> From him to clearer judgments we can say
> He shows a history couch'd in a play:
> A history of noble mention, known
> Famous, and true; most noble, 'cause our own;
> Not forg'd from Italy, from France, from Spain,
> But chronicled at home; as rich in strain
> Of brave attempts as ever fertile rage
> In action could beget to grace the stage. (Prol. 13–20)

Making a Jonson-like appeal to the wisdom of the audience, the prologue asserts that Ford has presented a history "couch'd" in a play. This phrase has occasioned some critical commentary, with some arguing that it suggests the hardening of a distinction between history and play that points to the difficulty of writing historical drama. For example, Taylor writes, "Historical drama is now an uneasy and discordant hybrid, an unstable and ephemeral synthesis

---

66. See Kamps's *Historiography and Ideology in Stuart Drama* for a discussion of how critics have misread these lines that resonates with my own position (197–8). "Wise industry" is almost Jonsonian in its conjoining of wisdom and hard work.
67. Without careful attention to the field in a specific moment, retrospective generic categories like "the history play" are almost inevitably anachronistic and distorting.

of antithetical modes of inquiry" (400).⁶⁸ Given the evidence of the rest of the prologue, it appears to be something simpler: a description of the play's subject. As the prologue continues, it describes the history as "noble," "true," and "our own": "Not forg'd from Italy, from France, from Spain, / But chronicled at home" (17–18). Again, we can read these lines as the usual kind of opening description of the play to come that makes claims for the value of the play. The prologue refers to the matter of the play being "chronicled at home," which seems to be a reference to the source materials and describes those materials as "rich" in "brave attempts." English history, in the prologue's words, is as fertile a source for drama as anything other countries can offer – other countries where numerous contemporary plays in many genres are set – making a claim for the play's value despite its lack of an exotic setting.

The prologue closes by returning to the subject of the play's difference from contemporary plays. It does not "limit scenes" in accordance with some kind of neo-Aristotelian version of the unities, because "the whole land / Itself appear'd too narrow to withstand / Competitors for kingdoms" (21, 22–3). This refusal to limit scenes works as a practical theory of representation that places the demands of the material ahead of any kind of demand from genre. Finally:

> Nor is here
> Unnecessary mirth forc'd, to endear
> A multitude. On these two rests the fate
> Of worthy expectation: truth and state. (23–6)

The return to the topic of mirth, or "antic follies," points to the prologue's effort to align the play with serious drama and makes an assertion both that such serious plays have been few and that this one is worth the expectation of the worthy.⁶⁹ The distinction is not about genre – or at least not about the putative strangeness of choosing to write a history play in the later 1620s – but about seriousness as opposed to triviality.

68. As if this was ever *not* the case for historical drama. Taylor references Kamps's book on how *Perkin* invites questioning whether the play is better thought of as history or as literature but curiously ignores Kamps's discounting of the "end of the genre" narrative in his book's conclusion.
69. The exclusion of "unnecessary mirth" may point back to the purging of such mirth from *Tamburlaine*, a purging meant to heighten the seriousness of that play.

Ford's use of native sources and his investment in their seriousness is explicit in the epistle to Cavendish:

> Out of the darkness of a former age (enlighten'd by a late both learned and honorable pen), I have endeavored to personate a great attempt, and in it a greater danger. In other labors, you may read actions of antiquity discours'd; in this abridgment, find the actors themselves discoursing. (7–11)

Ford has drawn his material from the "darkness" with the help of a "learned and honorable pen" in an effort to "personate" the action.[70] He makes a distinction between texts in which actions are "discoursed" and theatre where the "actors themselves" discourse. Playing on two senses of actor, Ford draws attention to a formal distinction but not one about substance. In history books, the author discourses about past actions; on stage, the actors personate the historical actors discoursing in their own voices. Once more, it is striking that, in contrast to the critical narrative of decline and disappearance, nowhere in the paratexts of this play can we find unambiguous statements that this play is reviving a dead or dying genre. Instead, the play situates itself in ways consistent with other plays and offers conventional justifications for itself.

The play's epilogue, unattributed like the prologue, returns to the traditional matter of such texts in its abstract reiteration of the play and a kind of justification for the play:

> Here has appear'd, though in several fashion,
> The threats of majesty, the strength of passion,
> Hopes of an empire, change of fortunes—all
> What can to theaters of greatness fall,
> Proving their weak foundations. Who will please,
> Amongst such several sights, to censure these
> No births abortive, nor a bastard brood
> (Shame to parentage or fosterhood),
> May warrant by their loves all just excuses,
> And often find a welcome to the Muses. (1–10)

Ford's epilogue describes the play's action – "threats of majesty, the strength of passion, / Hopes of an empire, change of fortunes" – as proof of the weak foundations of "theatres of greatness," in keeping with the tradition of the explanatory and moralizing epilogue. But

---

70. Probably a reference to Bacon's *History of the Reign of Henry VII* that aligns the play with a particular model of historiography.

then, in a peculiar address to the audience, the epilogue speaks to those who will "censure" the sights of the play as "no births abortive, nor a bastard brood / (Shame to parentage or fosterhood)." The epilogue addresses audience members ("censurers") who see the play as *not* filled with "births abortive" or a "bastard brood" and *not* embarrassing, rather than choosing to depict the "strange truth" of the play in more positive terms. Nor does it offer the more familiar apologies and submission to the judgment of the audience typical of theatrical epilogues. The negatives suggest that those who see the play as filled with "births abortive" are both more common and less discerning than those who do not. The wise censurers, who see the play as not a bad play, "may warrant by their loves all just excuses, / And often find a welcome to the Muses." They may sanction, as Anderson glosses "warrant," unspecified just excuses for the play and, more puzzlingly, find a welcome to the Muses. What does this mean? Why should just censurers be welcome to the Muses? Is the prologue using the Muses to refer to the theatre, to other plays? These questions are not susceptible to ready answers, but it does seem that the play does not see itself as ending anything and the epilogue, like some of the commendatory poems, seems to expect more such plays.

Ford's play is not some kind of outlier that proves the death of the genre of the history play, but the question of how to understand it and how to place it in the genre system remains open. The paratexts as much as the opening speeches locate it in a line of plays in varied forms on historical subjects, a tradition that Ford and, more importantly, the writers of the commendatory verse, treat as a living one. One example from inside the play should serve. When Henry VII enters being "supported" (stage direction), he speaks in ways that echo any number of worried monarchs from earlier plays on English history:

> Still to be haunted, still to be pursued,
> Still to be frighted with false apparitions
> Of pageant majesty and new coin'd greatness,
> As if we were a mockery king in state,
> Only ordain'd to lavish sweat and blood
> In scorn and laughter to the ghosts of York,
> Is all below our merits; yet we sit fast
> In our own royal birthright. The rent face
> And bleeding wounds of England's slaughter'd people
> Have been by us, as by the best physician,
> At last both thoroughly cur'd and set in safety;

And yet for all this glorious work of peace,
Ourself is scarce secure. (1.1.1–13)

The speech echoes Bolingbroke's lament at the beginning of *1 Henry IV* ("So shaken as we are, so wan with care") as well as Richmond's speech at the end of *Richard III* ("Now civil wounds are stopp'd, peace lives again").[71] Regardless of whether these thematic and verbal echoes are deliberate or an effect of the field, they indicate the play's engagement in it and its connection to a durable and apparently still vital tradition of drama about history. Ford's play, like Henry VII, sits fast in its "birthright," but at the same time "is scarce secure" because, like the King, the play exists in a competitive field where succession and legitimacy are a constant stake in struggles that define that field. One aspect of the play's "strange truth" is that both of its kings are "mockery kings" because both are representations, more fictions that lie like truth.[72]

Hybrid forms, yes; innovative, yes; untimely, no. Innovation is a consistent feature of the period's drama – looking backwards for material to deploy and transform (something Middleton is particularly noted for) – and to describe a play like *Hengist* as "untimely" or "late" is to mistake, in some ways, how genre works. Rather, the play registers something of the dynamism of the field in the later years of James' reign. Proceeding from what we know about the field at the time (1621 or so), instead of from generic categories or a narrative of a playwright's career, places these plays into their time and makes their common label as "untimely" untenable. The plays' innovations, rather than being an indication of some kind of step outside or beyond the drama of the time, are a product and marker of how they are engaged in the field. *Hengist* appears to have been well-received in its early performances. These putatively late plays found receptive audiences, which argues for their being of their time rather than being out of it.

---

71. The comparison between the more theatrically kingly Perkin and the business-like Henry VII rehearses distinctions made between figures like Richard II or Hotspur and Bolingbroke.
72. The play's subtitle, *A Strange Truth*, is worth keeping in mind in thinking about the historical drama more generally. The truth of Ford's play is strange partly because Perkin's story is strange but also because the play offers truths in the form of fiction.

Chapter 6

"When the bad bleed": Tenants to Tragedy

Thomas Middleton's Vindice asserts that murder is a (perhaps the) tenant to tragedy in his 1607 *The Revenger's Tragedy*, offering a straightforward, if minimalist, way to recognize tragedy. Tragedy's tenants change throughout the period, and if murder is a pretty constant one, others move in and out of tragedy.[1] Inventing such categories as the "tragedy of blood," "Jacobean tragedy," or "revenge tragedy" helps to specify some of those changes but does not do much to explain where they come from. As I have just argued, narratives of decline pervade discussions of the "history play" as well and are belied by both print and performance history. Placing plays before authors and before genre in this chapter locates them in the moment of production and reception before making larger conclusions about the shape of the field or about generic change more generally. These changes take place in a field that enables, structures, and is structured by such changes. Old plays like *The Spanish Tragedy* or *Titus Andronicus* remained popular enough to draw Ben Jonson's ire well into the seventeenth century in the induction to *Bartholomew Fair*. Multiple editions of both old plays (especially of Kyd's) in the first decades of the seventeenth century support Jonson's claims that they remained popular with the theatre-going public. The fact that these notionally out of date plays remained in the bookstalls suggests in turn that they remained in the repertory, which means that these plays from the 1580s and 1590s continued to shape part of the conversation in the field.[2]

1. Belsey's "Continuity and Change on the English Popular Stage" makes a complementary argument to my own, pointing out ways that changes in genres depend as much on continuity with as on ruptures from the past.
2. Peter Kirwan's chapter "*Mucedorus*," in Emma Smith and Andy Kesson's collection *The Elizabethan Top Ten: Defining Print Popularity in Early Modern England* (2013), discusses the relation between theatrical popularity and the print market.

This chapter opens with a brief discussion of the "invention" of revenge tragedy, an invention that only took place in the early twentieth century, to suggest that such labels are useful but do not necessarily reflect the thinking of the writers whose work falls under such labels. I turn to a series of inductions, prologues, choruses, and epilogues because they offer contemporary insight into how playwrights and acting companies saw the genre system. These performed paratexts offer representations of dramatic kinds, stage confrontations among them, and outline a hierarchy. Unlike the prefatory materials added by stationers for readers, they are designed to introduce plays to theatrical audiences. The chapter treats John Marston's *Antonio* plays, George Chapman's *Bussy* plays, Thomas Middleton's *Revenger's Tragedy*, and Shakespeare's (and Middleton's) *Timon of Athens* before returning to Middleton and his *Women Beware Women*. These plays are tragedies of one kind or another, but, as with most early modern plays, they are plays whose effects depend on the deployment of generic resources beyond the strictly tragic and as such intervene in the generic system. Indeed, these plays raise questions about what "strictly tragic" actually means. This chapter considers changes in the idea and practice of tragedy that took place at the end of the sixteenth century and the early seventeenth century in terms of the theatrical field.

I

The revenge tragedy, a distinct species of the tragedy of blood, may be defined as a tragedy whose leading motive is revenge and whose main action deals with the progress of this revenge, leading to the deaths of the murderers and often the death of the avenger himself.
A. H. Thorndike "The Relations of Hamlet
to Contemporary Revenge Plays" (1902)

To say that there are such things as "revenge tragedies" is not controversial, but the distinctness of the species that Thorndike specifies fades the closer one gets to examples. The essay's argument that these plays share concerns and features remains compelling and, whether recognized or not, continues to structure discussions of the drama of the period. This definition of "revenge tragedy" continues to have considerable, almost inescapable, force today. The story it tells shapes syllabi, anthologies of plays (like the often-assigned Oxford World's Classics *Four Revenge Tragedies* that sits on many an office shelf), and, more importantly, it has shaped criticism of early modern drama ever since. At the same time, that it took until 1902 to "create" the genre raises questions about how the playwrights writing those plays and the companies producing them thought about what they were doing. A discussion of Thorndike's essay introduces a consideration of how the field of dramatic production structured the production and reception of these plays in the years around 1600.³

At the risk of flippant generalization, Thorndike, like many critics from the early twentieth century, has been more cited – invoked might be a better word – than read in recent decades.⁴ This tendency is particularly interesting given the force of Thorndike's definition and his remarkable scholarship. That definition has had the effect of obscuring the rest of his argument. Thorndike's purpose in the piece is less to "create" a genre than to locate and discuss what he calls the "relations" between revenge plays and *Hamlet* with the goal of understanding the greatness of Shakespeare's play. His Shakespeare-centric approach is nevertheless quite sensitive to the fact that Shakespeare is working in the field of professional playwriting:

> In investigating the relations of Shakspere's *Hamlet* to the demands of the stage and to contemporary plays of this revenge type, we are not to look upon Shakspere as an imitator, but as an Elizabethan play-wright, using an old play for the basis of his work, writing in response to current demands, accepting much that was already familiar on the stage, and vitalizing all, and permeating all with his own individuality. We need not obscure in the least our appreciation of his work or our admiration of his powers, but we must also look upon him as likely to work in much the same way and to be influenced by the same conditions as his fellow Elizabethan dramatists. (127)

---

3. The chapter will necessarily spend a good deal of time with criticism of these plays, since so much of our sense of both what "tragedy" is and how it changes derives from critical traditions. As Bourdieu writes in "The Field of Cultural Production," genre is as much a product of reception (and perceptions about reception) as of production.
4. As an example, John Kerrigan's magisterial book *Revenge Tragedy from Aeschylus to Armageddon* (1996) refers to Thorndike in passing but neither discusses nor cites the piece in any substantial way. Other critics point to the essay as the creation of the genre but, again, without much in the way of substantive discussion.

The research program implied by this paragraph, setting aside the teleology, is fundamentally historicist, and the essay, given the constraints of available texts, does locate Shakespeare's play in the context of the field at the turn of the seventeenth century.[5] My interest in Thorndike's argument lies in the way that his definition of "revenge tragedy" works in the context of an argument about how Shakespeare's work emerged out of the theatres of the late sixteenth century, not as a stable descriptor of a recognizable kind of drama. At the end of his essay, Thorndike writes that:

> we have repeatedly emphasized the imaginative efforts of the other dramatists, just as, in order to make Shakspere's relations to them more patent, we have emphasized the respects in which he clearly followed them. If we have been fair in this effort to view the great man and the smaller men from the point of view of their contemporaries, we are safe in saying that Shakspere took the material which other men had used and were using, followed the fashion other men had set, developed the material in many respects as other men were developing it, strove to express what they were striving to express—and succeeded. He created an immortal work of art by his transcendent genius, but also in some considerable measure by availing himself of the experience of others and by doing the same things which other men were doing at the same time. (219–20)

For Thorndike, defining the "revenge play" is only a step towards understanding where and how *Hamlet* emerged out of the theatres of early modern London. He is not writing as a theorist of genre but as a critic of *Hamlet*. We have set aside his teleology and the "great man" and "smaller man" language, but his emphasis on looking at the drama "from the point of view of their contemporaries" remains a crucial and more important contribution than a definition which, however descriptive it is, has lost its provisional and thus productive quality as an instrument of research into genre.

The acceptance of Thorndike's definition obscures some important research questions that this chapter attempts to take up.[6] For example: What makes a tragedy Jacobean rather than Elizabethan?

---

5. Thorndike also attempts to locate the plays in the history of production, but, again because of the limits of available resources, works from a series of assumptions that later scholarship have put into question (particularly with regard to the textual history of *Hamlet*).
6. Ronald Broude's "Revenge and Revenge Tragedy in Renaissance England" points to the force of the term as well as the way it depends on a modern, colloquial, sense of what revenge means.

What does it mean to call plays produced into the 1630s, as Fredson Bowers does, "Elizabethan"? What makes a tragedy of revenge distinct from, say, a domestic tragedy or a *de casibus* tragedy, both of which often rely on revenge as a driver of plot? Why do early modern printers not use "revenge tragedy" on title pages? A search in the *Database of Early English Playbooks* (*DEEP*) for plays whose title page text includes the word "revenge" lists thirteen playbooks (nine individual plays) printed since the beginning of printing in England, and the majority include the word "revenge" in the title, rather than in any kind of generic attribution, even as a modifier of "tragedy" (see table 6.1). Neither Kyd's *Spanish Tragedy* nor Shakespeare's *Hamlet* appear in the search results. A search for "revenger" yields no hits and "revenger's" only Middleton's play. Harbage, Schoenbaum, and Wagonheim's *Annals* uses the unmodified "tragedy" to label these plays.

Seven of these plays were performed by 1611; of those seven, only three are public theatre plays recognizable as revenge tragedies. One is a university play, and one is a closet drama: Beaumont and Fletcher's *Cupid's Revenge* deals with divine punishment for abjuring Cupid, and Tourneur's *Atheist's Tragedy* is more an anti-revenge play than a "revenge tragedy." Shirley's and Glapthorpe's works are much later and appear well after the "originators" of the subgenre. That only Marston and Chapman's plays went into print almost immediately is a possible indicator of their popularity (though neither *Antonio's Revenge* nor *The Revenge of Bussy D'Ambois* went into more than one quarto edition).[7]

Period playwrights and printers produced these texts but appear not to have been interested in calling them "revenge tragedies." When early title pages do qualify the genre of tragedy, it is generally to add "history" or evaluative terms like "true" or "lamentable." "Revenge" never appears as a qualifier for tragedy in these texts. Period writers, stationers, and theatre companies did not approach plays with this kind of definition in mind.[8] Instead, as Thorndike recognized in 1902, if there are changes in the practice of the theatre

---

7. *Bussy D'Ambois* did appear in a second quarto, but not until 1641. Marston's plays appeared in collections printed in 1633 and 1652. We must account for the relative popularity of these plays in thinking through how they appeared and what impact they had on the drama. The essays in Kesson and Smith's edited collection *The Elizabethan Top Ten* (2013) have made an important contribution to this discussion as has the dialogue among Peter Blayney, Alan Farmer, and Zachary Lesser about the popularity of playbooks.
8. With the possible exception of writers like Ben Jonson.

Table 6.1 Plays Which Include *Revenge* in the Title[a]

Play	Printed	Company	Printed for	Printed by	Registered
Marston, *Antonio's Revenge*	Q1602 (Production 1600–1)	Children of Paul's	Thomas Fisher	Richard Bradock	SR October 24, 1601
Anon., *Caesar and Pompey, or Caesar's Revenge*	Q1606? (Production 1595?)	University Production: Trinity at Oxford	John Wright	George Eld	SR June 5, 1606
Tourneur, *Atheist's Tragedy, or The Honest Man's Revenge*	Q1611 (Production 1607–1611?)	King's Men	John Stepneth and Richard Redmer	Thomas Snodham	SR Sept 14, 1611
Chapman, *Revenge of Bussy D'Ambois*	Q1613 (Production 1610–11)	Children of the Queen's Revels	John Helme	Thomas Snodham	SR April 17, 1612
Stevens, *Cynthia's Revenge, or Maenander's Ecstasy*	Q1613	Closet	Roger Barnes	(Unknown)	No SR
Beaumont and Fletcher, *Cupid's Revenge*	Q1615 (Production 1607–8)	Children of the Queen's Revels	Josias Harrison	Thomas Creede	SR April 2, 1615
Chettle, *Hoffman, or A Revenge for a Father*	Q1631 (Performed 1602)	Admiral's Men	Hugh Perry	John Norton	SR February 26, 1630
Shirley, *The Maid's Revenge*	Q1639 (Production 1626)	Queen Henrietta's Men	William Cooke	Thomas Cotes	SR April 12, 1639
Glapthorpe, *Revenge for Honor*	Q1654 (Production 1637–1641)	(Unknown)	Richard Marriot	(Unknown)	SR November (December?) 29, 1653

[a] Drawn from *DEEP*.

that make it possible to see an emergent subgenre, those changes emerge from the dynamics of the theatrical field. In order to understand the conditions for the emergence (and successful reception of at least some of these plays), we need to be wary of anachronistic definitions that have guided a great deal of research on the drama of the early seventeenth century. The drive to categorize and subcategorize, while helping, sometimes, to better define the specific object of criticism, often also results in the loss of a sense of relation between the plays in those categories and to the cultural field more generally. The categorical drive also obscures what the plays are doing in the interest of attempting to define what they are.[9]

II

BALTHAZAR: Hieronimo, methinks a comedy were better.
HIERONIMO: A comedy?
   Fie! comedies are fit for common wits:
   But to present a kingly troop withal,
   Give me a stately-written tragedy;
   Tragadia cothurnata, fitting kings,
   Containing matter, and not common things.
                              Thomas Kyd, *The Spanish Tragedy* (1590)

Kyd's tragedy plays with the social meanings of classical genres as Hieronimo introduces the play in sundry languages that affords him his revenge. Hieronimo trades on Balthazar and Lorenzo's ideas about what tragedy means – fitting for a "kingly troop," unlike comedy – as an underhanded way to draw them into a play in which they will be murdered. Hieronimo's strategic use of comedy and tragedy is an example of the way that practice often contradicts or questions prescriptive senses of genre. Hieronimo puts assumptions about genre to work in service of his revenge plot and that practical attitude is one subject of this chapter. Staged conversations about or between genres

---

9. Linda Woodbridge's *English Revenge Drama* (2010) responds to this drive to define by arguing that it has "helped obscure the prevalence of revenge across many genres" (5). Her book is "inclusive because [her] quarry is not genre definition but the cultural work that literary revenge performs" (5). This chapter is likewise interested in what tragedy does and how that changes over time. Her list of revenge plays includes forty-eight plays, far more than the nine plays that mention revenge in titles or on title pages listed above.

offer insight into playwrights' sense of the shape of the genre system within which their plays were produced.

The induction of the incredibly popular *Mucedorus* (reprinted fifteen times before 1642) frames the play with a contention between Comedy and Envy.[10] Comedy's first speech promises mirth and laughter to the audience saying "Comedy, play thy part, and please; / Make merry them that comes to joy with thee" (A2r).[11] Envy enters with naked arms besmeared with blood to block Comedy's efforts: "What, all on mirth? I'll interrupt your tale / And mix your music with a tragic end" (A2r). Envy invokes tragedy as a way to stop Comedy's play, to "interrupt" and mar Comedy's plans for a pleasant tale with blood, severed limbs, and the "cries of many thousand slain" (A2v). Tragedy functions here as a tool Envy uses to wreck Comedy's play. The opposition is between Comedy and Envy, not, as one might expect, between Comedy and Tragedy and, more importantly, the play associates the materials of tragedy with one of the Seven Deadly Sins. Tragedy, far from being a dignified and serious genre expressing high ideals, becomes subordinate to the failed agenda of a deadly sin. At the end of the induction, Comedy dares Envy to do its "worst" and says:

> And though thou thinks't with tragic fumes
> To brave my play unto my deep disgrace,
> I force it not; I scorn what thou canst do.
> I'll grace it so, thyself shall it confess
> From tragic stuff to be a pleasant comedy. (A3r)

"Tragic fumes," in this induction, are more tools for Envy than anything else, and Tragedy appears not to have sufficient importance in itself to warrant a physical embodiment on the stage. Comedy's scorn for Envy's efforts also points to the mutability of genre: the "tragic stuff" will be shown to be or will become "pleasant comedy." Generic mutability is a constant feature of the drama of the period, and this induction like many others calls attention to what Lyly calls the "mingle-mangle" of genre on stage. At the close of the play, Envy concedes defeat at Comedy's hands but promises a "double revenge" at another time (F4r). Thus, the play's frame invokes tropes com-

---

10. See Kirwan, "*Mucedorus*," for an extended discussion of the play's popularity. As Kirwan notes, despite the play's long early modern publication history, it has few modern editions and a "negligible" stage history over the past 200 years (227).
11. The play was printed for William Jones. I have modernized the spelling.

monly associated with tragedy – blood, violence, sad cries and the like – but reduces them to methods Envy will use in a failed attempt to ruin the play Comedy plans to present. There might be "tragic stuff" but no tragedy.

The 1599 quarto of *A Warning for Fair Women* opens with an often-discussed induction starring History, Tragedy, and Comedy. Chapter Four argues that this debate between Comedy, History, and Tragedy offers more insight into the competitive field of dramatic production than into definitions of genre. History and Tragedy enter carrying appropriate props (History with drum and ensign and Tragedy with whip and knife) and proceed to argue about whose kind is most worthy of the stage. That History appears on an equal footing with Tragedy and Comedy is evidence that at least one playwright thought of it as a genre (and that audiences would see it that way as well).[12] History's popularity is one object of Tragedy's anger in the induction. Responding to Tragedy's criticism, History likens Tragedy to a "common executioner," which prompts Tragedy to threaten to whip both History and Comedy off the stage (Ind. 8).[13] Comedy goes on at some length describing representative tragic plays:

> How some damned tyrant, to obtain a crown,
> Stabs, hangs, impoisons, smothers, cutteth throats,
> And then a Chorus, too, comes howling in,
> And tells us of the worrying of a cat,
> Then of a filthy whining ghost,
> Lapt in some foul sheet, or a leather pelch,
> Comes screaming like a pig half sticked,
> And cries "*Vindicta*, revenge, revenge!"
> With that a little rosen flasheth forth,
> Like smoke out of a tobacco pipe, or a boy's squib.
> Then comes in two or three like to drovers,
> With tailors' bodkins, stabbing one another.
> Is this not trim? Is not here goodly things? (Ind. 55–67)

Comedy's speech caricatures tragedy as populated by contemptible (and trivial) figures. This demeaning description undercuts the seriousness of the genre and has teeth because the caricature offers a not totally inaccurate depiction of some real plays. Provoked by

12. Much of the critical discussion of these figures focuses on History being on stage with Tragedy and Comedy and on the trappings associated with the three figures. Critics take the drum and ensign of History to be a kind of symbolic definition of the content of the "history play": warfare.
13. I am citing from *A Warning for Fair Women* (2021).

such descriptions, Tragedy whips both Comedy and History. She (the printed text identifies Tragedy as female) resents and envies the popularity of the other genres.[14] As she says, "Tis you have kept the Theatres so long, / Painted in play-bills, upon every post, / That I am scorned of the multitude, / My name profaned: but now I'll reign as Queen" (Ind. 78–81). Once Comedy and History exit, Tragedy presents a play drawn from real events saying "I am not feigned," exiting saying "what I am, I will not let you know, / Until my next ensuing scene shall show" (Prol. 11–12). Tragedy thus produces what could be labeled a history play, using her resources to narrate a "not feigned" story. She refuses to be a howling Chorus, preferring to let the play reveal its tragic nature. After the play's final action, Tragedy returns to the stage as an epilogue.[15] The epilogue, understandably, offers a strongly positive description of tragedy and exhibits considerable tolerance for both comedy and history. Tragedy describes a moral agenda for the genre – sluicing forth sin and lancing the boils of lust – and, more interestingly, points to the constraints imposed by the truth of the story behind the play. Tragedy asks pardon for any errors in the "true and home-born" play presented in "such form as haply you expected" (Epil. 20) and closes by saying "what now hath fail'd, tomorrow you shall see, / Performed by History or Comedy" (Epil. 21–2). Tragedy asserts that multiple forms are valid, expresses a tolerance for both History and Comedy not seen in the induction, and emphasizes content and function over form. Tragedy's tolerance at least in part derives from the fact that the source material for the play is historical – "truth" – and represents a typically practical disposition towards generic distinctions. By invoking truth as an explanation for the "strange" fact "that one hath not avenged another's death" (Epil. 10–11), Tragedy places the play alongside a group of plays making tragedy out of true stories. These plays – *Arden of Faversham* being the first – have come to be called "domestic tragedies."[16] This label, like revenge tragedy, is a creation of criticism that productively identifies a shared set of concerns but is at the same time not one that seems to have occurred to printers, playwrights, or acting companies. The invocation of truth also lines the play up with the history that it pretends to temporarily banish from the stage.

14. Envy is personified on stage in multiple plays – Jonson's *Poetaster* being only one – and is involved in both the establishment and evaluation of generic categories in the way that it attempts to police borders and to guide judgment.
15. I discuss the epilogue in more detail in chapter four. My interest in this chapter is in the tolerance of mixture expressed in the speech.
16. I discuss *Arden of Faversham* in the third chapter of this book.

These complexities speak to the complexities of the generic system as well as the theatrical field.

The printed text of Heywood's *A Woman Killed with Kindness* (1603, Q 1607, Q2 1617), another play drawn from an historical narrative, includes a prologue and an epilogue that never directly mention any traditional genre. The prologue enters, as a

> harbinger, being sent
> To tell you what these preparations mean.
> Look for no glorious state; our Muse is bent
> Upon a barren subject, a bare scene. (Prol. 1–4).[17]

The play's subject is barren, the playwright's muse "dull and earthy," and the speech functions as an extended plea that the audience bear with the play. The instructions tell the audience not to expect any "rich display," as Kidnie's gloss to "glorious state" asserts, but to expect a smaller, simpler story. The audience is thus left to decide what kind of play it is. Nowhere in the whole text of the prologue does it mention any generic convention; instead, it plays on tropes of incapacity:

> We could afford this twig a timber-tree,
> Whose strength might boldly on your favours build;
> Our russet, tissue; drone, a honey-bee;
> Our barren plot, a large and spacious field;
> Our coarse fare, banquets; our thin water, wine;
> Our brook, a sea; 'ur bat's eyes' eagle's sight;
> O'r poet's dull and earthy Muse, divine;
> Our ravens, doves; o'r crow's black feathers, white.
>   But gentle thoughts, when they may give the foil,
>   Save them that yield, and spare where they may spoil. (Prol. 5–14)

The play's epilogue, which tells a story about divergent responses to the same wine as a way to frame responses to the play, makes no reference to genre either. Instead, the story about wine "alludes" (compares) to the play:

> Which some will judge too trivial, some too grave.
> You as our guests we entertain this day
> And bid you welcome to the best we have.
> Excuse us, then—good wine may be disgraced
> When every several mouth hath sundry taste. (Epil. 13–18)

---

17. I cite from M.J. Kidnie's edition of the play (2017).

This too is a conventional parting gesture for a play: asking for pity for the play but suggesting that those who dislike the "good wine" offered by the play have faulty tastes. This play, while critics and audiences received it as tragedy, does not frame itself in those terms and submits, however disingenuously, to the judgment of audiences without the help offered by generic labels.[18]

The later *Witch of Edmonton* (1621, Q 1658) calls itself a "known true story composed into a tragicomedy" on its title page, conflating multiple kinds in a confusing manner that is also consistent with the practice of the period. The 1658 quarto's prologue and epilogue appear to have been composed for a 1634 revival of the play, and it is unclear whether the play's initial performances included either a prologue or epilogue.[19] Winnifred speaks the epilogue, in character:

> I am a widow still, and must not sort
> A second choice without a good report;
> Which though some widows find, and few deserve,
> Yet I dare not presume, but will not swerve
> From modest hopes. All noble tongues are free;
> The gentle may speak one kind word for me. (Epil. 1–6)

She speaks both for herself – a widow expressing modest hopes for the future – and for the play, hoping that the "gentle may speak one kind word for me." Like many of the plays just discussed, this play, which critics usually describe as a domestic tragedy, never directly invokes that genre, leaving that judgment to the auditors and readers. Munro's argument in the introduction that we can describe the play as a domestic tragicomedy makes excellent sense and speaks to the "generic, theological, and theatrical ambiguities of the play" (52). The play dramatizes sensational events drawn from recent history whose outlines would have been familiar to audiences. Several of these plays are linked to "history plays," plays that do very much the same thing but with specific attention to political questions rather than witchcraft or the politics of marriage, and their generic ambiguity is not unlike that of the "history play."

This set of paratexts demonstrates the complexity of relations among the genres, the shifting nature of labels, and, most centrally, the practical disposition of the playwrights towards the categories used to label their work. *Mucedorus* in particular treats tragedy not

---

18. In fact, the words tragedy, tragic, or tragical appear nowhere in the play.
19. See the introduction to Lucy Munro's edition of the play (2017), especially 41–55. I am citing this edition.

as a genre but as a "fume," or set of tools that are meant to create tonal effects and disrupt a planned comic plot. Peter Berek's work on title pages and the uses of generic labels demonstrates that genre had a function for stationers as they marketed the plays they printed (and that printed generic attributions had a shaping effect on reading audiences). As he writes in "Genres, Early Modern Theatrical Title Pages, and the Authority of Print," "generic categories belong more to the 'aftermarket' of plays in print than to their initial appearance on stage," going on to state that:

> Philip Henslowe's diary . . . suggests that generic categories were not very important to his practical theatrical life. When he inventories the playbooks owned by the Admiral's Men, none of the titles has a generic designation. Only a very small number of the plays whose performances or acquisitions he lists are referred to by terms like "comedy" or "tragedy." (160–1)[20]

In a later article, Berek demonstrates that the use of *tragedy* and *tragical* on printed title pages was not initially associated with plays and that when those terms did get linked to plays they carried a weight of ideological association that has little to do with how literary critics understand genre. Before *Tamburlaine:*

> Forms of the word "tragedy" in titles first appear under Edward in Protestant tracts and Hall's chronicle. Through much of the sixteenth century the term continues to appear in the titles of narratives of Protestant martyrdom . . . in almost every instance where the word "tragedy" appears, its affiliations are Protestant or nationalistic or both. That is the context in which printed plays for the professional theater begin to appear. ("Tragedy and Title Pages" 21)[21]

---

20. Berek also makes the crucial point that labels like "tragedy" and "comedy" had a far broader application in the period than just drama, a point my discussion of Drayton's poems *Peirs Gaveston* and *Mortimeriados* elsewhere in this book underscores. The terms are used adjectivally more than they are as substantives. Berek's series of essays on genre and print are an important contribution to our understanding of how stationers deployed generic labels in what he calls the "aftermarket," and he makes cautious suggestions about the effect of those labels on production but notes that those effects would mostly occur later in the period after the establishment of a set of expectations about plays in print.
21. The two parts of *Tamburlaine*, as Berek writes, were called "tragical discourses" in Jones's edition, and *Hamlet* was later called a "tragical history." The process Berek describes is one where stationers appear to be working towards a set of terms while the plays themselves outpace efforts to label them, and until late in the period the plays stay ahead of the labels.

That context influences the uses of the word *tragedy* on early theatrical title pages and is in turn influenced by ideas about tragedy coming from the theatre. Title page conventions, of course, have more to do with the printing house than the playhouse – where, as an example, Henslowe's indifference to generic labels speaks to a practical disposition toward genre. This practical disposition underlies and makes possible the innovations that will be the subject of the rest of this chapter.

III

John Marston's Antonio plays – *Antonio and Mellida* (1599, Q 1602) and *Antonio's Revenge* (1600, Q 1602) – and Chapman's Bussy plays – *Bussy D'Ambois* (1603–4, Q1 1607, Q2 1608, Revised text Q 1641) and *The Revenge of Bussy D'Ambois* (1610, Q 1613) – are, as the titles indicate, two-part revenge-inflected plays produced by child companies around the turn of the seventeenth century. Both pairs of plays stress revenge in the second parts, though the plotting and potential for violence common to the so-called revenge tragedy run though both parts of both playwrights' plays. Marston's two plays use the resources of satire in ways that anticipate his later play *The Malcontent*, and Chapman draws on recent French history to comment on court life more generally. My interest lies in what we can infer about what the playwrights thought they were doing in producing these plays in the first decade of the seventeenth century, in how these plays respond to and attempt to intervene in the dramatic field. Marston's plays react to what the induction to *Antonio and Mellida* represents as older conventions, conventions that are out of date, and offer novel elements, some of which are picked up by other playwrights. Chapman's intervention is to revise a tragic stage tradition in service of a particular ethical and authorial project, and though Marston's intervention seems to have had a more durable impact, Chapman remains an important figure.

Much criticism of Marston's paired plays calls attention to questions about form and genre and locates them in the context of the child companies. R. A. Foakes, in "John Marston's Fantastical Plays: *Antonio and Mellida* and *Antonio's Revenge*," calls specific attention to the apparent parodic intent of the induction:

> The Induction draws attention to the child actors, and assumes on the part of the audience a knowledge of common practices at the public

theatres. The allusion to *The Spanish Tragedy* is followed by another to *Tamburlaine* ... By the end of the Induction, in fact, it is clear that the play will parody the old ranting styles, make the children outstrut the adult tragedians, who were still performing the plays of Kyd and Marlowe, and burlesque common conventions. (229)[22]

Foakes argues that Marston deploys the child actors as a sort of special effect designed to remind audiences at all times about the distance between the actors and the roles they play. The careful invocation of older tragic plays at the opening of *Antonio and Mellida* locates the play in the competition among theatres and, even though the play calls itself a comedy and closes with a more or less comic resolution, suggests the tragedy to come in *Antonio's Revenge*.[23] In "The Ironic Tragedies of Marston and Chapman," Allen Bergson argues that the plays

> share a tragic form or movement characterized by a pervasive irony which manifests itself in both structure and tone. [His] chief concern in the following paper will be to indicate the several ways in which the "ironic tragedies" of Marston and Chapman, all written for and performed in the private playhouses between late 1599 and 1608, reveal this coherent dramatic and imaginative pattern. (613)[24]

For Bergson, irony, the privy mark that allegedly made *The Knight of the Burning Pestle* unacceptable to its early audiences, here characterizes the form of these plays. In the later essay "Dramatic Style as Parody in Marston's *Antonio and Mellida*," Bergson characterizes both plays as a "pervasive literary parody" of the conventions of romantic comedy and, at least by implication, of tragedy (307–8). Treating the two plays as a single ten-act play, he makes sense of the improbable conversion of Piero at the end of *Antonio and Mellida* by

---

22. I am not entirely convinced that parody is the primary goal here, but Foakes's attention to the plays' engagement with the field is important.
23. The *Annals* call the play a "tragicomedy," a label Harbage, Schoenbaum, and Wagonheim use quite freely but one that does not get used on title pages as a generic label until 1623 (for Webster's *Devil's Law Case*). Fletcher's *Faithful Shepherdess*, whose paratexts are often described as one of the first discussions of tragicomedy, is labeled as "pastoral" in the *Annals*. Nathaniel Leonard's "Embracing the 'Mongrel': John Marston's *The Malcontent, Antonio and Mellida,* and the Development of Early Modern Tragicomedy" argues that *Antonio and Mellida*'s deployment of comic tropes at the play's close suggests that the play's happy closure is not sustainable and points to the tragedy of the next play.
24. Bergson includes Chapman's two Byron plays in this grouping.

reference to the opening of the second play, which depicts it as false and part of a larger, violent plan. These readings all depend on the survival of both "parts" of the play, and without *Antonio's Revenge*, we might think of *Antonio and Mellida* as a romance.

Marston's two plays are particularly theatrically self-conscious.[25] He reacts to what he treats as a codification of tragic elements in the contemporary theatre, as the way that he represents conventions in the paratexts of both plays demonstrates. *Antonio and Mellida* opens with a long induction, in which the actors talk about their roles (and, in some cases, their unhappiness with them) and, significantly, about both mode and acting styles. The actor playing Piero, the corrupt Duke, thinks his role will be simple to occupy: "Who cannot be proud, stroke up the hair, and strut?" (Ind. 14).[26] The actor playing Alberto, a virtuous counselor, responds:

> Truth. Such rank custom is grown popular;
> And now the vulgar fashion strides as wide
> And stalks as proud upon the weakest stilts
> Of the slight'st fortunes as if Hercules
> Or burly Atlas shoulder'd up their state. (15–19)

Alberto calls these gestures rank and vulgar, deployed indiscriminately for slight and serious materials alike, indicating that their meaning has been emptied out. Another actor, playing a "modern Bragadoch" (88) demonstrates his capacity for rant:

> By the bright honor of a Milanoise,
> And the resplendent fulgor of this steel,
> I will defend the feminine to death,
> And ding his spirit to the verge of hell
> That dares divulge a lady's prejudice. (81–5)

Prompted by this performance, Feliche responds: "Rampum, scrampum, mount tufty Tamburlaine! What rattling thunderclap breaks from his lips?" (86–7). The induction closes indicating hopes for a second part when the actor playing Feliche expresses anxiety about the play having space to "limn so many persons in so small a table

---

25. This is, of course, true of many of his plays – particularly *The Malcontent* – and his involvement in the Poet's War demonstrates the depth of his engagement in the struggles that shape the field of theatrical production.
26. I am quoting from G. K. Hunter's editions of both plays (1965).

as the compass of our plays afford" (132–3).²⁷ The actor playing Antonio responds:

> Right. Therefore I have heard that those persons, as he, you, Feliche, that are but slightly drawn in this comedy, should receive more exact accomplishment in a second part; which, if this obtain gracious acceptance, means to try his fortune. (132–8)

The actor here reassures his colleague, promising a sequel to this "comedy" that will offer a larger compass for other persons. He calls the current play a comedy, but offers no indication about the potential kind of the second part. The prologue that follows the induction makes no specific reference to dramatic kind, only wishes that the actors'

>   muse
> Had those abstruse and sinewy faculties,
> That, with a strain of fresh invention,
> She might press out the rarity of art,
> The pur'st elixed juice of rich conceit. (9–13)

But, lamentably, Marston lacks abstruse and sinewy faculties, and the prologue can only hope that the audience will make up for their deficiencies and "polish these rude scenes" (21).²⁸ The prologue does not offer any discussion of the play proper and only attempts to flatter the audience into accepting the play.²⁹

The play's trajectory towards the wedding promised at the end of the play is complicated by Piero's unexplained animosity towards Andrugio and his son Antonio, an animosity that results in Andrugio's deposition and presumed death and that forces Antonio to adopt a disguise as an Amazon. The lovers appear to have overcome the various crosses to the love story by the end of the play, but there are any number of indications of the potential shape of the play's sequel. One

---

27. The possessive ("our plays") Feliche uses here is interestingly ambiguous: is he referring to plays in general (as in "the two hours traffic of our stage") or narrowly to the plays put on by the Children of Paul's? Either way, the statement's meaning depends on the audience's sense of the scale of a play. Writing about Marston's *Malcontent*, Meghan Andrews points out how the additions to the play as performed by the King's Men were necessary because the child company plays were shorter than those performed by the adult companies.
28. This is humorous self-deprecation, since Marston *is* an abstract and sinewy playwright.
29. Antonio's opening speech functions as an introduction to the plot of the play, doing the work of a descriptive prologue.

of these is the play's recourse to Senecan quotation and imitation.[30] Piero quotes Seneca's *Thyestes* twice in the play. The first ("dimitto superos: summa votorum attigi" (l. 888) [I dismiss the gods, I have attained the height of my prayers]), appears in 1.1, when Piero is filled with pride at his victory over Andrugio. The second, also in 1.1 ("o me caelitum excelsissimum" (l. 911) [I am the highest of the gods]), follows confirmation that his letters promising rewards for the heads of either Andrugio or Antonio have been circulated. *Thyestes* is quoted frequently in *Antonio's Revenge* as well, as are some other Senecan texts. The Latin quotations in the play seem very likely to be a response to the way that Kyd's *Spanish Tragedy* makes use of Senecan materials.[31] Marston invokes both the content of these plays and the domestic tradition of citing them.

Despite being cautioned about the dangers of pride, Piero twice quotes Atreus' prideful utterances at the banquet where his brother will eat his children. The quotes have the immediate effect of exemplifying Piero's villainy and suggesting that his pride will be punished. Marston's choice of *Thyestes* points forward towards elements of *Antonio's Revenge*, particularly to Antonio's murder of Piero's son Julio, whose body is then served to Piero in the closing action of that play. Senecan tragedy runs through the whole of *Antonio and Mellida* even though the end of the play avoids a tragic denouement, providing a tragic undercurrent of allusion that partly explains it being labeled a tragicomedy and that also offers some support to the arguments of critics like Bergson who see the two plays as comprising one ten-act play.[32] Marston's experiment, successful enough to justify the sequel, is to produce a comedy whose resolution is undercut by the whole structure of the play as well as this pattern of Senecan allusion that points forward to that sequel and the more thorough Senecanism that characterizes it.

Antonio and Mellida ends with an armed epilogue whose words bear a structural resemblance to the prologue armed of *Troilus and Cressida*:

---

30. The first play uses Italian extensively in the romantic plot, but the Italian vanishes in *Antonio's Revenge*.
31. See chapter four above.
32. See Bergson, "Dramatic Style as Parody in Marston's *Antonio and Mellida*." Bergson calls the whole ten-act play *Antonio and Mellida*. The question of whether Marston composed the plays as one extended play remains an open one, but it seems improbable to me (and it seems like an unnecessary complication).

> Though I remain an armed Epilogue, I stand not as a peremptory challenger of desert, either for him that composed the comedy or for us that acted it, but a most submissive suppliant for both . . . what we are is by your favor. What we shall be, rests all in your applausive encouragements. (1–10)[33]

This epilogue offers traditional requests for applause and reminds the audience that the play they have just seen is a comedy. It makes only the vaguest promise of a sequel ("what we shall be") and no indication whatever of what that potential second part, to use the Induction's phrase, might be about or that it will be a tragedy.

When *Antonio's Revenge* appears on stage, the play leaves no doubt about its genre. While it lacks an induction, it does include a prologue and epilogue that name the play as tragedy, invoking the season as a justification for the dark mood of the play:

> The rawish dank of clumsy winter ramps
> The fluent summer's vein; and drizzling sleet
> Chilleth the wan bleak cheek of the numb'd earth,
> Whilst snarling gusts nibble the juiceless leaves
> From the nak'd shivering branch, and pills the skin
> From off the soft and delicate branch.
> O now, methinks, a sullen tragic scene
> Would suit the time with pleasing congruence. (Prol. 1–8)

After this mood-setting, the prologue goes on to hope that the audience is composed of people who are "nail'd to the earth with grief" and "pierc'd through with anguish" or have blood "whose heat is chok'd / And stifled with true sense of misery" (21–5).[34] The play that follows does not disappoint: it opens with Piero entering smeared with blood carrying his bloody poniard, accompanied by Strotzo (a strangler) carrying the cord appropriate to his name. As Hunter's introduction to his Regents Renaissance Drama edition of the play

---

33. The "not . . . either . . . but" construction has interesting resonances with *Troilus and Cressida*'s "not in confidence / Of author's pen or actor's voice, but suited / In like conditions as our argument" (Prol. 23–25). The epilogue is in armor because it is spoken by Andrugio, who ends the play in armor, and who will be murdered by the time the sequel play begins. The revenge in *Antonio's Revenge* is for his murder (and, in a double plot, for Feliche's, which also happens as the play begins).
34. The speech instructs those who are "uncapable of weighty passion," who do not want to "know what men were and are, / Who would not know what men must be" to "hurry amain from our black visag'd shows" (Prol. 18–20). The play's tragedy is weightier than the lighter offerings of comic shows.

notes, "direct quotation from Seneca appears in almost every scene; the Italian that decorated the love intrigue of *Antonio and Mellida* has disappeared and Latin reigns alone as the language of tragic passion" (xiii). The play's violence and consistently extreme plot align it with later examples of tragedy, but the fact that the main revenger survives the play and is offered the dukedom of Venice, only to refuse it, marks it as unusual.[35]

Marston's use of a closing masque of revengers is one of the most striking innovations of the play and is so striking that it has come to sometimes seem like a convention. As M. R. Golding writes:

> ... so impressive is the use of the masque as a revenge murder machine in these plays, that certain commentators have been led to think it the distinctive feature of almost all revenge tragedies. (44).

Golding points to some examples, including M.C. Bradbrook's 1952 second edition of *Themes and Conventions of Elizabethan Tragedy*. The essay goes on to state that only four extant plays use a masque in this way: *Antonio's Revenge, The Malcontent, The Revenger's Tragedy,* and *Women Beware Women* (45).[36] In *Antonio's Revenge,* the masque pretends to be in celebration of Piero's wedding to Antonio's mother (who is an active participant in the revenge), and the ghost of his murdered father is in the audience. The play in many languages that closes Kyd's *Spanish Tragedy* likewise is intended, however bizarrely, to be part of a wedding celebration, and its confusion of languages makes it more like a masque or a dumbshow than a play within a play, like Hamlet's *Mousetrap*. Marston's masque thus echoes but goes beyond Kyd's murder-play, putting *Antonio's Revenge* in dialogue with Kyd's still-influential work. Framing the masque, Galeatzo, son of the Duke of Florence, tells the conspirators in asides that he, Venice and (he hopes) Fortune support the planned violence. Andrugio's Ghost takes on a role structurally reminiscent of the ghost of Andrea in *The Spanish Tragedy*. He is "placed betwixt the music-houses" in a stage direction and tells the audience, "Here will I sit, spectator of revenge, / And glad my ghost in anguish of my foe" (5.3.53–4). This appreciation is almost precisely the attitude expressed by Andrea in Kyd's play and is one more signal of Marston's responsive reaction to Kyd's

---

35. This play belies the truism that "revengers always die."
36. Masques within plays are, of course, far more common, but their use as a "murder machine," to use Golding's phrase, is limited to these four. This fact might explain critical assumptions about the murder-masque being a convention rather than an exception.

work.³⁷ The maskers convince Piero to empty the room of witnesses so they can dine privately with him and as soon as they do "*the conspirators bind* Piero, *pluck out his tongue and triumph over him*":

> ANTONIO: Murder and torture; no prayers, no entreats.
> PANDULPHO: We'll spoil your oratory. Out with his tongue!
> ANTONIO: I have't, Pandulpho; the veins panting bleed,
>   Trickling fresh gore about my fist. Bind fast! So, so.
> GHOST: Blest be thy hand. I taste the joys of heaven,
>   Viewing my son triumph in his black blood. (5.3.63–8)

The maskers then torment the silenced Piero in various ways before finally showing him a dish containing his son's "limbs." Presenting the dish, Antonio tells him, "Look, look here: / Here lies a dish to feast thy father's gorge / Here's flesh and blood which I am sure thou lov'st" (5.3.78–80). Piero "condoles" his son's limbs, according to a stage direction and then the conspirators remind Piero of his crimes and repeatedly bid "pity, piety, remorse / Be alien to our thoughts" (5.3.89–90). Pandulpho, wishing that Piero would "die and die, and still be dying. / And yet not die till he hath died and died / Ten thousand deaths in agony of heart," prefaces the actual murder, committed by all the conspirators in a flurry of stabs (5.3.105–7).³⁸ This violence is extreme, particularly since this is a Paul's play with actors of similar ages to Piero's murdered son, and it seems designed both for shock value and to specifically outdo some earlier iterations of plays about revenge. Kyd's *Spanish Tragedy* draws on and transforms classical models of tragedy, and Marston's responsive reaction draws on both that classical tradition and Kyd's own work in producing his own version of revenge tragedy.

With Piero's death, Andrugio's ghost is satisfied and leaves the stage, offering a possibly disturbing proverb: "'Tis done; and now my soul shall sleep in rest. / Sons that revenge their father's blood are blest" (5.3.114–115).³⁹ The final moments of the play see the

---

37. Scholars have long recognized that Kyd's play was a direct influence on Marston's work. One example, Harry Levin's "An Echo from *The Spanish Tragedy*," argues that the Painter's lines in the additions to Kyd's play are echoed by Balurdo's commission of a painting in *Antonio and Mellida*. Most interestingly, Levin argues that what he calls the "transpositions" of the painter's scene register the "respective moods of a fast-changing period" and that they can serve as evidence of the shape of the field (302). The relationship between Andrugio's ghost and Old Hamlet is less direct.
38. Hieronimo and Bel-Imperia close their play in a flurry of stabs as well.
39. The vexed dating of both this play and *Hamlet* makes it difficult to say for

revengers claiming responsibility for the murder and the "glory of the deed" (5.3.120). Unlike most revenge plots, this play closes with the revengers being praised and rewarded because their deeds are judged to be just. The senators and Galeatzo all approve the murder based on their judgment of what appear to be either documents or testimony ("beadrolls of mischief, plots of villainy"), and award Antonio the rule of Venice. Antonio refuses, and along with the conspirators, departs to, in Pandulpho's words, "live enclos'd / In holy verge of some religious order, / Most constant votaries" (5.3.151–2) where they will meditate on their misery and contemplate "past calamities" (5.3.165). Rather than the deaths that punctuate Kyd's play, Marston's closes with contemplation. Revenge is, if not unambiguously praiseworthy, not punished by the immediate death of the revenger.[40] Both the masque and the fates of the revengers are interventions in the field, and I take up later responses – both Marston's own and that of other playwrights – below.

Antonio's final speech, which functions like an epilogue (much as his opening speech in *Antonio and Mellida* functions like a prologue), turns to Mellida's death and away from the spectacle of violence that closes the play. Instead of justice, the theme of the response to Piero's murder, Antonio claims that singing "Mellida is dead" will cause universal sadness and that "never more woe in lesser plot was found" (5.3.176). Hunter glosses *plot* as "area," but the theatrical sense of the word makes good sense here and is in keeping with the self-referential nature of the speech (and play) as a whole.[41] He hopes that when some future writer "dares once to engage his pen to write her death, / Presenting it in some black tragedy," it will be

> suck'd up
> By calm attention of choice audience;
> And when the closing Epilogue appears,
> Instead of claps may it obtain but tears. (5.3.183–6)[42]

certain if Marston is responding to Shakespeare or the other way around in this father-avenging plot overseen by a ghost. *Hamlet*'s revenge and ghost are quite different from what we see in Marston's play.
40. The masque staged at the close of *The Malcontent* looks to end in murder but does not, and Marston appears to be engaging in a kind of dialogue with his own work. Malevole/Altofronto chooses clemency and, unlike Antonio, does not have to retreat from the world.
41. The OED lists Beaumont's *Knight of the Burning Pestle* (1607, Q 1613) as a first instance of this sense of the word, at least suggesting that the pun was available to Marston.
42. The speech expresses hope that this writer will have a style "deck'd / With

The play's deep metatheatricality, a degree of self-reference that runs through Marston's work, appears to be another feature of his work that later writers respond to and is a feature of the field in general.

Chapman's Bussy plays, while they appear to have been theatrically successful, seem not to have had the same degree of influence on later work. In their first editions, Chapman's plays lack the introductory apparatus seen in Marston's plays. *Bussy D'Ambois* only acquires a prologue and epilogue in the 1641 Quarto which were probably added in the 1630s.[43] The reference to the death of Nathaniel Field (1619) in the prologue only indicates the date after which the prologue must have been written, and the references to two other actors who played the role of Bussy, one described as being too old now, support the idea that the prologue dates to the 1630s. *The Revenge of Bussy D'Ambois* never gets a frame at all, only a dedicatory letter from Chapman to Thomas Howard. Instead, the plays simply begin. That their initial presentations lack the kind of metatheatrical openings or comments on form that Marston seems to enjoy producing suggests that Chapman (and the acting company) either counted on audiences to recognize what kind of play they were about to see or did not think it necessary to explain it.

The prologue to the 1641 quarto of *Bussy D'Ambois* makes no programmatic statement about the play, but places it into the context of a debate over the right to perform it:

> Not out of confidence that none but we
> Are able to present this tragedy,
> Nor out of envy at the grace of late
> It did receive, nor yet to derogate
> From their deserts, who give out boldly that
> They move with equal feet on the same flat;
> We offer it, gracious and noble friends,
> To your review; we far from emulation,
> With this work entertain you, a piece known,
> And still believed in Court to be our own. (1–12)

The rest of the prologue speaks to the company's history of performing the play (the reference to Field and two other unnamed actors

---

freshest blooms of purest elegance" (5.3.182), unlike, for example, the muse the acting company apparently does have, at least according to the prologue. Marston cannot seem to resist metatheatrical self-reference.

43. Interestingly, the *Annals* call *Bussy D'Ambois* a "foreign history," not a tragedy, despite the 1641 quarto's self-description as tragedy. The *Annals* name *The Revenge of Bussy D'Ambois* as tragedy.

serve both as evidence of title and a claim about the popularity of the play).[44] Chapman's epistle in the quarto of *The Revenge of Bussy D'Ambois* asserts that the play was pleasing to the wiser sort. More importantly, it goes on to make comments about what it calls "autentical truth":

> And for the autentical truth of either person or action, who (worth the respecting) will expect it in a poem, whose subject is not truth, but things like truth? Poor envious souls they are that cavil at truth's want in these natural fictions; material instruction, elegant and sententious excitation to virtue, and deflection from her contrary, being the soul, limbs, and limits of an autentical tragedy.

Wise souls, not afflicted by envy, will not expect fidelity to "truth of either person or action" from what Chapman calls a poem because the proper concern of tragedy is not mimesis but offering moral instruction. Fidelity to truth, something extolled as a positive good in plays like *A Woman Killed with Kindness*, *Arden of Faversham*, and *A Warning for Fair Women*, looks to Chapman like a defect that detracts from the real nature of tragedy. This position is paradoxical, of course, since all his tragedies draw on recent French history for their plots.

Critics have traditionally seen Chapman's specific intervention in these plays in their effort to advance an ethical agenda that comes out of his commitment to stoicism. This agenda appears most clearly in *The Revenge of Bussy D'Ambois*, whose hero strives to remain above the corrupting political world he occupies.[45] Albert Tricomi argues that the revisions of *Bussy D'Ambois* seen in the 1641 quarto point to an attempt to make the play line up more directly with the stoic agenda of the sequel.[46] Much of the criticism of the plays is

---

44. Discussion of title to plays is not an unprecedented part of inductions – see Marston's *Malcontent*, which opens with dialogue explaining why a Paul's play is being performed by the King's Men – and moments like these offer a glimpse into the relationships among the various acting companies. Like Marston's, Chapman's play moves from a child to an adult company, and the existence of this prologue shows that the move needed explaining.
45. There is an extensive scholarship arguing this position, as Suzanne Kistler points out in her "'Strange and Far-Removed Shores': A Reconsideration of *The Revenge of Bussy D'Ambois*." Kistler's argument is that rather than offering an endorsement of stoic values, *The Revenge* depicts their profound failure by destroying Clermont despite (or because of) his ideals and by portraying his suicide as a moral failure.
46. Tricomi's conclusion is that "the revised version of *Bussy D'Ambois* is truer to the intentions and outlook of *The Revenge of Bussy D'Ambois* than it is to the

far more concerned with these questions – is Chapman endorsing stoicism? criticizing it? – than with locating it in the theatrical field. One exception is Richard Ide's 1984 essay "Exploiting the Tradition: The Elizabethan Revenger as Chapman's 'Complete Man,'" which argues that the *Revenge of Bussy D'Ambois*, while a failure, is a "bold, fascinating, and instructive failure" because of Chapman's effort to "renovate a sensational, melodramatic genre and its entire dramatic tradition to serve his ethical intention" (170). The play fails because, in Ides' view, it cannot bear the "weight" of that agenda. James Krasner's "*The Tragedy of Bussy D'Ambois* and the Creation of Heroism" (1989) argues that we can understand *Bussy* as a kind of position-taking in the field because it stages a conflict "between the artist and political myth-maker and the artist as aesthetic creator" that is also a feature of Chapman's translations (107).[47] Although Krasner's essay also puts Chapman's play into dialogue with *Antonio's Revenge* and *Hamlet* as part of a broader tradition of tragedies of revenge, his work remains author-focused and leaves institutional questions aside.

I have discussed these four plays at some length because their specific innovations move from the private theatres and the child companies to the adult theatres, and some of those changes become the hallmarks of what we have come to call either "Jacobean tragedy" or, often, "revenge tragedy." Marston and Chapman's responses to and deployments of Seneca, the court masque, and other plays contribute to both a shifting theatrical landscape and to later critical definitions of genres. Critical interest in genre, however useful in writing literary criticism, can obscure the field's dynamism since generic definitions offer an illusion of fixity that the practice of playwrights belies. Marston and Chapman's plays resist straightforward categorization, as do many plays of the period. The tenants to these tragedies move in and out of later plays, influencing both production and reception. Middleton's plays pick up some features from these plays and, as the field develops, introduce others. The murder-masque represents only the most obvious of these elements.

---

    values of the original *Bussy* itself" (305). Tricomi sees some of the revisions as being designed to improve stage effects, but others appear to him as intended to align the play's philosophical positions with the *Revenge*.

47. I use Bourdieu's term here even though Krasner does not because it offers the best description of the essay's thesis. Bourdieu discusses position-takings in the field of cultural production extensively in *The Field of Cultural Production*.

IV

> When the bad bleeds, then is the tragedy good.
> Middleton, *The Revenger's Tragedy* (1607)

Vindice's line – repeated in various forms at other points in the play – functions as a kind of literary criticism that evaluates "tragedy" in terms of how well it metes out punishment to the "bad." His position, which is also echoed in plays like Marston's *Antonio's Revenge*, does not depend on a clearly articulated definition of tragedy; instead, the key category is justice. In Middleton's play, as with a number of others, "tragedy" refers to a kind of play, but it also simply means "death" or "murder," as in a sword being the agent of a character's tragedy. In the course of his opening monologue, which functions in place of a chorus, Vindice prays to Vengeance:

> Vengeance, thou murder's quit-rent, and whereby
> Thou show'st thyself tenant to Tragedy,
> O, keep thy day, hour, minute, I beseech,
> For those thou hast determin'd!—hum, who e'er knew
> Murder unpaid? (1.1.39–43)

When Vindice says that murder is tenant to tragedy at the start of *The Revenger's Tragedy*, he is making an argument about the kind of play that he is in and the genre as a whole. Middleton produced plays critics have categorized as tragedy (of various subtypes), history, comedy (also of various subtypes), and tragicomedy – all the major modes of drama in the period. His best-known tragic plays – *The Revenger's Tragedy* and *Women Beware Women* – engage with generic questions in profound ways. *Revenger's* parody of revenge tragedy both calls attention to what had already become set pieces of the form and transforms them in the service of a more general questioning of the purposes of tragedy. Both look very specifically back to plays by Shakespeare and Marston – deploying set pieces or famous props from both playwrights' works. *Hengist, King of Kent*, as I discussed in chapter two, returns to the mode-mixing of 1590s historical drama. His city comedy, like that of Marston, Dekker and Jonson, represents London to itself. His play *The Old Law* dips into tragicomedy.[48]

---

48. See Gary Taylor's "Thomas Middleton: Lives and Afterlives" in *Thomas Middleton: The Collected Works* (2008) for an extended discussion of Middleton's life and the diversity of his work.

Scholars have more often discussed *The Revenger's Tragedy*, performed in 1605 or 1606 and printed in 1607, as parody, camp, or even black comedy than as a serious intervention in or meditation on early modern tragedy. The play makes use of a whole range of tropes from the English tragic tradition, often calling quite specific attention to them.[49] The spectacular and bizarre nature of its violence, its subversion of the revenge-masque trope common to Marston's revenge plays, and its Italian setting, among other details small and large, make clear that the play is a response to the theatrical moment's interest in revenge tragedy. Moreover, the play's extreme degree of self-consciousness also links it to a play like *Knight of the Burning Pestle* (performed for the first time in 1607, the year Middleton's play was published). A more focused parody than Beaumont's play, Middleton's play nevertheless works as a comment on the whole of the dramatic field.

While the question of Middleton's authorship of the play is at least sporadically open, there are compelling reasons to see the play as Middleton's. For the purposes of my argument about genre and generic change, Brian Jay Corrigan's arguments for Middleton's authorship in his 1998 essay "Middleton, *The Revenger's Tragedy*, and Crisis Literature" is particularly relevant. Corrigan discusses the traditional reluctance "to assign a tragedy to a playwright whose output up to 1606 had been comprised entirely of comedies and one history" and goes on to show that Middleton testified to have written a tragedy at this point in his career (285).[50] Middleton's early attachment to the Children of Paul's is also often adduced as evidence against his authorship of *The Revenger's Tragedy*. Corrigan argues that the play dates to the time when the Paul's company was on the verge of dissolution and that since there is evidence of his writing plays freelance later in his career it is not unreasonable to think that he could have written the play as an early speculative script for the adult companies (285–6). In other words, Middleton was working in a changing dramatic field and the play can be understood as an effort to respond to change.[51]

49. These references start at the very beginning of the play: Vindice's reference to Murder being "tenant to tragedy" in the initial speech of the play heads a long list of metadramatic commentary ("when the bad bleeds, then is the tragedy good" and so on).
50. The play is the lost "Viper and Her Brood," which was the object of some litigation.
51. These arguments against Middleton's authorship also depend on the assumption that the evidence we have is complete: in other words, since we only have

As Corrigan also argues, Middleton "had a metadramatic view of his composition" and occasionally wrote "crisis literature," which Corrigan defines as work that "comments self-consciously on the external times in which it is written" (287). The crisis here derives from the changing theatrical field, and Middleton's parody of *The Spanish Tragedy* represents part of his response to that crisis.[52] Corrigan's article locates the play in the field:

> Clearly Middleton was aware of the change in the condition of playwrighting and character construction and, as he had done before and would do again, wrote on that change as well to dismiss the old as to anticipate the new. (292)

Corrigan's essay spends less time on the details of how the play demonstrates its engagement in the field than on the history of criticism of the play. Middleton's play represents a particular kind of position-taking in the genre system.

Middleton's history with the Children of Paul's offers one way to characterize his involvement in the field and a link to some of the innovations discussed above. Beaumont, Chapman, Dekker, Fletcher, Marston, Middleton, and Webster are the named playwrights of surviving plays associated with the second Children of Paul's. Comedies dominate the surviving repertory, but Marston and Chapman's tragedies figure largely in the repertory, and as a more or less attached playwright Middleton would have been well aware of both men's work. This exposure helps explain his later tragedies' deployment of the masque as a vehicle for violence, and the three writers share a metadramatic sensibility as well as an interest in parody. The Paul's repertory seems to have had a shaping influence on both Marston and Middleton's later work for adult companies.

Leslie Sanders argues that *The Revenger's Tragedy* is "self-consciously and insistently theatrical" and that when we properly consider this theatricality "the play emerges as both a black parody of that highly popular form of renaissance entertainment, the revenge play itself, and as a profound examination of the implications of

---

Middleton comedies from this period, he must only have been writing comedies. The same goes for the child company argument.

52. The play is also, inevitably, a response to *Hamlet*. Scott McMillin's "Acting and Violence: *The Revenger's Tragedy* and Its Departures from *Hamlet*," argues that the whole play is a response to Shakespeare's play.

the genre's immense popularity" (25).[53] Sanders is less interested in locating the play in the immediate context of the theatre world of the early seventeenth century than in demonstrating how the play's sometimes (before 1974) overlooked theatricality represents a comment on tragedy. Vindice's opening monologue invokes an enormous array of theatrical tropes linked to multiple genres. Gloriana's skull is only the most tangible of these, and taken together they locate the play as a sophisticated satirical tragedy from the opening moments even before the character names solidify that identification. These links to satire extend beyond the allegorical naming of the characters and represent another connection to theatrical fashion of the first years of the seventeenth century and to the work of playwrights like Marston who was closely associated with stage satire. Middleton uses the extended parody of the play to raise serious questions about the drama of revenge.[54] I argue that we can see *The Revenger's Tragedy* as Middleton's version of *Hamlet*, produced through a response to Marston.

Vindice's opening speech deploys the language of character books, of allegorical drama, and of city comedy, before it transitions to a meditation on the transitory nature of life. As McMillin argues, figures of compression dominate the play's figural language, and "metalepsis seems the goal of play's figurative language" ("Acting and Violence" 281). This sort of compression affords Middleton the opportunity to cram an enormous range of references into small spans – even into props – creating a dense web of allusion. As only one example, the opening speech invokes a broad range of dramatic and poetic kinds through piling up synecdoche, amounting to a parodic snapshot of the theatrical field. Even Vindice's "Oh God!" could be a reference to Hamlet's first soliloquy, which is itself consumed with the horror of death and a squeamish fascination with lustful behavior by his elders.[55] Vindice's own horror of (and attraction to) lust is never far from the surface in the play, and in this speech the Duke's "palsy-lust" is what turns his "abused heart-strings to fret" (1.1.34, 13). He only turns directly to the skull he enters with when he starts to think of

---

53. Sanders's essay was influential in producing the still-current critical consensus about the play's parodic disposition.
54. Sanders makes a similar point, arguing that the play leads its audiences to become "aware of its zest for the horrible, and into applauding what it cannot condone in itself" (35).
55. The whole speech comments on and refracts Hamlet's "too too solid flesh" speech, and we can put even the comments on time into dialogue with Hamlet's thoughts about speed.

the incongruity of how the "parched and juiceless" Duke acts "like a son and heir" (1.1.9, 11).⁵⁶ His invocation of revenge comes after thoughts about the Duke's lust, not Gloriana's murder, and refers to Vengeance as "murder's quit-rent" (1.1.39). These lines refer to *Hamlet* but with a difference. Where Hamlet's quietus appears in the context of a nuanced meditation on the outcomes of action and inaction, Vindice's quit-rent appears as a straightforward, if long-delayed in this case, response to murder. Vengeance is not a problem, as in *Hamlet*, but is instead a simple effect of murder: murder must and will be repaid by revenge.⁵⁷ Vindice's invocation of "Tragedy" is not the kind of choric meditation on form typical of the paratexts discussed above. For him, "Tragedy" is simply a kind of story where revenge can take place. When he asks "who e'er knew / Murder unpaid?" he can only be referring to murders in revenge plays, because there are numerous examples of murder being unpaid.⁵⁸ Here, as elsewhere in the play, Vindice eschews deeper thought about consequence in favor of a more or less unreflective exchange of violence for violence. Middleton's characters avoid ontological and ethical questions, and the play instead focuses on sensational surfaces and the extremes of what revenge plots imply.

Critics have long noted the metadramatic nature of Middleton's play and the depth of its reference to the contemporary theatre world. From Vindice's early invocation of Tragedy to his (fulfilled) expectation of thunder as applause for his actions, Middleton constantly calls attention to the play as a performance. Hippolito, among other characters, admires the "quaintness" of his brother's malicious plotting "above thought" (3.5.108). In the absence of a programmatic prologue, reflective moments such as these serve as ways of guiding audience attention and as ways of identifying the play's place in the theatrical metadialogue. Both individual moments and the succession of scenes orchestrate the play's parody. For example, the murder of the duke by the Bony Lady's skull precedes the scene in which the head of Supervacuo becomes both an incitement to revenge and a weapon. Thus, the structure of the play itself calls for the audience's applause for the quaintness of its plotting. Rather than using

---

56. Vindice spends more time discussing his disgust for the Duke's lust than the Duke's murder of Gloriana, which he presents more as a consequence of lust than anything else.
57. Like both *The Spanish Tragedy* and *Titus Andronicus*, *The Revenger's Tragedy* shows the law to be useless in seeking justice.
58. He also ignores that it has taken him nine years (so far) to repay the murder of Gloriana.

a framing device to locate the play, Middleton uses allusion – structural or otherwise – and archly transparent references to the play's genre and the excesses of the plot to invoke, question, and alter the genre to which the play belongs. We see this citation as Hippolito simultaneously admires his brother's ingeneous murder weapon and bemoans "why, brother, brother," conveying at least a hint of chagrin (3.5.49).[59]

The (inadvertently) doubled murder masque is a more direct kind of position-taking since it invokes Marston's play and offers at the same time a more distanced reflection on the plays within the play in Kyd's *Spanish Tragedy* and Shakespeare's *Hamlet*. In 5.1, the death of the Duke is discovered, and Lussurioso takes power. One of the nobles of the court offers the Duchess comfort and then suggests revels to celebrate the new Duke's accession. In a nicely ironic moment, the noble tells the Duchess that "no doubt but time / Will make the murderer bring forth himself," which prompts Vindice to say in an aside "He were an ass then, i'faith!" (5.1.154–6). Time, of course, does see the murderer reveal himself, and Vindice becomes the ass he criticizes here. His self-revelation also fulfills the tragic convention that murder will out which Vindice invokes at the start of the play. At the same time, Vindice and Hippolito remark on the planned revels: "Revels!" both say in asides, and Vindice plans to "strike one strain more and then we crown our wit" (5.1.160, 166–8). Supervacuo and Ambitioso, the witless sons of the Duchess, also see the revels as an opportunity to remove Lussurioso. As Supervacuo says, "A masque is treason's licence: that build upon— / 'Tis murder's best face, when a vizard's on!" (5.1.178–9). Both cases are direct references to the ending of *Antonio's Revenge*.

In 5.2, Vindice introduces his plan to an array of nameless "lords," whose "wrongs are such, / [They] cannot justly be revenged too much" (5.2.8–9). He and the lords will preempt the official masque (itself intended by Ambitioso and Supervacuo as a vehicle for murder) with one of their own. Vindice's plan for the masque is remarkably detailed given the speed with which he must have developed it and is worth quoting in full:

---

59. To point to another example: in 4.2, Vindice and Hippolito talk about the effort involved in the multiple disguises Vindice puts on in the play and, later in the scene, make jokes about how Lussurioso tells Vindice of the deeds of Piato while hiring him to, as Vindice says, "kill myself." Scenes like this use theatrical self-consciousness as plot points and at the same time point out the absurdities of those plot points.

> Revels are toward,
> And those few nobles that have long suppressed you
> Are busied to the furnishing of a masque
> And do affect to make a pleasant tale on't.
> The masquing suits are fashioning; now comes in
> That which must glad us all: we to take pattern
> Of all those suits, the colour, trimming, fashion,
> E'en to an undistinguished hair almost.
> Then entering first, observing the true form,
> Within a strain or two we shall find leisure
> To steal our swords out handsomely,
> And when they think their pleasure sweet and good,
> In the midst of all their joys, they shall sigh blood! (5.2.10–22)

The description of the preparation and plan for the masque takes more time than the actual event in the next scene. Vindice's invocation of "the true form" in line 18 is thick with theatrical reference. They will observe traditional masque form but will also observe the true form of masque in plays about revenge when they draw "swords out handsomely" (5.2.20). When the stage audience thinks *their* pleasure is sweet and good, the masquers will satisfy the expectation of murder set up here by making Lussurioso "sigh blood," and that fulfillment will make the theatrical audience's pleasure sweet and good. Like the rest of the play, the scene invokes elements of tragic convention while at the same time undercutting some of the seriousness of those elements. The play ends with Vindice being punished for doing what almost all revengers do: publicizing his cause and responsibility for the deaths. The difference in Middleton's play is that Vindice is positioned to be able to survive his revenge because no one save Hippolito knows about it. That he confesses for no reason other than dramatic convention is a final intervention in the genre that indicates both the necessity of publicity to successful revenge and the absurdity of that necessity.[60]

In the *Revenger's Tragedy,* murder is only one of many tenants to tragedy, and the diversity of tenants functions to comment on and expand the already permeable boundaries of the genre. Permeable generic boundaries become more and more of a feature of the theatre of the period and, it seems to me, are as productive for the playwrights as it is puzzling to generations of critics who, for reasons having to do with our own field, have been compelled to label and

---

60. Hippolito's reaction ("'Sfoot, brother, you begun") reacts to this.

sort plays whose writers and producers did not, or at least not in the ways that later audiences and critics have.

V

> Our poesy is as a gum which oozes
> From whence 'tis nourished.
> Shakespeare and Middleton, *Timon of Athens* (1606–7)

Shakespeare and Middleton's collaborative play stands somewhere on the borders of tragedy and has long been regarded as a hybrid, much like *Troilus and Cressida*.[61] The satire is an outlier among the plays I discuss in this chapter since satire, rather than revenge, is the tenant to this tragedy and produces social criticism rather than the violence characteristic of the other plays. Rather than adapting the mode of Marston's or Middleton's tragedies of the same years, it turns back to the satirical invective of *Troilus and Cressida*, the play whose place *Timon of Athens* takes in the 1623 Folio.[62] The play's performance and publication history is just as murky as the earlier play.[63] There is no evidence of the play having been performed in either Shakespeare or Middleton's lifetime, and it seems to have been a late addition to the Folio. The oozing gum that nourishes this play seems not to have been especially palatable to audiences (and perhaps to the playwrights, if the idea that the play was abandoned unfinished has any truth to it). *Timon of Athens* engages with the satirical tone of much of the drama of the years around its apparent composition, but its tragical satire appears not to have resonated in the way the satirical comedy did.

61. Curiously, while *Troilus and Cressida*, printed among the tragedies in the 1623 Folio, is now typically collected with the comedies, *Timon of Athens* continues to be printed there, despite a critical consensus about how difficult it is to find a proper generic label for the play.
62. The play's inclusion in the Folio increases its impact on criticism, but it is difficult to see how a likely-unperformed and possibly abandoned play impacted the genre system. At the same time, the play can say something about what Shakespeare and Middleton thought might be successful in 1606 or 1607. Middleton's role in the play is fascinating, and both *The Revenger's Tragedy* and the later *Women Beware Women* appear to have blended comedy, satire and tragedy more successfully, if appearing in quarto can be taken as evidence of some amount of success.
63. See Anthony Dawson and Gretchen Minton's introduction to the Arden edition *Timon of Athens* (2008) for an extended discussion of the play's print and performance history. I cite from this edition.

Much of the criticism not concerned with questions of authorship has been interested in establishing or commenting on the play's genre, but as William Slights argues in an oft-cited essay:

> We seek in vain for the stamp of generic purity in the variegated *Life of Timon of Athens*. It is neither tragedy, nor comedy, morality nor history. Shakespeare has not ignored genre as a means of shaping his material, but he has used that tool of his craft in a far more flexible way than has generally been understood. His subject, an examination of the proper uses of authority in an established social order, was ideally suited to satire. His problem was to find or construct a dramatic form that would create multiple perspectives capable of challenging illegitimate claims to authority and strengthening what he saw as valid ones. (40–1)

The closest to a stamp of purity we can get is the play's inclusion among the tragedies in the Folio (an inclusion consistently replicated in modern editions of the plays). Slights's emphasis on the practicality of Shakespeare (and Middleton's) disposition towards genre is suggestive, as is his recognition that the play attempts to create multiple perspectives on a central question like many of the other plays discussed in this book.

Focused as it is on money and debt, the play necessarily circles around questions about value that link it to *Troilus and Cressida*. The exchange between Timon and the Jeweller has clear affinities with the ideas about value in the Trojan council scene in the earlier play:

> TIMON: If I should pay for't as 'tis extolled,
>   It would unclew me quite.
> JEWELLER: My lord, 'tis rated
>   As those which sell would give. But you well know
>   Things of like value differing in the owners
>   Are prized by their masters. Believe't, dear lord,
>   You mend the jewel by wearing it. (1.1.170–6)

Value, according to the Jeweller, is not innate to the thing valued but derives from the will of the purchaser. In *Timon of Athens* this position is a sales pitch for an overpriced piece of jewelry, not part of a debate about whether to end or continue the Trojan War. Entering immediately after this exchange, Apemantus serves as a less-bawdy Thersites to most of the other characters' less-violent Ajaxes. The gold that Timon discovers at the end of the play represents another kind of value supposedly innate and desired by every character who learns of it but worthless to Timon. Like *Troilus and Cressida*, *Timon of Athens* undercuts and destabilizes conventional notions about value and refuses even to gesture at offering solutions. That refusal of closure aligns it with others among Shakespeare's plays and may have contributed to its problematic reception.

Genera mixta offers a way to consider the kind of position-taking the play represents. In his essay, Slights identifies a series of genres that the play mixes – tragedy, comedy, morality, history – showing how the play actively resists easy categorization.[64] Many of Shakespeare's plays of the early seventeenth century also mix genres and resist categorization. In the years more or less immediately around the play's likely composition, Shakespeare had written *All's Well That Ends Well* (1604–5, F 1623), *King Lear* (1605, Q 1608, 1619, F 1623), *Macbeth* (1606, F 1623), *Antony and Cleopatra* (1606, F 1623), and *Pericles* (1607–8, Q 1609, 1609, 1611, 1619). *Coriolanus* likely dates to 1608 (F 1623). Dawson and Minton argue for a late date of 1607 for *Timon*, but the exact date is less important than the kinds of work surrounding the play. *All's Well*'s discomforting romantic plot blurs boundaries and expectations; *Lear* and *Macbeth*, while both more clearly tragic, also end ambiguously, on a note of diminishment in *Lear*'s case and anxious expectation in *Macbeth*'s.[65] *Antony and Cleopatra* draws on history, romance, and tragedy in producing another troubling play. And *Pericles*, another collaboration, was a wildly popular generic hybrid. Middleton had written a series of city comedies – (*Michaelmas Term* (1604, Q 1607, 1630), *A Trick to Catch the Old One* (1605, Q 1608, 1616), and *A Mad World My Masters* (1605–6, Q 1608) – before turning to tragedy in *The Revenger's Tragedy* (1606, Q 1607) and possibly *The Yorkshire Tragedy* (1605, Q 1608, 1619).[66] Middleton seems to have been branching out into tragedy at the same time that Shakespeare was producing several of his major tragedies and moving towards the plays we have come to see as romances. Like a number of these plays, *Timon* blends various modes, and the play attempts to carve out a space for a less comic, if not fully tragic, mode of satirical drama. Like *Troilus*, another play inflected by satire, it struggled to find an audience, but, unlike that play, that struggle may have

64. This resistance is another link to *Troilus and Cressida*.
65. The final lines of *Lear* project a lessened future, and in *Macbeth*, Fleance's line will supplant Malcolm's (if there is one), but the play gives no sense of how.
66. Some scholars see Middleton as a collaborator on both *All's Well* and *The Yorkshire Tragedy*. If this is right, the mixing of genres goes with the mixing of writers.

kept the play from being performed and printed at all until the 1623 Folio.

Timon's long speech that comprises the whole of 4.1 functions as a kind of synecdoche for the mixing of genres and effects in the whole play. The invective veers from curses that, as many critics note, resemble Lear's heath scenes to a description of the chaos that Ulysses imagines to be the consequence of disorder in *Troilus and Cressida*, and his invocation of the "cold sciatica," syphilis, echoes Pandarus' bequest of diseases at the end of that play:

> Instruction, manners, mysteries and trades.
> Degrees, observances, customs and laws,
> Decline to your confounding contraries—
> And let confusion live! Plagues incident to men,
> You potent and infectious fevers heap
> On Athens, ripe for stroke. Thou cold sciatica,
> Cripple our senators that their limbs may halt
> As lamely as their manners. (4.1.18–25)

Lear's desire that others feel what his misery resembles this wish as well, though Timon never makes the step from vindictiveness to empathy that Lear does. When composing the speech, Shakespeare and Middleton blended ideas, language, and images from a play that probably did not do well with one that, to all appearances, did. Like *Troilus and Cressida*, the play's conclusion resolves none of the issues set up in the beginning. Alcibiades, after all, does not propose to alter Athenian social arrangements, only to punish Athens for its offenses against him and Timon. If we accept a late date for *Timon*, the playwrights may have been attempting to use elements of *King Lear* in the service of satire rather than tragedy, revising, in a way, the generic intervention of *Troilus and Cressida* in hopes of a better reception. If the play precedes *Lear*, *Timon* may have shown that tragedy and satire remained unsuitable partners in a play. Either way, the play's fortunes suggest that the experiment was not a successful one.

As part of a conjectural argument for a late date for *All's Well That Ends Well*, Laurie Maguire and Emma Smith speculate that *A Mad World, My Masters* and *Timon of Athens* "investigate Middleton's diptych of comic and tragic satire respectively" and that Shakespeare's collaboration with Middleton influenced an *All's Well That Ends Well* written in 1607 (195). Where *A Mad World, My Masters* appeared in quarto with title page references to recent performances at Paul's and appeared to have influenced Jonson's

Volpone, All's Well only appears in the 1623 Folio, and there are no references to contemporary performance outside of a 1669 Lord Chamberlain's report that the play was in the repertory of the King's Men at Blackfriars.[67] Middleton's comedy appears to have found early success, where *Timon* did not, and it is at least arguable that *All's Well* did not either.[68] The relatively unsuccessful experiment of *Timon* suggests that the field lacked space for its kind of satirical tragedy, which does not resemble, say, the comical satire of plays like Jonson's *Volpone*. In a recent essay, Jens Elze places *Timon of Athens* between tragedy and romance, arguing that the play "helped prepare the field for Shakespearean romance." Elze writes:

> *Timon of Athens* was the catalyst in an increase and re-evaluation of human immanence, which eventually extended towards the full human manipulation of nature and towards the limits of dramatic conflict and irredeemably shifted Shakespearean drama from the conventions of tragedy towards the more loosely conscripted worlds and open temporalities of romance. (23)

Elze's essay uses the play's version of economic relations – where Timon's spendthrift generosity creates an economic world based on collaboration and reciprocity, which runs afoul of greed – to show how the play moves towards the more open world of romance. Satire as *Timon of Athens* practices it appears to have been an inappropriate tenant to tragedy but may have moved Shakespeare's practice towards other modes where different hybrids could find more welcome.

VI

> *Women beware Women*: 'tis a true text
> Never to be forgot. Drabs of state vexed
> Have plots, poisons, mischiefs that seldom miss
> To murder virtue with a venom kiss.
> Witness this worthy tragedy, expressed
> By him that well deserved among the best

---

67. See Wiggins and Richardson (5: 230), for references to Jonson's debt to Middleton's play(s). For the 1669 reference to *All's Well*, see Wiggins and Richardson (5: 197). *A Mad World, My Masters* was revived in the 1630s.
68. Neither *Timon* nor *All's Well*, unlike a number of the other Folio-only plays, has independent evidence of performance.

> Of poets in his time. He knew the rage,
> Madness of women crossed; and for the stage
> Fitted their humours, hell-bred malice, strife
> Acted in state, presented to the life.
> I that have seen't can say, having just cause,
> Never came tragedy off with more applause.
>
> Nathaniel Richards, dedicatory poem to the 1657 Quarto[69]

Nathaniel Richards' poem, titled "Upon the Tragedy of My Familiar Acquaintance, Thomas Middleton," locates Middleton's play in a series of contexts of evaluation. First, it indicates the veracity of the "text" of the title read as an aphorism. Then Richards calls the play a "worthy tragedy, expressed / By him that well deserved among the best of poets in his time" (5–6), offering both a judgment of the play and an endorsement of the author as highly ranked among his fellow poets. Finally, Richards informs the reader that "never came tragedy off with more applause," claiming the sanction of audience approval for the play (12). All three of these evaluative contexts depend on a sense of the play's effect on an audience: the truth of the text lies in the accuracy of the warning, the worthiness of the tragedy in the rank of the poet and the accuracy of the representation, and the success of the play, marked by applause, necessarily depends on the audience. The poem also attests to Middleton's awareness of the "rage, / Madness of women crossed" and his ability to properly represent them on stage. By this description, Middleton's play might appear to fit nicely into the Aristotelian description of the tragic – representing action of some amplitude, with proper language and spectacle, and inducing knowledge in the audience, witnessed by their applause. However, the play does contain elements of other genres, like city comedy, and because of this mixing later readers have seen it as being problematic in terms of form and effect.[70]

In his 1955 book *Middleton's Tragedies: A Critical Study*, Samuel Schoenbaum discusses *Women Beware Women* and *The Changeling* together, describing them both as "impressive" and "in their own

---

69. I cite the dedicatory poem from the 1657 edition (I have modernized the spelling). I will be citing the play proper from the Oxford *Complete Works of Thomas Middleton*.
70. For discussions of city comedy as a form see Knights's, Gibbons's, and Leinwand's work. Scholars closely associate city comedy with the first decades of the seventeenth century and with playwrights like Ben Jonson, Thomas Dekker, and Middleton. Jonson's *Volpone* and *The Alchemist* along with Middleton and Dekker's *Roaring Girl* might serve as exemplars.

ways, even masterpieces. Yet for masterpieces they are curiously imperfect and uneven" (102). This unevenness he attributes to several causes: that Middleton loses interest in the plays, that he becomes exhausted, or that he "was finding it increasingly difficult—possibly even distasteful—to try to reconcile the sensational melodrama of his age with the psychological drama toward which he aspired" (103). In consigning some of the play's so-called unevenness to a conflict between the playwright's desire to write one kind of play and the audience's desire for another, Schoenbaum describes a conflict of the type that Bourdieu discusses as productive of generic upheavals. Without speculating on Middleton's possible "distaste" for melodrama (a distaste I am not convinced he had), this idea provides a useful way to begin a closer examination of the play.

Women Beware Women dates to 1621, for Middleton a very busy year: he had collaborated with Shakespeare on *Measure for Measure*; Massinger's revision and retelling of his play *Trick to Catch the Old One* had appeared under the title *New Way to Pay Old Debts*; and he was at work on his city comedy *Anything for a Quiet Life*. He also was the playwright for the Lord Mayor's Show that year. The range of his work in just this one year demonstrates that Middleton was experimenting with city comedy, tragicomedy, and other forms. It is clear that this experimentation extends to the formal structure of *Women Beware Women*, which draws on historical materials for its plotline but transforms that material by presenting it through a series of shifting genres that move from comic to tragic.

As Schoenbaum and many other commentators note, Middleton draws on an Italian source for the main plot of the play: the history of Bianca Capello (1548–87), whose life served as a structural model for the Bianca of the play. Unlike Middleton's Bianca, the historical Bianca does not die on her wedding day but lives for almost ten years as the wife of the Grandduke Francesco de' Medici before succumbing to either malaria or poison on the same day as her husband.[71] Many of the details of the play's plot echo this historical narrative – from the secret wedding between Bianca and Leantio to the efforts to placate Leantio with offices. My interest here is in how the play transforms history into fiction by deploying the resources of multiple genres. The revisions of the historical plot depend in some degree on form and on dramatic economy: the historical story spans

---

71. Schoenbaum's discussion of the Bianca Capello story asserts that the tale was well-known but that Middleton likely drew on Celio Malespini's version of 1609. See Schoenbaum 104–109.

many years and ends inconclusively where Middleton's plot comes to a rapid and spectacular end. The play begins in the conventional territory of city comedy with the first characters we see being part of the merchant class but is inflected by motifs characteristic of other genres. I intend to argue that the play takes what are fundamentally comic materials and, by moving them into what might be considered the social and literary territory of tragedy, produces a play that mixes these forms to produce what Sidney might have considered a "right" play. I do not propose to offer a comprehensive reading of the play; my goal is to demonstrate the usefulness of genre theory for developing an understanding of how the play works.

Leantio enters with his mother and Bianca in 1.1 and introduces Bianca as his wife. For him, the marriage is a heroic act, his "masterpiece," while at the same time in need of concealment because her rich parents are against the marriage. He tells his mother:

> You must keep counsel, mother, I am undone else;
> If it be known, I have lost her. Do but think now
> What that loss is; life's but a trifle to't.
> From Venice her consent and I have brought her,
> From parents great in wealth, more now in rage;
> But let storms spend their furies now we have got
> A shelter o'er our quiet innocent loves.
> We are contented. Little money sh'as brought me.
> View but her face, you may see all her dowry,
> Save that which lies locked up in hidden virtues
> Like jewels kept in cabinets. (1.1.47–56)

Leantio presents the marriage as a love-match: it is her consent that brings her from Venice, and the parents' rage at the marriage will, in his view, expend itself while they enjoy their quiet loves. He attributes more value to her face and virtue than any dowry, and that will content both of them. The language of possession and wealth pervades his speech throughout this first scene, and Middleton appears to be linking this vocabulary with Leantio's social position. His scene-ending soliloquy, in which he decides to keep Bianca obscure, makes this linkage more explicit:

> ... 'tis great policy
> To keep choice treasures in obscurest places:
> Should we show thieves our wealth, 'twould make 'em bolder.
> Temptation is a devil will not stick
> To fasten upon a saint; take heed of that.
> The jewel is cased up from all men's eyes. (1.2.165–170)

This plan to keep her hidden from sight has comic antecedents, not least being Corvino in Jonson's *Volpone* whose efforts to hide Celia only result in the predations of Volpone and his own punishment as a fool. Leantio and his mother seem clearly to belong to the world of city comedy and, at least at the beginning of the play, so does Bianca.

The Duke and his family, however, are more closely associated with a court of the type seen in *The Revenger's Tragedy* – if perhaps a less universally pathological one. From the incestuous desire of Hippolito to the lust of the Duke, Middleton links the Florentine court to the tragic. Hippolito's words at the end of 1.2, after avowing his incestuous love for her to his niece Isabella, point to tragedy in no uncertain terms: "The worst can be but death, and let it come. / He that lives joyless, ev'ry day's his doom" (1.2.231–2). The satisfaction of his desire can only be tragic, despite the role of the clownish Ward and the weird intervention of Livia, his sister. The play brings these populations together at court in the second and later acts, and this movement is one of the elements that constitute it as tragedy.

Probably the best-known and most discussed example of this movement is the chess-playing seduction/rape scene in act 2. The Duke, after seeing Bianca at her window, is consumed with desire for her. This moment has a comic antecedent in Volpone's sighting of Celia from the street, which produces the same effect of lust in him. But, where *Volpone* avoids adultery and punishes lust, *Women Beware Women* does not avoid the adultery, and while lust *is* punished in the end, it is punished in a tragic mode. The sighting in the street here brings Bianca into the ambit of tragedy. After the Duke seduces (or rapes) her, she says:

> Now bless me from a blasting! I saw that now
> Fearful for any woman's eye to look on.
> Infectious mists and mildews hang at's eyes.
> The weather of a doomsday dwells upon him.
> Yet since mine honour's leprous, why should I
> Preserve that fair that caused the leprosy?
> Come, poison all at once! (2.2.419–24)

Bianca shifts from the language of domestic happiness she uses in the first act with Leantio and into the tragic register of disease and doomsday here. The Duke, far from being the goodly gentleman the Mother labels him in 1.3, is here surrounded by a cloud of corruption. In the aftermath of this violation, Bianca's character shifts: she becomes discontented with the "shelter o'er [her] quiet innocent loves" (1.1.153) and is cold to the husband she was reluctant to be parted from for even an hour in the first act.

Leantio's character and fate is likewise shaped by his movement from the comic world of the merchants to the tragic world of the court. When Livia falls in love with him, he accedes to her advances as a means of revenge on Bianca and as a means of social advancement. He banters with Bianca about their "advancement" in 4.1, and he leaves her with a warning that his revenge will come to her "at such an hour when thou least seest of all. / So to an ignorance darker than thy womb / I leave thy perjured soul. A plague will come" (4.1.103–5). His adoption of the language of revenge signals his absorption into the tragic plotline of the play, and his brief career as a courtier ends when Hippolito kills him in 4.2. Hippolito challenges Leontio in the name of his sister Livia's honor, and Leantio recognizes that had he remained a poor factor he would have been safe from such attacks:

> How close sticks envy to man's happiness!
> When I was poor, and cared little for life,
> I had no such means offered me to die;
> No man's wrath minded me. (4.2.32–5)

Should he have remained where he was, in other words, he would not have been exposed to a world in which such dangers are normal (and that he is ill-equipped for). He is the first direct casualty of the tragic aspect of the play, and his fate has much to do with his movement away from the social and generic world of comedy. Moreover, his death precipitates the series of killings in the final scene of the play: the multiple revenge plots all derive directly or indirectly from Livia's response to Leantio's death.

The change in Bianca's character and Leantio's fate, while both plausible for reasons deriving from the plot, are also supported by the movement from the territory of comedy, from trade and domesticity, to the world of the court, often the territory of tragedy. Middleton deploys the resources of different genres as the play moves to its tragic denouement. Using the effects made possible by the contrast between the comic elements of the first act and the developing tragedy of the rest of the play, he creates and intensifies a sense of imminent catastrophe, part of which depends on the audience's sense that characters like Leantio are doomed in the tragic world into which they enter when they move to the court. Schoenbaum recognizes something important about the play's intervention in the theatrical field when he suggests that the play at its most brilliant is "not too far removed from the spirit of comedy" (103). As he writes, the settings of the play are closer to those of city comedy, and the play develops a "blurring of the distinction between tragedy and comedy" (128–9). On the basis of this blurring, Schoenbaum argues that "In *Women Beware Women* Middleton appears to have been on the verge of creating a novel kind of drama—a drama that occupies a middle ground between comedy and tragedy" (103). The middling sort, represented by Leantio, and the better sort, represented by the Duke and his court, occupy that middle ground, and both bring with them plot elements and assumptions tied to generic expectations linked to their social locations that blend in this play that blurs boundaries between genres. The "lowering" of tragedy from the palaces of the nobility to the houses of the gentry represents Middleton's intervention into the genre system.

Bibliography

Abbott, Andrew. *The System of Professions: An Essay on the Division of Expert Labor*. U of Chicago P, 1988.

Alhiyari, Ibrahim. "Thomas Watson: New Birth Year and Privileged Ancestry." *Notes and Queries* 53.1 (2006): 35–40.

Alpers, Paul. "Narration in *The Faerie Queene*." *ELH* 44.1 (1977): 19–39.

Andrews, Meghan. "'Address to Public Council': The Additions to Marston's *The Malcontent*, the King's Men Repertory, and Early Modern Theatrical Economics." *Renaissance Drama* 45.2 (2017): 181–208.

Ankersmit, Frank. *Historical Representation*. Stanford UP, 2002.

Anonymous. *Arden of Faversham*, edited by Catherine Richardson, Arden Shakespeare, 2022.

———. *Edward III*, edited by Richard Proudfoot and Nicola Bennett, Arden Shakespeare, 2017.

———. *A Most Pleasant Comedy of Mucedorus, the king's son of Valencia, and Amadine, the king's daughter of Aragon*. London, 1598.

———. *A Warning for Fair Women*, edited by Ann C. Christensen, U of Nebraska P, 2021.

Arber, Edward. *A Transcript of the Registers of the Company of Stationers of London, 1554–1640 A.D.* London, 1875–94.

Aristotle, *The Poetics, Classical Literary Criticism*, translated by T. S. Dorsch, Penguin Books, 1965.

Asp, Carolyn. "Th' Expense of Spirit in a Waste of Shame." *Shakespeare Quarterly* 22.4 (1971): 345–57.

Bakhtin, M. M. *The Dialogic Imagination*. U of Texas P, 1981.

———. "Forms of Time and the Chronotope in the Novel: Notes towards a Historical Poetics." *The Dialogical Imagination: Four Essays*. U of Texas P, 1981, 84–258.

———. "Problem of Speech Genres." *Speech Genres and Other Late Essays*. U of Texas P, 1986, 60–102.

———. *Speech Genres and Other Late Essays*. U of Texas P, 1986.

Bate, Jonathan. *Shakespeare and Ovid*. Oxford UP, 1986.

Beaumont, Francis. *Knight of the Burning Pestle*, edited by Michael Hattaway, Bloomsbury New Mermaids, 1971.

Belsey, Catherine. "Alice Arden's Crime." *Renaissance Drama* 13 (1982): 82–102.

——. "Continuity and Change on the English Popular Stage." *Renaissance Drama* 45.2 (2017): 141–60.

Benson, C. David. *The History of Troy in Middle English Literature: Guido delle Collone's* Historia Destructionis Troiae *in Medieval England*. D. S. Brewer, 1980.

Bentley, G. E. *The Jacobean and Caroline Stage*. Oxford UP, 1941–1968. 7 vols.

Berek, Peter. "Genres, Early Modern Theatrical Title Pages, and the Authority of Print." *The Book of the Play: Playwrights, Stationers, and Readers in Early Modern England*, edited by Marta Straznicky, U of Massachusetts P, 2006, 159–75.

——. "Tragedy and Title Pages: Nationalism, Protestantism, and Print." *Modern Philology* 106.1, (2008): 1–24.

Berger, Harry, Jr. "Narrative as Rhetoric in *The Faerie Queene*." *Situated Utterances: Texts, Bodies, and Cultural Representation*, Fordham UP, 2005, 173–217.

——. *Situated Utterances: Texts, Bodies, and Cultural Representation*. Fordham UP, 2005.

——. "Sneak's Noise or Rumor and Detextualization in *2 Henry IV*." *The Kenyon Review* 6.4 (1984): 58–78.

Bergeron, David. "Shakespeare Makes History: *2 Henry IV*." *SEL* 31.2 (1991): 231–45.

Bergson, Allen. "Dramatic Style as Parody in Marston's *Antonio and Mellida*." *SEL* 11.2 (1971): 307–25.

——. "The Ironic Tragedies of Marston and Chapman: Notes on Jacobean Tragic Form." *Journal of English and German Philology* 69.4 (1970): 613–30.

Berthelette, Thomas, editor. *Jo. Gower De confessione amantis*. London, 1532.

——. Thomas, editor. *Jo. Gower De confessione amantis*. London, 1534.

Betteridge, Thomas and Greg Walker, editors. *Oxford Handbook of Tudor Drama*. Oxford UP, 2012.

Bevington, David. *Tudor Drama and Politics*. Harvard UP, 1968.

Blayney, Peter W. M. "The Alleged Popularity of Playbooks." *Shakespeare Quarterly* 56.1 (2005): 33–50.

——. "The Publication of Playbooks." *A New History of Early English Drama*, edited by John D. Cox and David Scott Kastan, Columbia UP, 1997, 383–422.

Blinde, Loren M. "Rumored History in Shakespeare's *2 Henry IV*." *English Literary Renaissance* 38.1 (2008): 34–54.

Blundeville, Thomas. *True Order and Methode of Writing and Reading Hystories*. London: 1574.

Boas, Frederick S. *University Drama in the Tudor Age.* 1914. Oxford UP, 1966.
Bodenham, John. *Belvedere, or The Garden of the Muses.* London, 1600.
Boose, Lynda. "The 1599 Bishop's Ban, Elizabethan Pornography, and the Sexualization of the Jacobean Stage." *Enclosure Acts,* edited by Richard Burt and John Michael Archer, Cornell UP, 1994, 185–200.
Borges, Jorge Luis. *Fictions.* Grove, 1962.
Bourdieu, Pierre. *Distinction: A Social Critique of the Judgment of Taste.* Harvard UP, 1987.
———. *The Field of Cultural Production.* Columbia UP, 1993.
———. "The Field of Cultural Production, or: The Economic World Reversed," *The Field of Cultural Production,* Columbia UP, 1993, 29–73.
———. *Invitation to Reflexive Sociology.* U of Chicago P, 1992.
———. "Principles for a Sociology of Cultural Works." *The Field of Cultural Production,* Columbia UP, 1993, 176–91.
———. *The Rules of Art: Genesis and Structure of the Literary Field.* Stanford UP, 1996.
Bowers, Fredson. *Elizabethan Revenge Tragedy, 1587–1642.* Princeton UP, 1940.
Braden, Gordon. *Renaissance Tragedy and the Senecan Tradition.* Yale UP, 1985.
Briggs, Julia. "*Hengist, King of Kent*: Middleton's Forgotten Tragedy." *Review of English* 41.164 (1990): 479–95.
Brink, Jean R. *Michael Drayton Revisited.* Twayne, 1990.
Bromham, Tony, and Zara Bruzzi. *The Changeling and the Years of Crisis, 1619–1624.* Pinter, 1990.
Broude, Ronald. "Revenge and Revenge Tragedy in Renaissance England." *Renaissance Quarterly* 28.1 (1975): 38–58.
Bruster, Douglas. "The Representation Market of Early Modern England." *Renaissance Drama* 41.1–2 (2013): 1–23.
Bullough, G. R. *Narrative and Dramatic Sources of Shakespeare.* Columbia UP, 1957–75. 8 vols.
Burke, Peter. *The Renaissance Sense of the Past.* Arnold, 1969.
Cartwright, Kent. *Theatre and Humanism.* Cambridge UP, 1999.
Cavell, Stanley. *Disowning Knowledge in Six Plays of Shakespeare.* Cambridge UP, 1987.
Chakravorty, Swapan. *Society and Politics in the Plays of Thomas Middleton.* Oxford UP, 1996.
Chambers, E. K. *The Elizabethan Stage.* Clarendon Press, 1923. 4 vols.
Chapman, George. *Bussy D'Ambois.* London, 1607.
———. *Bussy D'Ambois,* edited by Maurice Evans, New Mermaids, 1996.
———. *The Revenge of Bussy D'Ambois.* London, 1613.
———. *The Revenge of Bussy D'Ambois. The Plays of George Chapman: The Tragedies,* vol. 1, edited by Marc Parrot, Russell and Russell, 1961, 75–148.

Charnes, Linda. *Notorious Identity*. Harvard UP, 1993.
Chatterley, Albert. "Watson, Thomas (1555/6–1592)." *Oxford Dictionary of National Biography*. Oxford UP, 2008, www.oxforddnb.com/view/article/28866.
Chaucer, Geoffrey. "Knight's Tale." *The Riverside Chaucer*, edited by Larry D. Benson. Houghton Mifflin, 1987, 37–65.
——. *Troilus and Criseyde*. *The Riverside Chaucer*, edited by Larry D. Benson. Houghton Mifflin, 1987, 471–586.
Cheney, Patrick. *Shakespeare's Literary Authorship*. Cambridge UP, 2008.
Chettle, Henry, and Thomas Decker. *Troilus and Cressida*. London 1599.
Cobb, Christopher. *The Staging of Romance in Late Shakespeare*. U of Delaware P, 2007.
Cohen, Ralph. "History and Genre." *New Literary History*, vol. 17, no. 2, 1986, 203–18.
——. "Introduction: Notes towards a Generic Reconstitution of Literary Study." *New Literary History* 34.3 (2003): v-xvi.
Colie, Rosalie. *The Resources of Kind: Genre Theory in the Renaissance*, edited by Barbara Lewalski. U of California P, 1973.
Comensoli, Vivian. *"Household Business": Domestic Plays of Early Modern England*. U of Toronto P, 1996.
Cooper, Helen. *The English Romance in Time: Transferring Motifs from Geoffrey of Monmouth to the Death of Shakespeare*. Oxford UP, 2004.
——. "*Pericles* and other Gowers, 1592–1640." *A Companion to Gower*, edited by Siân Echard, D. S. Brewer, 2004, 99–113.
Corrigan, Brian Jay. "Middleton, *The Revenger's Tragedy*, and Crisis Literature." *Studies in English Literature* 38.2 (1998): 281–95.
Croce, Benedetto. *Aesthetic*. Macmillan and Company, 1909.
Crocker, Holly. "'As false as Cressid': Virtue Trouble from Chaucer to Shakespeare." *Journal of Medieval and Early Modern Studies* 43.2 (2013): 303–34.
Dane, Joseph A. *Who Is Buried in Chaucer's Tomb? Studies in the Reception of Chaucer's Book*. Michigan State UP, 1998.
Danto, Arthur. *Narration and Knowledge*. Columbia UP, 1985.
DEEP: Database of Early English Playbooks. Eds. Alan B. Farmer and Zachary Lesser. Created 2007. Accessed 6 December 2022. http://deep.sas.upenn.edu
Davis-Brown, Kris. "Shakespeare's Use of Chaucer in *Troilus and Cressida*: 'That the Will is Infinite, and Execution Confined.'" *South Central Review* 5.2 (1988): 15–34.
Dekker, Thomas, and John Webster. *Famous History of Sir Thomas Wyatt*. London, 1607.
Dekker, Thomas, John Ford, and William Rowley. *The Witch of Edmonton*, edited by Lucy Munro, The Arden Shakespeare, 2017.
Derrida, Jacques. *Archive Fever*. U of Chicago P, 1995.
——. "The Law of Genre." *Critical Inquiry* 7.1 (1980): 55–81.

——. *Spectres of Marx*. Routledge, 1993.
Devitt, Amy. "Generalizing about Genre: New Conceptions of an Old Concept." *College Composition and Communication* 44.4 (1993): 573–86.
Dewar-Watson, Sarah. "Ford's *Perkin Warbeck* as Historical Tragedy." *The Genres of Renaissance Tragedy*, edited by Daniel Cadman, Andrew Duxfield, and Lisa Hopkins, Manchester UP, 2019, 184–95.
Dimmick, Jeremy. "Gower, Chaucer, and the Art of Repentance in Greene's *Vision*." *Review of English Studies* 57.231 (2006): 456–73.
Dimmock, Wai-Chee. "Genre as World System: Epic and Novel on Four Continents." *Narrative* 14.1 (2006): 85–101.
Dolan, Frances. "The Subordinate('s) Plot: Petty Treason and the Forms of Domestic Rebellion." *Shakespeare Quarterly* 43.3 (1992): 317–40.
Donaldson, E. Talbot. *The Swan at the Well: Shakespeare Reading Chaucer*. Yale UP, 1985.
Dowden, Edward. 1877. *Shakspere*. 2nd ed., London: Macmillan, 1890.
——. 1875. *Shakspere, A Critical Study of His Mind and* Art. Capricorn Books, 1962.
Drayton, Michael. *Mortimeriados*. London, 1596.
——. *Peirs Gaveston*. London, 1596.
Dubrow, Heather. "The Arraignment of Paridell: Tudor Historiography in *The Faerie Queene*, III.ix." *Studies in Philology* 87.3 (1990): 312–27.
——. *Genre*. Routledge, 1982.
Dudgeon, Cheryl. "The Arraignment of Paridell: Tudor Historiography in *The Faerie Queene*, III.ix." *Studies in Philology* 87.3 (1990): 312–27.
——. "Forensic Performances: Evidentiary Narrative in *Arden of Faversham*." *Justice, Women, and Power in English Renaissance Drama*, edited by Andrew Majeske and Emily Detmer-Goebel. Fairleigh Dickinson UP, 2009, 98–117.
Duff, David, editor. *Modern Genre Theory*. Longman, 2000.
Dutton, Richard, and Jean E. Howard, editors. *A Companion to Shakespeare's Works, Vol. II: The Histories*. New York: Blackwell, 2003.
Echard, Siân. "Gower in Print." *A Companion to Gower*, edited by Siân Echard, D. S. Brewer, 2004, 115–35.
Edelman, Charles. "*The Battle of Alcazar, Muly Molocco*, and Shakespeare's *2* and *3 Henry VI*." *Notes and Queries* 49.2 (2002): 215–18.
Elliot, John. *Ortho-epia Gallica*. London, 1593.
Elliott, John R., Alan H. Nelson, Alexandra F. Johnston, and Diana Wyatt, editors. *Oxford*. Toronto and London: U of Toronto Press and The British Library, 2004. 2 vols.
Else, Gerald. *Aristotle's* Poetics: *The Argument*. Harvard UP, 1957.
Elze, Jens. "Contained Immanence: Shakespeare's *Timon of Athens* between Tragedy and Romance." *Anglia* 134.1 (2016): 1–24.

Erne, Lukas. *Beyond* The Spanish Tragedy: *A Study of the Works of Thomas Kyd*. Manchester UP, 2001.

Ewald, Helen Rothschild. "Waiting for Answerability: Bakhtin and Composition Studies." *College Composition and Communication* 44.3 (1993): 331–48.

Farmer, Alan B. and Zachary Lesser, editors. "The Popularity of Playbooks Revisited." *Shakespeare Quarterly* 56.1 (2005): 1–32.

Farrell, Joseph. "Classical Genre in Theory and Practice." *New Literary History* 34.3 (2003): 383–408.

Federico, Sylvia. *New Troy: Fantasies of Empire in the Late Middle Ages*. U of Minnesota Press, 2003.

Felperin, Howard. *Shakespearean Romance*. Princeton UP, 1972.

Fishman, Burton J. "Pride and Ire: Theatrical Iconography in Preston's *Cambises*." *Studies in English Literature* 16.2 (1976): 201–11.

Fletcher, John. *The Faithful Shepherdess*. London, 1610.

———. "John Marston's Fantastical Plays: *Antonio and Mellida* and *Antonio's Revenge*." *Philological Quarterly* 41.1 (1962): 229–39.

Ford, John. *Perkin Warbeck*. London, 1634.

———. *Perkin Warbeck,* edited by Donald K. Anderson, U of Nebraska P, 1965.

Forni, Kathleen. *The Chaucerian Apocrypha: A Counterfeit Canon*. UP of Florida, 2001.

Forse, James. "*Arden of Faversham* and *Romeo and Juliet*: Two Elizabethan Experiments in the Genre of 'Comedy-Suspense.'" *Journal of Popular Culture* 29.3 (1995): 85–102.

Fowler, Alastair. *Kinds of Literature: An Introduction to the Theory of Genres*. Harvard UP, 1982.

Foxe, John. *Acts and Monuments*. London, 1563.

Fraser, Russell, and Norman Rabkin, editors. *Drama of the English Renaissance*. MacMillan, 1976. 2 vols.

Frow, David. *Genre*. Routledge, 2005.

Frye, Northrop. *Anatomy of Criticism*. Princeton UP, 1957.

———. *A Natural Perspective*. Harcourt, 1965.

———. *A Secular Scripture*. Harvard UP, 1976.

Gager, William. *Meleager*. Oxford, 1593.

Gibbons, Brian. *Jacobean City Comedy*. Routledge, 1980.

Gieskes, Edward. "'materia conveniente modis': Early Modern Dramatic Adaptations of Ovid." *Ovid and Adaptation in Early Modern Theatre*, edited by Lisa Starks, Edinburgh UP, 2020, 238–53.

———. *Representing the Professions*. U of Delaware Press, 2006.

Goldberg, Jonathan. *Voice Terminal Echo: Postmodernism and English Renaissance Texts*. Methuen, 1986.

Golding, M. R. "Variations in the Use of the Masque in English Revenge Tragedy." *Yearbook of English Studies* 3 (1973): 44–54.

Grant, Teresa. "History in the Making: The Case of Samuel Rowley's *When You See Me, You Know Me* (1604/5)." *English Historical Drama, 1500–1660: Forms Outside the Canon*, edited by Teresa Grant and Barbara Ravelhofer, Palgrave Macmillan, 2008, 125–57.

Green, Richard Firth. *A Crisis of Truth: Literature and Law in Ricardian England*. U of Pennsylvania P, 1999.

Greene, Robert. (1592). *Greenes Vision. The Life and Complete Works in Prose and Verse of Robert Greene*, edited by A. B. Grosart, vol. 12, Russell and Russell, 1964, 191–281.

———. *The Scottish History of James the Fourth*, edited by Norman Sanders, Methuen, 1970.

———. *Pandosto*. London, 1588.

Griffin, Benjamin. *Playing the Past: Approaches to English Historical Drama, 1385–1600*. Brewer, 2001.

Guillory, John. *Cultural Capital: The Problem of Literary Canon Formation*. U of Chicago P, 1993.

Gurr, Andrew. *The Shakespearian Acting Companies*. Oxford UP, 1996.

Halasek, Kay. *A Pedagogy of Possibility: Bakhtinian Perspectives on Composition Studies*. Southern Illinois UP, 1999.

Harbage, Alfred, Samuel Schoenbaum, and Sylvia Stoler Wagonheim, editors. *Annals of English Drama, 975–1700*. 3rd ed., Routledge, 1989.

Heinemann, Margot. *Puritanism and Theatre*. Cambridge UP, 1980.

Helgerson, Richard. "Murder in Faversham." *The Historical Imagination in Early Modern Britain: History, Rhetoric, and Fiction, 1500–1800*, edited by Donald R. Kelley and David Harris Sacks, Cambridge UP, 1997, 133–58.

Henryson, Robert. *The Testament of Creseide*. London, 1598.

Henslowe, Philip. *Diary*, edited by R. A. Foakes, Cambridge UP, 2002.

Herman, Peter C. "'Is This Winning?' Prince Henry's Death and the Problem of Chivalry in *Two Noble Kinsmen*." *South Atlantic Review* 62.1 (1997): 1–31.

Heywood, Thomas. *The First Part of If You Know Not Me, You Know Nobody*. London, 1606.

———. *The Second Part of If You Know Not Me, You Know Nobody*. London, 1606.

———. *A Woman Killed with Kindness*, edited by M. J. Kidnie, Arden Shakespeare, 2017.

Hieatt, A. Kent. "The Genesis of Shakespeare's Sonnets: Spenser's *Ruines of Rome: By Bellay*." *PMLA* 98.5 (1983): 800–14.

Hill, Eugene D. "The First Elizabethan Tragedy: A Contextual Reading of *Cambises*." *Studies in Philology* 89.4 (1992): 404–33.

———. "Parody and History in *Arden of Feversham* (1592)." *Huntington Library Quarterly* 56.4 (1993): 359–82.

Hillman, David. "The Gastric Epic: *Troilus and Cressida*." *Shakespeare Quarterly* 48.3 (1997): 295–313.

Hirrel, Michael J. "Thomas Watson, Playwright: Origins of Modern English Drama." *Lost Plays in Shakespeare's England*, edited by David McMinnis and Matthew Steggle, Palgrave, 2014, 187–207.

Hoeniger, F. David. "Gower and Shakespeare in *Pericles*." *Shakespeare Quarterly* 33.4 (1982): 461–79.

Holinshed, Raphael. *The Chronicles of England, Scotland, and Ireland*. London, 1587.

Holland, Samuel. *Don Zara del Fogo*. London, 1656.

Hopkins, Lisa. *From the Romans to the Normans on the English Renaissance Stage*. Medieval Institute Publications, 2017.

Howard, Jean. *Theatre of a City: The Places of London City Comedy, 1598–1642*. U of Pennsylvania P, 2007.

Hutson, Lorna. *The Invention of Suspicion: Law and Mimesis in Shakespeare and Renaissance Drama*. Oxford UP, 2007.

Ide, Richard S. "Exploiting the Tradition: The Elizabethan Revenger as Chapman's 'Complete Man.'" *Medieval and Renaissance Drama in England* 1 (1984): 159–72.

James, Heather. *Shakespeare's Troy: Drama, Politics, and the Translation of Empire*. Cambridge UP, 1999.

Jameson, Fredric. "Magical Narratives: Romance as Genre." *New Literary History* 7.2 (1975): 135–63.

———. *The Political Unconscious: Narrative as a Socially Symbolic Act*. Cornell UP, 1981.

Jonson, Ben. *Five Plays*, edited by G.A. Wilkes, Oxford UP, 1988.

———. "Ode: To Himself." *The New Inn*. London, 1629.

———. *Workes*. London, 1616.

Kalas, Rayna. "The Technology of Reflection: Renaissance Mirrors of Steel and Glass." *Journal of Medieval and Early Modern Studies* 32.3 (2002): 519–42.

Kamps, Ivo. *Historiography and Ideology in Stuart Drama*. Cambridge UP, 1996.

Kerrigan, John. *Revenge Tragedy from Aeschylus to Armageddon*. Oxford UP, 1996.

Kesson, Andy. *John Lyly and Early Modern Authorship*. Manchester UP, 2014.

Kesson, Andy, Callan Davies, and Lucy Munro, project team. *Before Shakespeare*, 2016, https://beforeshakespeare.com/. Accessed 14 June, 2022.

Kesson, Andy, and Emma Smith, editors. *The Elizabethan Top Ten*. Routledge, 2013.

Kewes, Paulina. "The Elizabethan History Play: A True Genre?" *A Companion to Shakespeare's Works: The Histories*, edited by Richard Dutton and Jean Howard, vol. 2, Blackwell, 2003, 170–93.

Kiefer, Frederick. "Rumor, Fame, and Slander in *2 Henry IV*." *Allegorica* 20 (1999): 3–44.

King, Ros. "*Arden of Faversham*: The Moral of History and the Thrill of Performance." *The Oxford Handbook of Tudor Drama*, edited by Thomas Betteridge and Greg Walker, Oxford UP, 2012, 635–52.

Kinney, Arthur, editor. *Renaissance Drama: An Anthology of Plays and Entertainments*. Wiley-Blackwell, 2000.

Kirwan, Peter. "*Mucedorus*: The Popular Play." *The Elizabethan Top Ten: Defining Print Popularity in Early Modern England*, edited by Emma Smith and Andy Kesson, Routledge, 2013, 223–34.

Kistler, Suzanne. "'Strange and Far-Removed Shores': A Reconsideration of *The Revenge of Bussy D'Ambois*." *Studies in Philology* 77.2 (1980): 128–44.

Kistner, A. L. and M. K. Kistner. "What is *Hengist, King of Kent*?" *Arbeiten aus Anglistik un Amerikanistik* 7.2 (1982): 147–59.

Knights, L. C. *Drama and Society in the Age of Jonson*. Chatto and Windus, 1937.

Knutson, Roslyn. "Pembroke's Men in 1592–3, Their Repertory and Touring Schedule." *Early Theatre* 4 (2001): 129–38.

———. "Play Identifications: *The Wise Man of West Chester* and *John a Kent and John a Cumber*; *Longshanks* and *Edward I*." *Huntington Library Quarterly* 47.1 (1984): 1–11.

———. *Playing Companies and Commerce in Shakespeare's Time*. Cambridge UP, 2001.

———. *The Repertory of Shakespeare's Company, 1594–1613*. U of Arkansas P, 1991.

Krasner, James N. "*The Tragedy of Bussy D'Ambois* and the Creation of Heroism." *Medieval and Renaissance Drama in England* 4 (1989): 107–21.

Krier, Theresa, editor. *Refiguring Chaucer in the Renaissance*. UP of Florida, 1998.

Kyd, Thomas. *The Spanish Tragedy*, edited by Clara Calvo and Jesús Tronch, Arden Shakespeare, 2013.

———. *The Spanish Tragedy*, edited by J.R. Mulryne, A & C Black, 1989.

Lane, Jeremy. "Between Repression and Anamnesis: Pierre Bourdieu and the Vicissitudes of Literary Form." *Paragraph* 35.1 (2012): 66–82.

Leonard, Nathaniel. "Embracing the 'Mongrel': John Marston's *The Malcontent, Antonio and Mellida,* and the Development of Early Modern Tragicomedy." *JEMCS* 12.3 (2012): 60–87.

Lesser, Zachary. "Walter Burre's *The Knight of the Burning Pestle*." *English Literary Renaissance* 29.1 (1999): 21–43.

Lethbridge, J. B., editor. *Shakespeare and Spenser: Attractive Opposites*, Manchester UP, 2008.

Levin, Harry. "An Echo from *The Spanish Tragedy*." *Modern Language Notes* 64.5 (1949): 297–302.

———. "Women in the Renaissance Theatre Audience." *Shakespeare Quarterly* 40.2 (1989): 165–74.

Levine, Nina. *Practicing the City: Early Modern London on Stage*. Fordham UP, 2016.

Leinwand, Theodore. *The City Staged: Jacobean Comedy, 1603–1613*. U of Wisconsin P, 1986.

Lindenberger, Herbert. *Historical Drama: The Relation of Literature and Reality*. U of Chicago P, 1975.

Lodge, Thomas. *The Wounds of Civil War*. London, 1594.

Longstaffe, Stephen. "What is the English History Play and Why are They Saying Such Terrible Things About It?" *Renaissance Forum: An Electronic Journal of Early Modern Literary and Historical Studies* 2.2 (1997), https://www.academia.edu/41699521/What_is_the_English_History_Play_and_Why_are_They_Saying_Such_Terrible_Things_About_It. Accessed 9 February, 2023.

Lopez, Jeremy. *Constructing the Canon of Early Modern Drama*. Cambridge UP, 2014.

Lyly, John. *Midas*. London, 1952.

Maguire, Laurie, and Emma Smith. "'Time's Comic Sparks': The Dramaturgy of *A Mad World, My Masters* and *Timon of Athens*." Taylor and Henley, 181–95.

Marlowe, Christopher. *All Ovids Elegies*. London: 1603.

———. *Edward II*, edited by Martin Wiggins and Robert Lindsey, A & C Black, 1997.

Marston, John. *Antonio and Mellida*. London, 1602.

———. *Antonio and Mellida*, edited by G. K. Hunter, U of Nebraska P, 1965.

———. *Antonio's Revenge*. London, 1602.

———. *Antonio's Revenge*, edited by G. K. Hunter, U of Nebraska P, 1965.

———. *Malcontent*. London, 1604.

———. *Scourge of Villainy*. London, 1598.

McInnis, David. *Shakespeare and Lost Plays: Reimagining Drama in Early Modern England*. Cambridge UP, 2021.

McMillin, Scott. "Acting and Violence: *The Revenger's Tragedy* and Its Departures from *Hamlet*." *SEL* 24.2 (1984): 275–91.

———. "The Book of Seneca in *The Spanish Tragedy*." *Studies in English Literature, 1500–1900* 14.2 (1974): 201–8.

McMillin, Scott, and Sally Beth MacLean. *The Queen's Men and Their Plays*. Cambridge UP, 1998.

McMullan, Gordon. *Shakespeare and the Idea of Late Writing*. Cambridge UP, 2007.

Meres, Francis. *Palladis Tamia*. London, 1598.

Middleton, Thomas. *Hengist, King of Kent*, edited by Grace Ioppolo. Taylor and Lavagnino, 1448–87.

———. *A Trick to Catch the Old One*, edited by Valerie Wayne. Taylor and Lavagnino, 373–413.

———. *Women Beware Women*, edited by John Jowett. Taylor and Lavagnino, 1488–1541.

Middleton, Thomas, and William Rowley. *The Changeling*. London, 1652.
Miola, Robert. *Shakespeare and Classical Comedy*. Oxford UP, 1994.
——. *Shakespeare and Classical Tragedy*. Oxford UP, 1992.
Miskimin, Alice. *The Renaissance Chaucer*. Yale UP, 1975.
Montrose, Louis. "Of Gentlemen and Shepherds: The Politics of Elizabethan Pastoral Form." *ELH* 50.3 (1983): 415–59.
Moretti, Franco. "Conjectures on World Literature." *New Left Review* 1 (2000): 54.
——. *Graphs, Maps, Trees*. Verso, 2005.
Mowat, Barbara. "'What's in a Name?': Tragicomedy, Romance, or Late Comedy." *A Companion to Shakespeare's Works: The Poems, Problem Comedies, Late Plays*, edited by Richard Dutton and Jean Howard, vol. 4, Blackwell, 2003, 129–49.
Mulready, Cyrus. *Romance on the Early Modern Stage*. Palgrave, 2013.
Munro, Lucy. "'Nemp your Sexes!' Anachronistic Aesthetics in *Hengist, King of Kent* and the Jacobean 'Anglo-Saxon' Play." *Modern Philology* 111.4 (2014): 734–61.
——. "Speaking History: Linguistic History and the Usable Past in the Early Modern History Play." *Huntington Library Quarterly* 76.4 (2013): 519–40.
Nashe, Thomas. "Excerpt from *Pierce Penniless*." *The Norton Anthology of English Literature*, edited by M.H. Abrams and Stephen Greenblatt, vol. 1, 6th ed., W. W. Norton, & Co., 1993, p. 1010.
Nelson, Alan H. editor. *Cambridge*. U of Toronto Press, 1989. 2 vols.
——. "The Universities and the Inns of Court." *The Oxford Handbook of Early Modern Theatre*, edited by Richard Dutton, Oxford UP, 2009, 280–91.
Newcomb, Lori Humphrey. *Reading Popular Romance in Early Modern England*. Columbia UP, 2001.
Norland, Howard B. *Drama in Early Tudor Britain, 1485–1558*. U of Nebraska P, 1995.
——. *Neoclassical Tragedy in Elizabethan England*. U of Delaware P, 2009.
Norton, Thomas, and Thomas Sackville. *The Tragedie of Gorboduc*. London, 1565.
Owens, Rebekah. "Parody and *The Spanish Tragedy*." *Cahiers Elisabéthains* 71.1 (2007): 27–36.
Parks, Joan. "History, Tragedy, and Truth in Marlowe's *Edward II*." *SEL* 39.2 (1999): 275–90.
Patterson, Annabel. *Reading Holinshed's Chronicles*. U of Chicago P, 1994.
Patterson, Lee. *Chaucer and The Subject of History*. U of Wisconsin P, 1991.
Pearsall, Derek. "The Gower Tradition." *Gower's Confessio Amantis: Responses and Reassessments*, edited by A.J. Minnis, D. S. Brewer, 1983, 179–98.
Peele, George. *Edward I*, edited by G. K. Dreher. Adams Press, 1974.
Preston, Thomas. *Cambises*, edited by James R. Siemon. *The Routledge*

Anthology of Early Modern Drama, edited by Jeremy Lopez, Routledge, 2020, 5–48.
Prince, Michael. "Mauvais Genres." *New Literary History* 34.3 (2003): 452–79.
Puttenham, George. 1589. *The Art of English Poesy*, edited by Frank Whigham and Wayne A. Rebhorn, Cornell UP, 2007.
Quinn, Kelly. "Mastering Complaint: Michael Drayton's *Peirs Gaveston* and the Royal Mistress Complaints." *English Literary Renaissance* 38.3 (2008): 439–60.
Reiss, Timothy. *The Meaning of Literature*. Cornell UP, 1992.
Ribner, Irving. *The English History Play in the Age of Shakespeare*. Methuen, 1957.
Ricouer, Paul. *Memory, History, Forgetting*. U of Chicago P, 2005.
——. *Time and Narrative*. U of Chicago P, 1984–8. 3 vols.
Roebuck, Thomas. "Middleton's Historical Imagination." Taylor and Henley, 116–29.
Rutter, Tom. "*Hamlet,* Pirates, and Purgatory." *Renaissance and Reformation* 38.1 (2015): 117–39.
Rosmarin, Adena. *The Power of Genre*. U of Minnesota P, 1985.
Rowley, Samuel. *When You See Me, You Know Me*. London, 1605.
Sanders, Leslie. "The Revenger's Tragedy: A Play on the Revenge Play." *Renaissance and Reformation* 10.1 (1974): 25–36.
Schoenbaum, Samuel. *Middleton's Tragedies: A Critical Study*. Columbia UP, 1955.
Seneca His Tenne Tragedies, translated by Jasper Heywood, London, 1581.
Seneca. *Hercules Furens, Seneca His Tenne Tragedies*, translated by Jasper Heywood, London, 1581.
——. *Thyestes*, edited by Rudolf Peiper and Gustav Richter, Teubner, 1921. *Perseus Project*, Tufts University, http://data.perseus.org/citations/urn:cts:latinLit:phi1017.phi008.perseus-lat1:1-67.
Shakespeare, William. *Hamlet*, edited by Harold Jenkins, Routledge, 1982.
——. *Henry V*, edited by Herschel Baker. *The Riverside Shakespeare*, edited by G. Blakemore Evans et al., 2nd ed., Houghton Mifflin, 1996, 930–75.
——. *King Henry IV, Part 2*, edited by James Bulman, Bloomsbury Arden, 2016.
——. *King Henry IV, Part 2*, edited by A. R. Humphrey, Arden Methuen, 1966.
——. *Pericles*, edited by Suzanne Gossett, Arden Shakespeare, 2004.
——. *The Second Part of Henry IV*, edited by Giorgio Melchiori, 2nd ed., Cambridge UP, 1989.
——. *Timon of Athens*, edited by Anthony Dawson and Gretchen Minton, Arden Shakespeare, 2008.
——. *Troilus and Cressida*, edited by David Bevington, 3rd series, Arden Shakespeare, 1998.

Shakespeare, William, and John Fletcher. *Henry VIII*, edited by Gordon McMullan, Arden Shakespeare, 2000.

——. *The Two Noble Kinsmen. The Norton Shakespeare*, edited by Stephen Greenblatt, et al., 2nd ed., Norton, 2008, 451–536.

——. *The Two Noble Kinsmen*, edited by Eugene Waith. Oxford UP, 1998.

Shapiro, Barbara. *A Culture of Fact: England, 1550–1720*. Cornell UP, 2003.

Sidney, Sir Philip. *A Defence of Poetry*, edited by J.A. Van Dorsten, Oxford UP, 1996.

Siemon, James R., editor. *Cambises, The Routledge Anthology of Early Modern Drama*, edited by Jeremey Lopez, Routledge, 2020, 5–48.

——. "Sporting Kyd." *English Literary Renaissance* 24.3 (1994): 553–82.

——. *Word Against Word: Shakespearean Utterance*. U of Massachusetts P, 2002.

Slights, William W. E. "*Genera mixta* and *Timon of Athens*." *Studies in Philology* 74.1 (1977): 39–62.

Smith, Bruce R. *Ancient Scripts and Modern Experience on the English Stage*. Princeton UP, 1988.

Smith, Emma. "Hieronimo's Afterlives." *The Spanish Tragedy with the First Part of Jeronimo*, edited by Emma Smith, Penguin, 1988, 133–59.

——, editor. *The Spanish Tragedie* with Anonymous *The First Part of Jeronimo*, by Thomas Kyd. London: Penguin, 1988

Speght, Thomas, editor. *The Workes of Chaucer*. London, 1598.

Speller, John. *Bourdieu and Literature*. Open Book Publishers, 2001.

Spenser, Edmund. *The Faerie Queene*, edited by Thomas P. Roche and C. Patrick O'Donnell, Penguin Books, 1979.

——. "A Letter of the Authors," *Edmund Spenser's Poetry*, edited by Hugh MacLean and Anne Lake Prescott, W. W. Norton, 1993, 3.

Spikes, Judith Doolin. "The Jacobean History Play and the Myth of the Elect Nation." *Renaissance Drama* 4 (1977): 117–49.

Stapleton, Michael. *Marlowe's Ovid: The Elegies in the Marlowe Canon*. Routledge, 2014.

Stevens, Martin. "Hamlet and the Pirates: A Critical Reconsideration." *Shakespeare Quarterly* 26.3 (1975): 276–84.

Sutton, Dana, editor. *The Plays of William Gager*. The Philological Museum at Birmingham University, https://philological.cal.bham.ac.uk/gager/plays/index.html.

Taylor, Gary. "Thomas Middleton: Lives and Afterlives." Taylor and Lavagnino, 25–58.

Taylor, Gary, and Trish Thomas Henley, editors. *The Oxford Handbook of Thomas Middleton*. Oxford UP, 2012.

Taylor, Gary, and John Lavagnino, editors. *Thomas Middleton: The Collected Works*. Oxford UP, 2007.

Taylor, Miles. "The End of the English History Play in *Perkin Warbeck*." *Studies in English Literature, 1500–1900* 48.2 (2008): 395–418.

Thompson, Ann. *Shakespeare's Chaucer: A Study in Literary Origins*. Barnes and Noble, 1978.

Thorndike, A. H. "The Relations of *Hamlet* to Contemporary Revenge Plays." *PMLA* 17.2 (1902): 125–220.

Tricomi, Albert H. "The Revised Version of Chapman's *Bussy D'Ambois*: A Shift in Point of View." *Studies in Philology* 70.3 (1973): 288–305.

"*Troilus and Cressida*." *Lost Plays Database*, https://lostplays.folger.edu/Troilus_and_Cressida#Critical_Commentary. Accessed 6 June, 2021.

Turner, Henry. *English Renaissance Stage*. Oxford UP, 2006.

Van Es, Bart. *Spenser's Forms of History*. Oxford UP, 2002.

Voloshinov, V. N. *Marxism and the Philosophy of Language*. Harvard UP, 1986.

Walsh, Brian. *Shakespeare, the Queen's Men, and the Elizabethan Performance of History*. Cambridge UP, 2009.

Watson, Thomas. *Hekatompathia, or Passionate Century of Love*. London, 1582.

Webster, John. *The White Devil*. London, 1612.

Whipday, Emma. "Everyday Murder and Household Work in Shakespeare's Domestic Tragedies." *Staged Normality in Shakespeare's England*, Palgrave Shakespeare Studies, 2019, 215–36.

White, Hayden. *The Content of the Form*. Johns Hopkins UP, 1990.

Wiggins, Martin and Catherine Richardson. *British Drama: 1533–1642: A Catalogue*. Oxford UP, 2012–9. 9 vols.

Winston, Jessica. *Lawyers at Play: Literature, Law, and Politics at the Early Modern Inns of Court, 1558–1581*. Oxford UP, 2016.

Woodbridge, Linda. *English Revenge Drama*. Cambridge UP Press, 2010.

Woolf, D. R. "From Hystories to the Historical: Five Transitions in Thinking about the Past, 1500–1700." *Huntington Library Quarterly* 68.1–2 (2005): 33–70.

———. "Genre into Artifact: The Decline of the English Chronicle in the Sixteenth Century." *The Sixteenth Century Journal* 19.3 (1988): 321–54.

W. S. *The True Chronicle History of the whole life and death of Thomas Lord Cromwell*. London, 1602.

Zucker, Adam. *Places of Wit in Early Modern English Comedy*. Cambridge UP, 2011.

Index

Abbott, Andrew, 23n34
All Is True see *Henry VIII*
Alpers, Paul, 86–7
Ankersmit, Frank, 157n2, 168n12
Arden of Faversham (Anon.), 148–54
   dramatization of law, 153–4
   see also domestic tragedy;
      Holinshed's *Chronicles*
Aristotle, 8–9

Bakhtin, Mikhail, 3, 17–18
   literary change, 29–31, 76–7, 85, 134, 138
   speech genres, 21–2
   utterances, 17–20, 44, 134
Beaumont, Francis, *Knight of the Burning Pestle*, 53–4, 67–8
Belsey, Catherine, 150n64, 152–3
Benson, C. David, 200
Berek, Peter, 251
Berger, Harry, 86–7
Blundeville, Thomas see historiography
Bourdieu, Pierre
   artistic production and change, 22–9, 79
   field, 3–4, 25–8, 56–7, 79–80, 135
Braden, Gordon, 128, 137; see also Seneca
Bussy D'Ambois see Chapman, George

Cambises, King of Persia, 119–127
   genre, 120–1
   reception, 122–4
   see also Seneca; university drama
Chapman, George, Bussy plays *(Bussy D'Ambois* and *The Revenge of Bussy D'Ambois)*, 243, 261–3
Charnes, Linda, 50n24, 115n56, 201n5
Chaucer, Geoffrey
   author function, 46–8, 60, 75–6
   reception, 45–6
   Knight's Tale, The, 73
   Troilus and Criseyde, 46–8, 49–51, 199, 200–2
Chaucer, Geoffrey (as character)
   in Greene's *Vision*, 61–4
   in Henryson's *Testament of Creseide*, 46–7, 197, 199
   in Shakespeare's *Troilus and Criseyde*, 45, 47
   in Shakespeare's *Two Noble Kinsmen*, 45, 60, 72–4, 76
chronicle play, 152, 152n68, 172
city comedy, 32, 276n70, 278–281; see also comedy
Cohen, Ralph, 10–11, 11n19
Colie, Rosalie, 10n16, 11–12
comedy, 29–30, 51, 58, 168
   reception, 52–3
   see also city comedy
Cressida (character comparison), 48, 49

Dekker, Thomas, and Webster, Ben see *History of Sir Thomas Wyatt*
Derrida, Jacques, 2n4, 11n19, 168n12
Dimock, Wai-Chee, 16
distant reading see Dimock, Wai-Chee; Moretti, Franco
Dolan, Frances, 152–3

domestic tragedy, 148–53, 182–3, 248–50; *see also Arden of Faversham*; *Edward II*
Donaldson, E. Talbot, 48, 49, 73
Dowden, Edward, 37–42, 80
Drayton, Michael
  Mortimeriados, 177
  Peirs Gaveston, 173–7
Dudgeon, Cheryl, 153n70

Edward II, 178–84
  genre, 171–3
  see also Marlowe, Christopher
Edward III (Anon.), 178
English history play, 152, 197–8, 207–8, 229–31

Famous History of Sir Thomas Wyatt, 211–14
  reception, 211
Farrell, Joseph, 9
Federico, Sylvia, 200, 201, 202n7
Fletcher, John
  Faithful Shepherdess, 69–71
  and Shakespeare, William *see Two Noble Kinsmen*
foil *see* mirror imagery
Ford, John, *Perkins Warbeck, A Strange Truth*, 199, 228–37
Fowler, Alastair, 14–15

Gager, William
  Hippolytus, 136
  Meleager, 130–2
  see also Seneca; university drama
genre, theory of, 1–32, 35, 264–7
  effect, 5–6, 11–14, 42–3, 157
  history of, 8–17
  innovation and history, 3, 7–8, 10–17, 19–22, 57, 84, 237
  mixta, 4–8, 70–1, 144–8, 273–5
  purity, 1–4, 272
  staged definitions, 70–1, 110, 150–1, 168–70, 184–6, 246–51
Gower, John
  author function, 64–5
  Confessio Amantis, 64–6
Gower, John (as a character)
  in Greene's *Vision*, 60–1, 62–4
  in Shakespeare's *Pericles*, 59–60, 65–9
Greene, Robert
  James IV, 126–7
  Vision, 61–4
Gregory of Tours *see* historiography

Hamlet, 79–80, 96–109, 241–2
  genre, 96
Hengist, King of Kent, 157, 223–8
  genre, 223–4
  reception, 237
Henry VIII (aka *All Is True*), 217–23
  genre, 41, 197, 207–8
  truth, 198–9, 220
Henryson, Robert, *Testament of Creseide*, 46–7, 198, 202; *see also* Chaucer, Geoffrey (as character)
Henslowe, Philip, 133, 142–7, 172, 251–2
Heywood, Jasper, 121, 129–30, 138; *see also* Seneca
Heywood, Thomas, 131, 154, 207, 214
  If You Know Not Me, You Know Nobody (1 and 2), 207n19, 214–15, 222
  Woman Killed with Kindness, A, 249–50
historiography, 158–67
  Blundeville, Thomas, 164–6, 183, 188n48
  Gregory of Tours, 158–9
  Nashe, Thomas, 162–3, 194
  Puttenham, George, 161–2, 230
  Sidney, Sir Philip, 159–60
  Spenser, Edmund, 160–1, 163
  Woolf, D. R., 163–4
History of Sir Thomas Wyatt, 211–14
history (dramatic genre)
  comedy in, 163
  definition, 51–2, 155–8, 163, 167–8, 184–5, 206
  emerging, 157–8
  "late," 197–9, 206–8, 215–18, 227–9
Holinshed's *Chronicles*, 153–4, 167–8, 184n38; *see also Arden of Faversham*
Hutson, Lorna, 153–4

Inns of Court, 24n35, 44n15, 118, 120n3, 128–9, 144n48, 193; *see also* university drama

James, Heather, 200n4
Jameson, Fredric, 12–14, 228

Kalas, Rayna, 91n22
Kewes, Paulina, 156–7, 158n3
kind *see* genre theory
Knight of the Burning Pestle see Beaumont, Francis
Knutson, Roslyn, 52, 148, 172, 177n26
Kyd, Thomas, 133, 135; see also *Spanish Tragedy*

lies like truth, 191–2, 193–5, 213–14, 215–17; *see also* Walsh, Brian
Lodge, Thomas, *The Wounds of Civil War*, 182–3
looking glass *see* mirrors, imagery with

McInnis, David, 154
McMillin, Scott, 141, 267
Marlowe, Christopher, Ovid, 9–10; *see also* domestic tragedy; *Edward II*
Marston, Antonio, Antonio plays (*Antonio and Mellida, Antonio's Revenge*), 252–61
masque, 180, 258–60, 263, 265, 269–70
"Mayor of Queenborough, The" see *Hengist, King of Kent*
Meres, Francis, 130–1, 132–3
metatheatricality, 87–8, 184–94, 225–8, 253–61, 266–70
Middleton, Thomas see *Hengist; Revenger's Tragedy; Women Beware Women*
Mirrors, imagery with, 90–2, 99–102, 104, 108–9
Moretti, Franco, 16–17
Mortimeriados see Drayton, Michael
Mowat, Barbara, 38n3, 42, 58
Mucedorus, 246–7, 250–1
Munro, Lucy, 223n42, 250

Nashe, Thomas, *Pierce Penniless*, 162; *see also* historiography

neoclassical drama *see* university drama
Norland, Howard B., 119–20, 127, 129, 131, 132

1 Henry IV, 119
Ovid, 9–10, 85n13
  influence, 47–8, 64, 94, 114n53, 127–8, 131–2, 177

pastoral, 70–1
Patterson, Annabel, 153, 167, 192n38; *see also* Holinshed's *Chronicles*
Peele, George, *Edward I*, 177–8
Pericles, 65–9
  genre, 39–41, 67
  reception, 69, 118
  see also Gower, John
pirates *see* romance
Preston, Thomas *see Cambises, King of Persia*
Puttenham, George, *Art of English Poesy*, 43–4, 91–2; *see also* historiography; mirrors, imagery with

Revenge of Bussy D'Ambois (The) see Chapman, George
revenge tragedy, 129, 240–5, 26
  reception, 242–5
  see also tragedy
Revenger's Tragedy, The, 239, 264–71
  genre, 264–5
Ribner, Irving, 172–3, 197–8, 215, 217, 231n61
Ricouer, Paul, 168n12; *see also* historiography
romance
  definition, 38–44, 57
  drama, 44–67, 80–2, 106, 126–7
  medieval verse, 80–1
  pirates, 105–7
Rowley, Samuel *see When You See Me, You Know Me*

satire, 58–9, 267, 271, 275
  The Revenger's Tragedy, 267
  Troilus and Cressida, 51–2
Seneca, 121, 129–30, 136, 141–2, 256
Shakespeare, William, 122

exceptionalism, 80, 122, 156, 207, 242
reception, 44, 51–5
and Fletcher, John see *Henry VIII*; *Two Noble Kinsmen*
and Middleton, Thomas see *Timon of Athens*
see also plays by title
Siemon, James R., 121, 135
Sidney, Sir Philip
Defence for Poesy see historiography
"mongrel tragicomedy," 5–6, 72n50
Spanish Tragedy, The, 133–48, 189–91, 245–6, 258
reception, 142–4, 239
reaction to tradition, 134–42
see also Seneca; university drama
Spenser, Edmund
Faerie Queene, The, 86–7, 88–96
Faerie Queene, The, in *Hamlet*, 97–9
Faerie Queene, The, in *Troilus and Cressida*, 109–14
"poet historical" see historiography
stichomythia, 128, 130, 138–9, 141; see also Seneca; university drama

Thomas, Lord Cromwell, 208–11
Thompson, Ann, 73
Thorndike, A. H., 240, 241–2, 243
Timon of Athens, 271–5
genre, 40–1, 271–2, 273
reception, 275
tragedy
definition, 4, 8–9, 29–30, 168, 239–40, 250–2, 270–1
reception, 52–5, 145–8
see also revenge tragedy
tragicomedy, 4, 6, 58–9, 71–2
Troilus (character comparison), 49–51, 110, 115–16
Troilus and Cressida, 109–18, 202–6
genre, 57–9, 204, 206
reception, 43, 44, 51–3, 55–7
see also Troy

Troy
as England's mythic origin, 112–13, 167–8, 200–3
in *Faerie Queene, The*, 109–15
in *Troilus and Cressida*, 115–17, 204–5
in *Troilus and Criseyde*, 200–3
truth, 173, 183–4, 198–9
literary, 47–8, 98–104, 169–70, 262
historical, 153, 159–67, 186–9, 199–202, 217–23, 247–9, 276–8
see also lies like truth
2 Henry IV
history and metatheatricality, 184–94
lies like truth, 193–5
reception, 185
Two Noble Kinsmen, 44, 72–6

university drama, 127–42, 177, 255–6, 263

Virgil see university drama
Voloshinov, V. N., 17–19, 186; see also Bakhtin, Mikhail

W. S. see *Thomas, Lord Cromwell*
Walsh, Brian, 166–7; see also historiography
Warning for Fair Women, A (Anon.), 168–70, 247–8
Watson, Thomas, 139–41
Webster, Ben, and Dekker, Thomas, see *History of Sir Thomas Wyatt*
When You See Me, You Know Me, 215–17
White, Hayden, 160n7, 164n9, 230n58; see also historiography
Winston, Jessica, 24n35
Witch of Edmonton, 250
Women Beware Women, 275–81
genre, 276–7
Woolf, D. R., 163–4; see also historiography

EU representative:
Easy Access System Europe
Mustamäe tee 50, 10621 Tallinn, Estonia
Gpsr.requests@easproject.com